THE
BOER WAR
GENERALS

PETER TREW

WRENS
PARK

First published in 1999 by
Sutton Publishing Limited · Phoenix Mill
Thrupp · Stroud · Gloucestershire · GL5 2BU

This edition first published in 2001 by
Wrens Park Publishing, an imprint of W.J. Williams & Son

British Library Cataloguing in Publication Data
A catalogue record for this book is available from the British Library

ISBN 0 905 778 677

Typeset in 10/12pt New Baskerville.
Typesetting and origination by
Sutton Publishing Limited.
Printed in Great Britain by
J.H. Haynes & Co., Sparkford.

Contents

List of Maps

Chronology

A Chronology of the South African War 1899–1902

1899 **9 October**. Transvaal issues ultimatum.
11 October. Boer Republics at war with Britain.
12 October. Boers enter Natal and cross Western Transvaal border. De la Rey captures armoured train at Kraaipan.
16 October. Kimberley invested.
20 October. Battle of Talana.
21 October. Battle of Elandslaagte.
24 October. Battle of Rietfontein.
30 October. Battle of Ladysmith (Modderspruit). De Wet captures Carleton's column at Nicholson's Nek.
31 October. Buller arrives in Cape Town.
1 November. Boers seize Norvalspont Bridge and invade Cape Colony.
15 November. Armoured train wrecked at Chieveley and Winston Churchill captured.
20 November. French arrives at Naauwpoort.
22 November. Buller leaves Cape Town for Natal.
23 November. Battles of Belmont and Willow Grange.
25 November. Battle of Enslin (Graspan).
28 November. Battle of Modder River.
10 December. Gatacre is repulsed at Stormberg.
11 December. Battle of Magersfontein.
15 December. Battle of Colenso.
18 December. Roberts is appointed Commander-in-Chief in South Africa with Kitchener as Chief of Staff.

1900 **10 January**. Roberts and Kitchener arrive in Cape Town.
18 January. Dundonald in action at Acton Homes.
24 January. Battle of Spion Kop.
5 February. Buller captures Vaalkrantz.
7 February. Buller evacuates Vaalkrantz.
11 February. Start of Roberts's flank march on Bloemfontein.
15 February. French relieves Kimberley; Roberts in Jacobsdal; De Wet captures supply convoy at Waterval Drift.
16 February. Cronjé evacuates positions at Magersfontein.

1900 **18 February**. Battle of Paardeberg; Lyttleton captures Monte Cristo.

19 February. Accidental death of Ignatius Ferreira, Chief Commandant of the Free State forces.

27 February. Cronjé surrenders to Roberts at Paardeberg. Battle of Pieter's Hill.

28 February. Relief of Ladysmith.

7 March. Battle of Poplar Grove.

10 March. Battle of Driefontein (Abraham's Kraal).

13 March. Roberts enters Bloemfontein.

18 March. Boer *krygsraad* in Kroonstad.

27 March. Death of Joubert; Louis Botha appointed acting Commandant-General of the Transvaal forces.

31 March. De Wet defeats Broadwood at Sannah's Post and captures waterworks.

4 April. De Wet captures British detachment at Mostert's Hoek near Reddersburg.

5 April. Gen de Villebois-Mareuil killed in action near Boshof.

23 April. Ian Hamilton recaptures the waterworks at Sannah's Post.

3 May. Roberts occupies Brandfort.

7 May. Last meeting of Transvaal Volksraad.

12 May. Roberts occupies Kroonstad.

14 May. Buller drives Boers from the Biggarsberg.

17 May. Relief of Mafeking.

19 May. Buller occupies Newcastle.

22 May. Roberts resumes advance from Kroonstad.

24 May. Roberts proclaims annexation of Orange Free State.

29 May. Battle of Doornkop outside Johannesburg.

30 May. President Kruger and Transvaal government leave Pretoria for Machadodorp.

31 May. Roberts occupies Johannesburg; 500 Irish Yeomanry surrender to Piet de Wet at Lindley.

2 June. Buller and Chris Botha in abortive peace talks at Laing's Nek.

5 June. Roberts occupies Pretoria.

7 June. De Wet overwhelms British post at Roodewal (Rooiwal) Station and captures stores.

8 June. Buller breaks through at Botha's Pass.

11 June. First day of battle of Diamond Hill (Donkerhoek); battle of Allemans Nek.

12 June. Second day of battle of Diamond Hill (Donkerhoek); Buller occupies Volksrust.

11 July. Actions in the Western Transvaal at Zilikats Nek and Dwarsvlei.

1900   **15 July**. President Steyn and De Wet escape from the Brandwater Basin.
21 July. Roberts begins advance along Delagoa Bay Railway to Komatipoort.
27 July. Roberts occupies Middelburg.
30 July. Prinsloo surrenders to Hunter in the Brandwater Basin.
4 August. De la Rey surrounds Col Hore at Brakfontein on the Elands River.
14 August. De Wet escapes through Olifants Nek.
16 August. Kitchener relieves Hore at Brakfontein.
27 August. Battle of Bergendal.
1 September. Roberts proclaims annexation of the Transvaal.
6 September. Buller occupies Lydenburg.
13 September. French occupies Barberton.
24 September. Pole-Carew occupies Komatipoort.
25 September. Dissolution of British Parliament.
8 October. Milner appointed administrator of the Transvaal and Orange Free State.
19 October. President Kruger sails for Europe from Lourenço Marques in the *Gelderland*.
20 October. De Wet surrounds Barton at Frederikstad.
25 October. De Wet retires from Frederikstad.
27 October. Steyn and Botha join De la Rey and Smuts at Syferfontein to review strategy.
6 November. De Wet defeated at Bothaville.
16 November. De Wet forces Springhaans Nek and goes south to attempt an invasion of the Cape Colony.
23 November. De Wet captures Dewetsdorp.
29 November. Kitchener succeeds Roberts as Commander-in-Chief in South Africa; action at Rhenoster Kop.
3 December. De la Rey captures supply convoy at Buffelspoort.
5 December. De Wet abandons invasion of Cape Colony.
13 December. De la Rey and Beyers capture Clements's camp at Nooitgedacht.
14 December. De Wet returns northwards through Springhaans Nek.
16 December. Hertzog and Kritzinger invade the Cape Colony.
29 December. Ben Viljoen captures British post at Helvetia.

1901   **7 January**. Botha and Viljoen attack Belfast and other stations on the Delagoa Bay Railway.
10 January. Murder of Morgendaal, Boer peace emissary, in De Wet's laager near Kroonstad.
27 January. Start of French's drive in the Eastern Transvaal.

1901 **29 January**. Start of the Third (Great) De Wet hunt; Knox engages De Wet at Tabaksberg.

31 January. Smuts captures British post at Modderfontein.

6 February. Botha attacks Smith-Dorrien's camp at Lake Chrissie.

10 February. De Wet invades the Cape Colony at Sand Drift.

13 February. Kitchener proposes a meeting with Botha to discuss peace terms.

14 February. Plumer engages De Wet at Wolvekuil near Philipstown.

27 February. De Wet and Hertzog return to the Orange Free State via Botha's Drift.

28 February. Botha and Kitchener discuss peace terms at Middelburg.

3 March. De la Rey's attack on Lichtenburg is repulsed.

11 March. De Wet reaches Senekal; end of Third (Great) De Wet hunt.

16 March. Botha refuses peace terms offered by Kitchener.

8 May. Milner goes to England on leave.

10 May. Meeting of Boer leaders at Immigratie, near Ermelo.

29 May. Dixon repulses Kemp's attack at Vlakfontein.

6 June. De la Rey and De Wet attempt unsuccessfully to rescue a women's convoy at Graspan, near Reitz.

12 June. Muller cuts up Victorian Mounted Rifles at Wilmansrust.

20 June. Meeting of Boer leaders at Waterval, near Standerton.

11 July. Most of Free State government is captured in Reitz. Steyn escapes.

7 August. Kitchener issues proclamation threatening banishment of Boer leaders still in the field after 15 September.

3 September. Smuts invades the Cape Colony at Klaarwater Drift.

7 September. Botha sets out to invade Natal.

17 September. Botha cuts up Gough's force at Blood River Poort; Smuts cuts up 17th Lancers at Modderfontein in the Elands River Valley.

26 September. Botha attacks unsuccessfully Forts Itala and Prospect in Zululand.

30 September. De la Rey attacks Kekewich's camp at Moedwil.

9 October. Emily Hobhouse is prevented from landing in Cape Town when she tries to return to South Africa.

11 October. Commandant Lötter is executed in the Cape Colony; Scheepers is captured.

24 October. De la Rey attacks Von Donop at Kleinfontein.

30 October. Benson killed after Botha attacks his column at Bakenlaagte.

7 November. Ian Hamilton is appointed Kitchener's Chief of Staff.

16 December. Kritzinger is captured in the Cape Colony.

25 December. De Wet captures yeomanry camp at Tweefontein.

1902   **18 January**. Scheepers is executed at Graaff Reinet.

25 January. Ben Viljoen is captured at Lydenburg; offer of mediation by Dutch government.

6 February. Start of first 'new model' drive in North-Eastern Free State.

13 February. Start of second drive.

23 February. De Wet and President Steyn break through the British cordon at Langverwacht.

25 February. De la Rey captures Von Donop's convoy at Yzerspruit.

27 February. Execution of 'Breaker' Morant and Lt Handcock in Pretoria.

7 March. De la Rey defeats and captures Methuen at Tweebosch.

17 March. President Steyn and De Wet join De la Rey at Zendelingsfontein.

24 March. First drive in the Western Transvaal.

26 March. Death of Cecil Rhodes.

31 March. Kemp, Celliers and Liebenberg attack Cookson at Boschbult.

1 April. Maritz captures Springbok near Okiep.

4 April. Smuts surrounds Okiep.

6 April. Kritzinger is acquitted of charges of murder.

7 April. Ian Hamilton takes command in the field in the Western Transvaal.

9 April. Transvaal and Free State government representatives meet at Klerksdorp.

11 April. Kemp leads a charge of 700 men against British columns at Roodewal (Rooiwal).

12 April. Boer government representatives meet Kitchener in Pretoria.

14 April. Boer government representatives meet Kitchener and Milner in Pretoria.

18 April. Boer government representatives leave Pretoria to consult the commandos.

15 May. Opening of Vereeniging Conference of Boer district delegates.

31 May. Peace treaty signed in Pretoria.

Photographic Sources

Plates between pages 146 and 147

By permission of the Officers of the Corps of the Royal Engineers: photograph no. 13. Courtesy of the Director, National Army Museum, London: nos 4 and 11. Courtesy of the Cape Town Archives Repository (accession number in brackets): nos 1 (J476), 2 (AG15377), 3 (AG10481), 6 (J238), 7 (AG10489), 9 (AG3295), 10 (AG276), 12 (AG14231), 16 (AG10535) 17 (L819), 18 (J1163), 19 (AG10490), 20 (L436), 21 (AG3017), 22 (AG15334), 23 (AG2478), 25 (AG15378), 26 (AG13792), 27 (L1366), 30 (AG15332). E. Hobhouse, *The Brunt of War and Where it Fell*, London, Methuen, 1902 (facing p. 297): no. 27. L. Penning, *Verdedigers en Verdrukkers*, Den Haag, J.N. Voorhoeve, 1902, (facing p. 61) no. 5 and (facing p. 96) no. 8. H.W. Wilson, *After Pretoria*, London, The Amalgamated Press, 1902, (p. 703) no. 14 and (p. 715) no. 29. Author's photographs: nos 15, 24 and 28.

Introduction

This book had its origin in my interest in a war which was little more than a generation away during my childhood in South Africa. Surviving blockhouses were reminders of it, and another reminder hung in the library of my school in Cape Town – a framed note from Col Baden-Powell thanking the boys for their Mafeking Day telegram. There was also a family interest. My Australian grandfather had served in the war, first under Gen Plumer and later in the South African Constabulary and had stayed on in South Africa. He served as commandant of Louis Botha's bodyguard in the 1914 rebellion and the 1915 German South West Africa campaign. Regrettably he left little in the way of reminiscences of the Boer War, although he wrote two books about his subsequent career as a police officer.

The seven generals who are the subject of this book had in common the fact that they exercised independent command at some point during the South African war of 1899–1902. I had originally intended to include generals French and Methuen on the British side and Piet Cronjé on the Boer side, but that would have resulted in an unacceptable degree of duplication in the narration of events. As it is, some duplication has been unavoidable in the interests of maintaining continuity, but I have tried to minimise it by the use of cross-referencing. In the case of the Tugela campaign, however, because of its importance in the careers respectively of Buller and Botha, I have tried to tell the story from each of their points of view in the appropriate chapters. I have treated Smuts somewhat differently from the others. Although he played a significant part in the events leading up to the war, in its conduct and in the final peace negotiations, he did so primarily as a senior State official, albeit a very young one. He was a comparatively junior general, but he did exercise independent command for the last nine months of the war during his invasion of the Cape Colony. Because his contribution to the war features in six out of the nine other chapters I have devoted the chapter in his name mainly to a brief survey of his remarkable postwar career.

The significance of the Boer War in their personal careers varied for each of the seven men concerned. For Christiaan de Wet alone, perhaps, it was a time of fulfilment when all his special gifts came into play. For Smuts and Botha it was a preparation for their future careers as politicians; for De la Rey, who hated war, it was a heavy but unavoidable duty which he discharged with distinction. For Kitchener it was a tedious and exhausting interlude which delayed his appointment as Commander-in-Chief in India; for Roberts it was a final triumph, which lost its gloss when the war dragged on for a year and a half after his departure; for Buller, it was the graveyard of his reputation. Of the seven only two, Roberts and Smuts, died full of years and honour. Kitchener was drowned at sea and De la Rey was shot accidentally. De Wet, prematurely aged, and Buller, discredited but cheerful and active, died in their sixties. Botha was only fifty-seven when he died, exhausted by the burdens of office and heartbroken by his rejection by many of his own people.

For South Africa the war left a legacy of bitterness, but probably hastened its development as a modern industrial state. For the black population it created disappointment that a British victory resulted in no improvement in their lot. It brought about something not far removed from the hopes of Milner and Chamberlain – a union of the four South African states playing a full part within the British Empire, including fighting on Britain's side in two world wars – but they might have been surprised that for the best part of half a century it was governed by three former Boer generals. While Botha, Smuts and eventually Hertzog strove for reconciliation between the white races in South Africa, the forces of extreme Afrikaner nationalism were at work and triumphed in 1948 when Smuts was defeated and the Nationalists came to power, leading South Africa into the cul-de-sac of apartheid and, for a generation, out of the British Commonwealth. The preoccupations and passions which led to the war were real enough to those who had to make the decisions, but few of them would have guessed that before the twentieth century was over, the torch of political power in South Africa would be carried by neither Boer nor Briton but by the descendants of those black South Africans who toiled, suffered, and in many cases fought in the white man's war.

In writing this book I have drawn heavily on the work of those who have preceded me and I hope that I will be found to have acknowledged my sources adequately in the notes and bibliography. Apart from those staple contemporary sources *The Times History* and *The Official History* I am indebted among later works in particular to Professor J.H. Breytenbach's *Die Geskiedenis van Die Tweede Vryheidsoorlog in Suid-Afrika 1899–1902*, to Professor S.B. Spies's *Methods of Barbarism?* and to his joint editorship with Gail Nattrass of Jan Smuts's *Memoirs of the Boer War*, to Professor C.J. Barnard's *Generaal Louis Botha op die Natalse Front 1899–1900* and to a number of the works of Johannes Meintjes. Many people have helped me. I am beholden to William Lane for making available to me and allowing me to quote from the diary of his grandfather John Moody (Jack) Lane; this is due to be published by the Van Riebeeck Society as *The War Diary of Burgher Jack Lane, 16 November*

Introduction

1899 to 27 February 1900. I have acknowledged separately those who have allowed me to reproduce illustrations. Richard Wallington read the drafts, made useful suggestions and alerted me both to military solecisms and to grammatical infelicities. Any that remain are my responsibility. My father Antony Trew advised me on some of the chapters before he died and I am much indebted to my son-in-law Glen Miller for his work on the maps. I am grateful to Major Paul Naish for an enjoyable and informative day at Colenso and Spion Kop, and to Warham Searle for help with maps and photographs in Cape Town. My thanks are due also to the staff at the National Army Museum, the London and British Libraries, the Public Record Office and the House of Lords Record Office, the National Museum of Military History in Johannesburg, the State Library in Pretoria and the National Archives in Pretoria and Cape Town.

Finally, this book is dedicated to my wife, Jo, with my thanks for her help, support and forbearance during the five years it took me to write it.

Note on Spelling

I have used the contemporary spelling for place names associated with the better known military actions using *The Times History* as a guide. Where that spelling differs markedly from the modern form I have used both old and new in the index e.g. Paardeberg (Perdeberg). In the spelling of ordinary words I have preferred Afrikaans to Dutch except for those Dutch words like kopje and laager which have found their way into the Oxford English Dictionary. After Roberts' annexation of the Orange Free State in May 1900 the British renamed it the Orange River Colony. I have disregarded that change of name partly in the interests of simplicity and partly because I am persuaded by the argument that the annexation, like Roberts' later annexation of the Transvaal, was premature and therefore probably invalid in international law.

CHAPTER ONE

Background

The Origins of the War[1]

In South Africa at the end of the nineteenth century there coexisted four states with varying degrees of autonomy. The Cape Colony and Natal were self-governing British colonies, while the Transvaal and Orange Free State were Boer republics founded by the Voortrekkers, whose independence had been recognised respectively in the Sand River Convention of 1852 and the Bloemfontein Convention of 1854. However, the Transvaal had been annexed by Britain in 1877, ostensibly to protect it from incursions from native tribes, but had fought to regain its independence in the First Boer War in 1881. After the British setback at Majuba in that war Gladstone had balked at the implications of trying to achieve a military defeat of the Transvaal forces and had opted for a political settlement which largely restored to the Transvaal its independence, subject to British 'suzerainty', as defined in the Pretoria Convention of 1881. That convention was replaced by the London Convention of 1884 in which all mention of suzerainty was removed but in which Britain retained a measure of control, most importantly a right to veto external treaties.

Paul Kruger had come into political prominence after the annexation, and during the First Boer War was one of a triumvirate of Transvaal leaders. He was elected President in 1883 and re-elected in 1888, 1893 and 1898. He was a formidable personality, deeply religious and, despite his lack of a formal education, a shrewd politician. The annexation of 1887 had been the culmination of a failed attempt by Lord Carnarvon, British Colonial Secretary from 1874 to 1878, to establish a South African federation of the four states with a view to consolidating British supremacy in the subcontinent. That failure and the humiliation of Majuba were of little practical consequence as long as the Transvaal remained a poor, sparsely populated and backward pastoral republic, but the discovery on the Witwatersrand in 1886 of the richest goldfield in the world changed things in a number of ways. It attracted not only massive British and European investment, but a large influx of expatriates (Uitlanders). It provided the previously poor republic with the revenues to arm itself with the most modern weapons and it made the Transvaal potentially the economic and political hub of South Africa.

In parallel with those developments, Cecil Rhodes, as much an imperialist as a businessman, was establishing control of Rhodesia, and in

1

the scramble for Africa, Germany was in the forefront of countries with territorial ambitions in the continent. The question of British supremacy, which had lain dormant since Majuba, became central to the politics of Southern Africa. It was Rhodes who revived the idea of a South African federation, which he saw as including Rhodesia. From 1890 to 1896 he was Prime Minister of the Cape Colony, an office he held by virtue of the support of the Afrikaner Bond, the principal political grouping of Dutch-speaking citizens of the colony, many of whom shared his vision of a union of the white races of Southern Africa.[2] This could not be said of Kruger's Transvaal which was determined not only to preserve its qualified independence under the London Convention but also to progress to full sovereignty. The first clash between these opposing ambitions came in 1895 with the so-called Drifts Crisis, the culmination of a railway tariffs war in which Kruger sought to discriminate against the Cape Railway in favour of the newly opened lines from Durban and Delagoa Bay. The latter was of particular importance to the Transvaal as it was its only link to the sea which did not cross British territory. When the Cape Railway sought to circumvent the discrimination by transferring goods onto ox-wagons at the Transvaal border for the final part of the journey to Johannesburg, Kruger retaliated by closing the drifts across the Vaal River. The British government intervened on the grounds that Kruger had breached the London Convention and when diplomatic means failed threatened to use force. The fact that Kruger backed down and that the Orange Free State had not supported him encouraged Britain to underestimate his resolve in future disputes.

Joseph Chamberlain, the Colonial Secretary who led the British government's intervention in the Drifts Crisis, had resigned as a member of Gladstone's government in 1886 on the issue of Irish Home Rule. As leader of the Liberal Unionists he had become a member of Lord Salisbury's coalition government which came into office in June 1895. He had declined the office of Chancellor of the Exchequer in favour of the comparatively minor office of Secretary of State for the Colonies. Probably the most influential member of the government after Salisbury, he was an avowed imperialist who believed that the consolidation of the empire was vital to Britain's survival as a major power. He saw the creation of a South African federation as a desirable step in that process. The provinces of Canada had been united in one dominion by 1870 and the six Australian colonies were moving towards a federal constitution. It was not necessarily a requirement of a South African federation that the Transvaal and the Orange Free State should give up their republican status, but simply that Britain should be acknowledged as the paramount power.

The position of the Uitlanders featured largely in the growing tension between Britain and the Transvaal. It was represented by both sides that Uitlanders outnumbered Boers, a convenient exaggeration since it justified British indignation about their grievances and Boer fears about their potential political influence. No figures are available for the white population of the Transvaal as a whole immediately before the war, but working backwards from the 1904 census figures, Professor J.S. Marais concluded that there were more Boer men, women and children than Uitlanders in the Transvaal, but in terms of adult males only, more Uitlanders. In Johannesburg, however, there was a clear preponderance of Uitlanders. A local authority census in 1896 put the total white population within a 3-mile radius at just under 51,000 with a slightly larger number of non-whites, mostly Bantu. Of the whites only 6,205 were Transvaalers and of the remainder the great majority were British or South African colonials.[3] As the new-found prosperity of the Transvaal was based on the efforts and the tax contributions of the Uitlanders, they understandably sought not only adequate public services but a right to vote. They perceived the Kruger government as corrupt and inefficient and the police as arrogant and ineffective. Kruger's system of granting concessions for essential services and supplies of all sorts increased the working costs of the mines and the cost of living generally. For his part the old president feared that his republic would be overwhelmed by an alien culture and in 1890 the residential qualification for full voting rights was increased from five years to fourteen. As a sop he created a subordinate chamber with limited powers called the Second Volksraad for which Uitlanders were given voting rights after two years' residence.

The Uitlander grievances provided the background to Dr Jameson's ill-fated raid, launched from Mafeking on 29 December 1895. It was intended to support a local rebellion in Johannesburg planned for 28 December and was organised, with the active involvement of Cecil Rhodes, by the Uitlander Reform Committee in which mining interests were predominant. The committee, whose membership included nationalities other than British, was seeking a reformed Transvaal republic, but Rhodes had a wider agenda – the furtherance of his cherished plan for a South African federation. By the date planned for the start of the rebellion the committee was in disarray, unable to decide whether the Transvaal or the British flag should be raised over Johannesburg.[4] Despite messages urging delay, Jameson started out on his raid and with his 470-strong force was surrounded at Doornkop, 14 miles south-west of Johannesburg, where he surrendered on 2 January 1896 to a superior Boer force under Piet Cronjé. He and his associates were sent to England for trial by the imperial government, where they received lenient sentences. His accomplices in Johannesburg were treated more harshly. It was soon established by a select committee of the Cape House of Assembly that Cecil Rhodes was fully implicated in the raid.[5] He lost the support of the Afrikander Bond and resigned as Prime Minister of the Cape Colony. The question of Chamberlain's involvement was skirted around by the House of Commons select committee which investigated the raid – a committee of which Chamberlain himself was a member and which was dubbed 'the Committee of No Enquiry'.[6]

In May 1897 Sir Alfred Milner took up his appointment as British High Commissioner in South Africa and Governor of the Cape Colony. He had spent the previous five years as chairman of the board of the Inland Revenue in London and before that had served as Under-Secretary of Finance in Egypt. He was an avowed imperialist, but like Chamberlain a consolidationist rather than an expansionist.[7] If he lacked Chamberlain's political skill he made up for it in single-mindedness. He had been a brilliant student at Oxford from which he took 'an accumulation of prizes but no large stock of general ideas'.[8] He was to play a dominant part in the events which led to war. In the immediate aftermath of the Jameson Raid, Chamberlain had taken up the complaints of the Uitlanders but had backed off from intervening in the internal affairs of the Transvaal and had been dissuaded by Milner's predecessor, Sir Hercules Robinson, from reinforcing the British garrison in South Africa at that time. Kruger had toyed with and then rejected the idea of accepting an invitation to visit Britain. In the latter half of 1896 Chamberlain had alleged breaches by the Transvaal of the London Convention in respect of an extradition treaty with the Netherlands and its internal legislation concerning aliens, undesirables and the press. In March 1897 the Transvaal and the Orange Free State had entered into a new treaty of mutual support in which President Steyn had secured the insertion of a clause requiring consultation in the hope of exerting a moderating influence on his sister republic. In April 1897 British military strength in South Africa was increased to 8,000 men and 24 field guns.

Kruger's convincing re-election as President in 1898 dashed Milner's hopes that the Transvaal problem would be solved by his removal from office and from this time onwards he concluded that matters must be brought to a head, if necessary by a resort to force or at least the threat of it. In part he was prompted by the fear that unless the question of British supremacy was resolved soon the Transvaal would emerge as the leader of an Afrikaner-dominated South African federation. While that might have been a valid fear for the longer term there was at that time no cohesive force of Afrikaner nationalism in South Africa. It took the Boer War and Milner's postwar attempt to suppress Afrikaner culture to create it. For the time being Chamberlain restrained Milner's impatience. In a favourable development for Britain in August 1898 Germany effectively renounced the possibility of intervention in a war between Britain and the Transvaal as a *quid pro quo* for agreement on the possible division of territory in Portugal's African colonies. In November that year Milner visited England to confer with the Colonial Office. While he was there tension increased in the Transvaal as the result of the shooting while resisting arrest of an Uitlander called Edgar, after apparently leaving another man dead in a drunken brawl. Kruger's intention to extend the dynamite monopoly for another twelve years – a matter of great concern to the mining industry because of its effect on working costs – was taken up by Chamberlain as an alleged breach of the London Convention, but it was the question of the franchise which was the main source of discord as events moved towards war.

One of the far-reaching consequences of the Jameson Raid was the disillusionment of a brilliant young Cape Afrikaner, who had been an admirer of Cecil Rhodes and a supporter of his pan-African ambitions. Jan Christian Smuts was born on the farm Bovenplaats near Riebeek West in the Malmesbury district of the Cape Colony on 24 May 1870, the son of a member of the Cape legislative assembly. Academically gifted, he won a scholarship which enabled him to go to Christ's College, Cambridge, where in 1894 he was first in both parts of the law tripos. Returning to the Cape after Cambridge he practised unsuccessfully at the bar. His first venture into politics was to speak in Kimberley in October 1895 in defence of Rhodes, who had been attacked publicly by Olive Schreiner* and her husband. Two months later the Jameson Raid left him with a bitter sense of betrayal. Early in 1897 he left the Cape Colony for good and went to the Transvaal where he attracted the attention of President Kruger. In June 1898, at the age of twenty-eight he was appointed *staatsprocureur* (State Attorney) and at the same time abandoned his British Nationality.[9] He soon made his mark by taking over control of the detective force and eliminating corruption. He assisted in the writing of *A Century of Wrong*[10] which was issued under the name of F.W. Reitz, the State Secretary, a bitter polemic on the alleged perfidy of Britain in its dealings with Dutch-speaking South Africans over the previous 100 years. Despite this Reitz and Smuts played a constructive rôle in an attempt to avert war.

Milner returned to South Africa in January 1899 and in March he forwarded to the Colonial Office a 21,000-signature petition organised by the South African League, which since 1897 had been active in articulating Uitlander discontent. The petition rehearsed their grievances and sought the intervention of the British government. Milner followed this up with a series of dispatches, culminating on 4 May with one in which he referred to British subjects being kept permanently in the position of helots. A contemporary writer commented that 'the helot wore his golden chains with insolent composure of demeanour'.[11] It was agreed that Kruger and Milner should meet, which they did from 31 May at a conference in Bloemfontein, where Milner refused to discuss anything but the franchise issue. Proposal and counter-proposal

---

* A prominent South African writer, pacifist and feminist.

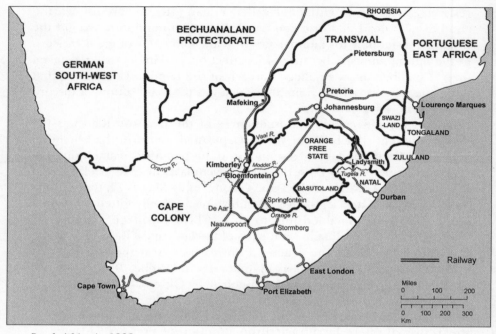

South Africa in 1899

produced no agreement and at the end Kruger exclaimed despairingly 'It is our country that you want.'[12] Thereafter Milner worked relentlessly to engineer a confrontation. The Transvaal government continued to seek a settlement and on 31 August Smuts put forward a proposal which appeared to give Milner all that he had been demanding at the Bloemfontein Conference – a five year retroactive franchise with a quarter of the seats in the Volksraad allocated to the Witwatersrand. However, it was subject to conditions which were unacceptable, particularly the dropping of Britain's claim to suzerainty. By now Milner had persuaded Chamberlain, who in turn persuaded the Cabinet, that it might be necessary to go to war. On 8 September it was decided to increase the number of British and colonial troops in South Africa to 27,000.[13] Both sides prepared ultimatums. For Chamberlain and Milner there was a problem of how to convince the man in the street that the question of the franchise for Uitlanders was worth going to war for. Kruger came to their rescue and on 9 October issued his ultimatum first. He had decided that the only alternative to war was the surrender of his country's independence. The Orange Free State, as it was bound to do by treaty, joined in and on 11 October 1899 Britain was at war with the Boer republics.

THE ARMIES AND THEIR WEAPONS

Although essentially a European army, the British Army was unique in the breadth of the demands made on it. Whereas the continental armies were geared to the possibility of war in Europe against potential adversaries who could be expected to fight in much the same way and on terrain which was reasonably familiar, the British Army had to be able to operate throughout a vast empire in a wide variety of conditions. Its strength was its versatility, its weakness its deficiencies in staff work and intelligence. Compared with Germany, which employed on its General Staff 300 officers at an annual cost of £270,000, Britain employed in its nearest equivalent to a General Staff, the Mobilisation and Intelligence Division – seventeen officers at a cost of £11,000.[14] Giving evidence to the 1903 Royal Commission, L.S. Amery, editor of *The Times History*, stated that in the months leading up to the war he employed more information gatherers in South Africa in his capacity there as *The Times* correspondent, than the British Army employed intelligence officers.[15] In 1898 the Transvaal Intelligence Department was spending on its secret service agents in Johannesburg, the Cape and Natal, and in England, at least twenty times as much as British Intelligence was, on its secret service in South Africa.[16]

For both officers and men ceremonial duties and the usual chores of Army life took precedence over formal military training, to which an average of only two months was allocated in a year. The men were recruited from among the urban unskilled and were below the national average in terms of intelligence and physique, but the latter deficiency was remedied by good food and gymnastic exercises.[17] Capt S.L.'H. Slocum, the American military attaché with the British forces, wrote of British officers and men: 'They have not the individuality or resources of our men, but for indomitable courage, uncomplaining fortitude and implicit obedience they are beyond criticism.'[18] The strengths of British officers reflected the demands made on them by worldwide service. They were skilled in logistics and the knowledge of what could be expected of men in widely varying conditions. At the start of the Boer War they were poor tacticians as a result of their addiction to parade-ground formations and frontal attacks, but this did not apply to officers who had served on the North-West Frontier of India and in particular to Lord Roberts. His main successes in Afghanistan were based on well-planned flank attacks.

The Boer republics were too poor to afford professional standing armies, apart from very small corps of artillerymen. Instead they relied on the commando system, which had evolved since the time of the Great Trek from the custom of mutual cooperation among neighbours in response to a common threat or to gather food in hunting expeditions. They would ride out together as equals, having chosen one among them to take charge. The system had been honed in a succession of minor wars, mostly against natives but some against the British, to the point where it was enshrined in the constitutions of the republics and part of the fabric of civic duty. Essentially it was a system of conscription since it placed on every male between the ages of sixteen and sixty the obligation of military service when called on by the State.[19] That obligation embraced whites and non-whites, but since by law only the former were allowed to bear arms the commandos were composed entirely of white men. Non-whites were employed on transport and scouting duties, as trench diggers and generally as hewers of wood and drawers of water.[20] Each district, of which there were twenty-two in the Transvaal and nineteen in the Orange Free State provided one commando under a commandant elected by his peers.[21] There was no exact equivalence in rank between a commandant and his British counterpart since commandos varied in size from 300 to 3,000 men.[22] The districts were subdivided into up to four field-cornetcies or wards under an elected field-cornet, whose responsibility it was to maintain a list of men liable to military service, and to implement the call to arms. He was also responsible for commandeering transport if there was insufficient from government sources. In military terms the rank of field-cornet was roughly equivalent to captain in the British Army but the comparison was not exact since the field-cornet had certain civic duties in peacetime.[23] Burghers liable for military service were required to maintain a rifle in working order with thirty rounds of ammunition. In the Free State, farm dwellers were also required to provide a horse with saddle and bridle, but there was State assistance for those who could not afford it. There was exemption from commando service for certain categories like legislators, State officials and ministers of the Church.[24] In the Transvaal the most senior military official was the publicly elected Commandant-General who was responsible to the State President and the Executive Committee. In times of war he was required to convene a *krygsraad*, or council of war, before making important operational decisions. There was no such official in the Free State but the commandants elected one of their number as the Chief Commandant and he exercised much the same function as his Transvaal counterpart, but without the *krygsraad* obligation, although he was free to consult his officers if he wished.[25]

In going on commando burghers retained their civic rights and there was no formal system of military discipline as in the British and European armies. Patriotism made up for this to some extent, but Boer commanders often experienced difficulty in mustering their full strength, in keeping burghers at the front when things were going badly – notably during Roberts's advance through the Free State – and in getting their men to follow up successes by pursuing the enemy. There are accounts of practically every well-known Boer general resorting to the use of his riding whip to encourage his men in the heat of battle. There was little in the way of military training, but in peacetime burghers were required to present themselves at regular *wapenskouings* (musters) or shooting practice. There were prizes to encourage good marksmanship.[26] Riding and shooting were skills which most Boers acquired from an early age, and since they had learnt to shoot by hunting game in the days before the advent of the high-velocity rifle they were also skilled in making use of all available natural cover to get near their prey.[27] Many of the British officers who gave evidence to the 1903 Royal Commission on the war in South Africa were asked how they rated Boer marksmanship compared with that of British soldiers. The general opinion was that it was better; that it was best at the usual range for shooting game, namely 200–300 yd, and that the skill was to a large extent due to keenness of sight, developed from childhood in the open country in which most Boers grew up, an advantage denied to most British boys. As Archibald Hunter put it, ' . . . if he is born in Stepney or Hackney, in a narrow lane, how is he going to have any eyesight?'[28] Officers who had been in South Africa at the time thought that the standard of Boer shooting had fallen off in the twenty years since the First Boer War, possibly because of the declining prevalence of big game.[29]

If the burgher army was under-officered by British standards this was compensated for by the high degree of personal initiative shown by many Boers. It was commonly said that every Boer was his own general.[30] This is not surprising since the ethos of the commando system was the association of equals united in a common purpose. However, there are exceptions to all generalisations and Christiaan de Wet later recorded his irritation at the succession of burghers asking him for instructions on trivial matters during the action at Sannah's Post.[31] The shooting and riding skills of the Boers were complemented by the high degree to which their ponies were adapted to war in South Africa. Unlike the horses used by the British, at least in the early stages of the war, they were trained to remain where they were when their masters dismounted to fight and they did not require to be fed, but grazed off the veld.[32] Winston Churchill described the burgher army as 'the finest mass of rifle-armed horsemen ever seen, and the most capable mounted warriors since the Mongols',[33] probably a fair assessment of the best of the Boers when he was in South Africa and even more so of the hard core of 'bitter-enders' who went on fighting long after their cause was ostensibly lost.

At the outbreak of the Boer War the number of burghers liable for military service was about 32,000 in the Transvaal and 22,000 in the Free State, a total of 54,000[34] which was supplemented by the full-time artillery corps, the police and foreign volunteers. The State Artillery Corps, of which the Transvaal force was much the larger, had a combined strength with reservists of about 1,000. In contrast to the burgher army these small professional forces were smartly uniformed, disciplined and trained in the European tradition, and skilled in the use of modern artillery weapons. Although separate forces they came under the operational control of the burgher army. The uniformed police accounted for a total of 1,400 men, again with the greater part coming from the Transvaal and of those most coming from Johannesburg.[35] During the war they were organised and fought in the same way as burgher commandos but their discipline gave an edge to their fighting ability. Foreign volunteers from a number of European countries and from America accounted for 2,000 to 2,500 men, the largest contingents coming from Germany and France.[36] The smaller Irish corps, led by an American West Pointer, Col J.Y.F. Blake, made a notable contribution to the Boer cause during Roberts's advance from Bloemfontein by its skill in demolition work.

By tacit agreement between the two sides the Boer War was to be a white man's war.[37] This required no policy decision on the Boer side since it was illegal in both republics for non-whites to bear arms. Britain accepted the same restraint informally, largely in deference to the views of the colonial governments in South Africa. In doing so she denied herself not only the opportunity of arming non-white South Africans but also of employing her well-trained native Indian and Egyptian armies. Even the offer of a Maori contingent by New Zealand was declined.[38] In reality the Boer War was a white man's war only to the extent that the vast majority of armed participants on both sides were white. Both sides employed large numbers of black non-combatants. In the British Army alone there were 14,000 non-white transport riders.[39] From early on in the war both sides complained that the other was using armed non-whites. Roberts gave strict orders against this for the first twelve months of the war, but they were probably ignored in some cases by local commanders. Smuts admitted that Piet Cronjé had placed armed Africans in forts during the siege of Mafeking.[40] If the Boers captured armed Africans they would usually shoot them. As the guerrilla war progressed the British Army made increasing use of African scouts. After a Boer proclamation in July 1901 to the effect that all Africans found working for the British would be shot, whether armed or not, Kitchener allowed scouts to be armed. Later the policy was extended to include non-whites guarding the blockhouse lines. Towards the end of the war he revealed that some 10,000 non-whites had been armed by the British. Lloyd George suggested that the figure was 30,000 without revealing his sources.[41] After the war when a Transvaal ordinance required the handing in of arms owned by non-whites, 50,000 weapons were collected.[42] Apart from the direct employment of Africans in their respective armies, both sides relied on the goodwill of tribal chiefs within and on the borders of the republics.

In some cases the British enjoyed their active collaboration since the chiefs believed that that a victorious Britain would improve the lot of Africans, an expectation in which they were largely disappointed.

The staple field artillery weapon of the British Army was the 15-pounder breech-loading gun, organised in batteries of eight. The Horse Artillery used 12-pounders. At the smaller end of the scale the Army was provided with the Maxim machine-gun using .303 rifle ammunition and the Vickers-Maxim automatic gun of 37-mm (1½-in) calibre. Better known as the 'pom-pom' this gun worked on the same principle as the Maxim machine-gun, using belts of twenty-five percussion shells with fixed brass cartridge cases. This was ordered early on in the war after Buller had been impressed by its effect when used by the Boers, and it was first used by the British at Paardeberg.[43] Vickers themselves thought little of this gun, devised originally for use by the Navy against torpedo boats, and had not pushed it. Before the war it had been bought only by China and by the Boers. It was not an efficient weapon of destruction but its noise and rapidity of fire had a damaging effect on the morale of those at the receiving end.[44]

For heavy artillery the Army had at first to look to the Navy which landed 4.7-in quick-firing guns on extemporised mountings from warships. These were capable of firing a 50 lb shell up to 10,000 yd (the difference between breech-loading (BL) and quick-firing (QF) guns was that in the former, charge and projectile were loaded separately, whereas in the latter they were integral). The Navy also provided 12-pounder QF guns with both long and short barrels.* The involvement of the Navy resulted primarily from the initiative of Rear Adm Sir Robert Harris, Commander-in-Chief at the Cape, who concluded in July 1899 while on a cruise up the East Coast that war with the Boers was probable.[45] He furnished the Army with a list of ordnance that he could make available and then despite assurances that help was unlikely to be required, started training a 500-strong naval brigade for service ashore.[46] In the event three naval brigades with a mixture of 4.7-in and 12-pounder guns served in the early part of the war. The Western Brigade joined Methuen after initial service at Stormberg. The Ladysmith Brigade arrived by train from Durban with its guns at 9.30 a.m. on 30 October 1899 at the height of the battle of Ladysmith when the British Army was in dire peril. The sailors were in action later in the morning covering the Army's retreat into the town, in which the brigade remained throughout the siege. The Natal Brigade served with Buller throughout his Natal campaign and later in the

* The latter featured for many years in the annual field gun competition at the Royal Tournament.

Transvaal. By the end of 1900 all naval units had returned to their ships.[47] Once the usefulness of 4.7-in guns had been established they were provided from Britain on 6-in Howitzer mountings.

Whereas the British Army had the use over the course of the war of some 500 guns,[48] the Boers started with the use of under 100, together with 55 later captured from the British.[49] The Boer field guns were the 75-mm (2.95-in) Creusot and the 75-mm Krupp, similar in their general characteristics to the British 15-pounder except that the Creusot had a very much higher muzzle velocity, nearly 2,000 ft per second compared with 1,500. As to their relative merits, 15-pounders captured by the Boers were said by some officers to have caused more annoyance to British troops than any other Boer gun.[50] Experience in South Africa taught the British artillery two things fairly quickly – firstly, that preliminary bombardment of enemy positions was ineffective, and secondly, that close coordination between artillery and infantry was essential. After the initial debacle at Colenso, Buller's Natal Division achieved a high degree of coordination, culminating in the final set-piece battle at Bergendal in the Transvaal where the last shell fell 10 yd ahead of the leading infantry.[51] Thomas Pakenham credited Buller with the development of the creeping barrage.[52]

In the early part of the war the British used their guns in batteries. The Boers, having far fewer guns generally, used them singly from well-concealed positions with little coordination. An exception was the battle of Spion Kop when the Boers brought a number of guns to bear on the summit with devastating results. The Boer heavy guns were four 6-in Creusot siege guns removed from their location in forts for service in the field. Known by the British as 'Long Toms' they fired a 94-lb shell up to 11,000 yd. Although both Mafeking and Ladysmith were bombarded regularly by these guns during the sieges they were relatively ineffective. The Boers had difficulty using timed fuses and therefore tended to use common shells rather than shrapnel. The use of pom-poms by the Boers has been referred to above and they had not only the .303 Maxim like the British, but the larger .45-calibre weapon as well. As the war went on the Boers relied increasingly on captured British guns.

The war was pre-eminently one in which the magazine-loading high-velocity rifle came into its own. Kitchener's victory at Omdurman in 1898 was ample testimony to its deadly defensive power, but the 27,000 dervishes who were killed and wounded there were armed with swords, spears and outdated rifles.[53] In South Africa the British Army faced an opponent whose weapons and skill in using them were at least equal to its own. The officers who gave evidence to the 1903 Royal Commission were more or less equally divided as to the relative merits of the ten-round British .303-calibre (7.7-mm) rifle (Lee-Metford and Lee-Enfield) and the five-round .276-calibre (7.0-mm) Mauser used by the Boers. The Mauser scored on individual features – clip loading which gave a higher rate of fire,[54] better sighting[55] and a softer trigger[56] – but the British rifle was thought to stand up better to the wear and tear of campaigning.[57] After the Mauser ammunition ran out the captured British rifle became the main weapon for the Boers. Ian Hamilton and Plumer agreed that some of the Boers – Plumer thought a majority – preferred it to their own rifle.[58] After the war the British adopted clip loading for the Lee-Enfield.

TRANSPORT, COMMUNICATIONS, AND MEDICAL CARE

Modern and ancient methods of transport were used side by side during the South African War. The railways made it possible to move troops and supplies quickly over great distances, but away from them the roads were little more than tracks and both sides were reliant on animal-drawn transport. The ox-wagon was the traditional form of transport in South Africa, having the great advantage that oxen grazed off the veld, unlike mules for whom forage had to be provided; but the mule was faster and more versatile and for the British Army was the more suitable near the fighting line. However, through long experience the Boers were considerably more skilled in the use of ox-wagons than the British, and this was one of the reasons why Christiaan de Wet was able consistently to outpace his pursuers in the first of the so-called De Wet hunts. The Boer commandos were mounted from the start and so increasingly as the war progressed was the British Army. It was a disastrous war for horses. Some 350,000 perished on the British side and probably 100,000 on the Boer.[59]

Permanent and field telegraph lines provided effective communications to both sides during the war. Even after the end of the conventional phase the Transvaal government was able by this means to keep in touch with the commandos under Botha and De la Rey.[60] Telephones were used extensively by the British to link the blockhouse lines. In the open landscape and clear atmosphere of South Africa the heliograph could also be used to relay signals over great distances. Early in the war the British intercepted a large amount of radio telegraphy equipment consigned to President Kruger but attempts to put it to use were unsuccessful.[61]

Compared with the enormity of what was to come in the First World War the casualties in the Boer War were light. Just under 8,000 British soldiers were killed or died of wounds, compared with 4,000 Boer combatants. Over 13,000 British soldiers died of disease, of which the largest single killer was typhoid, then known as enteric fever.[62] In organisational terms the British Army was well provided with medical services in South Africa. Shortly before the war the Army Medical Service had been reorganised on military lines as the Royal Army Medical Corps.[63] Medical care was provided by a hierarchy of general hospitals, field hospitals and bearer companies. The best medical arrangements were those available during Buller's Natal campaign, due variously to the quality of the medical staff, the relatively static nature of the fighting and Buller's personal interest in the care of the wounded. The care facilities in Bloemfontein were at first inadequate to cope with the typhoid epidemic which afflicted Roberts's army during its halt there, mainly because of the difficulty of getting in supplies by the single railway line from the Cape Colony. Medical care for the Boer commandos was provided by the Transvaal Red Cross and the Free State's own ambulance corps. Both received valuable help from foreign volunteer ambulance units and from individual doctors who chose to work independently among the commandos.[64]

Notes

1. I am indebted in this section to J.S. Marais, *The Fall of Kruger's Republic* (1961), G.H.L. Le May, *British Supremacy in South Africa 1899–1907* (1965) and Iain R. Smith, *The Origins of the South African War 1899–1902* (1996).
2. Smith, p. 62.
3. Marais, pp. 1–3.
4. Wheatcroft, pp. 173–7.
5. Marais, p. 71.
6. Ibid., pp. 72–6.
7. Smith, p. 147.
8. Le May, *British Supremacy*, p. 8.
9. DSAB.
10. Smith, p. 424, n. 17.
11. Hobson, p .61.
12. Le May, *British Supremacy*, p. 21.
13. Maj Gen Sir Frederick Maurice and M.H. Grant, *History of Warfare in South Africa* (1906–10), referred to as *The Official History* in the main text and hereafter as *OH* in the notes: *OH* i, 1.
14. L.S. Amery (ed.), *The Times History of the War in South Africa* (1900–9), referred to as *The Times History* in the main text and hereafter as *TH* in the notes: *TH* ii, 39.
15. Cd. 1791 *Royal Commission* Q.20443 (Amery).
16. *TH* ii, 84.
17. *TH* ii, 33.
18. Slocum and Reichmann, p. 79; quoted in *TH* ii, 34.
19. Breytenbach i, p. 32; *TH* ii, 72.
20. Ibid., i 35–6; *TH* ii, 87.
21. Ibid., i 34–5.

22. *TH* ii, 73.
23. Breytenbach i, pp. 37–8; *OH* i, 75.
24. Ibid., i, 32–3.
25. Ibid., i, 44–5.
26. Ibid., i, 32.
27. Ibid., i, 29–30.
28. Cd. 1791 *Royal Commission* Q.14586 (Hunter).
29. *TH* ii, 74–5.
30. *TH* ii, 96.
31. De Wet, pp. 89–90.
32. *TH* ii, 75.
33. Churchill, *My Early Life*, p. 110.
34. Breytenbach i, pp. 35–6.
35. *TH* ii, 79.
36. Breytenbach i, pp. 62–8; *TH* ii, 86.
37. *TH* ii, 30.
38. Warwick, *Black People*, p. 16.
39. Ibid., p. 21.
40. Ibid., p. 26.
41. Ibid., pp. 22–5.
42. Ibid., p.165.
43. *TH* vi 476.
44. Cd. 1790 *Royal Commission* Q.1687, 1739–45 (Brackenbury *et al.*); Slocum and Reichmann, p. 40.
45. Cd. 1791 *Royal Commission* Q.18962 (Harris).
46. *OH* i, 116.
47. *OH* i, 119–21.
48. *TH* vi, 469.
49. *TH* vi, 472.
50. Cd. 1791 *Royal Commission* Q.18494 (Marshall).
51. *OH* iii, 402.
52. Pakenham, p. 457.
53. See Chapter Five pp. 94–6.
54. Cd. 1791 *Royal Commission* Q.16974, p. 288 (Colvile).
55. Ibid., Q.15972, p. 240 (Hildyard).
56. Ibid., Q.16327 (Barton).
57. Ibid., Q.16614 (Paget) and Q.18080 (Plumer).
58. Ibid., Q.14086 (Hamilton) and Q.18080 (Plumer).
59. *TH* vi, 417.
60. *TH* ii, 82.
61. *TH* vi 361.
62. Boer casualties *TH* v, 601. British casualties *TH* vii, 25 (Appendix III).
63. *TH* vi, 502.
64 . Breytenbach i, pp. 71–4.

CHAPTER TWO

Buller

In 1899 few British soldiers stood as high in public esteem as Gen the Rt. Hon. Sir Redvers Buller VC, KCB, KCMG. A big, red-faced and imperturbable man with small twinkling eyes, he had served with distinction in a number of campaigns and his administrative gifts had been apparent in important posts at the War Office. A later Secretary of State for War described him as one of the most capable of businessmen among soldiers.[1] But for a change of government in 1898, he would almost certainly have become Commander-in-Chief of the Army.[2] A biography published shortly after his arrival in South Africa listed him as one of a line of Devon-born naval and military heroes, along with Sir Francis Drake, Sir Richard Grenville, Sir John Hawkins, Sir Walter Raleigh and the Duke of Marlborough.[3]

He was born the second son of a rich landowning family at Downe House, Crediton on 7 December 1839. His father was an MP and his mother was a niece of the Duke of Norfolk. Her death when he was sixteen, and the death six months later of his favourite sister Julia, are said to have affected him greatly. He was educated at Harrow, briefly, and at Eton. His military career began on 23 May 1858 when he was gazetted an ensign in the 60th Rifles. He went first to India and then in 1860 to China, where he was in action for the first time, taking part in operations leading to the capture of the Taku forts. Also serving in those operations was Garnet Wolseley, then a brevet lieutenant-colonel, who would later become a dominant influence in Buller's career.

In 1862 he went to Canada as a lieutenant to join the 4th Battalion commanded by Col Robert Hawley, a gifted officer who recognised and fostered Buller's potential. In 1870 Wolseley, now a full colonel, commanded an expedition to Manitoba to put down a rebellion led by a French Canadian, Louis Riel. Inhabitants of a little colony known as the Red River Settlement had objected to its transfer to dominion government and seized Fort Garry near Winnipeg. As a newly gazetted captain Buller commanded a company in the 1,200-man force. There was no fighting – Riel had left by the time they got there – but the expedition involved a journey of 1,200 miles, the last 550 miles by lake and river in specially constructed boats 25–30 ft long. Frequent waterfalls necessitated dragging the boats and carrying the supplies overland for distances varying from 150 yd to 2 or 3 miles.[4] These circumstances could almost have been devised to demonstrate Buller's qualities – his willingness to identify with his men and share their hardships, his resourcefulness and his great physical strength. Wolseley said of him in his memoirs: 'I think he was the only man with us of any rank who could carry a 100 lb barrel of pork over a portage on his back . . . full of resource, and personally absolutely fearless, those serving under him trusted him fully.'[5] In contrast to his physical robustness it is said of him that at this time he revelled privately in Greek and Latin verse and that he carried in his kit the Bible and Bacon's essays.[6]

From Canada Buller went in 1873 to the Staff College but he broke off his course there to follow Wolseley, who had been sent to command an expedition against the dominant Ashanti tribe on the Gold Coast. Wolseley, then at forty the youngest general in the Army, decided that he needed exceptional officers to help him in this task and who better than those who had been with him on the Red River expedition and whose nerve he had seen proved 'in the midst of physical dangers which silence men of ordinary manufacture'.[7] Buller, still a captain, was appointed Deputy Assistant Quartermaster General and also Chief of the Intelligence Department. Wolseley's objective was the Ashanti capital Kumasi, 130 miles inland, which was occupied and destroyed by early February 1874 after two minor battles. The campaign was a triumph, not so much of fighting as of organisation, road building (including 237 bridges),[8] supply and healthcare. It earned Wolseley the GCMG and the KCB, a parliamentary vote of thanks and a grant of £25,000. For his part in the war Buller was made a CB. A coterie of the officers who had served in the war came to be known as the Wolseley or Ashanti 'Ring'. Seven of them, including Buller, became generals and one a field marshal.[9]

On his return to England Buller was appointed Deputy Assistant Adjutant General at the Horse Guards where he gained a reputation for thoroughness.[10] In the same year he inherited Downe House on the death of his elder brother Wentworth and became a wealthy man. In 1878 he volunteered to assist Col Evelyn Wood VC, a fellow member of the Wolseley Ring, in South Africa. He went out 'on special service' and took command as a major of the Frontier Light Horse which, with considerable attention to detail, he welded into an efficient fighting force.[11] He spent four months in Kaffraria* taking part in the 9th Frontier War, helping to put down a rebellion of the Gaika and Galeka tribes led by the old chief, Sandile, with whose death the war came to an end.

Later that year he moved to Natal for service in the Zulu War in which the British forces were commanded by Lord Chelmsford and the Zulus by the warrior king, Cetewayo. Buller was not involved directly in either of the two actions for which that war is best remembered – the disaster at

---

* Later the Transkei and now part of the Eastern Cape Province.

Isandlwana, in which virtually the whole of a British force of 1,300 was killed, and the subsequent heroic stand at Rorke's Drift. His force, part of the 4th Column commanded by Evelyn Wood, was expanded in size from 200 to 800 and included a small contingent of Boers from the Utrecht district of the Transvaal led by Piet Uys, a son of one of the original Voortrekkers. A war correspondent wrote of Buller at this time: 'I found Buller there in command of some 800 volunteer irregular horsemen – or perhaps rather mounted infantry; a strange, wild, heterogeneous band, whom Buller held in sternest discipline, and made do wonders of fighting and marching by sheer force of character. A stern-tempered ruthless, saturnine man, with the gift of grim silence not less than a gift of curt forcible expression on occasion, Buller ruled those desperadoes with a rod of iron.[12]

Buller had been gazetted a lieutenant-colonel in November 1878 and in March the following year was awarded the Victoria Cross for his part in the escape from Mount Hlobane. With a small force he had occupied this 3-mile long narrow plateau standing 1,200 ft above the surrounding country and had to leave it quickly on the approach of a Zulu force of 20,000.[13] He was the last man down as his force descended via a series of rocky ledges and he personally rescued from pursuing Zulus two officers and a trooper who had lost their mounts. Piet Uys was killed trying to help his youngest son. Buller wrote of him, 'He was my guide, counsellor and friend. His loss is a most serious one to all South Africa and irreparable to me. He really was the finest man, morally speaking, that I ever met.'[14] Three months later he carried out vital reconnaissance the day before the battle of Ulundi which ended the war, narrowly escaping an ambush by 4,000 Zulus.[15] Chelmsford, who held Buller in high regard, described this as 'one of the finest episodes in this eventful war.'

On his return home Buller was promoted to the rank of full colonel, was made a CMG and appointed ADC to the Queen. His reputation as a fighting soldier was now firmly established. After a short spell as Quartermaster-General of the North British District and then in the same role at Aldershot he went back to South Africa in 1880, following the outbreak of the First Boer War. He arrived in Cape Town to take up an appointment as Military Secretary to the C-in-C of the Cape as Gen Sir George Pomeroy Colley was advancing on Laing's Nek in an attempt to break through from Natal into the Transvaal. On 27 February Colley was killed and his force defeated on the summit of Majuba. That battle effectively ended the war, as Gladstone preferred a negotiated peace to the cost of ultimate victory, but for what remained of the war Buller became Chief of Staff, with the local rank of major-general, to Evelyn Wood who had succeeded to Colley's command. Before leaving South Africa at the end of 1881 Buller wrote, prophetically, expressing his relief that the war had not been pressed to a conclusion: 'It would also have been a war from which little credit could be gained, and which would have been an unpleasant one to fight out; for the Boers had no strategical point the occupation or destruction of which would render a continuance of the struggle hopeless, we should have had to reduce them by harrying their farms and burning their homesteads. . . .[16]

On 10 August 1882 Buller married Lady Audrey Townshend, a widow with four children, but he broke off his honeymoon to join Wolseley in Egypt as head of the Intelligence Department. Arabi Pasha, a young Egyptian colonel of modest origins, having effectively seized power there was considered a threat to British interests, and to the security of the Suez Canal in particular. The resulting war was brief even by Victorian standards, and apart from its military success it was an impressive display of logistics involving the assembly of a force of nearly 35,000 men from Britain and from her foreign bases. The force from Britain required sixty-nine transport vessels of which eleven carried rolling stock.[17] The main Egyptian stronghold was at Tel-el-Kebir, 30 miles west of the Suez Canal on the railway line from Ismailia to Cairo. The canal was secured by 21 August and Tel-el-Kebir fell three weeks later after fierce fighting following a night march. Buller had personally reconnoitred the enemy positions during the days before, and was responsible for the direction and timing of the march.[18] Wolseley entered Cairo on 15 September. His reward was promotion to full general and a grant of £300,000. Buller received the KCMG.

In 1884 Buller took part in another brief campaign as one of two brigade commanders under Maj Gen Sir Gerald Graham in the expedition to the Red Sea port of Suakin in the Sudan. He fought in successful actions against the forces of the Mahdi's formidable lieutenant, Osman Digna, at El Teb on 29 February and at Tamai on 13 March. In his dispatch Gen Graham wrote of him: 'The 1st Infantry Brigade was commanded by Brigadier-General Sir Redvers Buller, VC, etc. who by his coolness in action, his knowledge of soldiers, and experience in the field, combined with his great personal ascendancy over both officers and men, has been most valuable.'[19]

He returned to Egypt in September 1884 as Wolseley's Chief of Staff in the ill-fated expedition for the relief of Gen Gordon in Khartoum at the confluence of the Blue and the White Niles, 1,800 miles upstream from Cairo. As a result of Gladstone's procrastination, funds had not been authorised for the expedition until August, some five months after Gordon's first request for help. The expedition used conventional transport, railway and steamer, for the first 800 miles to Wadi Halfa on the Sudanese border. Thereafter the main striking force was to travel in 800 specially built 30 ft boats similar to naval whalers, each boat carrying 12 men and provisions for 100 days. The river route had been chosen in preference to the much shorter route across the desert from Suakin, partly because of the strong advocacy of Wolseley and Buller on the strength of their experience in Canada on the Red River expedition, and partly because the capture of Berber by the Mahdi's forces had made the desert route less attractive. As a contingency against the possibility that river transport might not prove practicable an alternative force mounted on camels was also assembled.

Buller's task as Chief of Staff was to deliver the river and land forces to Korti, the advanced base for the striking force, about fifty miles below the fourth cataract. It was clear when Wolseley and Buller arrived there that the rescue of Gordon was going to be a race against time and the land force was therefore ordered to short circuit the great northern loop of the Nile and cross the desert to Metemmeh, 160 miles away. Because there were not enough camels for men and supplies it was necessary to make a preliminary trip to establish a supply base halfway at Gakdul Wells and the desert column finally set out from there in mid-December. It consisted of 1,800 British troops, 350 Egyptians and 3,000 camels[20] and was commanded by Maj Gen Sir Herbert Stewart. In a battle at Abu Klea, approximately thirty miles short of Metemmeh, the column was attacked on 17 December by a force of about 12,000 dervishes, who were repulsed with heavy casualties despite breaking the British square. Stewart's second in command, Col Fred Burnaby, was killed in the action and he himself was fatally wounded the following day outside Metemmeh. The command now devolved upon Col Sir Charles Wilson, an intelligence officer with no experience of fighting. He decided not to attack Metemmeh and fell back on Gubat where four of Gordon's steamers had arrived. Wilson set sail with two of these on 24 December, arriving off Khartoum on the 28th to learn that it had fallen two days earlier and that Gordon had been killed.

Buller was sent to take command of the demoralised desert column which he led back over the 100 miles from Gubat to Gakdul. By his own account he vacillated over whether to attack Metemmeh, as Wolseley had instructed, decided against it but then wished he had and finally on reflection thought he had done the right thing.[21] Wolseley endorsed his decision,[22] but Buller's critics have cited this as the first example of his discomfort with the responsibilities of independent command. The government abandoned its resolve to crush the Mahdi at this time and British forces were withdrawn to Egypt in May 1885.

Buller relinquished his appointment as Chief of Staff at the end of October and returned to the War office, where he was to remain until 1897, apart from a year in Ireland, mainly as Under Secretary, from 1886 to 1887. Initially Deputy Adjutant-General, he was Quartermaster-General from 1887 to 1890 and thereafter Adjutant-General. With previous appointments these brought his total time at the War Office to 15½ years, or one-third of his Army service. He was more than a competent administrator. With Wolseley and Evelyn Wood he was one of a trio of reformers, who thought deeply about the Army, its training and its organisation. His name is linked in particular with the creation in 1888 of the Army Service Corps. In this Buller unified as an integral part of the Army the supply and transport functions which had hitherto been provided largely by private contractors answerable to civil servants. He also established the machinery of supply and transport on a mainly regimental basis. Roberts scrapped this on his arrival in South Africa in favour of a centralised basis as being better suited to the needs of his great flank march, but Buller's system was restored in 1909 and used in the First World War.[23] In June 1898 Buller was appointed commanding officer at Aldershot, the Army's main training establishment, where in the manoeuvres that year he had his first opportunity of commanding a large body of men. He and the Duke of Connaught opposed one another, each with 20,000 men. By all accounts Buller did not distinguish himself.[24]

In the spring of 1899 Buller was sent for by Lord Lansdowne who told him that he had been selected as the best officer to act as Commander-in-Chief in South Africa in the event of war. He demurred on the grounds that he had never held independent command and suggested that the better arrangement would be Wolseley as C-in-C with himself as Chief of Staff.[25] Despite his misgivings he was persuaded to accept the role of intended C-in-C, which remained confidential and gave him little authority in the matter of preparations. He did, however, persuade the government that the core of the strategy should be an advance on Pretoria via Bloemfontein, but he was less successful when he urged the importance of taking immediate steps to protect the Cape Colony and Natal.

Boer forces invaded Natal two days after the Transvaal government's ultimatum of 9 October 1899 and Buller sailed from Southampton in the *Dunottar Castle* on the 14th. When he disembarked at Cape Town on 31 October Mafeking and Kimberley were besieged and Sir George White was hemmed in at Ladysmith with 12,000 troops, including virtually all the mounted troops in South Africa. There was considerable anxiety about a possible rebellion of Boer sympathisers in the Cape and the 400-mile frontier was protected by a mere 4,000 troops. Buller spent the first three weeks in Cape Town preparing for the arrival of the Army Corps which was following him, and he set in train the recruitment of local volunteer forces. Having decided that Kimberley and Ladysmith must be relieved before he could proceed with his planned advance on Bloemfontein he assigned two brigades under Lord Methuen to the first task and three brigades under Gen Clery to the second. He sent Gen French, who had escaped on the last train from Ladysmith, to Naauwpoort in the Cape Midlands to await the assembly of mounted infantry regiments and ordered Gen Gatacre with two battalions to Queenstown to protect the Eastern Cape. In the third week of November he decided, apparently in response to urging by the generals assigned to Natal,[26] that he should take personal command of the Ladysmith relief operation and he sailed from Cape Town on the 22nd. After disembarking in Durban on 25 November he immediately travelled to Pietermaritzburg where he spent the next ten days on administrative matters, paying particular attention to the hospital arrangements. On 5 December he went to Frere where the force for the relief of Ladysmith was assembling.

To the task ahead of him he brought an unrivalled knowledge of the Boers and of the difficulties of the Natal terrain. Between him and Ladysmith lay the winding Tugela River, flowing strongly from its source in the Drakensberg only 30 miles to the west. Beyond the river was a complex of hills stretching from Acton Homes in the west to Colenso in the east, at that time little more than a village south of the river on the railway line to Ladysmith. Some of the hills were almost mountains, rising up to 1,500 ft above the river. The principal features, from west to east, were the 3-mile Tabanyama or Rangeworthy plateau, Spion Kop, the Brakfontein ridge, the Vaalkrantz gap and the Tugela heights which, with Hlangwane Hill across the river, formed an amphitheatre of hills overlooking Colenso. Immediately to the east of Colenso the river flowed northwards for 3 miles through a gorge flanked on the right by Hlangwane before flowing eastwards again over a waterfall. Despite the fact that there had been a British garrison in the area for fifty years there were no adequate maps. This 30-mile combination of river and unsurveyed hills gave an immense advantage to the defending Boers, whose divided command was increasingly dominated by the 37-year-old Louis Botha. He made the most of a slender force of 8,000 men ranged against Buller's 18,000, rising later to 30,000. Until his last battle for Ladysmith, when he erred the other way, Buller consistently overestimated the strength of the Boers. As a result he was never aware that he had that overwhelming superiority in numbers that an attacking general normally looks for. Given his abhorrence of casualties and his awareness that a serious reverse could lead to the loss of Natal it is understandable that he displayed at times a degree of caution that seems excessive with the advantage of hindsight.

At the start of the Tugela campaign Buller's first instinct was to attack by means of a flank march on Potgieter's Drift, 25 miles to the west of Colenso, but he changed his mind on hearing of the British defeats at Stormberg and Magersfontein. As Commander-in-Chief he was anxious to get back to Cape Town and a determined frontal attack on Colenso appeared to him to be a quicker if more difficult option. He had also anticipated meeting on his flank march a Boer force demoralised by the relief of Kimberley, now deferred by the defeat at Magersfontein, and he was reluctant to overstretch his lines of communication.[27] In this change of plan he confirmed Botha's hunch that the British would want to stay

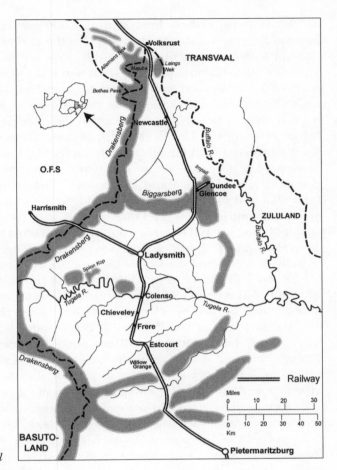

Northern Natal

near the railway line. In anticipation the Boers had mined the Colenso
road bridge, intending to blow it up once the British had crossed the
river and they were entrenched in force on its north bank and in the hills
overlooking the village. Buller may have been encouraged in his change
of plan by the fact that bombardment of the Boer positions on 13 and
14 December had provoked no response. The Boers sat tight in their
trenches, fortified, perhaps, by Cronjé's special message from
Magersfontein about the harmlessness of artillery fire.[28]

Buller's battle orders, preserving the fiction that Clery was still in
command and issued in his name, envisaged forcing the passage of the
Tugela by means of a three-pronged attack. The 5th (Irish) Brigade,
commanded by Maj Gen Sir Fitzroy Hart, was to cross via a drift to the
west of Colenso; the 2nd Brigade under Maj Gen Hildyard was to advance

23

on the Colenso railway bridge; and 1,000 men from the Mounted Infantry Brigade, commanded by Maj Gen the Earl of Dundonald were to attempt to secure a position for artillery on the slopes of Hlangwane. That this hill position – in being separated from their main force by the river – was the weakest link in their position and dangerously exposed, was only too apparent to the Boers and to some of Buller's officers who volunteered to take it by night, but Buller decided against taking it before crossing the Tugela. The 4th Brigade under Maj Gen the Hon. Neville Lyttleton, and the 6th Brigade under Maj Gen Barton were to act in support as necessary, the former between Hart and Hildyard and the latter between Hildyard and Dundonald. The artillery which had not been allocated to individual brigades, including six naval guns, was to be under the control of Col C.J. Long.

At 4.30 a.m. on 15 December the British columns began their advance down the 4-mile plain which sloped gently to the Tugela. The imprecision of Buller's orders and the lack of an accurate map led quickly to the first of the day's disasters when Gen Hart, a fiercely courageous officer addicted to the virtues of close formations, unwittingly led his brigade into a salient formed by a loop in the river in search of the bridle drift referred to in his orders.[29] There it came under heavy Boer fire from three sides. The river was swollen, possibly because the Boers had dammed it,[30] and was probably impassable even if the elusive drift had been found. However, a few brave men made the attempt to cross. Some were drowned; the handful who got across made their way back again. At 7.15 a.m. Buller, aware of Hart's predicament, ordered his retirement which was accomplished with the help of Lyttleton's brigade.

The origins of the second disaster lay partly in a fashionable theory that artillery should come into action ahead of the infantry, partly in some ambiguity in Buller's orders and partly in the difficulty of judging distance with a morning mist on the river. Col Long, a fiery artillery officer who had distinguished himself at Omdurman, had been ordered to advance under cover of Barton's brigade east of the railway line and to open fire at 'medium range' in order to prepare the way for Hildyard's advance on Colenso. An enthusiastic supporter of the guns in front theory he had interpreted 'medium range' with some liberality and from 6 a.m. onwards his three horse-drawn field batteries and even the six ox-drawn naval guns began to draw ahead of Barton's brigade. Riding ahead of the guns Long misjudged the distance and got considerably closer than he intended, halting the batteries at a point probably 1,000 yd from the river.[31] There he drew up the twelve field guns in perfect formation. The naval guns were some way behind and to the left. The Boers had held their fire during Long's advance, but as soon as he halted, the batteries came under heavy fire from both artillery and at least 1,000 rifles. In spite of this they kept up a concentrated reply to the Boer fire, until they ran out of ammunition at about 7 a.m. At this point the gunners retired to the safety of a nearby donga taking the wounded with them. Long himself had been seriously wounded in the liver, but refused attention until his men had been seen to.

The plight of Long's batteries came to Buller's attention after he had commanded Hart to retire. He ordered Hildyard to halt his advance on the Colenso railway bridge and to send two battalions in support of the guns. He himself rode down to a donga about 800 yd behind the guns,[32] where he countermanded an order to get more ammunition to them and instructed one of his ADC's to attempt to rescue them. The ensuing attempt was heroic, tragic and probably unnecessary. It cost the life of Lord Roberts's only son Freddy and other volunteers in return for the recovery of only two guns. At worst all the guns could have been recovered with relative impunity at dusk. At best, resupplied with ammunition and with the support of the infantry and the naval guns which were still in action, they could have continued with their allotted task.

Meanwhile, Hildyard's two battalions sent in support of the guns, the Queens and the Devons, had occupied Colenso and had succeeded in driving the Boers from the trenches nearest the river, but they had been unable to progress further for lack of artillery support. At 10.30 a.m. they had received Buller's order to retire as soon as the guns were recovered, followed half an hour later by the order to retire in any event. On the extreme right Dundonald had gained a foothold to the south of Hlangwane but had been held up by Barton's unwillingness to support him without orders from Buller. He was recalled after Buller had decided at 11 a.m. to abandon the ten remaining guns, and extricated his force with difficulty, incurring as many casualties as he had in the advance.

The retirement of the British forces was accomplished by the middle of the afternoon but small pockets of men remained behind, either because they had not received the order or because they chose to defer retirement until dusk. Some escaped and some were captured. The Boers delayed crossing the river in any strength until the 4.7-in naval guns had been drawn back. At about 5 p.m. they collected the ten abandoned guns and took sixty-four gunners prisoner.[33] Thus ended the battle of Colenso, with British casualties of 1,127, nearly half of which had been incurred by Hart's brigade.[34] The Boer losses were 7 killed and 21 wounded.[35] Buller blamed Hart and particularly Long for the debacle but after the war Botha described Long as 'one man who saved the British army that day' since his impetuosity had sprung the carefully laid Boer trap.[36]

After the battle Buller sent three messages, the first two of which sealed his immediate fate and the third of which played a part in his ultimate downfall. At 5 p.m., back at Chievely, he telegraphed Lansdowne with a brief report of his 'serious reverse'. This was followed up late that night by telegram in which he expressed the view that he ought to 'let

Ladysmith go'. The following morning he sent a message by heliograph to Sir George White in Ladysmith in which he suggested 'firing away as much ammunition as you can and making the best terms you can'. White, who at first did not believe that the message was genuine, replied to the effect that his position was rather better than Buller assumed, adding 'the loss of 12,000 men here would be a heavy blow to England. We must not yet think of it.' The reaction from the British government was swift. At a meeting of available Cabinet ministers on 17 December it was decided that Buller should be superseded as Commander-in-Chief in South Africa by Lord Roberts, with Lord Kitchener as his Chief of Staff. The decision was announced by the War Office on the grounds that the situation in Natal called for Buller's undivided attention. Far from being incensed, as Wolseley had predicted, Buller was relieved in both senses of the word.

During the period of inactivity which followed the battle of Colenso, Lt Gen Sir Charles Warren RE joined Buller in Natal. Then aged fifty-nine, he had an unusually varied background. He had served twice in South Africa, though not in the First Boer War, and he had been an unsuccessful commissioner of the Metropolitan Police during the time of the Jack the Ripper murders. Later he had served in Singapore as GOC and had irritated Buller, then at the War Office, by pressing on him copies of his acerbic correspondence with the Governor. He had retired after a spell in command of the Thames District. He had the reputation of being clever but ill-tempered and difficult to get on with. As an engineer his forte and chief interest were in logistics and the minutiae of military operations. He had been appointed to command the 5th Division as part of the decision to expand the strength of the British Army in South Africa following Roberts's appointment. After some confusion as to where it should best be employed the 5th Division arrived at Estcourt on 8 January 1900, bringing the strength of Buller's force up to 30,000. While Buller had not resented being superseded as C-in-C he did resent the fact that Warren held a 'dormant' appointment as his successor and friction between the two men was a significant factor in the next phase of the Tugela campaign.

Buller had decided to revert to his original plan to attack via Potgieter's Drift, and on 10 January, the day on which Roberts and Kitchener arrived in Cape Town, his force set out for Springfield 16 miles to the west and merged with Warren's en route. Barton's brigade was left behind to cover Colenso. The combined force of 23,000 men, together with its impedimenta carried in 650 ox-wagons, formed a train 17 miles long, making its way ponderously through the mud and slush resulting from heavy rain. Dundonald went on ahead with his mounted infantry and, finding the Springfield bridge over the Little Tugela intact, he disregarded his orders and occupied the undefended high ground on

Spearman's Farm which overlooked Potgieter's Drift. He was joined there on the 12th by Lyttleton's brigade and by Buller who spent about an hour surveying the scene through a telescope.

At that point the Tugela wound in a series of great loops in a 4-mile wide basin, flanked by Spearman's Farm to the south and by the Brakfontein ridge to the north. Between Brakfontein and Spion Kop to the west of it lay the road from Potgieter's Drift to Ladysmith, whose rooftops were visible 17 miles away, from Spearman's Farm. The Boers, having had ample warning of the British movements, were digging in on Brakfontein and there were probably 2,000 of them facing Spearman's Farm at that stage. Buller abandoned his intention to cross by Potgieter's Drift and on the 14th instructed Warren to reconnoitre Trichardts Drift 5 miles further upstream, and 3 miles south of the shoulder which separated Tabanyama from Spion Kop. Warren confirmed that a crossing there was feasible.

Buller decided to split the command. Warren was to take charge of the turning movement on the extreme left and Lyttleton was to command a containing force on the right with the intention that they should link up behind Brakfontein. Buller thus effectively relinquished operational control but he did not resist the temptation to intervene as events unfolded. On the 16th the 4.7-in naval guns were installed on Mount Alice at Spearman's Farm and proceeded to bombard Brakfontein. Lyttleton crossed the river at Potgieter's Drift and occupied a group of small kopjes known as the Maconochie Kopjes. Warren's force reached Trichardt's Drift that night. Had he seized the opportunity of crossing immediately he would have found a negligible Boer force opposing him, but like Buller he consistently overestimated the Boer strength and in any event he was more concerned about getting his wagons across than with making contact with the enemy. That was something he was in no hurry to do as it was one of his theories that soldiers should have a period of getting accustomed to the enemy before going into battle. The whole of the next day was spent in constructing two pontoons and the whole of the 18th in crossing the river, an operation to which Warren gave his personal supervision. Dundonald infuriated him by setting off with 1,200 mounted infantry along the road to Acton Homes to the west of Tabanyama where it joined the road from the OFS to Ladysmith. He ordered him to return 500 men to guard the cattle. Continuing with his reduced force Dundonald ambushed and overcame a 250-strong Boer patrol and took up a commanding position in some nearby kopjes. By his initiative he had secured a foothold which with speedy reinforcement could have provided the basis for outflanking the Boers and relieving Ladysmith. Warren was adamant in refusing reinforcements, proclaiming that 'Our objective is not Ladysmith; our objective is to effect junction with Sir Redvers Buller's force and then to await orders from him.'[37]

Taking advantage of Warren's leisurely preparations the Boers were now digging in on Tabanyama, Botha having cancelled his intended leave on instructions from President Kruger. After a frigid meeting with Dundonald on the 19th, after which he excluded him from his councils, Warren devoted his energies to a series of indecisive attempts on Tabanyama. The main features of the southern flank of this 3-mile plateau were a series of spurs projecting from a forward crest, between which and the summit, where the Boers were entrenched, was an open slope varying in width from 600 to 2,000 yd. Three Tree Hill, one of the central spurs, and part of the forward crest was taken relatively easily, but crossing the long slope to the summit would have entailed very heavy casualties. Despite the fact that Dundonald, using his initiative once again, had taken the westernmost spur known as Bastion Hill, Warren shied away from the idea of attacking the Boer's relatively weak right flank, fearing that it would overextend his line of communications. He favoured an attack via the central ravine which entered deep into the plateau immediately to the west of Three Tree Hill, but only after three to four days of artillery bombardment.

Buller had become incensed by Warren's dithering. He advocated an attack on the extreme left but was not prepared to impose his will on Warren or to supersede him. Instead he told Warren that unless he attacked immediately he would order his forces back across the Tugela. Since Warren was against the flank attack, and had persuaded his subordinate generals to the same view, and since Buller was against his plan to attack the centre, Warren suggested that the only alternative was to take Spion Kop. Buller told him to get on with it. Since Spion Kop had not featured in Buller's plans, little thought had been given to the implications of taking it and its true shape could not adequately be appreciated from the British positions to the south and west. As Warren did not ask for, and Buller did not offer him, the use of the observation balloon, and as there was no adequate map, neither general was aware of features which were to play a key role in the battle for the hill's possession.

From above, the western part of Spion Kop looked like a three-legged starfish with the main summit, Warren's objective, forming the central hub with spurs projecting to the north-east, north-west and south-west. The north-easterly spur merged into a high narrow saddle which, curving round to the east, linked the main summit to a long thin plateau bearing three consecutive peaks, the nearest and highest of which was a mile away and about 250 ft lower than the main summit. The Boers saw these as a triple (*Drieling*) kopje, but only the first two were visible from the south and the British referred to them as the Twin Peaks. The north-westerly spur was a narrow plateau extending about half a mile from and about 150 ft lower than the main summit bearing at its far end a small kopje known as Conical Hill. The south-westerly spur descended by a series of

28

shelves towards Trichardts Drift. It was this spur that Warren chose for the ascent since elsewhere on the British side the ascent was steep, with a sheer cliff below the main summit on the upper part of its southern flank. On their side the Boers had a shorter but steeper climb to the top. The main summit itself, 1,470 ft above the Tugela, was in the shape of an equilateral triangle with its apex to the north and its highest point nearer the south. Two features in particular were to prove to be critical. Firstly, because of the steepness of the slopes on the northern side of the hill they could not be seen from the highest point on the summit and could only be commanded from the summit's northern crest. Secondly, about 250 yd from the summit on the north-easterly spur was a small aloe-covered kopje known as Aloe Knoll, which effectively commanded the summit and the northern slopes.

Buller had understood that the attack was to take place on the night of 22 January and was annoyed the next day to find that Warren had delayed it to allow time to reconnoitre the ascent. He gave Warren the option of attacking that night, the 23rd, or withdrawing his force. At Buller's suggestion Warren appointed Maj Gen Sir E.R.P. Woodgate to lead the attack in place of his first choice, Maj Gen J. Talbot Coke. Neither was ideal to lead an assault on a mountain since Coke was still lame from a broken leg and Woodgate was fifty-five years old and in poor health. Woodgate's force was 1,700 strong, drawn from the Lancashire Fusiliers, the Royal Lancaster Regiment and the South Lancashire Regiment, together with half a company of Royal Engineers and 200 men, without their horses, from Thorneycroft's Mounted Infantry, a volunteer force raised in Johannesburg and Natal. Buller assigned Col à Court (later Repington) of his own staff to act as a liaison officer with Woodgate. The force assembled at dusk to the south of Three Tree Hill and started out for Spion Kop at about 9 p.m. led by Col Thorneycroft, a massive man, 6 ft 2 in tall and 20 st in weight. The ascent although slow went well. A small contingent of Boers near the top was quickly put to flight and at 3.30 a.m. Woodgate instructed his force to give three cheers as a signal to those below that they had occupied the summit. However, all was not well. It had been intended that each man should bring up one sandbag, but these had been forgotten. The mountain gun intended to go with them was still on its way from Frere. The engineers had jettisoned some of the trenching tools on the way up[38] and as it turned out they were not suited anyway to the hard ground on the rock-strewn summit. Crucially no telegraph line had been laid since it was intended to rely on visual signalling.

A heavy mist had settled on the summit shortly before the British arrival, reducing visibility to about 20 yd. Without further reconnaissance the force proceeded to dig in where it had arrived, constructing a V-shaped trench with its apex to the north, about 400 yd in extent and about 200 yd back from the northern crest line. Because of the difficulties of digging the trench was a shallow ditch behind a parapet of stones and rubbish about 18 in high.[39] The protection on the extreme right was particularly sparse. Thorneycroft's mounted infantry were in the centre with the Lancashire Fusiliers on the right and the rest on the left.

The Boer's initial reaction to the news of the capture of the summit of Spion Kop was one of panic since they assumed that this was part of a wider breakthrough, but they were rallied by their more resolute leaders and by Botha in particular. Both Gen Joubert and President Kruger sent telegrams making it clear that Spion Kop was to be retaken. Under cover of mist, which remained after the break of day, about 250 burghers began to climb into attacking positions from 6 a.m. The Carolina Commando, an elite force[40] led by Commandant H.F. Prinsloo, occupied Aloe Knoll. Others took up positions on Green Hill at the eastern end of Tabanyama and on Conical Hill.

When the mist lifted temporarily at around 7.30 a.m. it was clear to the British that their trench was too far back and detachments were sent forward to defend the true crest line as best they could. It was too late to dig in and in any event the ground near the edge was even harder than at the summit, so the troops had to rely for shelter on whatever rocks they could find. At 7.45 a.m. Woodgate sent à Court down to report to Buller and Warren and to request Lyttleton's cooperation on the right. When the mist lifted finally at about 8.30 a.m. the Boers opened fire. The British found themselves exposed to a 120-degree arc of rifle and artillery fire and in particular to crossfire from Green Hill on the left and from Aloe Knoll on the right; The latter took a devastating toll of the Lancashire Fusiliers, seventy of whom were found after the battle with wounds on the right side of the head.[41] At 7.45 a.m. Woodgate was mortally wounded and the command devolved on Col Blomfield of the Lancashire Fusiliers who was himself wounded shortly afterwards. The command then passed to Col Crofton of the South Lancaster Regiment whose first action was to send a signal to Warren. This was passed verbally, against the rules, by a signalling officer to a flag signaller and in the process was changed from Crofton's intended 'General Woodgate Dead. Reinforcements urgently required' to 'Reinforce at once or all lost. General Dead.' This message was to have far-reaching consequences after its receipt by Warren and Buller, but in the meantime the action on the summit became intense, with bitter fighting for the possession of the crest line. The Boer artillery, well served by efficient signalling, was able to sweep the summit with common shell and shrapnel with such accuracy that the Boers in the vicinity were unharmed.

Warren and Buller were at vantage points 6 miles apart, Warren 2 miles west of the summit near Three Tree Hill and Buller 4 miles south-east near the signalling station on Mount Alice. Although further away Buller had much the better view and unlike Warren could see Aloe Knoll and the Twin Peaks. When heavy fire moved the signallers round to the southern slope of the summit most messages were relayed to Warren via Mount Alice where Buller saw them first. Col à Court passed Woodgate's generally reassuring message on to Warren at 9 a.m. and telegraphed it to Buller. He then rode across to join Buller. Crofton's apparently desperate message was received at 9.50 a.m. As a result of this, Coke, whom Warren had earlier instructed to send up two battalions to reinforce the summit, was now instructed to send further reinforcements so that by around 11 a.m. the Imperial Light Infantry, the Middlesex Regiment and finally the Dorsets, accompanied by Coke himself, were all on their way to the top. Warren's final words to Coke as he left were, 'Mind. No surrender!'

Lyttleton had started a demonstration against Brakfontein at daybreak that morning which had been called off at 8 a.m. on Buller's orders for fear of widening the engagement. Warren passed Crofton's message on to Lyttleton at 10 a.m. and shortly afterwards he received a request for help from an unidentified person on Spion Kop. In response he sent in support two squadrons of Bethune's Mounted Infantry and the Scottish Rifles, and they crossed the river below Mount Alice at around midday. They were followed by the 60th Rifles who were also intended to reinforce Spion Kop but Lyttleton judged that the summit was in danger of becoming overcrowded and he diverted them to the Twin Peaks. His eight naval guns and two howitzers on the Maconochie Kopjes had opened fire on the eastern ridge at about 10.30 a.m. as had the naval 4.7-in guns on Mount Alice, the latter effectively harassing the Boers on Aloe Knoll. They were stopped within half an hour at the request of Warren who thought that Woodgate had occupied the eastern ridge as well as the western summit and was unaware of the existence of Aloe Knoll. Apparently out of courtesy Buller chose not to intervene.[42]

At around 11.45 Buller, who by his own account[43] could see that the British on the summit had given way – and influenced both by the note of panic in Crofton's garbled message and by à Court's praise for Thorneycroft – signalled to Warren, 'Unless you put some really good hard fighting man in command on the top you will lose the hill. I suggest Thorneycroft.' Warren took this suggestion as an order and complied immediately informing Thorneycroft by heliograph that he was in command on the summit with the local rank of brigadier general. He was unable to inform Coke, but assumed he would be told when he got to the top. Thorneycroft received this message verbally some time between midday and one o'clock. From about this time the intensity of fire increased and the Boers began to encroach on the right and centre of the main trench. At around 1 p.m. a number of men on the extreme right, where the casualties had been particularly heavy, began to raise and wave handkerchiefs and Boers came over the crest to take them prisoner. They were interrupted by the arrival of Thorneycroft, revolver in hand and hobbling with a twisted knee, who shouted, 'I'm in command here.

Take your men back to hell, sir! I allow no surrender.'[44] Some 167 men disregarded him and allowed themselves to be led off, but the remainder followed him back as he extricated himself, 'in order not to get mixed up in any discussion'.[45]

The Boers now began to take possession of the vacated trench but just at that moment the Middlesex reinforcements arrived. Thorneycroft gathered them together with his own men and charged, clearing the trench and sending the Boers back over the crest. From this time on the main burden of the fighting fell on the reinforcements from the Middlesex Regiment, the Imperial Light Infantry and the Scottish Rifles. The timely arrival of some of them on the summit helped to contain further threats to the main trench and others were engaged in fierce fighting for the possession of the eastern slope below the crest line, under the control of Col Hill of the Middlesex. They were gradually forced back but were able to hold the line on the south-eastern slope. At about 4.30 p.m. Botha accepted that his attempt to take the summit had failed and he redoubled the efforts of his artillery in the hope of forcing the British to withdraw. His guns were few in number, but placed behind Tabanyama to the north-west and below the Twin Peaks to the east, they operated unmolested by British artillery. Until nightfall they were able, therefore, to rain down shells with precision on an overcrowded summit. There were now 2,000 men there, excluding 400 killed and wounded, with shelter for only 1,000.[46]

The 60th Rifles had continued their advance towards the Twin Peaks, and splitting the battalion into two halves began their ascent at about 2 p.m. Col Buchanan-Riddell led the attack on the eastern peak and Maj Bewicke-Copley the attack on the western peak. Buller almost immediately instructed Lyttleton to withdraw them and, having received a pessimistic assessment of their chances from one of his staff officers on Spion Kop, he ordered them to retire at 3 p.m. However, his directive was ignored and under covering fire from the supporting infantry and naval guns the ascent continued and both peaks were taken around 5 p.m. Shortly afterwards, Buchanan-Riddell was shot through the head while standing on the skyline. Despite the success of the operation Buller made his displeasure clear to Lyttleton, who finally recalled the 60th Rifles at 6 p.m., explaining that it would be impossible to support them. The positions were vacated after dark.

The resolute defence of the summit was conducted against a background of inadequate communication with Warren and continuing confusion as to who was in command. Thorneycroft had heard nothing since the message about his appointment had been passed to him verbally and it was not until 2.30 p.m. that he was able to send a report to Warren, the burden of which was summed up in the last sentence: 'If you wish to make a certainty of the hill tonight you must send more infantry

32

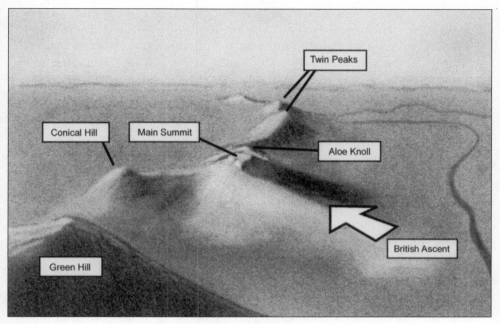

A bird's eye view of Spion Kop from the South-West

and attack the enemy's guns.' This had been delivered by hand to Warren at 4 p.m., having been seen by Coke on its way down. Coke had spent most of his time since leaving Warren directing the deployment of reinforcements from the lower slopes and he did not reach the summit until the late afternoon. On the way up he had stopped at 3.50 p.m. to send a message asking for more doctors, food and water and giving the approximate bearing of the Boer guns behind Tabanyama.[47] He sent another message at 5.50 p.m. via Col Morris in which he echoed Thorneycroft's insistence on the necessity of silencing the Boer guns and unambiguously referred to 'withdrawal', as an option. Morris delivered this to Warren at 8 p.m., shortly after it had been signalled by lamp and added his own impression that the situation was critical. At 6.30 p.m. Thorneycroft sent a further message, similar in content to Coke's, but without an explicit reference to withdrawal, which was not received by Warren until 2 a.m. It was not until Winston Churchill arrived shortly after Morris that Warren appears finally to have accepted the seriousness of the situation. Churchill, back in Natal after his escape from Pretoria, was now both a war correspondent and an honorary lieutenant in the South African Light Horse. He had gone to the summit on his own initiative at 4 p.m. On his return he sought out Warren and, narrowly averting arrest for impertinence, implored him not to allow another

Majuba.[48] At 8.30 p.m. Churchill left with a message from Warren's staff informing Thorneycroft about the preparations in hand, including sending up guns to the summit, and seeking his views. Warren sent a further message at 9.0 p.m. via Col Sim of the Royal Engineers, urging Thorneycroft to hold the hill at all costs. At the same time he sent a message to Coke instructing him to come and see him.

All this was too late. Thorneycroft, whose personal courage was beyond question and whose leadership had been decisive in holding the summit all day, had heard nothing from Warren since his appointment. With no basis for believing that effective steps would be taken to silence the Boer guns he saw no prospect of averting another day of slaughter. Hard pressed in the firing line all day he had been unaware of the capture of the Twin Peaks. Col Cooke of the Scottish Rifles and Crofton, summoned to an informal council, did not dissent when he declared, 'Better six good battalions safely down the hill than a mop up in the morning.'[49] Exercising what he believed to be his authority for the safety of the troops on the hill he ordered their retirement, which started at 8.15 p.m. Col Hill demurred when Thorneycroft encountered him on the way down but he yielded to the force of Thorneycroft's personality. Further down the hill Thorneycroft brushed aside the messages borne by Churchill and Sim. Only a comparatively junior officer, Capt Hill of Gen Coke's staff, made a determined effort to halt the retirement, pointing out to all commanding officers that it had been ordered without the authority of either Coke or Warren, but he was unable to contact Warren because there was no oil for the signal lamp. Coke reached Warren's headquarters, relocated to avoid stray shell fire, at about 2 a.m. having spent two hours in the dark looking for it. He was followed shortly afterwards by Thorneycroft.

Buller described Thorneycroft as having 'exercised a wise discretion'[50] in the absence of timely preparations for the second day's defence. Roberts described his assumption of responsibility and authority as 'wholly inexcusable'.[51] Whatever its merits or justification, Thorneycroft's decision had been unnecessary. The day's fighting had taken a heavy toll of Boer morale and in particular those in the vicinity had been unnerved by the British occupation of the Twin Peaks. Many feared that a breakthrough to Ladysmith was imminent and melted away in panic. Only Botha was confident that the British would vacate the summit and persuaded part of his force to remain at the bottom of the hill. At 3.30 a.m. a few burghers who went up in search of a fallen comrade found the summit deserted.

Buller resumed command at dawn and ordered a withdrawal across the Tugela. Including the Twin Peaks operation total British casualties were 1,439, including 384 killed, and in addition 300 were taken prisoner. The Boer casualties were estimated at 400. Out of Buller's total force of 23,000 only some 3,000 men had been involved in the battle of Spion Kop while the rest stood idly by. Of all the generals present only Lyttleton seems to have recognised that an attempt to occupy the hill could only have succeeded as part of a wider operation. Buller had spent the day of the battle in the rôle of an umpire, apparently unwilling to command or to allow anyone else fully to command. Roberts was unsparing in his judgement, 'whatever faults Sir Charles Warren may have committed, the failure must also be ascribed to the disinclination of the Officer in supreme command to assert his authority and to see what he thought best was done, and also to the unwarrantable and needless assumption of authority by a subordinate Officer'.[52]

After the withdrawal Buller's force rested while its numbers were restored by the arrival of reinforcements. The man himself was torn by conflicting considerations. On the one hand White could not hold out for much longer at Ladysmith without having to kill his horses; on the other Roberts counselled a defensive stance until his own planned advance on Bloemfontein drew Boer forces away from Natal. Buller rejected a War Office proposal that White should break out of Ladysmith and attempt to join him with 7,000 men, and his own instinct prompted him to a further attempt at breaking through. He announced on 28 January that he had found a new key to the relief of Ladysmith. He had in mind the road from Schiet's Drift to Ladysmith some five miles to the east of the Twin Peaks at the point where it passed through a narrow defile, flanked on the west by a low hill called Vaalkrantz and on the east by a slightly higher one known as Green Hill. Vaalkrantz, an extension of the Brakfontein ridge, lay on the north-east edge of the easternmost big loop of the Tugela. At the bottom of that loop, 2 miles south of Vaalkrantz, lay the twin hills known as Swart Kop, to which some of the naval guns from Spearman's Farm were now moved. The total of all guns available to Buller approached seventy. Green Hill was a westerly extension of a massive hill called Doornkop and was separated from the northern end of it by a broad ravine known as Doornkloof.

Following the battle of Spion Kop Louis Botha had gone to Pretoria and many Boers had left the area for a rest. Only some 4,000[53] remained on the Upper Tugela and of those approximately 500[54] were near Vaalkrantz under the command of Ben Viljoen, a young newspaper editor and member of the Volksraad. Alarmed by the size of Buller's force ranged against him he had asked Joubert for reinforcements, but had received instead a visit from Lucas Meyer who chided him for his lack of faith. However, he was reinforced by 350 men, who camped in Doornkloof, and a 5.9-in Long Tom was dispatched to Doornkop. Compared with Buller's massive arsenal the Boers initially had about ten guns between the Twin Peaks and Doornkop.

The battle of Vaalkrantz started at 7 a.m. on 5 February 1900 with an elaborate demonstration against Brakfontein by Woodgate's Lancashire Brigade, now commanded by Col Wynne, formerly Buller's Chief of Staff.

Under cover of this operation, which was carried out at extreme rifle range and which scarcely elicited a Boer response, a pontoon was built by midday near Munger's Drift, south of Vaalkrantz. Lyttleton's, Hildyard's and Hart's brigades were to cross here in order to seize the Vaalkrantz gap and to secure a passage for the cavalry. It was not until 2 p.m. that Buller allowed Lyttleton's brigade to lead off. Hildyard's brigade had been followed only by the Devons when Buller became concerned about the intensity of the Boer defence and aborted the attack, or, as Conan Doyle put it, yielded, as he had done at Colenso, to a 'sudden impulse to drop his tools in the midst of his task and do no more for the day'.[55] Lyttleton pressed on and after heavy fighting Vaalkrantz was taken by the Durham Light Infantry at 4.30 p.m., followed by the Rifle Brigade, the Scottish Rifles and the 60th Rifles. The Devons, whom Lyttleton had taken under his wing, occupied the lower slopes. Buller's decision meant that by nightfall the British held Vaalkrantz but not Green Hill, enabling the Boers to move in reinforcements and guns. In the morning there was an artillery battle. The British had many more guns but the Boers' were better placed. There was, however, one spectacular British success when a naval 4.7-in shell from Mount Alice 5 miles away blew up the Long Tom's ammunition wagon on Doornkop. Lyttleton and his men were now in a position much like that at Spion Kop, isolated from the rest of the force and exposed to artillery fire from three sides, but fortunately Vaalkrantz offered better shelter.

It had been a premise of Buller's plan, based on a farmer's description, that Vaalkrantz would provide an artillery platform to deal with Boer defences at Roodepoort, 5 miles ahead on the way to Ladysmith, but it proved to be a long ridge unsuitable for the purpose.[56] He now realised that he could reach Ladysmith only by forcing his way through with heavy losses – by his own estimate from 2,000 to 3,000 men – and he telegraphed Roberts to this effect asking what he should do. Roberts replied: 'Ladysmith must be relieved, even at the loss you anticipate. I would certainly persevere, and my hope is that the enemy will be so severely punished as to enable White's garrison to be withdrawn without great difficulty. Let your troops know that the honour of the Empire is in their hands, and that I have no possible doubt of their being successful.'[57]

Botha returned at midday and took command of the Boer forces. At about 3.30 p.m. a Boer attempt to storm Vaalkrantz under cover of a grass fire was repulsed by the 60th Rifles and at 5 p.m. Hildyard relieved Lyttleton via a new pontoon immediately below the hill. Buller's indecision continued the following day and at 4 p.m. he called a council of all his generals telling them that Roberts was in favour of pressing on, without disclosing the details of his message. Only Hart and Warren were for pressing on. The others settled for Warren's second choice which was to go back to Colenso and attack via Hlangwane. The retirement to

Chievely began at 7 p.m. Ben Viljoen, who had shown conspicuous personal courage in rescuing one of the Boer guns during the battle, said later that the retreat from Vaalkrantz remained as much of a mystery to him as the abandonment of Spion Kop.[58]

On his departure from Vaalkrantz Buller informed White of his intention to break through via Hlangwane within days, but his resolve weakened under the influence of Natal's fierce February heat and his renewed misgivings about the magnitude of the task. He expressed these in telegrams to Roberts, doubting on the one hand whether he could succeed without reinforcements and asking on the other that he should not be condemned to inactivity. In his final reply, sent on 15 February, Roberts put the responsibility firmly back on Buller:

> My reason for telling you to remain on the defensive is to be found in your own statements that you are too weak to relieve Ladysmith without reinforcements, and that the fall of Ladysmith is only a question of days. As, however, I have no reinforcements to send to Natal, any operations of the success of which you are not absolutely confident, seem to me to be only a useless waste of force. You should wait and see whether my advance into the Free State will draw away forces from your front and so simplify your task. I do not require that you should remain absolutely inactive all the time, provided that you keep clear of complications which result in heavy losses. Harass the Enemy as much as you can. I leave you liberty of action and rely on your assurance that you will not sacrifice the troops uselessly.[59]

Relieved by this message of the necessity of waiting for reinforcements Buller now embarked on his final and successful attempt to break through to Ladysmith. He had first to gain control of the area east of Colenso but the capture of Hlangwane would no longer suffice since the Boer defences now extended 2 miles eastwards from that hill to Green Hill* and thence were drawn back north-eastwards for a further 2 miles to Monte Cristo, the central hill in a 6-mile chain running back south-eastwards from the Tugela. To the south-east of Monte Cristo lay the hill called Cingolo, joined to it by Cingolo Nek, and it was these two hills that Buller now intended should be attacked by the 2nd Division and Dundonald's Mounted Infantry Brigade. Since Clery was unfit, Buller persuaded Lyttleton to turn down an opportunity to join Roberts and instead to command the 2nd Division in the attack. Lyttleton's laconic reason for his acceptance was that Buller's new ideas 'appeared so sound that I doubted if they were his own, and I decided to stay on with him on these terms'.[60]

* Other hills of this name featured in the Spion Kop and Vaalkrantz operations.

The Boer strength in Natal was now down by about one-third to around 11,000 men, as a result of defections and transfers to the Free State. Of these 4,000 were under Joubert at Ladysmith, 5,000 under Botha on the Upper Tugela and 2,000 under Lucas Meyer in the Colenso area.[61] Joubert asked Botha to assume overall command on the Tugela but neglected to tell Meyer, and Botha was wary of upsetting his old chief. The Boers manning the defences to the east of Colenso were connected with their compatriots by two inadequate bridges, one of which consisted of no more than planks and sleepers across some rapids.

On 12 February Dundonald drove off a small Boer patrol to enable Buller to carry out a prolonged inspection of the Boer positions by telescope from Hussar Hill, about three miles south-east of Hlangwane. The British reoccupied Hussar Hill on the 14th and Buller ordered Lyttleton to commence the attack on the right at 5 a.m. on the 17th. Lyttleton's brigade commanders were Hildyard, Barton and Col Norcutt. He was supported by Warren on the left and by approximately fifty guns. Dundonald was ordered to cover his extreme right, and exceeding his orders once again, went on ahead and around midday cleared the Boers off the summit of Cingolo, where he was joined about two hours later by men of the Queen's* in Hildyard's brigade. Buller called off the fighting at about 5 p.m. on account of the heat. In anticipation of an attack on the following day many Boers left Monte Cristo during the night.[62]

On the 18th Lyttleton brought the whole of his division into action, attacking Cingolo Nek and Monte Cristo on the right and Green Hill on the left. Monte Cristo was taken in the early afternoon and Boer resistance crumbled when the British opened fire on their laager in the plain below. However, they were able to retreat unmolested to their Tugela crossings since Buller forbade their pursuit for fear of getting embroiled with reinforcements. A small rearguard of Boers was dislodged from Hlangwane the following day and by the 20th Buller had complete possession of the area to the east of Colenso.

Of the possibilities now open to him Buller rejected a wide detour to the east and a crossing to the north and chose as the most convenient a crossing immediately to the west of Hlangwane about one mile north of Colenso. He was attracted by the possibility of using the main road, which followed the railway line to Ladysmith, and was encouraged by misleading intelligence reports to believe that only a rearguard of Boers now remained on the left bank of the Tugela. In fact, some 4,000 to 5,000 Boers were now deployed on a 6-mile front from the heights west of Colenso to Pieter's Hill. Botha commanded the Boer right and Lucas Meyer the left.

* The Royal West Surrey Regiment.

A pontoon bridge was constructed west of Hlangwane during the morning of 21 February, with the intention that as troops crossed they should turn right and follow the river. However, the first battalion across, the Somerset Light Infantry, came under heavy rifle fire when it deployed to protect the bridgehead kopjes and was pinned down for the rest of the day. Crossing continued overnight so that by daylight on the 22nd there were eleven battalions and forty guns in the restricted low-lying area behind the Colenso kopjes and they were joined by four more battalions during the morning. It was clear by now that there was going to be no easy march to Ladysmith and over the next few days there was heavy fighting concentrated on a 4-mile line of hills lying close to the river on its north-easterly course, from a point about two miles north of Colenso. From the south these successively were the three Wynne Hills, Inniskilling Hill – also known as Hart's Hill – Railway Hill and Pieter's Hill.

Later that day Wynne's brigade attacked the low-lying hills that now bear his name. He was wounded early on and the command passed to Col Crofton as it had done at Spion Kop. It was later assumed by Col Walter Kitchener, the younger brother of Lord Kitchener. Fighting continued during the night and by the following day the British had secured a precarious presence on the hills without gaining possession. Buller now delayed the advance and ordered Hart to attack Inniskilling Hill, the next in line. His Irish Brigade was joined for the purpose by two battalions of Norcutt's brigade. The hill was bombarded heavily by British artillery while Hart's troops advanced slowly along the river bank towards the low ground at the foot of the hill which came to be known as Hart's Hollow, losing men as they crossed an exposed railway bridge over the Langverwacht Spruit. The Irish Brigade, without waiting for Norcott's battalions, started the attack at about 5 p.m., coming under intensive fire from Boers on the hill itself and from adjoining hills. The Irish Brigade succeeded in clearing the Boer's forward position but were beaten back from the summit. The casualties were very heavy, amounting to 30 per cent of the troops involved and 50 per cent in the case of the Inniskilling Fusiliers. The following day the lower slopes proved to be untenable and the force retired to the shelter of Hart's Hollow.

Buller now ordered a renewed attack on Inniskilling Hill to be carried out simultaneously with an attack on the adjoining Railway Hill, both attacks to be under the direction of Warren. As he did not receive the message until 4 p.m. it was agreed that the attacks should be postponed until the following day, Sunday 25 February. Since the start of the fighting on the 21st the British had lost 1,300 men and many of the wounded had been left out in exposed positions. Botha and Lucas Meyer refused a formal armistice to collect the wounded, but on the Sunday both sides ceased firing informally. The wounded were collected and fraternisation took place. The absence of a formal armistice was to Buller's advantage since it enabled him to make dispositions for a new plan which was taking shape in his mind. This was to be a coordinated attack on three hills, starting on the extreme right, for which it would be necessary to construct a new pontoon opposite Hart's Hollow over the still water below the waterfall.

By the morning of 26 February seventy-six guns were in position on the right bank of the Tugela and preparations continued during the day. It is not surprising that the Boers interpreted these movements of men and equipment back across the river as the start of yet another British retreat and Botha alerted Joubert to this possibility saying that it would not be clear what was happening until the following morning. Buller put the final touches to his plan, having ridden the entire length of the right bank as far as Monte Cristo with Warren and some of the staff. The pontoon was to be thrown across the Tugela early on 27 February and Pieter's Hill, Railway Hill and Inniskilling Hill were to be attacked in echelon by Barton's, Kitchener's and Norcutt's brigades respectively under the overall command of Warren. Lyttleton's division was to cover the left as far as Colenso.

The pontoon was in position by 10.30 a.m. on the 27th and Barton's brigade started crossing at 11 a.m. under cover of artillery and rifle fire from Dundonald's brigade on the right bank. As they crossed news was received from Roberts of Cronjé's surrender at Paardeberg. Pieter's Hill was a 400–500 ft high plateau on which there were a number of small kopjes and Barton had secured all but the northernmost of these by 3 p.m. when Kitchener was ordered to attack Railway Hill. He had taken this by about 5 p.m. when Norcutt was instructed to attack Inniskilling Hill which he took by nightfall. It was only on the northernmost kopje on Pieter's Hill that the Boers held out but they had vacated it by midnight. There was no further resistance and the Boers retreated in confusion. Botha tried to form a rearguard but gave up when he learnt that Joubert had joined the retreat. Buller declined to pursue the fleeing Boers despite the urging of his generals and staff. As he explained to the 1903 Royal Commission: 'All that I know worth knowing about rearguards I learned from the Boers when I commanded in 1879; and I was, and am still, deeply impressed with the belief that unless there is some paramount object to be gained, an attempt to force a Boer rearguard is merely a waste of men.'[63] He entered Ladysmith formally on 1 March having been preceded by Dundonald on 28 February.

Some 16,000 Boers consolidated along the Biggarsberg, a range of hills 20 miles north of Ladysmith, but by the middle of April more than half of them had been drawn away by Roberts's advance.[64] Buller waited in Ladysmith until early May when, in a series of flanking movements, he drove the Boers northwards to the vicinity of Laing's Nek near the Transvaal border. While waiting to concentrate his forces there in early

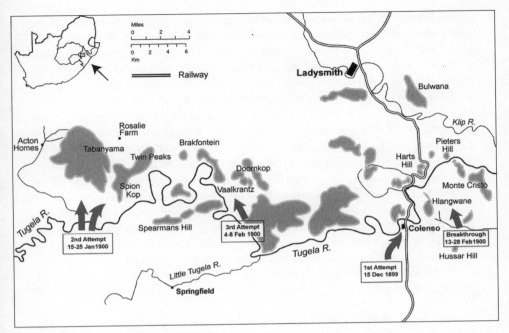

Buller's attempts to relieve Ladysmith

June he spent three days in the shadow of Majuba attempting to persuade Gen Christiaan Botha to surrender, but neither Roberts nor Louis Botha would endorse the proposed terms. On 8 June Buller fought his way through the Drakensberg escarpment into the Free State at Botha's Pass and on 11 June in another successful action he broke through into the Transvaal at Alleman's Nek, thus outflanking Laing's Nek. By now his army, profiting from its experience in the Tugela campaign, had become a highly effective fighting force, particularly in the coordination of artillery and infantry. Even Buller's severest critics found little fault with him during this phase of the war, one observer commenting that 'Speed and decision replaced pottering and lethargy; instant and continuous success were the fruits.'[65] This confident handling of his troops was apparent again in August when he joined Roberts's forces driving the Boers eastwards along the Delagoa Bay railway. On 27 August, in the final large-scale battle of the war, it was Buller who found and overcame a vulnerable salient in the Boer line at Bergendal near Belfast, with the result that Botha vacated extensive positions he had expected to hold for a month. Subsequently, he dislodged Botha from the mountainous country around Lydenburg.[66] He relinquished his command on 6 October and left South Africa shortly afterwards.

On his return to England Buller resumed his previous appointment as the commanding officer at Aldershot. In September 1901 he was attacked, in an anonymous letter to *The Times* by L.S. Amery, on his conduct at and immediately after the battle of Colenso. This was prompted by plans to reorganise the home regular Army into an expeditionary force of three Army corps which were to be trained and commanded by the generals who would lead them in battle. The implication of this was that, in a future war, Buller would command the First Army Corps for which he was responsible at Aldershot. Provoked by Amery's attack Buller made an ill-judged after-lunch speech defending his conduct on the Tugela and in particular his telegram to White after Colenso. The speech was a gift to his enemies both in the press, whom he had always treated with disdain, and at the War Office. On the grounds that he had breached the prohibition on public comment by serving officers he was relieved of his command and retired on half pay.[67] He devoted himself to the management of his estate in Devon and died in 1908. In 1905 a 13-ft high equestrian statue was erected to him in Exeter bearing the legend 'HE SAVED NATAL'.

It has been Buller's misfortune to be remembered mainly for his performance during ten weeks of a military career spanning forty years and to be judged by his failures during those weeks rather than by his ultimate success in relieving Ladysmith. *The Times History* was particularly severe in its assessment of him, describing the Tugela campaign as a 'display of supreme military incapacity'.[68] Recent historians have been kinder to him, emphasising his considerable qualities, not least of which were his personal courage, his great administrative ability and his genuine concern for the welfare of his men. Although he changed his opinion later in life,[69] the young Winston Churchill – presumably a good judge of men even at the age of twenty-five – held him in high esteem, writing shortly before the final breakthrough to Ladysmith, 'Knowing the General and his difficulties, I am inclined to ask, not whether he might have succeeded sooner, but rather whether anyone else would have succeeded at all.'[70] He was also respected by the Boers who called him 'the Red Bull'[71] and feared him and French more than any other British generals. In 1906 a number of Boers who fought on the Tugela were prepared to swear affidavits in connection with a court case in England to the effect that Buller's campaign was well conducted and that he could not have relieved Ladysmith sooner.[72] De Wet commented that Buller had to operate against stronger positions than any other English general.[73] He was probably the most controversial of the Boer War generals and no doubt the debate will continue. Perhaps the most enduring evidence in his favour is that although many of his officers were critical of him he never forfeited the respect and affection of the ordinary soldiers who served under him.

Notes

1. Midleton, p. 81.
2. Melville i, p. 275.
3. Jerrold, p. 17.
4. Ibid., p. 52.
5. Wolseley, i, p. 178.
6. Lt Col I.G. Thomas in *RCT Review* vol. 1, 18 (November 1974).
7. Wolseley, i, p. 278.
8. Farwell, *Eminent Victorian Soldiers*, p. 213.
9. Bond, p. 179 fn.
10. Jerrold, p. 80.
11. Ibid., p. 85.
12. Archibald Forbes quoted by Jerrold, p. 132.
13. Jerrold, p. 120.
14. Melville, i, p. 116.
15. Laband, p. 268 n. 55.
16. Melville, i, p. 153.
17. Bond, p. 257.
18. Melville, i, p. 166.
19. Ibid., i, p. 188.
20. Ibid., i, p. 211.
21. Ibid., i, p. 237.
22. Ibid., i, p. 242.
23. Ibid., i, p. 301.
24. Lyttleton, p. 243.
25. Ibid., p. 201.
26. Melville, ii, p. 67.
27. Ibid., ii, p. 94.
28. *TH* ii, 234.
29. For details of the confusion as to the identity of drifts and bridges see Pemberton, pp. 128–9.
30. Wilson, *Flag to Pretoria*, p. 74.
31. Pemberton, p. 137.
32. Symons, p. 163.
33. Pemberton, p. 147.
34. *TH* ii, 456.
35. Breytenbach ii, p. 322.
36. Fitzpatrick, *SA Memories*, p. 153; Pemberton, p. 148.
37. *TH* iii, 223.
38. Col W.H.H. Waters and Col H. Du Cane (translators), *The German Official*

Account of the War in South Africa (1904–6), referred to in the main text and the notes hereafter as *German Official Account*: *German Official Account* ii, p. 144

39. Ransford, p. 67.
40. Ibid., p. 71.
41. *TH* iii, 255 n.
42. Symons, p. 221.
43. Cd. 968 (*Spion Kop Dispatches*) p. 23.
44. From a Boer account quoted by Pemberton, p. 181.
45. Cd. 968 (Spion Kop Dispatches), p. 28.
46. *TH* iii, 276.
47. *TH* iii, 278.
48. As related by Capt Levita, one of Warren's staff officers. See Symons, p. 232 and Pemberton, pp. 193–4.
49. Wood (ed.), p. 218.
50. Cd. 968 (*Spion Kop Dispatches*), p. 24.
51. Ibid., p. 4.
52. Ibid., p. 5.
53. Symons, p. 249.
54. *German Official Account* ii, p. 203.
55. Doyle, p. 275.
56. *German Official Account* ii. p. 198.
57. *TH* iii, 323–4.
58. Viljoen, p. 94.
59. Quoted in *German Official Account* ii, p. 225.
60. Lyttleton pp. 221–2; Symons p. 261.
61. *German Official Account* ii, p. 227.
62. Ibid., ii, p. 237.
63. Cd. 1791 *Royal Commission* Q.14963 (Buller), p. 182; Buller, *Evidence*, p. 39.
64. Melville ii, p. 225.
65. 'Linesman', p. 167.
66. For a fuller account of the Bergendal and Lydenburg operations see Chapter Seven pp. 18–20.
67. Powell, pp. 196–200.
68. *TH* iii, 549.
69. Powell, p. 161.
70. Wood, p. 240.
71. 'Linesman', p. 140.
72. Charles Dudley in the *Army Quarterly and Defence Journal*, vol. 114, 3 (July 1984).
73. De Wet, p. 31.

CHAPTER THREE

Roberts, Part 1

India and Afghanistan

Frederick Sleigh Roberts was born on 30 September 1832 in Cawnpore, India, the first son of Lt-Col Abraham Roberts* by his second wife. Delicate in health as a young child he nearly died from an attack of 'brain fever' which left him permanently without the sight of his right eye. He was sent home to England to be be educated and after a year at Eton went to Sandhurst at the age of fourteen, where he spent two years. Lacking the wealth to launch him on a career as an officer in the Queen's Army, his father entered him in the service of the East India Company. After a year at the Company's military school at Addiscombe, near Croydon, he was appointed a second lieutenant of artillery on the Bengal establishment. He was then nineteen years old and had already acquired the nickname 'Bobs'.[1] On his arrival in India in April 1852 he spent four months at the headquarters of the Bengal Artillery at Dum-Dum near Calcutta. He found this dull and depressing, most of the force garrisoned there having been sent to Burma. When his father was appointed commander of the Peshawar Division Roberts joined him there as his ADC after a journey of three months. He spent a happy year absorbing his father's knowledge of the North-West Frontier and Afghanistan, where many years later he was to make his reputation.

He served throughout the Indian Mutiny of 1857–8 and, although employed mainly as a staff officer, was never slow to take an opportunity of joining in the fighting, notably during the siege of Delhi and at Khudaganj, between Cawnpore and Fategargh, where on 2 January 1858 he took part in an action which won him the Victoria Cross. The citation read:

> On following up the retreating enemy . . . Lieutenant Roberts saw in the distance two sepoys going away with a standard. He put spurs to his horse and overtook them just as they were about to enter a village. They immediately turned round and presented their muskets at him and one of the men pulled the trigger, but fortunately the cap snapped, and the standard bearer was cut down by this gallant young officer, and the standard taken possession of him by him. He also on

---

* Later Gen Sir Abraham Roberts GCB (1784–1873).

the same day cut down another sepoy who was standing at bay, with musket and bayonet keeping off a sowar.* Lieutenant Roberts rode to the assistance of the horseman and, rushing at the sepoy, with one blow of his sword cut him across the face, killing him on the spot.[2]

By the end of his involvement in the campaign he had had two horses killed under him, and three badly wounded.[3] In addition to his VC he had been mentioned in dispatches seven times.[4] This record was all the more remarkable considering that Roberts was only 5 ft 3 in tall[5] and blind in one eye as a result of his childhood illness. Having become an excellent horseman before the Mutiny and having now demonstrated his personal bravery in action he had fulfilled two essential requirements for a successful career in the Victorian Army. Apart from these achievements he had learnt valuable lessons from his own observations during the Mutiny. He had seen that trouble had been averted where prompt and firm action had been taken and that the lack of it, whether through complacency, indecision or sentimentality, had led to disaster.

The strain of campaigning had told on Roberts' delicate health and he accepted the opportunity to go home on extended sick leave. After fifteen months in England and Ireland, during which he met and married Miss Nora Bews, he returned to India to take up a promised appointment in the Quartermaster-General's Department, and in November 1860 was gazetted as brevet major. Apart from three short spells of active service, two in India and one in Abyssinia, Roberts was to spend nineteen years in the Quartermaster-General's Department, rising in due course to be its head. In addition to matters of supply the department was responsible in those days for operations, plans and intelligence so that, apart from active service in the field, it was one of the best preparations for high command. By January 1875 Roberts was the Quartermaster-General with the local rank of Major General. The year 1878 brought within prospect the fulfilment of his youthful ambition for a career on the North-West Frontier. The election of a Conservative government under Disraeli four years earlier had led to the reappraisal of British policy towards Afghanistan, the buffer state between India and Russian expansionism. The policy of 'masterly inactivity' espoused by the Liberal government gave way to a 'forward policy' based on active promotion of British influence. Lord Lytton,† a minor diplomat and poet, had come to India as Viceroy in 1876 with instructions to implement the forward policy, one very much in accord with the temperament and perceptions of Roberts, in whom the new Viceroy found a congenial adviser. When Lytton proposed the formation of a new frontier district to the west

---

* Indian mounted soldier.
† The son of Edward Bulwer-Lytton, the novelist.

of the River Indus Roberts was a natural choice as the Chief Commissioner Designate and, pending confirmation of Lytton's proposal, he accepted an appointment as commanding officer of the Punjab Frontier Force.

In September 1878, in what he admitted was an attempt to force the issue of relations with Afghanistan,[6] Lytton arranged to send a British special mission to Kabul. When that overture was rebuffed on Russian advice by Sher Ali, the Amir of Kabul, Lytton ordered on 21 November an advance towards Afghanistan by three forces: from Quetta towards Kandahar with a force of 13,000 men under Maj Gen Michael Biddulph, pending the return from England of Maj Gen Donald Stewart; through the Khyber Pass with a force of 16,000 men under Lt Gen Sam Browne'* and through the 60-mile long Kurram Valley to the Shutargardan Pass with a force of 7,000 men under Roberts.[7] Although Roberts's force was the smallest of the three, particular importance was attached to it since success in gaining possession of the Shutargardan Pass would directly threaten Kabul and Ghazni.[8] At the end of November Roberts learnt that an Afghan force was concentrating on the Peiwar Kotal, a pass at 9,000 ft above sea level at the end of the Kurram Valley and 2,000 ft above the floor of the valley. Realising that a frontal attack on so commanding a position could not succeed Roberts left a small force in front of the pass, making ostentatious preparations as for a frontal attack, and on the night of 1 December led a flank march up a tree-covered spur to the right called Spingawi. Despite incipient mutiny by some of his Pathans, who did not want to fight their fellow Muslims, Roberts overcame the enemy's defences at the top of Spingawi at dawn and had put to flight by nightfall the Afghans on the Peiwar Kotal itself. After a few days he pressed on without resistance to the Shutargardan Pass, 11,000 ft above sea level. From here he was able to look down on the Logar Valley which presented an unrestricted route northwards to Kabul, but his orders did not allow him to go further for the time being and he returned to the Kurram Valley.

Early in January 1879 Roberts entered the Khost Valley, an offshoot of the Kurram, with orders to dislodge the Amir's administration there and deny him supplies. Here he had his first experience of public controversy. In an unfortunate incident six prisoners were killed and thirteen wounded while escaping which, together with the destruction of villages as reprisals for attacks on Roberts's camp, gave rise to questions in Parliament.[9] The smallness of his force made it impossible for him to maintain a British presence in the Khost Valley and by the end of January he had returned to the Kurram. At the end of 1878 Sher Ali had fled to Russian territory; he died on 21 February 1879, leaving the government of Afghanistan in the hands of his son, Yakub Khan, with whom a treaty was signed at Gandamak

---

* The inventor of the uniform belt of that name.

on 26 May 1879, providing *inter alia* for the establishment of a permanent British mission in Kabul. The man chosen to head the mission was Maj Cavagnari, now Sir Louis, whose earlier rebuff at the frontier had led to war and who had negotiated the Treaty of Gandamak. In mid-July Roberts, who believed that the Treaty of Gandamak was premature because the Afghans had not 'had the sense of defeat sufficiently driven into them',[10] took leave of Cavagnari and his escort at the Shutargardan Pass with a sense of foreboding. Cavagnari reported favourably on his reception in Kabul and Roberts, having been invited to serve on a commission of inquiry into Army expenditure and organisation, returned to Simla leaving his force behind in the Kurram Valley. In August he was made a KCB and accorded the thanks of both Houses of Parliament for his work as commander of the Kurram Field Force.

Early in September 1879 Sir Louis Cavagnari, the members of the mission and his 75-man escort were massacred in the British residency in Kabul by Afghan soldiers who had mutinied for their pay. If Yakub Khan was not actually implicated in the murders, he had failed lamentably to accord the mission the protection which he owed it and the British response was to mount a punitive expedition to Kabul. Since Roberts's Kurram Field Force was the only one of the three original invasion forces still in place he was appointed to command the expedition, with the local rank of lieutenant-general. His force, with a strength of 7,500 men and 22 guns,[11] was renamed the Kabul Field Force, with Herbert Macpherson and T.D. Baker as his infantry brigade commanders, both of whom had seen a great deal of service. His cavalry commander was Brig Gen Dunham Massy who had little experience of war in that capacity. While Roberts set out for Kabul Sir Donald Stewart reoccupied Kandahar, which he had vacated in accordance with the Treaty of Gandamak.

On learning of the approach of Roberts's force Yakub Khan had gone out to meet it, and at his own request remained with the British force. As he did so ostensibly as an ally Roberts was able to represent that he was acting in support of the Amir's authority, but his presence was a source of anxiety and almost certainly a source of intelligence to the enemy. Three days later, on his forty-seventh birthday, Roberts ignored Yakub Khan's advice to wait and began his advance through the Logar Valley towards Kabul, having issued a proclamation stating the purpose of his expedition and issuing a warning against any attempts to resist it. On 5 October his leading brigade reached Charasia, 12 miles from Kabul, where the Logar River flowed through a gorge in a ridge of hills rising 1,000–2,200 ft above the plain. At dawn the following day Afghan forces in considerable strength were apparent on both sides of the gorge, their principal position extending for 3 miles along the ridge to the left of the river as seen by the British. With a feint towards the gorge and a flank attack on the enemy's extreme right, in which Highlanders, Gurkhas and the Punjab Infantry bore the brunt of the fighting, Roberts succeeded in turning the Afghans off the hills. Apart from the fact that it cleared Roberts's way to Kabul the battle was noteworthy as being the first occasion on which the Gatling gun was used in action. It was here also that Colour-Sgt Hector MacDonald* earned his commission and Maj George White† his VC.

Although Roberts's formal entry into Kabul did not take place until 13 October, he went two days earlier to the Bala Hissar, a massive fortress on the south-eastern corner of the city, within which he saw evidence of the massacre in the British residency. Here on the 12th with much ceremony he read a proclamation to the people of Kabul, giving details of how he intended to exact retribution for the massacre. On 16 October there were two massive explosions in the Bala Hissar, starting a fire which threatened a magazine containing 250 tons of explosive. The fire was contained but Roberts decided to vacate the fortress and to quarter his force in the cantonment at Sherpur, a village to the north of the city.

The instructions dated 29 September 1879 from the government of India which Roberts had received before setting out for Kabul, required him both to investigate the causes and circumstances of the massacre of Cavagnari's mission and to inflict appropriate punishment 'upon the Afghan nation in proportion as the offence was national and as the responsibility falls on any particular community, while it must also involve condign punishment of those individuals who may be found guilty of any participation in the crime'. He was instructed that the punishment of those individuals 'should be swift, stern and impressive without being indiscriminate or immoderate'.[12] To implement these instructions Roberts appointed two commissions, each with three members, the first to act as an investigatory tribunal to inquire into the causes and circumstances of the massacre and the second as a military tribunal to try and punish individuals. Col C.M. Macgregor, Roberts's Chief of Staff, was the senior member of the first and Gen Massy president of the second. By the end of November eighty-seven individuals had been tried by the military tribunal and executed.[13] Roberts did not, as he was authorised to do, impose any collective punishment on the Afghan nation and in particular on the people of Kabul. On the contrary he established a charitable hospital and dispensary in the city.

Early in December 1879, incited by an aged mullah, Mushk-i-Alam, and other religious leaders, large numbers of tribesmen began to converge on Kabul from the north, south and west.

---

* Later Maj Gen Sir Hector MacDonald ('Fighting Mac') who commanded the Highland Brigade during the Boer War.
† Later Gen Sir George White VC, the defender of Ladysmith.

On 23 December they launched a massive and fanatical but unsuccessful attack on the Sherpur cantonment in which Roberts had concentrated his forces after a failed attempt to thwart the advance. The issue was decided when he dispersed the attackers by sending out a force to attack them in flank, after which they were pursued by Massy's cavalry. After this repulse, in which the Afghans lost 3,000 men,[14] the rising collapsed. Three days later Roberts issued a proclamation granting an amnesty to those involved, apart from a few named ringleaders. A fort and villages belonging to Kohistani ringleader, Mir Bacha, were destroyed, Roberts believing that it was necessary to make an example of him.[15] In Britain, reports of those reprisals added fuel to criticism in sections of the press and Parliament of Roberts's conduct of martial law. His memorandum dated 27 January 1880 in which he justified his actions[16] was received by the War Office less than two weeks before the dissolution of Parliament on 24 March. In the press of business the new Liberal government did not make a time for it to be debated. Although Macgregor had at the time recorded in his diary his anxiety about the individual trials[17] and later about the Kohistan reprisals,[18] he subsequently expressed the view that Roberts had given a complete reply to the allegations and shown 'that every man was fairly tried'.[19] Roberts was finally vindicated in the House of Commons by the Secretary of State for War in a debate on Afghanistan in May 1881.[20]

The winter snows ensured comparative peace in Afghanistan for the first three months of 1880. At the end of March Sir Donald Stewart was ordered to leave Kandahar for Kabul, reaching it in early May, having fought off attacks on the way. As the senior officer Stewart took over command of Northern Afghanistan from Roberts, leaving him in command of the troops in Kabul. The new Liberal government in Britain reversed the forward policy in Afghanistan and a decision was taken to withdraw British troops as soon as the vacancy left by Yakub Khan's abdication as Amir of Kabul could be filled . Abdur Rahman, the British-sponsored candidate, finally agreed to accept the role and at a durbar arranged by Stewart he was formally recognised as the new Amir on 22 July 1880.

Lytton was succeeded as Viceroy by the Marquess of Ripon and one of his last acts as Viceroy was to dissuade Roberts from seeking to leave Kabul. Roberts soon had cause to be grateful for that advice. On 27 July Gen Burrows, attempting to defend Kandahar, was defeated decisively at Maiwand by Ayub Khan, a rival claimant to the amirship of Kabul, and returned to Kandahar with the loss of 1,000 of his 2,500 men. Roberts was chosen to lead a relief expedition from Kabul.

The venture bore Roberts's usual stamp of meticulous and detailed preparation, supervised by himself, down to the precise weight of kit allowed to each man – 30 lb for British soldiers, 20 lb for native soldiers and 10 lb for camp followers. The column, designated the Kabul-Kandahar Field Force, set out on its 320-mile march on 8 August, a force of just under 10,000 men with 18 guns and nearly 8,000 camp followers. Because of the roughness of the terrain no wheeled guns or vehicles were taken, transport being provided by 2,800 ponies, 4,500 mules and 950 donkeys. After Ghazni food and forage had to be gathered *en route*, often from standing crops. Firewood for cooking was a problem, it being necessary sometimes to purchase houses and break them up. Uncertain water supplies and frequent dust storms added to the hardships of the march which started each day at 4 a.m. Temperatures ranged from freezing at night to 43°C (110°F) during the day. For the last four days of the 23-day march Roberts was so ill that he had to be carried in a doolie,* but he was able to summon up the strength to sit on his horse for the entry into Kandahar on 31 August. He was appalled by the low morale of the besieged force despite the massiveness of the city walls and was particularly incensed by its failure to raise the Union flag until his relief column was in sight. Ayub Khan's force was occupying the jagged Babi Wali ridge of hills 2 miles to the north-west of the city and was entrenched in strength on either side of the Kotal (pass) intersecting the ridge. Careful reconnaissance later on the day of Roberts's arrival satisfied him that the Afghan position could be turned in a repeat of the tactics he had used successfully at the Peiwar Kotal and Charasia. Early on 1 September he threatened the heavily defended Babi Wali Kotal but sent the bulk of his force in a flank attack around the Afghan right. Ayub Khan's force was taken in reverse and routed after a charge by Highlanders supported by Gurkhas and Pioneers. He left behind his camp with all its supplies, thirty of his own guns and two guns captured from the British at Maiwand.[21]

Having accomplished all that there was for him to do in Afghanistan Roberts returned via Quetta to Simla where a medical board granted him sick leave. The symptoms described in his medical report were suggestive of what today would be recognised as a duodenal ulcer.[22] In England he received a hero's welcome. He had been made a GCB shortly after the battle of Kandahar and received a much appreciated letter from the Queen. He was surprised at the public adulation, believing his march from Kabul to Kandahar to be a lesser achievement and less dangerous than his earlier march from Kurram to Kabul. In May 1881 he received the thanks of both Houses of Parliament. However, he was disappointed when the rewards for the Second Afghan War were announced in September 1881. These gave to Sir Donald Stewart and himself a baronetcy and a grant of

* Covered litter.

£12,500, a substantial sum in those days,* but only half the amount awarded to Wolseley for the less impressive Ashanti campaign.

Roberts had been nominated as Commander-in-Chief of the Madras presidency before leaving India but after the humiliating British defeat by the Boers at Majuba on 27 February 1881 he was sent to South Africa with the intention that he should take over the command of the troops there and the governorship of Natal. By the time he reached Cape Town peace terms had been agreed and he went back to England after a stay of only 24 hours. He returned to India in November 1881 to take up the Madras command. During four uneventful years there his health improved and he was able to devote thought and energy to reforming military efficiency and ameliorating the lot of the common soldier. Having noted how often a soldier's career was blighted by harsh punishment in its early years he impressed on his commanding officers the desirability for greater leniency in the treatment of young offenders.

When he visited India before the advent of a new Conservative government under Lord Salisbury in June 1885, Lord Randolph Churchill had been impressed by Roberts and on becoming Secretary of State for India in the new administration he was influential in the decision to appoint him Commander-in-Chief in November 1885 in succession to Sir Donald Stewart, and in preference to the rival claims of Wolseley. Widespread lawlessness in Burma required Roberts's presence in that country from October 1886 to February 1887. He took direct command of the 25,000 troops sent there to restore order following the death from fever of Gen Macpherson. As a member of the Viceroy's Council Roberts worked closely first with the Earl of Dufferin and then with Lord Lansdowne, who later became Secretary of State for War, continuing in that role up to the end of the first year of the Boer War. Roberts used his position on the council to promote the reinstatement of the forward policy on Afghanistan by the building of road and rail links to strategic points on the North-West Frontier, strengthening the defences of the main garrisons and fostering good relations with the border tribesmen. He continued to work for improved military efficiency and a better life for soldiers. Well ahead of his time he realised that the introduction of the high-velocity breech-loading rifle would change the nature of warfare and he introduced more realistic and rigorous training in musketry as well as in gunnery.

In 1891 Roberts accepted an appointment as Adjutant-General at the Horse Guards but had to forego it when he was asked to stay on in India

* Approximately £500,000 at 1990s prices.

for a further two years because of the difficulty in choosing his successor. The real reason was Lord Salisbury's determination to deny the succession to the Queen's son, the Duke of Connaught.[23] In 1892 he was raised to the peerage as Baron Roberts of Kandahar and Waterford and in 1893 declined a further two-year extension, feeling that after seven years as C-in-C it was time to leave. He was unemployed for two years, living with his family in Kingsbury, Middlesex and devoting much of his time to writing articles and his two-volume *Forty-One Years in India*. He was thought to be too senior for the appointment he would most have liked – commanding officer at Aldershot. He declined an appointment as Governor of Gibraltar or Malta on the grounds that he could not afford it.[24] He was promoted field marshal in May 1895 and in the same year, following Wolseley's appointment as Commander-in-Chief of the Army, Roberts succeeded him as C-in-C of Ireland. In this comparative backwater he spent four happy years, where he could reasonably have expected to have ended his long career. In June 1897, to vocal public acclaim, he led the colonial half of the 50,000-strong diamond jubilee procession through London. This was the last occasion on which he appeared on his grey Arab, Vonolel, who had carried him from Kabul to Kandahar, and who was awarded the Afghan War Medal by special order of the Queen.*

On 11 October 1899 the Transvaal government's ultimatum to Britain expired and the country was at war. Roberts soon became alarmed at the pessimistic tone of Buller's dispatches from South Africa, fearing that his lack of confidence would infect the Army, with potentially disastrous results. He offered his services as the supreme commander there, despite his long-held belief that commanders in the field should be comparatively young men, noting that none of the generals in South Africa had had any experience of independent command. Lord Salisbury, the Prime Minister, declined this at first on the grounds that at sixty-seven, Roberts was too old. However, with news of the Black Week disasters at Stormberg, Magersfontein and Colenso, Salisbury was persuaded by Lansdowne that Roberts should go to South Africa as Commander-in-Chief, but he stipulated that he must have a younger man as Chief of Staff. The choice fell on the 49-year-old Lord Kitchener whom Roberts had met in Ireland two years earlier. There had been an immediate rapport between these two very different men and Kitchener had offered his services as Chief of Staff if Roberts were ever again appointed to command in the field. In addition to this heavy new responsibility Roberts now had to bear the burden of the grievous news

---

* The horse died in 1899 at the age of twenty-seven and was buried in a corner of the grounds of the Royal Hospital in Chelsea.

that his son Freddy* had died of wounds after attempting to save the guns at Colenso. It was little consolation that he was awarded the first posthumous VC. Roberts sailed from Southampton in the *Dunottar Castle* on 17 December and with Kitchener, who joined the ship at Gibraltar, he arrived in Cape Town on 10 January 1900.

Notes

1. James, p. 12.
2. Quoted by James, p. 51.
3. De Watteville, p. 49.
4. James, p. 54.
5. Farwell, *The Great Anglo-Boer War*, p. 152.
6. Lytton to Cranbrook, 23 September 1878, quoted in Balfour, *Lytton Administration*, p. 285.
7. Roberts, p. 346.
8. Balfour, *Lytton Administration*, p. 298.
9. *Hansard 3rd Series*, Vol. 243 1312–13 Mr G. Anderson MP (Glasgow), HC 1878–79 (100) LVI, pp. 757–66, HC 1878–79 (234) LVI, pp. 767–72; Hanna, ii, p. 213.
10. Roberts, p. 376.
11. Ibid., p. 387.
12. Balfour, *Lytton Administration*, pp. 372–4.
13. Ibid., p. 375.
14. Roberts, pp. 454–5.
15. Hensman, pp. 276–7. Robson, p. 149.
16. Robson, *Roberts in India*, pp. 164–8.
17. Macgregor, ii, pp. 135–6.
18. Ibid., ii, p. 171.
19. James, p. 144.
20. *Hansard 3rd Series*, Vol. 260 1866; James, p. 173.
21. Roberts, p. 490.
22. James, p. 164.
23. Ibid., pp. 222–3.
24. Symons, p. 19.

* Lt the Hon. F.H.S. Roberts.

CHAPTER FOUR

Roberts, Part 2

South Africa and After

Roberts and Kitchener arrived in Cape Town barely a month after the Black Week defeats at Stormberg, Magersfontein and Colenso. The generals concerned remained in the vicinity of those setbacks – Gatacre near Stormberg, Methuen entrenched on the Modder River and Buller about to make another attempt to break through to Ladysmith. In addition Maj Gen John French was near Colesberg with three cavalry brigades and one and a half battalions of infantry. Like Ladysmith, Mafeking and Kimberley were still under siege, a fact of small strategic significance but an affront to British pride and damaging to morale. Roberts's task was to instil coherence and momentum into a campaign which had become fragmented and bogged down in failure after only three months. When Buller had left England in October 1899 to take up his appointment as Commander-in-Chief in South Africa, it had been intended that his 47,000-strong Army Corps should march on Pretoria, either through Natal or through the Cape Colony and the Orange State. He had chosen the latter plan but had deferred it in order to relieve Kimberley and Ladysmith. In doing so he had broken up the Army Corps and weakened his own ability to exercise central control by going to Natal in order to take charge himself of operations there. Before he reached Cape Town Roberts had decided to resurrect Buller's plan, believing that by advancing in force through the Free State towards Bloemfontein he would draw Boer forces away from Kimberley and Natal and make the Boer positions south of the Orange River untenable.[1] Buller had envisaged using all three of the railway lines which converged on the Orange River from the principal ports of the Cape Colony: the Eastern Line from East London via Stormberg, which crossed the Orange at Bethulie; the Midland Line from Port Elizabeth via Naauwpoort and Colesberg, which crossed the river at Norvalspont: and the Western Line via De Aar and Orange River Station. The Eastern and Midland Lines had the advantage of going directly to Bloemfontein, whereas the Western Line went to Kimberley, but Roberts rejected the direct routes as the bridges in both cases were now held by the Boers. He decided, therefore, to use the western Line to assemble a large force on the Western border of the Free State, and then to undertake a 100-mile flank march across open country to Bloemfontein. This had the added advantage of making possible the early relief of Kimberley.

Roberts spent nearly a month in Cape Town preparing for his advance. To increase the mobility of his army he recruited irregular mounted infantry units locally and required every regular infantry battalion to provide one company of mounted infantry. Many of the soldiers who made up these new mounted units had first of all to learn how to ride. Roberts scrapped the existing decentralised 'regimental' system of transport and supply – one of the fruits of Buller's long spell at the War Office – and centralised it. This was not only more in accord with his own experience in India and with Kitchener's in the Sudan, but he was convinced that it was essential for a large force engaged in a long march across open country and reliant on its own supplies. Worried about the mistaken tactics which he believed had contributed to the Black Week defeats he issued two detailed memoranda espousing among other things the virtues of extended order and flank attacks. He did not underestimate the military skills of the Boers:

> We have to deal with an enemy possessing remarkable mobility, intimately acquainted with the country, thoroughly understanding how to take advantage of ground, adept in improvising colour, and most skilful in the use of their weapons.
>
> Against such an enemy any attempt to take a position by direct attack will assuredly fail. The only hope of success lies in being able to turn one or both flanks, or what would in many instances be equally effective, to threaten to cut the enemy's line of communication.[2]

In the short time available Roberts also tried to remedy the defects of British military intelligence and, in particular, the inadequacy of the available maps, one consequence of which was uncertainty about the availability of water on the way to Bloemfontein. This obliged him to move his starting point further north and to plan an advance along the Modder River, extending still further his long line of communication and bringing him closer to Cronjé's force at Magersfontein than he would have wished. In making his plans he had to take into account Milner's fears about the possibility of a rebellion of Boer sympathisers in the Cape Colony, fears which had been reinforced by the friendly reception accorded the Boer invaders of the Eastern Cape. While Roberts acknowledged those fears as valid he decided that he must give priority to the 'bolder course' of mounting his offensive.[3] However, he sent reinforcements under Maj Gen R.A.P. Clements to French at Colesberg, and to keep open the railway link with Gatacre at Stormberg, he sent Lt Gen Thomas Kelly-Kenny with the greater part of his newly arrived 6th Division to Naauwpoort Junction on the Midland Line. At the end of January Roberts's estimate of British fighting strength in South Africa was approximately 35,000 men with 120 guns in Natal, and 52,000 men with 150 guns in the Cape Colony.[4]

Paramount in Roberts's preparations was the need for secrecy. Contrary to what he planned, the Boers believed that any British offensive was likely to be centred on one of the three major railway lines and it was important that they were encouraged in that belief. Partly with that in mind, but also to counter Boer raids from the west on Methuen's line of communication and to discourage rebellion in the North-Western Cape Colony, Roberts ordered the building of a small fort at Koedoesberg Drift on the Riet River, 20 miles west of Modder River Station. The task was given to the Highland Brigade under Maj Gen Hector MacDonald which was confronted there on 5 February 1900 by Boer forces under Christiaan de Wet and Andries Cronjé. The fighting was inconclusive and the British force was withdrawn on 8 February as more important work was in store for it.

Roberts's preparations were complete by 6 February and that evening he and Kitchener left Cape Town secretly to join a train just outside the city. They arrived on the 8th in Methuen's camp on the Modder, near and to the south of which the field force for the flank march was assembling, as it had been for the past week. Only a handful of people were privy to Roberts's plans and false information had been disseminated to suggest an intended concentration 150 miles from the Modder River at Naauwpoort on the Midland Line. Roberts's field force, as constituted by 13 February, was 45,000 strong with 100 guns and comprised 4 infantry divisions, 3 cavalry brigades and 1 mounted infantry brigade all under French (who had been withdrawn from Colesberg), 2 brigades of mounted infantry commanded by colonels Hannay and Ridley, and 5 small colonial mounted units. The 1st Infantry Division under Methuen was to remain on the Modder to contain Cronjé and then to occupy Kimberley and secure the Western Railway, the 6th Division under Kelly-Kenny had been moved round from Naauwpoort, the 7th Division under Lt Gen Charles Tucker had just arrived from England, and the 9th Division, which was assembled at the last moment and included Hector MacDonald's Highland Brigade and the Royal Canadian Regiment, was commanded by Lt Gen Sir Henry Colvile. Of the total force, 37,000, including 7,000 non-combatants, took part in the flank march; 1,100 mule wagons and 600 ox-wagons made up the supply train.[5]

The starting point for the march was to be the farm Ramdam, 12 miles east of Graspan station and 7 miles into the Orange Free State. It had the advantage of an abundant water supply and had been the site of a Boer laager the previous year during Methuen's advance to the Modder River. In its final form Roberts's plan required that the Cavalry Division should relieve Kimberley, securing the drifts across the Riet and the Modder Rivers on the way. The relief of Kimberley had become urgent following a report from Col Kekewich, the military commander, that Cecil Rhodes had called a public meeting at which he would recommend surrender.

Rhodes vehemently denied that intention after Roberts had authorised
Kekewich to arrest him if necessary. The infantry divisions were to follow
the cavalry – Tucker's 7th first, then Kelly-Kenny's 6th followed by
Colvile's 9th – and to occupy Jacobsdal on the other side of the Riet
River. The mounted infantry was to secure the right flank of the initial
movement.

The Cavalry Division, accompanied by seven batteries of horse artillery
and three field batteries, set out from Ramdam towards Waterval Drift on
the Riet River, 12 miles away, early in the morning of 12 February 1900.
The Boers had deduced from a report the day before of troop
movements from Graspan to Ramdam that the British intended an
advance eastwards to Koffiefontein and it was to thwart this that two small
forces under Christiaan de Wet were in the vicinity of the Riet River. The
Free State commandant, W.J. Lubbe, with 400 men awaited French on
the near side of the river in hills to the north–west of Waterval Drift while
De Wet himself with 450 men was preparing to intercept the British on
the road to Koffiefontein.[6] When Lubbe opened fire at about 6 a.m.
French left one brigade at Waterval Drift to engage him and took the
main body of the Cavalry Division across the river 5 miles upstream to De
Kiel's Drift. De Wet, who had responded to Lubbe's call for help by
occupying hills on the far side of Waterval Drift, moved eastwards again
when he realised that most of the cavalry were crossing at De Kiel's Drift.
He took up a position on the south side of the river at Wintershoek,
commanding the Koffiefontein road, where he was joined by Andries
Cronjé with 325 men, bringing the number of men at his disposal to
nearly 1,200.[7]

By ordering the 7th Division to delay its departure from De Kiel's Drift,
Roberts succeeded in reinforcing De Wet's belief that the British
objective was Koffiefontein and in keeping De Wet at or near
Wintershoek instead of using the whole of his force to impede French's
advance to the Modder River.[8] French went on to occupy Rondavel Drift
and Klip Drift, 2 miles apart on the Modder River, late on 13 February.
Earlier he had shaken off a small force sent by De Wet to delay him by
ordering his two brigades on the right to feint towards Klipkraal Drift, 8
miles east of Rondavel Drift.[9] Even allowing for the fact that it was the
hottest time of the year, the heat must have been exceptional since nearly
every account of the advance of Roberts's army refers to it. The *Daily
Mail*'s special correspondent wrote: 'The heat, which became insufferable
at five o'clock in the morning, reached broiling point by nine o'clock,
and knew no abatement until the sun sank. The parched veldt, suffering
from an almost rainless summer, had turned its surface into powder, and
the hot wind, playing with this, half smothered the troops in floury dust
almost continuously during daylight each day, and once during an entire
night.[10]

The 30-mile march from the Riet to the Modder in such heat was an ordeal for French's horses, some newly arrived from England and not yet acclimatised, and others still suffering from an exhausting journey from Naauwpoort. Between 11 and 13 February the Cavalry Division lost 460 horses, of which 50 had died, 14 had strayed and the remainder were unfit to proceed.[11]

When the large numbers of wagons accompanying the 7th Division caused acute congestion both at De Kiel's Drift and at Waterval Drift the 6th Division was diverted to Wegdraai Drift 12 miles downstream from Waterval and only 5 miles from Jacobsdal. As a result it got ahead of the other divisions. The 9th Division crossed at Waterval Drift on 14 February but did not receive Roberts's order that all wagons which had not crossed the Riet should be returned to Ramdam. As a result they were all taken across and 200 were still at Waterval Drift when the 9th Division set off for Wegdraai. On 15 February De Wet, who had remained in the vicinity, swooped on the inadequately protected supply park and captured 170 wagons, thus depriving Roberts of 150,000 rations for his men, 30,000 forage rations and 500 slaughter cattle, the equivalent of four days' supplies.[12] Roberts decided that he could spare neither the troops nor the time to recover the convoy without endangering the momentum of his advance; he therefore abandoned it, believing that for him his troops would make the strenuous efforts required of them on reduced rations – 2½ biscuits and ½ lb of meat a day, according to a Canadian soldier writing home to his mother.[13] On 14 February the 6th Division had occupied Jacobsdal, in which only Boer women and children remained, and had gone on to relieve French at Klip Drift early the following morning.

French was now in a position to advance to Kimberley. The Cavalry Division moved off in column of brigade masses at 9.30 a.m. on 15 February 1900. For the first two miles it moved north-eastwards, parallel to the river and protected on the left by a line of kopjes. First off was the 3rd Brigade under Col J.R.P. Gordon, who had arrived from India four days earlier. A mile behind was the 2nd Brigade under Col R.G. Broadwood, followed by Col T.C. Porter's 1st Brigade and Col E.A.H. Alderson's Mounted Infantry Brigade. French was with Broadwood. As Gordon's brigade approached the head of the bend in the river where it was to turn left for Kimberley it came under heavy Boer rifle fire from a kopje to the north-east and from artillery to the north-west. The route to Kimberley lay through a shallow valley about two miles wide, rising to a low ridge 1½ miles ahead, which was occupied by Boer riflemen. French called his brigadiers together and, judging that the ridge ahead was lightly held, ordered Gordon to extend his brigade into line and to take it at a gallop. At the same time he sent the artillery to engage the Boers to the left and right. Gordon set off immediately in a cloud of dust, followed half a mile behind by Broadwood. As the cavalry bore down on them the Boers scattered, with

59

a few stragglers either speared by the Lancers or taken prisoner. Porter's and Alderson's brigades followed and the division reformed at Roodekalkfontein before going on to reach Abon's Dam, about halfway to Kimberley, at midday. Here there was enough water for the men but not for the exhausted horses. The 'gallop' through the Boer defences had in fact been a steady canter, at a speed estimated by Gordon at 14 mph* which he judged to be the fastest his enfeebled horses could sustain.[14] The division halted 6 miles north of Abon's Dam to establish heliographic communication with Kimberley but French could not persuade the town garrison that he was not a Boer impostor.[15] He decided to press on and after repelling a half-hearted Boer attack entered the town at about 6 p.m.

French's total casualties in the charge through the Boer defences had been only two killed and seventeen wounded,[16] but the toll taken of his horses all but destroyed the mobility of his force. As a measure of the damage to the horses of the whole division, the 9th Lancers, who set out from Methuen's camp at Modder River with 420 horses, had only 105 left fit for duty.[17] Thomas Pakenham described the action as 'a magnificent but quite unnecessary dash to self-destruction across the veld'.[18] It was unnecessary, perhaps, on the assumption that Rhodes would have behaved responsibly despite Kekewich's fears, but Roberts was probably wise not to gamble on that assumption. Whatever the merits of Roberts's decision, the Klip Drift charge enhanced French's reputation as a general and attracted warm praise in due course from *The Times History*, *The Official History* and the *German Official Account*, the latter describing it as 'one of the most remarkable phenomena of the war'.[19]

Piet Cronjé's success at Magersfontein had been followed by several weeks of relative inactivity for his force, as for Methuen's. The main Boer laager remained near Brown's Drift on the Modder, but on medical advice, was moved 2 miles downstream in the interests of sanitation.[20] In expectation of a renewed attack most of Cronjé's force continued to man the trenches at Magersfontein, which were shelled on most days by the British. On the whole this caused little damage because lookouts were able to spot the flash of the guns and the Boers had time to get into their trenches before the shells arrived.[21] During this period they were buoyed up by false optimism, encouraged by their success at Magersfontein and by favourable news from the Natal front. On New Year's Day 1900 Cronjé boasted that he had declined an offer of reinforcements from Piet Joubert, the Commandant-General: 'Men I don't require and guns I will take from the British.'[22]

* The average speed of racehorses around the Grand National course is 22 mph and in a competitive sprint 40–45 mph.

The demonstration ordered by Roberts at Koedoesberg Drift in early February probably had the desired effect of reinforcing Cronjé's obstinate belief that the British would not stray far from the railway, despite a warning by De Wet that Methuen would not attack Magersfontein again, and that Cronjé would be outflanked.[23] Cronjé had earlier refused permission to De Wet and De la Rey to take 1,500 men to cut off Methuen's communications south of the Orange River.[24] He was determined to keep the whole of his force of 8,000 men under his own control. It is unlikely that he was aware of the full extent of the massing of British troops to the south of the Modder River but he learnt quickly of the start of Roberts's advance from Ramdam on 12 February. He believed at first that the British movements were a feint to lure him out of his positions at Magersfontein, but began to realise the seriousness of the situation very early in the morning of 14 February when he received reports from De Wet near the Riet River and Hertzog on the north bank of the Modder near Rondavel Drift. He sent out from Magersfontein all the men who still had serviceable horses, under commandants C.C. Froneman and Tollie de Beer, in order to oppose the advance of the British cavalry hoping that, in cooperation with De Wet, they would eventually be able to drive them back.[25] The 15th was a day of intense activity. Early in the morning Cronjé ordered the removal of the laager from its position near the river at Brown's Drift to a large pan on the farm Bosjespan 6 miles to the north-east. His 450 wagons had reached the new position by the afternoon. Remaining with the laager were a number of women and children who had come to visit their menfolk during the long period of inactivity. They included Mrs Cronjé and were joined by others fleeing from the British advance on Jacobsdal.[26] That morning, 6 miles to the east of the new laager, French's Cavalry Division had broken through Froneman's defences to relieve Kimberley later in the day.

During the afternoon of 15 February there was a stream of visitors to Cronjé's tent. The calamitous way in which all his confident expectations had been overturned seemed for the moment to have unhinged him. One witness described him as sitting in his tent, quite broken, with his wife stroking his head;[27] another as being as helpless as a little child.[28] Among the visitors at a chaotic *krygsraad* was 'the French Colonel', the Comte de Villebois-Mareuil, serving as a volunteer in the Boer forces. He advised Cronjé to send his wagons and unmounted men on ahead and then to fight a rearguard action with his artillery and mounted men until reinforcements were able to reach him. When it was clear that his advice was not going to be taken he left and rode off in the direction of Kimberley.[29]

That night the men in the Magersfontein positions were called in, the laager was broken up and the convoy, leaving seventy-eight wagons behind at the pan, set off eastwards in the moonlight towards the gap between French to the north and Kitchener on the river with the 6th Division. Of the original 8,000 men who had fought at Magersfontein only 5,000 now accompanied him; 2,000 to 3,000 had been detached for service with Ignatius Ferreira near Kimberley and with De Wet to the south. Others had melted away to their farms. About one-third of those now with him were unmounted, some men having unwisely sent their horses off to good grazing about four miles from Magersfontein.[30] Many of the horses that were present were in poor condition and the same was true of the trek oxen. The 16th was spent near Klipkraal Drift on the Modder where a line of kopjes provided protection from British forces to the west, which had spotted a great cloud of dust thrown up by the retreating convoy early that morning. Boers manning the kopjes fought a successful rearguard action, thwarting British efforts to get round their flanks, and the convoy was on the move again after dark. On the afternoon of the 17th it outspanned about five miles east of Paardeberg at Wolvekraal near Vendutie Drift. Once across that drift Cronjé might well have escaped with his convoy to Bloemfontein. But he was too late.

On 16 February, the day after his relief of Kimberley, French had made an abortive attempt to capture the Boers to the north of the town, together with their guns, but he did little more than further exhaust his horses. Responding to an urgent message from Kitchener on the 17th to prevent Cronjé crossing the Modder River, French had succeeded in getting guns and cavalry units into position to the north of the Boer convoy during the day and had shelled it. In the meantime, the British infantry was converging from the west on both sides of the river, some of it through prodigious feats of marching. Since he was not prepared to abandon his women and children or his wagons Cronjé now had no option but to stand and fight, hoping that somehow Ferreira and De Wet, together with reinforcements from Natal and Colesberg, might come to his rescue. Some 400 men slipped away during the night, either to join up with other fighting units or to go home. Those who had been out defending the convoy against French thought it wiser to continue the fight outside the laager. Those who remained spent the night digging in on both sides of the river.

The scene was set for the battle of Paardeberg which took place on Sunday 18 February 1900.[31] As the representative of Roberts, who had been taken ill at Jacobsdal, Kitchener effectively commanded the British forces, although he was outranked by other generals present. By the evening the attackers had succeeded, albeit with heavy casualties, in getting around both of the Boers' extended flanks and surrounding the laager. For most of the day the Boer positions, and the laager in particular, were shelled heavily. Cronjé lost 300 men killed and wounded, but the bombardment took a much greater toll of wagons – two-thirds of which were destroyed – and animals: horses, mules, oxen and sheep.[32]

The British lost 1,200 killed and wounded – 8 per cent of the 15,000 men engaged – proportionately much the same as the Boer losses.[33] During the battle other Boer units were active to the south of the river and the day ended with De Wet in possession of the commanding Kitchener's Kopje, 2 miles south-east of the laager. Kitchener had failed to take the laager, but there was now little doubt about the eventual outcome. Roberts, having recovered from his chill, arrived the following day with reinforcements. One of his first actions was to revoke a 24-hour armistice which had been granted to Cronjé to bury his dead, believing it to be a device to gain time for the Boer relieving forces,[34] and to demand his surrender. Cronjé's refusal was mistranslated as a reluctant acceptance, but a second message, sent after troops who were marched down to the river to take prisoners had been fired on, left no doubt: 'During my lifetime I will never surrender. If you wish to bombard, fire away. *Dixi.*'

Roberts decided against a further attempt to take the laager by force but the bombardment continued daily. Cronjé remained defiant and issued orders that any burghers seen attempting to surrender were to be shot.[35] On the 20th commandants Froneman and Potgieter, with 100 men, succeeded in galloping away from the laager under covering artillery fire from De Wet on Kitchener's Kopje. Heavily outnumbered, De Wet seized an opportunity to escape from the kopje on the following day but remained in the vicinity, determined to find a way of rescuing Cronjé. Reinforcements from Natal had by now brought the strength of Boer forces immediately outside the laager to nearly 4,000 but an attack along a line from Kitchener's Kopje to Koedoesrand Drift proved unsuccessful. On Sunday 25 February there was a respite in the bombardment. During the night Danie Theron, an emissary from De Wet, had succeeded in getting through the British lines and crossing the river, now swollen by heavy rains, to urge Cronjé to break out under cover of an attack by De Wet. The river rose even further during the day, frustrating an attempt to construct a bridge. The project was postponed and there was little support for it at a *krygsraad* the following day. The British bombardment had started again and morale in the laager was now at a low ebb. At a further *krygsraad* later in the day Cronjé yielded to what had become irresistible pressure from his men and it was decided to surrender at 6 a.m. the following day, 27 February.[36] Early that morning, before the decision was known to the British, the Royal Canadian Regiment, assisted by the Gordon Highlanders, had trenched up to within 80 yd of the western side of the Boer defences.

At daybreak Cronjé's secretary, G.R. Keizer, went across to the British lines with a white flag. He bore with him a letter from Cronjé to Roberts which, translated, read as follows: 'Herewith I have the honour to inform you that the Council of War which was held here last evening, resolved to surrender unconditionally with the force here, being compelled to do so under existing circumstances. They therefore throw themselves on the clemency of her Britannic Majesty. As a sign of surrender a white flag will be hoisted from 6 a.m. today. The Council of War requests that you give immediate orders for all further hostilities to be stopped, in order that more loss of life may be prevented.'[37] Cronjé himself went across later and was received by Roberts at 8 a.m. Both of them must have been acutely aware of the significance of the occasion, heightened by the fact that they met on Majuba Day. For the Boers it had destroyed effectively any hope of winning the war by conventional means. For Britain it had ended a run of disasters which had cast doubt on her military competence. The two sat down and arranged the details of the surrender. Then they breakfasted separately under the trees by the river bank.[38]

The unwounded Boer prisoners numbered just under 4,000, approximately two-thirds of whom were from the Western Transvaal commandos and the remainder from the Free State. They included nine commandants and the formidable Maj Albrecht, head of the Free State Artillery. Before the day was out they were on their way to Klip Drift, where they were marshalled before being sent on to Cape Town.[39] Most of the women and children went to Jacobsdal, but a few accompanied their husbands as far as Cape Town.[40] Cronjé and his wife travelled south by a special train and were accommodated in the admiral's quarters in the cruiser HMS *Doris* at Simonstown[41] before being sent, as were all Cronjé's men, to captivity in St Helena. At his request he was accompanied there by his wife, his grandson and his secretary.

Anxious as he was to press on to Bloemfontein, Roberts was obliged to stay on for a week near Paardeberg in order to rest the exhausted cavalry and artillery horses. He also needed a few days to switch his main supply route from the Kimberley line to the Bloemfontein line. The loss of wagons as a result of De Wet's raid at Waterval Drift had largely been made good by replacements from Modder River and from the De Beers Company in Kimberley, together with the seventy-eight wagons abandoned by Cronjé at Bosjespan on his flight from Magersfontein. The day after Cronjé's surrender Roberts moved his encampment a few miles upstream, largely for sanitary reasons. He took advantage of the delay to reorganise the mounted infantry and on 1 March he rode across to Kimberley with Kitchener to discuss with Methuen preparations for the relief of Mafeking.

Nine miles upstream from Paardeberg lay the Boer laager near the drift known to the Boers as Modderrivierpoort, on the farm Poplar Grove. Here De Wet, now the acting Chief Commandant of the Free State forces, was consolidating his commandos. On 27 February President Steyn had visited the laager to try and encourage the burghers into a further attempt to relieve Cronjé. A few hours later he heard the news of

Cronjé's surrender and, on his way back to Bloemfontein, the news not only of the Boer retreat from Ladysmith but also of the British reoccupation of Colesberg and advance towards the Orange River. In response to Steyn's urgent appeal for help in this bleak change of fortune, President Kruger joined him in Bloemfontein where they resolved on 5 March to stop Roberts's advance at all costs.[42] They also sent a joint telegram to Lord Salisbury effectively suggesting peace with a return to the *status quo ante*, but Salisbury's reply on 12 March dashed any hopes of peace with independence.[43]

Estimates of the fighting strength available to De Wet vary from 2,500 to 9,000 men, but allowing for desertions was probably around 5,000 with seven guns.[44] The men were mostly Free Staters with some Transvaalers. De la Rey, with part of his commando, was still in Bloemfontein awaiting the arrival of his unmounted men and transport from Colesberg. The Boer positions straddled the roads to Bloemfontein on both sides of the river and curved round to the west. North of the river the right flank rested on Loog Kop, also known as Leeuw Kop, a flat-topped hill commanding the drift at a range of 4,500 yd. It was protected by the presence, 4 miles to the north-west at Panfontein, of a commando with three guns under Commandant Kolbe.[45] South of the river the Boer positions ran south-westwards to Table Mountain, also known as Bles Kop, from which the line was extended southwards for 5 miles to a clump of hills called the Seven Kopjes, visible to the British across 5 miles of open plain. From one extremity to another the Boer positions extended for 25 miles. De Wet's headquarters were just south-east of the drift[46] and he himself commanded the forces south of the river. His brother Piet de Wet was in command on the northern side. In contrast to its excellence later in the war, De Wet's scouting at Poplar Grove was poor and as late as 5 March he believed that Roberts intended to bypass Bloemfontein and make straight for the Transvaal. He seriously contemplated attacking what he believed to be a small residual force left behind by the British.[47]

For his part Roberts was determined to turn Poplar Grove into another Paardeberg and to capture a large part of the Boer force assembling there. With the reinforcements which had arrived after 18 February he now had 30,000 men and 116 guns. On the afternoon of 6 May he assembled his commanding officers and, instead of issuing formal orders for the attack planned for the following day, read out to them a memorandum which was then distributed with a sketch plan. His address was discursive and in parts imprecise, but his intentions were clear. The essence of the plan was to outflank the Boers to the south and then, having forced them on to the river, to bombard them into submission. French was to take the Cavalry Division, with two brigades of mounted infantry and seven batteries of horse artillery, on a 17-mile detour around the Seven Kopjes in order to reach the river behind the Boer positions and cut off the retreat to Bloemfontein. Kelly-Kenny's 6th Division, with artillery and one brigade of mounted infantry, was then to attack from the south-east, rolling up those positions from the Seven Kopjes to the river. Tucker's 7th Division was to attack from the west along the south bank and Colvile's 9th Division was to do the same along the north bank, both assisted by artillery and mounted infantry.[48]

The plan was sound on the assumption that French would be well on his way to outflanking the Boer positions before daybreak. Although Roberts might not have been fully aware of the fragile state of their morale, it was almost a foregone conclusion that the Boers would not stand and fight once they realised that they were being outflanked. His instructions did not specify starting times for individual divisions, although this was apparently mentioned in conversation afterwards, but Kelly-Kenny left the conference believing that his 6th Division was to set out at 2 a.m. while French believed that the Cavalry Division should start at 3 a.m. and issued orders accordingly. That was probably too late in any event, but because of the exhausted and emaciated condition of his horses – one week's rest had not been enough – he halted twice on the way so that the Boers on the Seven Kopjes had ample time to see what was happening. Predictably they withdrew and their departure led the Boers on Table Mountain to retire as well. The 6th Division was also too late in starting its attack, partly because at first its way was blocked by the Cavalry Division and partly because of Kelly-Kenny's natural caution. The result was that the Boers had left their positions before he got to them. The Boer retreat was orderly at first, and skilful placing of flank guards to the south effectively frustrated French's attempt to stop it. De Wet was distracted from the task of commanding his army by the inopportune arrival that morning of President Kruger to try and stiffen the burghers' resistance. He was not at first aware of what was happening and by the time the old president had been bundled off to Bloemfontein for his own safety it was too late to prevent the orderly retreat becoming a rout on both sides of the river. When fleeing Boers overtook Kruger's carriage not even he could stop them. Given the state of French's horses it is questionable whether Roberts's plan could have succeeded. Furthermore, French himself did not show his characteristic dash and determination on this occasion. He was said to have been 'off his game',[49] supposedly because he was upset at Roberts' having upbraided the Cavalry Division for exceeding its meagre allocation of 3 lb of oats per horse, an unjust accusation based on inaccurate figures.[50] Twenty miles further on at Abraham's Kraal and Driefontein the Boers offered more determined resistance three days later, but they delayed Roberts for only a day and he entered Bloemfontein on 13 March.[51]

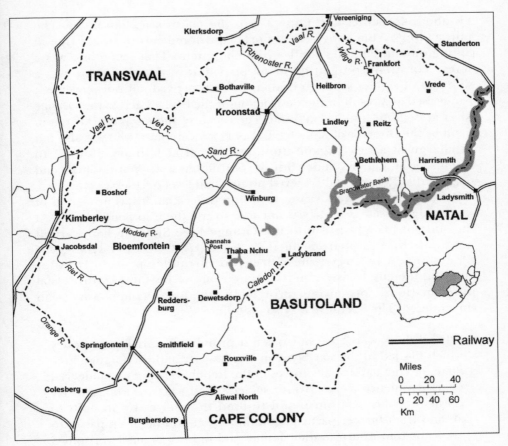

Orange Free State

Roberts spent six weeks in Bloemfontein resting and replenishing his army. In that primary purpose the interlude was successful, but it was marred by a serious outbreak of typhoid among his troops. It was here also that Roberts showed the first signs of his underestimation of the Boer will to resist, placing too much faith in civil and political measures and failing to get to grips with incipient guerrilla war in the Orange Free State. When he entered Bloemfontein, Roberts had only five days' supplies for his 34,000 men and virtually no forage for his 11,500 horses, and reinforcements were on the way. Before advancing to Pretoria he judged that he would require reserves equivalent to thirty days' supply for 100,000 troops. While he able to secure some supplies locally most had to come in by rail from the Cape Colony, where the stockpile was growing steadily, but East London, the nearest port, was 402 miles away, Port

67

Elizabeth 450 miles and Cape Town, the main base, 750 miles. The railway lines from those three ports converged into a single line at Springfontein, 90 miles south of Bloemfontein. That fact alone was a severe constraint on getting in supplies, but in addition there was a shortage of rolling stock and, when Roberts arrived, all rail movement had ceased as a result of the destruction of the bridges across the Orange River at Bethulie and Norvalspont. The repair of these was quickly put in hand by the Director of Railways, Lt-Col Percy Girouard, who was also put in charge of a new organisation, the Imperial Military Railway, to administer all railways under British control, but it was not until the end of April that Roberts had achieved his planned level of reserves.[52]

Roberts had acquired a taste for using proclamations as a weapon of war in Afghanistan and he was not slow to use them in South Africa. At the start of his advance into the Orange Free State he had warned burghers to desist from further hostility. On the outskirts of Bloemfontein he urged the citizens to surrender peacefully. After entering the city he issued on 15 March one of his most controversial proclamations, promising protection to Boer combatants who surrendered. The operative text was as follows:

> All Burghers who have not taken a prominent part in the policy which has led to the war between Her Majesty and the Orange Free State, or commanded any forces of the Republics, or commandeered or used violence to any British subjects, and who are willing to lay down their arms at once, and to bind themselves by an oath to abstain from further participation in the war, will be given passes to allow them to return to their homes and will not be made prisoners of war, nor will their property be taken from them.[53]

The initial response to Roberts's offer was sufficiently encouraging to lead him to underestimate the will of the Free State Boers to continue the struggle. As the war progressed many of those who surrendered their arms and took the oath of neutrality were persuaded by De Wet and others to rejoin the commandos.

Militarily, the interlude at Bloemfontein was a time of relative inactivity. In a small action north of the city on 29 March British forces secured Karee Siding, later to be the bridgehead for Roberts's advance. However, placing too much reliance on the apparent success of his proclamations in persuading burghers to surrender, Roberts allowed the Boer forces from the Stormberg and Colesberg areas of the Cape Colony to return unchallenged along the Basutoland border to the east of Bloemfontein – 5,500 men in all, accompanied by 1,000 native Africans, 10,000 oxen and 800 wagons.[54] For their part the Boers did little to implement a decision taken at a *krygsraad* at Kroonstad on 17 March to concentrate on offensive action by small commandos against British lines of supply, but De Wet did score two notable successes. On 31 March at Sannah's Post, 20 miles east of Bloemfontein, he ambushed a force under Broadwood and captured the city's waterworks. On 4 April at Mosterts Hoek near Reddersburg he surrounded and captured a 500-strong force under Capt McWhinnie, retiring from Dewetsdorp.[55] These actions contributed to the downfall of two British generals who failed to intervene although they had forces nearby – Colvile in the first case and Gatacre in the second. Gatacre, who had already blotted his copybook at Stormberg, was sent home, as was Colvile after another failure to intervene two months later.

Typhoid, or enteric fever as it was then known, was endemic in South Africa and was a hazard which had been anticipated to the extent that some 20,000 soldiers had been inoculated on the voyage out, although the practice had been discontinued.[56] It was already present in the Army to a limited extent before Roberts had arrived in South Africa and its incidence increased in all operational areas at about the time of the occupation of Bloemfontein, but it was there that the epidemic was most acute. Within ten days of the British arrival in the city there were over 1,000 men in hospital and when Roberts began his advance to Pretoria early in May he had to leave 4,500 men behind, quite apart from those who had been moved to hospitals elsewhere. Conan Doyle, who helped out there as a doctor, estimated that there were from 6,000 to 7,000 cases in total in Bloemfontein.[57] In his evidence to the Royal Commission Roberts gave the figure as 4,667, of whom 891 died.[58] The seriousness of the epidemic there is thought to have been attributable partly to the drinking of water from the Modder River at Paardeberg. Not only was typhoid present in Cronjé's laager but the river was polluted after the battle by the corpses of men and animals. Christiaan de Wet's successes at Waterval Drift and Sannah's Post are also thought to have aggravated the outbreak, in the first case by forcing Roberts's army onto reduced rations during the exertions of the march to Bloemfontein and in the second case by depriving the city of its main water supply for a month, leaving it to rely on tainted wells. The build-up of hospital facilities was constrained, like the getting in of supplies generally, by reliance on a single-line railway from the Cape Colony, and sick men had to be treated in overcrowded and unsuitable conditions. W. Burdett-Coutts MP, whom *The Times* had sent out as a special correspondent in January 1900 to report on medical arrangements, wrote from Bloemfontein at the end of April:

On that night (Saturday, the 28th of April) hundreds of men to my knowledge were lying in the worst stages of typhoid, with only a blanket and a thin waterproof sheet (not even the latter for many of them) between their aching bodies and the hard ground, with no milk and hardly any medicines, without beds, stretchers, or mattresses, without pillows, without linen of any kind, without a single nurse amongst them, with only a few ordinary private soldiers to act as 'orderlies', rough and utterly untrained to nursing, and with only three doctors to attend on 350 patients . . . The tents were bell tents such as were mentioned in a former letter as affording sleeping accommodation for from six to eight orderlies when working and in sound health. In many of these cases there were ten typhoid cases lying closely packed together, the dying against the convalescent, the man in his 'crisis' pressed against the man hastening to it. There was not room to step between them. . . .[59]

By the beginning of May Roberts had secured the South-Eastern Free State to his satisfaction and was sufficiently confident about the safety of the railway line south of Bloemfontein to begin his delayed advance to Pretoria. On 3 May he took a train to Karee Siding where he joined the central column of the main Army which was to advance along the line of the railway. In this column was Tucker's 7th Division, the 11th Infantry Division commanded by Lt Gen Reginald Pole-Carew, and Hutton's Mounted Infantry Brigade. French's Cavalry Division was to take up position on his left front* and Ian Hamilton, newly promoted major-general, with a mixed force of infantry and mounted men, including Broadwood's 2nd Cavalry Brigade, on his right front. To prevent a renewal of Boer activity in the South-Eastern Free State Hamilton was followed by Colvile's 9th Division and Lt Gen Sir Leslie Rundle was put in charge of the Eastern Free State. Kelly-Kenny was left behind at Bloemfontein in charge of the Southern Free State. To the west Lt Gen Sir Archibald Hunter's 10th Division was to advance to the Transvaal border from Kimberley and at the same time to send a small column under Lt-Col Brian Mahon to relieve Mafeking after joining hands with a column already near the besieged town under Lt-Col Herbert Plumer. Methuen's 1st Division was to the east of Hunter near Boshof. Hunter and Hamilton had been transferred at Roberts's request from the Natal Army after the relief of Ladysmith in which both had rendered useful service during the siege. Hunter, who had been sent to South Africa originally as Buller's Chief of Staff, was a close associate of Kitchener, under whom he had commanded the Egyptian Army at the Atbara and at Omdurman. Ian Hamilton was an ardent admirer and protégé of Roberts, under whom he had fought in Afghanistan, later acting as his

---

* French had first to refit in Bloemfontein after coming in from the Eastern Free State and did not join Roberts until 8 May.

ADC in India. He had served in South Africa in the First Boer War and was badly wounded at Majuba.

Buller's Natal Army supported the advance, acting independently, but, in the course of frequent exchanges of telegrams, Roberts found it difficult to get him to conform to any particular plan. Buller felt unable to do the two things that Roberts most desired of him, to support him in the Free State and to cross the Vaal at the same time as the main Army. Buller was still in Natal when Roberts occupied Pretoria, but they finally agreed that Buller should advance directly towards the Delagoa Bay Railway to support Roberts's advance to the border of Portuguese East Africa. Roberts was reluctant to coerce the man whom he had succeeded as Commander-in-Chief. The two men represented rival cliques in the British Army – Roberts was the most distinguished 'Indian' and Buller was a prominent member of the 'Wolseley Ring'. They had never met and neither fully understood the other's problems. Roberts said of Buller in a letter to Lansdowne on 1 April: 'He certainly is an extraordinary man. His first intentions are generally correct, but his second thoughts invariably lead him astray. . . . You will see from the telegrams which have passed between us, what difficulty I have had to keep him from changing his mind. I can never feel sure that he will carry out anything that has been decided upon, even though the idea may have originated with himself.'[60]

If Roberts was frustrated by what he saw as Buller's vacillation and tendency to dream up difficulties, for his part Buller maintained that Roberts had kept him idle at Ladysmith when he had wanted to advance. Of the two Buller had much the more difficult terrain ahead of him[61] but Roberts carried the responsibility for the whole of the British campaign in South Africa, a responsibility which Buller had accepted with misgivings in the first place and which he had yielded up to Roberts without regret. Roberts would have liked to replace him but accepted that he was virtually unsackable because of his continuing popularity with a large section of the Army and his public image as a dogged soldier who had persevered and succeeded in the face of great difficulties.[62] There was also a more personal reason which might have inhibited Roberts's dealings with Buller. He would have been less than human if privately he had not attributed his son Freddy's death to Buller's handling of the battle of Colenso.

Roberts, French and Hamilton had between them 38,000 men and 100 guns opposed by not more than 3,000 Transvaalers and 5,000 Free Staters.[63] Apart from a series of small rivers there was no natural line of defence as there had been at Magersfontein and there was little the Boers could do but fight a series of holding actions, always withdrawing in time to save their guns and transport. The first of these actions was fought near

Brandfort by De la Rey on 3 May, followed by actions on the Vet River on 5 May and on the Sand River, in defence of Kroonstad, on the 10th. Here Louis Botha took over from De la Rey, who returned to his native Western Transvaal to oppose the relief of Mafeking. Using his almost invariable method of attack, Roberts extended his line over a wide front with his flanks thrown forward. Making skilful use of their meagre resources the Boers were able to thwart the attempts to outflank them, by French to the west and by Hamilton to the east. However, in so doing they were obliged to weaken their centre so that Roberts had no difficulty in breaking through. On 12 May he occupied Kroonstad, having covered a distance of 128 miles in 10 days. The Free State government, condemned henceforth to a peripatetic existence, moved its capital successively to Lindley, Heilbron and Frankfort. Roberts was now 870 miles from his main supply base in Cape Town and he found it necessary to spend 10 days in Kroonstad, replenishing supplies and making arrangements to deal with a renewed outbreak of typhoid.[64] His most urgent task was the repair of the railway line to Bloemfontein which had been blown up in seventeen places, including the bridges over the main rivers. Much of the skilled demolition work had been carried out by the Irish Brigade, commanded by Col J.Y.F. Blake, a West Pointer fighting for the Boers.[65]

For the crossing of the Vaal, Roberts concentrated his forces west of the railway line, bringing Ian Hamilton's column across from the east to act in concert with French and at the same time bringing Methuen in eastwards from Boshof to back them up. Two of French's cavalry brigades crossed into the Transvaal on 24 May and on the same day, the Queen's birthday, Roberts proclaimed the annexation of the Orange Free State 'to Her Majesty's Dominions'.[66] He crossed the Vaal near Vereeniging on 27 May with the 7th and 11th Divisions and the 3rd Cavalry Brigade, and advanced the next day towards Germiston, about eight miles east of Johannesburg. French and Hamilton worked their way round to the south-west of Johannesburg where a ridge of rocky hills called the Klipriviersberg was occupied by Botha with a force reduced by desertions to about 5,000. To the west of him Doornkop was occupied by Gen Sarel Oosthuizen. Botha repelled French's attack on the Klipriviersberg on 28 May and initially his way was blocked on the 29th at Doornkop by Oosthuizen, but during the afternoon Hamilton came to his assistance, launching a determined frontal attack against Oosthuizen's positions in which the Gordon Highlanders played the leading part, assisted by the CIV (City Imperial Volunteers). Under the combined impact of this attack and a flank attack by French's cavalry the Boers withdrew, removing the last obstacle to the occupation of Johannesburg. On 30 May French and Hamilton remained to the west of Johannesburg. Roberts was on the opposite side at Germiston where, in response to a flag of truce, he met Dr Krause, the Acting Commissioner of Johannesburg, to whom he gave an undertaking to delay his occupation of the town for 24 hours to enable the armed burghers to escape, in return for an undertaking that the gold mines would be left intact. The Boers had, in fact, already agreed among themselves, on Botha's insistence, not to destroy the mines. When Botha met Roberts in London after the war he told him that he had spent the night of 29 May in Germiston, within a few hundred yards of where Roberts had been sleeping, and that he had made his escape by joining a British patrol, passing himself off as one of the many colonial troops with the British forces, and galloping off at an opportune moment.[67]

Roberts received the formal surrender of Johannesburg on 31 May 1900 and entered the town at noon, later establishing his headquarters at Orange Grove, a suburb 3 miles to the north on the road to Pretoria. He was now in a vulnerable position with his main supply base over 1,000 miles away and dependent over much of that distance on a single railway line. Renewed Boer activity in the Free State added to his anxieties. However, he resisted advice to pause in Johannesburg and consolidate, believing it essential to press on and follow up his successes. Not least of his considerations was the presence in Pretoria of 4,000 British prisoners of war and the possibility that the Boers might move them elsewhere if given time. He resumed his advance on 3 June. Kruger's government had already accepted the futility of attempting to defend Pretoria. Kruger and members of the Executive Council had left the capital on the 29th, taking with them the State archives and available money in order to establish a new seat of government at Machadodorp, 150 miles to the east of Pretoria on the Delagoa Bay Railway, pausing at Middelburg on the way. The guns had been removed from the expensively built forts around Pretoria. On 1 June Botha, De la Rey and other senior Boer commanders had met at the telegraph offices in the town where, dismayed at the extent of the demoralisation of the rank and file, they sent a telegram to Kruger at Middelburg, in which they tentatively suggested peace negotiations. Kruger immediately consulted Steyn. By the time the Transvaal military leaders reconvened the following day for a *krygsraad* in the hall of the Second Volksraad, the mood had changed. Even before the content of the Free State President's scornful response to Kruger was made known some of the junior Transvaal commanders had castigated their seniors for their faint-heartedness, and those present applied themselves to practical measures for the defence of Pretoria.[68] It was agreed that the objective would be solely to delay the British for a day to ensure the removal of ammunition and of the cash remaining in the custody of the bank. Botha accordingly established a line of defence along both banks of Six Mile Spruit, a stream 6 miles south of the city, with a second line of defence under De la Rey along a line of hills at Quaggaspoort, site of one of the disarmed forts. By now desertions had whittled down his available forces to between 1,500 and 2,000.

Roberts's forces were deployed to the south and west of Pretoria. Apart from a small force which made a half-hearted attempt to destroy the railway line he sent nothing to the east of the town. He had convinced himself that the occupation of the Boer capital, which was now inevitable, would end the war. On 4 June the Boer holding action at Six Mile Spruit achieved the desired delay. In the evening Lt-Col H. de B. de Lisle, whose mounted infantry regiment had followed the retreating Boers to within 2,000 yd of Pretoria, sent an officer under a flag of truce into the town, demanding its surrender in Roberts's name. This produced a reply from Botha offering to meet Roberts the next morning to consult about the surrender of the town or the removal of women and children. In response Roberts undertook not to move his forces any closer than the position reached by de Lisle before meeting Botha at 9 a.m., provided he received from Botha during the night an offer to surrender Pretoria unconditionally. Botha replied: 'With reference to your verbal demand, this serves to state that I have resolved not to defend the town any further, and I trust you will protect the women and children and private properties. This is, of course, because I understand from your message that you will not give us reasonable time to remove the women and children, such as was granted by us at the time to the officer commanding at Ladysmith.' Roberts did not respond to Botha's comment about the women and children but after the war suggested to the Royal Commission that conditions were not the same as they had been at Ladysmith, and that if the Boers had any fears for their women and children they would not have waited to remove them until the British were 'at the very gates of the city'.[69]

Roberts entered Pretoria at 9 a.m. to meet officials at the railway station, the Boer army having left during the night. At 2 p.m. he made his formal entry, marked by the hoisting of Lady Roberts's silk Union flag on the Raadzaal and a march past by Pole-Carew's and Ian Hamilton's divisions, after which he moved into the British residency. Within a day or two he had been persuaded by prominent locals, including Abe Bailey the mining magnate, that Botha was interested in discussing peace terms. The involvement of Botha's English-speaking wife, Annie, lent credibility to their advice. She called on Roberts on 8 June having, with his permission, visited Botha the day before in his camp 15 miles east of Pretoria. According to Roberts she told him that Botha was most anxious to meet him, and at her request he gave her a letter to convey to her husband proposing a meeting at 11 a.m. the following day at the house of Sammy Marks,* not far from Botha's camp. Botha replied:

* A prominent businessman well disposed to the Kruger government.

74

From your unsigned letter, dated this day, delivered to me by your messenger, it appears as if I had expressed a wish to have a personal interview with your Excellency. This, however, is wrong, as I, on my side, was brought under the impression by Mr De Souza* as well as by others, that your Excellency wished to have an interview with me to make certain proposals to me. The nature of these proposals were so entirely unknown to me personally, as also to the go-between who brought them, that I could not believe that they came from your Excellency, and I expressed the feeling to these people that if you wished to see me on any subject your Excellency could personally propose an interview. I do not see any reason for departing from this position.

Roberts concluded that Botha had changed his mind because of the successes of the De Wet brothers in the Free State – Piet de Wet's capture of the yeomanry unit at Lindley on 29 May and Christiaan's coup at Roodewal Station on 7 June[70] – but Botha did not hear of the latter until 10 June.[71] According to Smuts a number of people, apart from Mrs Botha, came to see Botha with passes from Roberts or his staff, 'some of them of local consequence', and did their best to persuade him to end the war, even to the extent of offering personal inducements.[72] Botha was promised that he would not be sent to St Helena and both he and De la Rey were offered annuities of £10,000† each if they laid down their arms.[73] Smuts was inclined to believe that Roberts neither authorised nor even knew about these crude attempts to subvert the Boer leaders, but he criticised Roberts for his choice of agents and for his insensitivity in using Mrs Botha as an intermediary.

Roberts persevered for another few days with another peace initiative, prompted by a family friend of the Bothas and aimed at President Kruger himself, but it came to nothing. It is not clear what prompted these interchanges between the two sides. Smuts thought that captured telegraph clerks had revealed to the British the content of the defeatist telegram sent to Kruger by the despondent Transvaal generals on 1 June.[74] Whatever it was that led to Roberts's peace initiatives they gave Botha an opportunity to play for time while he built up his strength to the east of Pretoria. Since the low point of 1 June the Boer commanders had recovered their nerve and Botha had managed to assemble a force of 6,000 men and 23 guns[75] along the eastward extension of the Magaliesberg which straddled the railway line along which Kruger and his government had escaped at the end of May. Mindful of Roberts's almost

---

* One of the Boer officials.
† About £400,000 at 1990s prices.

invariable outflanking tactics Botha spread his force over a front of 30 miles with its centre on the 6-mile plateau known as Diamond Hill, approximately 20 miles east of Pretoria. De la Rey commanded the Boer right and Botha himself the centre and left. Of the 200,000 British troops in South Africa Roberts was able to put only 14,000 men to oppose them, after providing for garrisons in captured towns, the protection of his 1,000-mile supply route from the Cape and the containment of guerrilla activity in the Free State.

The battle of Diamond Hill, or the battle of Donkerhoek as it was known to the Boers, began on Monday 11 June 1900. As Botha had anticipated, Roberts planned to throw his flanks forward, under French on the British left and Broadwood on the right, initially holding back the centre under Pole-Carew and Ian Hamilton. So successful were Botha's defensive measures on the first day that the British flanks were almost outflanked themselves. French, with a much depleted force, was in particular difficulty against De la Rey, who had allowed him to enter unopposed the Kameelfontein Valley which he commanded on three sides. French was obliged to dismount his men in order to return the Boer fire and to abandon his assigned task of turning the Boer right. Although he had no reserve ammunition his men were well protected and his casualties were light, so that at the end of the day he disregarded Roberts's instruction to withdraw if the enemy were too strong and decided to remain in position overnight. The attempt to turn the Boer left had also failed so that Roberts was in two minds as to whether to continue the action but, concluding from reports that an infantry attack against the Boer left centre might succeed, he ordered Ian Hamilton to carry it out the following day. By early afternoon on the 12th Ian Hamilton had managed to clear the Boers off part, but not all, of the Diamond Hill plateau. During the day De La Rey had brought more artillery to bear on French and by the afternoon had thirteen guns in action against him.[76] Deciding that the time had come to attack he asked Botha for reinforcements, intending to overpower French before attacking Roberts's weak centre and then Ian Hamilton's force. Botha ordered Tobias Smuts, who held the positions immediately to the north of the railway line, to send men to De La Rey, but just as they were leaving he countermanded the order, having learnt that Ian Hamilton had now taken the whole of the Diamond Hill plateau. Deciding that the loss of this position rendered the remainder of the Boer line untenable he withdrew all his forces overnight. Casualties were relatively low on both sides.

If, as a result of the battle of Diamond Hill, Roberts had succeeded in disposing of any further serious Boer threat to Pretoria, he had also failed to achieve a decisive victory. He now planned to gain possession of the Transvaal sector of the Delagoa Bay Railway which ran between

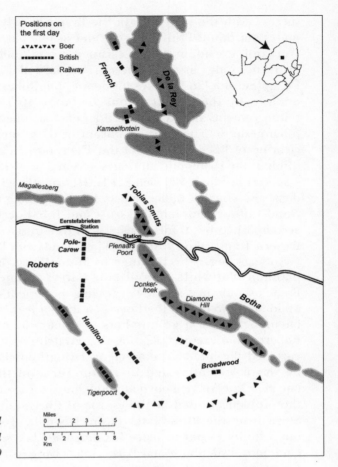

Positions on
the first day

▲▼▲▼▲▼ Boer
▪▪▪▪▪▪▪▪ British
══════ Railway

French

De la Rey

Kameelfontein

Magaliesberg

Tobias Smuts

Eerstefabrieken
Station

Pole-
Carew

Station

Pienaars
Poort

Roberts

Donker-
hoek

Diamond
Hill

Botha

Hamilton

Broadwood

Tigerpoort

Miles
0 1 2 3 4 5

0 2 4 6 8
Km

The Battle of Diamond Hill
(Donkerhoek) – 11 and
12 June 1900

Pretoria and Lourenço Marques in Portuguese East Africa. Not only
would this deprive the Boers of their only supply route from the outside
world, but it would also provide the British Army with a new supply route
and, coupled with the opening up of the Natal line through to
Johannesburg, end Roberts's perilous reliance on the single line from the
Cape via Bloemfontein. Furthermore, it was on the Delagoa Bay line at
Machadodorp – 150 miles from Pretoria and 120 miles from
Komatipoort, on the border of Portuguese East Africa – that President
Kruger and his colleagues conducted the business of government from a
railway carriage.

Before Roberts could begin his advance he had first to deal with the
Boer forces still at large in the North-Eastern Free State. That operation,
under the overall command of Archibald Hunter achieved partial

success, with the surrender in the Brandwater Basin of over 4,000 men under Marthinus Prinsloo at the end of July but, crucially, Christiaan de Wet and President Steyn escaped with 2,600 men.[77] There were distractions also in the Western Transvaal following the return there of De la Rey, with Jan Smuts as his deputy, but Roberts used the delay forced on him by these distractions to build up his supplies and await reinforcements and to fend off Boer encroachments towards Pretoria and Johannesburg. The most significant of these small actions involved the clearing of Boer forces from the Tigerpoort ridges, parallel and to the south of the Diamond Hill ridges – from 5 to 11 July and again on 16 July – actions in which Maj Gen E.T.H. Hutton played a prominent part. The delay also enabled Buller to get on with opening up the 120 miles of the Natal railway between Volksrust and Johannesburg, a task which he accomplished by 26 July, leaving him free to start his advance across the Eastern Transvaal on 7 August to join hands with Roberts.

Roberts began his advance to Middelburg on 23 July. Initially, he planned that while he and Pole-Carew advanced along the railway, French should make a wide encircling movement to the south and east of Middelburg to cut off the Boers' escape – a feasible plan since Botha was encumbered by large numbers of women and children deported by Roberts from Pretoria. Fearing that French might get into difficulties he curtailed the intended movement, laying himself open to criticism that he was more interested in gaining ground than in destroying the enemy.[78] Roberts remained at Middelburg for a month, largely because of the problems caused by the escape of Christiaan de Wet and President Steyn from the Brandwater Basin. His delay gave Louis Botha ample opportunity to put in place his defences. For some time he had been equipping Lydenburg and Barberton – lying in mountainous country to the north and south respectively of the railway line beyond Machadodorp – as ultimate rallying points. Between them and Roberts he chose the Dalmanutha plateau on the edge of the Highveld near Belfast to establish a line of defence. It had the twin advantages of a level field of fire to the west and shelter in the valley behind it for men and horses.[79] To the north lay mountainous country and to the south bogs and streams which effectively inhibited cavalry movements.

Buller had begun his advance to join Roberts on 7 August with 9,000 men and 42 guns, a force in which the main element was Lyttleton's 4th Infantry Division, supported by the cavalry brigades of major-generals Lord Dundonald and J.F. Brocklehurst. He had left much of his field army behind to guard Natal and the Transvaal section of the recently opened up Natal Railway. Having to subsist away from the railway he had a large supply train, 761 wagons in all, but for the first time he emulated Roberts and left his tents behind. Proceeding by way of Amersfoort and Ermelo he reached Twyfelaar, 18 miles south of the Delagoa Bay Railway, on

15 August and made contact with the right wing of French's cavalry. By the 25th Buller was 12 miles south of Belfast and he, French and Pole-Carew met in that town that day to receive Roberts's orders.

Botha had spread his estimated 5,000- to 7,000-strong force thinly over a 50-mile front with half on the left wing and half on the centre and right. He had 20 guns, including 4 Long Toms brought together for the first time. Roberts's and Buller's combined forces totalled 18,700 men with 82 guns and 25 machine-guns.[80] Buller was to attack the Boer left and French's cavalry, supported by Pole-Carew's infantry, was to attempt to turn the Boer right. It was Buller who found the key to breaking through Botha's defences when he spotted a boulder-covered kopje which formed a salient on the farm Bergendal near the Boer centre. The kopje was held by only 74 men – members of the Johannesburg police – with 100 men of the same force on the farm behind. The adjoining positions were manned by seasoned fighting men but they were of little help because of the lack of communication trenches. The battle of Bergendal resolved itself into a contest between the seventy-four policemen and two of Buller's infantry battalions advancing 1,500 yd over open ground after an intensive three and a half hour artillery bombardment of the isolated kopje. Buller's capture of the Bergendal kopje and the threat posed by French to the north led to the collapse of the entire Boer line and an orderly retreat. Roberts, believing that the war was all but over, annexed the Transvaal to the British Crown by proclamation on 1 September.[81] While Buller and French went to Lydenburg and Barberton respectively in pursuit of retreating Boers, Pole-Carew continued the advance along the railway line to Komatipoort, which he reached on 24 September. With the Boer capitals and all the major railway lines now in British possession the conventional phase of the war was effectively at an end.

If, on the whole, the hallmark of Roberts's conduct of military operations was his decisiveness, he was less sure-footed in his implementation of measures impacting largely on the civilian population. These included the burning of farms, the destruction of crops and livestock, the use of hostages to protect trains, the expulsion of Boer families from British-occupied areas and the use of concentration camps. Some of these measures are more commonly associated with Kitchener's time as Commander-in-Chief but, as Professor S.B. Spies has demonstrated, all were initiated by Roberts.[82] He was operating here in a grey area of morality and international law, and he was torn between his frustration at the Boers' refusal to give up the struggle when the ultimate result was no longer in doubt, and his own chivalrous instincts. He vacillated between severity and leniency according to whether he had been advised most recently by the hawks or the doves on his own side. Milner, alarmed at the potential political consequences of some of the measures, was generally on the side of the doves.

Farms had been destroyed legitimately from the beginning of the war where they had featured in military operations and where they had been the scene of Boer abuses of the white flag. Boer property had also suffered from too liberal an interpretation of instructions to British troops to requisition supplies as they moved through the country and some of the locally raised colonial units had been among the worst offenders in this respect.[83] It was not until June 1900 when railway communications had become vital to the British war effort that Roberts gave the practice of farm burning official sanction as one of a number of measures against civilians to discourage Boer attacks on trains.[84] This policy was founded on the belief that, after the annexation of the Free State to the Crown in February 1900, attacks on trains in British-occupied territory were not military operations but acts of brigandage. However, that annexation, like the later annexation of the Transvaal, was almost certainly in breach of international law on the grounds that it was proclaimed long before the achievement of complete military victory.[85] The Boers regarded the annexations as invalid from the start and the British effectively conceded the point when it was agreed in May 1902 that the Vereeniging Peace Treaty should be signed by the Boer leaders as representatives of the two republics. In fact, by September 1900 Roberts had discarded the notion that Free State combatants were rebels.[86] The first farm to be burnt under the new policy was Christiaan de Wet's farm[87] in the Northern Free State which lay close to a section of the railway line which had suffered greatly from his depredations. Once farm burning had been sanctioned officially the severity of its application varied widely from commander to commander – just as at the level of individual soldiers and junior officers there were those to whom these measures were repugnant and those who carried them out with zest. Capt March Phillipps of Rimington's Guides, who disapproved of the practice, wrote of operations in the Northern Free State in November 1900:

> We usually burn from six to a dozen farms a day; those being about all that in this sparsely-inhabited country we encounter. I do not gather that any special reason or cause is alleged or proved against the farms burnt. If the Boers have used the farm; if the owner is on commando; if the line within a certain distance is blown up; or even if there are Boers in the neighbourhood who persist in fighting – these are some of the reasons. . . . Anyway we find that one reason or another generally covers pretty nearly every farm we come to, and so to save trouble we burn the lot without enquiry; unless indeed, which sometimes happens, some names are given in before marching in the morning of farms to be spared.[88]

In the same month Roberts responded to a suggestion by Broadwood, one of the moderates, that there should be some uniformity of practice on farm burning and he issued the following clarification of the policy which he had introduced five months previously:

> As there appears to be some misunderstanding with reference to burning of farms and breaking of dams, Commander-in-Chief wishes following to be lines on which General Officers Commanding are to act: No farm is to be burnt except for an act of treachery, or when troops have been fired on from the premises, or as punishment for breaking of telegraph or railway line, or when they have been used as bases of operations for raids, and then only with direct consent of General Officer Commanding, which is to be given in writing, the mere fact of a burgher being absent on commando is on no account to be used as reason for burning the house. All cattle, wagons and foodstuffs are to be removed from all farms; if that is found to be impossible, they are to be destroyed, whether owner be present or not.[89]

Under Kitchener's regime the deterrent effect of farm burning ceased to be its sole justification as it became part of a policy of systematic destruction of the countryside intended to deny commandos the means of sustenance. After the war, when the Boer generals were seeking charitable funds in Europe, Milner did not dissent from the assertion in their appeal that a total of 30,000 houses were destroyed or seriously damaged during the war.[90]

Another of the measures introduced by Roberts in June 1900 was the practice of instructing civilians to travel on trains to discourage attacks on them, a 'human shield' policy in all but name. This was a less drastic response than farm burning but no less controversial. When, as was bound sometimes to be the case, candidates for this rôle were surrendered burghers, the practice was in breach of previous promises to protect them, apart from which they were hardly the sort of people whose presence on a train would deter a Boer attack. Roberts was never very happy about the policy, whose chief advocate was Girouard, the Military Director of Railways. He yielded to the wiser counsels of his political secretary, G.V. Fiddes, and withdrew the measure by proclamation only two months after its introduction.[91] It was later reintroduced by Kitchener.[92]

After the occupation of Johannesburg and Pretoria the British had perforce to accept responsibility for the feeding of many Boer families without means of support who had fled to those towns and surrounding areas. Roberts took the view that this was rightly the responsibility of the Boer combatants and ordered the expulsion during July and August 1900 of some 2,500 Boer women and children from Pretoria, the

Witwatersrand and Middelburg to the Boer positions on the Delagoa Bay Railway. Although some care was taken to ensure that only those in good health were sent, and in particular to avoid sending pregnant women, they were transported mostly in open railway trucks in bitterly cold weather for lack of any other rolling stock. The expulsions were deeply resented by the Boers who saw Roberts's true intention as being to use their families as a means of bringing pressure on them to surrender. They also complained, probably with justification, that the British had moved troops under cover of the expulsions. Roberts responded to Botha's complaints by blaming him and his burghers for continuing the war after the ultimate issue was no longer in doubt. The refugees ended up in Barberton where French found them when he occupied the town in September. The policy of attempting to force their dependants onto Boer combatants was abandoned as impracticable by the end of 1900, but in any event was overtaken by the policy of sending them to concentration camps.[93]

'Refugee camps' were established from September 1900 in the Free State to provide surrendered burghers and their families with protection from their fellow countrymen. While entry to them as originally conceived was voluntary, they were readily adapted to the purpose of enforced accommodation of Boer families rendered destitute by the destruction of their farms. They came in due course to be known as 'concentration camps' a name borrowed from the Spanish who in 1896 had accommodated all non-combatants in camps during the suppression of a rebellion in Cuba.[94] By the time of Roberts's departure from South Africa there were camps in both republics. In addition there were camps in the Cape Colony and Natal for civilian deportees from the republics.[95]

Roberts handed over his command to Kitchener on 29 November 1900, convinced that he was leaving him little more to do than mop up scattered guerrilla activities. His return home was delayed by a riding accident in which he broke his arm, but on 11 December he sailed from Cape Town with his wife and daughters in HMS *Canada*. Soon after the ship's arrival in the Solent on 2 January 1901 Roberts, his arm still in a sling,[96] was taken across to the Isle of Wight for an audience with Queen Victoria at Osborne, then only three weeks from the end of her long life. She awarded him the Order of the Garter, which she recorded 'quite overcame him, and he said it was too much'. She also told him she was going to confer an earldom on him, with the remainder to his daughter.[97] This was followed the next day by a triumphal progress through London in which 14,000 troops lined the streets. In recognition of his services Parliament made him a grant of £100,000.*[98]

* Approximately £4 million at 1990s prices.

Roberts now took up his appointment as Commander-in-Chief of the Army, an office which he held until February 1904, for him a period of frustration and declining influence. Despite the imposing title the incumbent had no operational control and was little more than the government's chief military adviser. Despite those difficulties he was able to initiate a number of important though modest administrative reforms, chiefly affecting the conditions and comfort of soldiers. In the autumn of 1901 he played a part in Buller's dismissal,[99] saying after Buller's injudicious speech in his self-defence that either Buller or he must go.[100] In late 1902 and early 1903 he gave evidence to the Royal Commission into the war in South Africa under the chairmanship of Lord Elgin. He submitted two detailed narratives of the operations under his command up to and including the battle of Diamond Hill and gave evidence for three days on a wide range of topics affecting the fighting efficiency of the Army in South Africa, and the lessons to be drawn for the future. Three subjects were, for him, of particular importance, the first of which, the organisation of the War Office, bore directly on his own future employment. The other two, Britain's preparedness for war and the proper use of cavalry, provided the basis of continuing debates in which he played a leading part almost to the end of his life.

Among the members of the Royal Commission was Viscount Esher, who took a keen interest in matters of Army reform. He perceived, as Roberts had not, that the office of Commander-in-Chief was obsolete and that it needed only a small extension of the subdivision of responsibilities proposed by Roberts to create a board to run the Army, analogous to the Board of Admiralty which ran the Navy.[101] After the Royal Commission had reported, Esher was appointed chairman of a commission to consider the matter with Adm Sir John Fisher* and Sir George Sydenham Clarke, then Governor of Victoria, as fellow members. The commission reported in February 1904 and duly recommended the replacement of the office of Commander-in-Chief by a seven-man Army Council.[102] Roberts accepted the recommendations with good grace; they were close to his own ideas although he had earlier expressed the view that the Army would take orders more readily from an individual than from a board.[103] He retired but agreed to remain on the Defence Committee. In the years leading up to the First World War he played a leading part in the continuing debates on how best to maintain adequately trained reserves – he campaigned vigorously for compulsory military training – and on military tactics, with particular reference to the rôle of the cavalry.

In his eighty-second year Roberts was drawn into the events surrounding the so-called 'Curragh incident', the nearest approach to a mutiny by

* Later Admiral of the Fleet Lord Fisher of Kilverstone.

officers in the British Army, and one which led to the resignation of Sir John French, by now a field-marshal and Chief of the General Staff, and of Col J.E.B. Seeley, the Secretary of State for War. Following the introduction in April 1912 by Asquith's Liberal government of a Home Rule Bill, intended to apply to the whole of Ireland, Roberts had identified himself closely with the Ulster Unionist cause, but he was also concerned that any attempt to use the Army to enforce Home Rule would damage it profoundly. When, in March 1914, a security alert in Ulster raised the possibility of Army involvement the Commander-in-Chief in Ireland, Gen Sir Arthur Paget, met his senior officers in Dublin on the 20th, having been briefed in Whitehall. He handled the meeting ineptly and that evening Brig Gen Hubert Gough, commanding officer of the 3rd Cavalry Brigade, based mainly at the Curragh near Dublin, reported that in addition to himself sixty officers, including the colonels of the three regiments in his brigade, preferred to accept dismissal rather than be involved 'in the *initiation* of active military operations against Ulster'.[104] Roberts, whom Gough consulted after the event, was believed by Seeley to have incited the resignations, and Asquith at the height of the crisis described him as being 'in a dangerous condition of senile frenzy',[105] but Roberts protested to the King that he had not been in touch with Gough for years and that he had always advised officers not to resign over the Ulster question.[106] When it emerged that the resignations had been provoked by Paget's mishandling, Gough was invited to resume his command as if nothing had happened, but he refused to do this until he had extracted an undertaking from the government to the effect that the Army would not be used under any circumstances to enforce the Home Rule Bill on Ulster.[107] In doing so he was probably advised by the politically adroit Director of Military Operations at the War Office, Sir Henry Wilson, himself a Protestant Irishman, who was working covertly with the Conservative opposition.[108] Seeley and French, who had exceeded their authority in accommodating Gough, resigned when the government repudiated the undertaking.

The outbreak of war pushed Irish affairs into the background for the time being. Within five months of the Curragh incident, French was commanding the British Expeditionary Force in France and within 2½ years of it Gough was a full general commanding the Fifth Army. When Kitchener was appointed Secretary of State for War in August 1914, Roberts went to congratulate him and to offer his services as Commander-in-Chief of Home Forces. The offer was declined but he was appointed Colonel-in-Chief of Overseas Forces in England. In November of that year he went to France, accompanied by his daughter Aileen, to inspect the Indian Division. He spent his last night in England in Ian Hamilton's house in London. While in France he caught a chill, developed pneumonia and died two days later on 14 November 1914 at

St Omer. His body was brought back to England and he was buried with due ceremony in St Paul's Cathedral.

Few people would claim today that Roberts was a great general, but throughout his career he did well, militarily, in whatever he was asked to do and, like many who excel in their professions, he made it look easy. In South Africa he never underestimated the fighting skill of the Boers and his flank march on Bloemfontein was a bold and successful venture, but when he had achieved victory in conventional terms he misjudged badly both the extent of the Boers' determination to go on fighting and their capacity to do so. He was not alone in that misjudgement and if the war proved to be a very difficult one to finish, the fault lay more with those who started it than with those who had to fight it.

Notes

1. Cd. 1790 *Royal Commission* Q.10843 (Roberts), p. 461.
2. Ibid., Appendix H, p. 532 and Roberts Papers NAM 7101-22-119 (Proclamations, Army Orders, Circulars), pp. 49–50, 55–6.
3. Cd. 457 (Roberts Dispatch No. 2), p. 8.
4. Cd. 457 (Roberts Dispatch No. 1), p. 7.
5. *TH* iii, 375–7.
6. Ibid., iv, 174–5.
7. Goldmann, p. 84.
8. Breytenbach iv, p. 184.
9. Ibid., iv, p. 199.
10. Ralph, pp. 310–11.
11. Anglesey iv, p. 132.
12. *TH* iii, 400.
13. Miller, p. 90.
14. Anglesey iv, p. 135.
15. Goldmann, p. 84.
16. *TH* iii, 395 n.
17. Anglesey iv, p. 137.
18. Pakenham, p. 327.
19. *German Official Account* i, p. 145.
20. J.M. Lane Diary, 18 December 1899.
21. Ibid., 16 December 1899 and 7 February 1890.
22. Ibid., 1 January 1900.
23. De Wet, p. 38.

24. De Wet, pp. 36–7.
25. Breytenbach iv, p. 192.
26. J.M. Lane Diary, 15 February 1900.
27. Sternberg, p. 172.
28. J.M. Lane Diary, 15 February 1900.
29. Ibid., 15 February 1900.
30. Ibid., 16 February 1900.
31. See Chapter Six, pp. 102–8.
32. J.M. Lane Diary, 18 February 1900.
33. *TH* iii, 445.
34. Cd. 457 (Roberts Dispatch No. 3), p. 14.
35. J.M. Lane Diary, 22 February 1900.
36. *TH* iii, 482.
37. Cd. 457 (Roberts Dispatch No. 3), p. 15.
38. National Army Museum, Photograph 20863, Acc. No. 7306-51; Cronjé breakfasted with the British staff and Roberts with his own staff.
39. Menpes, Chapter XV pp. 198–215; Menpes met and sketched prisoners at Klip Drift.
40. *TH* iii, 484 n.
41. Wilson, *Pretoria*, p. 134.
42. *TH* iii, 553.
43. Breytenbach v, pp. 23–5; Pakenham, pp. 387–8.
44. Ibid., v, pp. 37–8.
45. Ibid., v, pp. 41–2; *TH* iii, 554–5.
46. Ibid., v, p. 43.
47. Ibid., v, pp. 31–3.
48. The full text of Roberts's memorandum is in *OH* ii, 190–2 and in *TH*, iii, 557–9.
49. Maydon, p. 174.
50. Amery, *My Political Life* i, pp. 131–2.
51. See Chapter Nine, p. 223–4.
52. *TH* iv, 11–14.
53. Cd. 426 p. 3 III quoted in Spies, *Barbarism*, p. 34.
54. *TH* iv, 7–8.
55. See Chapter Eight, pp. 183–4.
56. *TH* vi, 522.
57. Doyle, p. 371.
58. Cd. 1790 *Royal Commission* Q.10493 (Roberts).
59. *TH* vi, 524.
60. Quoted by James, p. 316.
61. Powell, *Buller*, pp. 81–2.
62. Newton, pp. 181–2 quoted in Powell, *Buller*, p. 181.
63. *TH* iv, 113–4.
64. Cd. 1791 *Royal Commission* Q.13127 (Roberts), p. 51.

65. Breytenbach, v, pp. 484–5.
66. Cd. 426, p. 6 XI.
67. Cd. 1791 *Royal Commission* Q.13127 (Roberts), p. 56.
68. Spies and Nattrass, pp. 42–6.
69. Cd. 1791 *Royal Commission* Q.13127 (Roberts), pp. 57–8.
70. Ibid., Q.13127 (Roberts), p. 58.
71. Barnard, *Boer Commanders*, p. 156.
72. Spies and Nattrass, p. 59.
73. Spies, *Barbarism*, p. 92.
74. Spies and Nattrass, p. 59.
75. *TH* iv, 280.
76. *TH* iv, 291.
77. See Chapter Eight, pp. 11–12.
78. *TH* iv, 404–5.
79. Reitz, *Commando*, p. 119.
80. *OH* iii, 392 and *TH* iv, 441.
81. Cd. 426, p. 17 XXX.
82. Spies, *Barbarism*, chapters 1–5.
83. Ibid., pp. 42–3.
84. Ibid., pp. 102–3.
85. Ibid., p. 62.
86. Ibid., p. 145.
87. Ibid., p. 102.
88. Phillipps, p. 201 quoted in Spies, *Barbarism*, p. 125.
89. Cd. 426, p. 23 XL quoted in Spies, *Barbarism*, p. 127.
90. Spies, *Barbarism* p. 118.
91. Ibid., pp. 103–7.
92. Ibid., pp. 240–4.
93. Ibid., p. 128.
94. Ibid., p. 148.
95. Ibid., pp. 143–53.
96. Buckle, p. 638.
97. Ibid., p. 638.
98. James, pp. 369–71.
99. See Chapter Two, p. 42.
100. Symons, p. 289.
101. Cd. 1791 *Royal Commission* Q.13229 (Roberts).
102. James, p. 397.
103. Ibid., p. 394.
104. Jenkins, p. 309; Farrar-Hockley, *Goughie*, p. 97.
105. Asquith to Venetia Stanley 21 April 1914, quoted in Jenkins, pp. 309–10.
106. James, pp. 467–8; Holmes, p. 182.
107. Farrar-Hockley, *Goughie*, p. 111.
108. Holmes, p. 169; Ensor, p. 478.

CHAPTER FIVE

Kitchener, Part 1

Egypt and the Sudan

Kitchener had a hold on the imagination of the British public unrivalled by any soldier since the Duke of Wellington. His 'Your Country Needs YOU' poster which summoned Britain's young men to war in 1914 survives – albeit in parody – to this day, probably the best known advertisement ever devised. Aloof and austere, he was never liked by his fellow officers, apart from those close to him, and, indeed, never sought popularity. As for private soldiers he was seldom known to have spoken to one, except in the line of duty.[1] Although his features were later coarsened by the desert sun he was strikingly handsome, with blue eyes set wide apart above his great moustache. Tall and lean with a commanding presence he inspired loyalty partly through fear and partly through respect for his success. He compensated for his tactical deficiencies with immense drive, energy and grasp of detail. Often described as a great organiser he was, in fact, a chaotic administrator. His office was usually a shambles and he was loath to delegate, but he excelled at getting things done on the grand scale. Ian Hamilton, who was his Chief of Staff at the end of the Boer War, described him as 'a Master of Expedients',[2] L.S. Amery as 'essentially a hustler, one who could achieve results by force of will power and dominating personality.'[3] He was more than a soldier – with Cromer, Curzon and Milner he was one of the four eminent 'pro-consuls' of the British Empire at the height of its power; and he was later a Cabinet minister as Secretary of State for War from 1914–16. Although he made a vital contribution in that rôle to Britain's eventual victory by his creation of a great citizens' army he was disliked, distrusted and outclassed by the professional politicians with whom he had to work. He was happiest in the hot places of the world and went for many years without spending a winter in Britain. It was a cruel irony that he perished in the cold waters of a northern sea.

Although of English stock Kitchener was born and spent the first thirteen years of his life in Southern Ireland. His father was Lt Col Henry Horatio Kitchener, a retired Army officer who felt keenly the fact that he had never been in action. Kitchener's mother was born Frances Ann Chevallier, the daughter of a clergyman whose family home was Aspall Hall in Suffolk. It was her ill health in India that had prompted the colonel's return to England and subsequent retirement. With money to invest after the sale of his commission he had bought advantageously the 2,000-acre[4] Ballygoghlan estate on the borders of Counties Kerry and Limerick near the River Shannon, whose owner had been bankrupted by the great potato famine of 1846–7. While restoring the house his wife stayed with a friend in Gunsborough Villa near Listowel and it was in this house that the future field-marshal was born on 24 June 1850. His parents' third child and second son he was christened Horatio Herbert and was known by his second name. Two sons were born later. The family divided its time between Ballygoghlan and Crotta House which Col Kitchener added to his holdings in 1857. The colonel was an eccentric with strong views on discipline and education. Because of his aversion to schools the children were taught inadequately by a series of tutors and governesses. Kitchener enjoyed helping with the practical work of the estate. Among his siblings he was closest to his sister Millie, who remained his confidante for the rest of his life, and his youngest brother Walter,* who later served under him in the Sudan and South Africa.

In 1863 the health of Kitchener's mother began to deteriorate with the onset of tuberculosis and early in 1864 his father sold his Irish properties profitably and moved the family to Switzerland, hoping to find a cure, but she died at the end of the year. The family stayed on in Switzerland and Kitchener and his two younger brothers went to boarding school at the Chateau du Grand Clos near the eastern end of Lake Geneva. By hard work he was able to repair the shortcomings in his education, discovering an affinity for mathematics and languages. He became fluent in French and acquired some knowledge of German.[5]

With the help of coaching, first by a cousin in Cambridge and then from a well-known Army 'crammer' in London, Kitchener passed the entrance examination to the Royal Military Academy, Woolwich in 1868 and spent two years there without making any particular impression. As was usual for newly commissioned officers in the Royal Engineers Kitchener spent two years at the Royal School of Military Engineering at Chatham, where he enjoyed the practical nature of the regime. On leaving Chatham in April 1873 he was appointed an ADC to Brig Gen George Greaves at the annual manoeuvres of the Austrian Army. Here he attracted the attention of the Emperor Frans Joseph when Greaves fell ill and Kitchener deputised for him at official functions. In October he was appointed to a mounted troop of the Royal Engineers at Aldershot. Neither regimental life nor Aldershot were to his taste, but he worked hard and attracted a glowing report from his commanding officer. He left Aldershot in November 1874 and spent the next eight years out of the mainstream of Army life engaged mainly on

---

* Maj Gen F.W. Kitchener, 1858–1911, who at the end of his career was Governor of Bermuda.

survey work, first in Palestine and then in Cyprus. His work in Cyprus was interrupted by an eight-month spell from April 1879 as a military vice-consul at Kastamuni in Anatolia under the Consul-General Col Charles Wilson RE. Here he reported on the suffering of the people under the Turkish government as a result of corruption and maladministration.[6] In July 1882, in an attempt to get involved in the campaign against Arabi Pasha in Egypt, he incurred the displeasure of the High Commissioner of Cyprus, Maj Gen Sir Robert Biddulph, when under the pretext of taking a week's leave he went to Alexandria and then overstayed his leave by three weeks, having used his fluent Arabic to assist the Navy in its intelligence work. He resumed his survey work in Cyprus, his relationship with Biddulph cooler as a result of his deception but not irreparably damaged. He still hoped for employment in Egypt where, after Wolseley's decisive defeat of Arabi Pasha at Tel-el-Kebir and the subsequent British occupation of Egypt, Maj Gen Sir Evelyn Wood VC was given the task of creating a new 6,000-strong Egyptian Army in which he was to be Sirdar, or Commander-in-Chief. Biddulph released him to take up an appointment in February 1883 as second in command of the Egyptian cavalry with the local rank of major, or bimbashi, having been gazetted a captain in the British Army on 4 January 1883. Although it might have seemed incongruous for a sapper to be appointed to a cavalry regiment Kitchener had become a good horseman while in Cyprus and he soon displayed an outstanding capacity for training initially unpromising raw material. He acquired a reputation for obsessively hard work, taciturnity and unsociability.

Kitchener first came to public notice as a result of his part in the Gordon relief expedition.[7] From March 1884, as Gordon's predicament in Khartoum became more acute, Kitchener was diverted from his regimental duties and attached to an intelligence group preparing for possible conflict in the Sudan. His activities, some undertaken on his own initiative, included reconnaissance, the raising of a force of 1,500 Bedouin irregulars to guard the Egyptian border east of the Nile, intelligence gathering and the canvassing of support of tribes opposed to the Mahdi, by bribery if necessary. His work took him into desert areas in Upper Egypt and the Sudan, usually in Arab dress and with a small escort of Arabs.[8] After seeing, by chance, the torturing to death of a spy, he took with him a vial of poison to avoid the same fate.[9] He also established and maintained a link, through Arab messengers, with Gordon. His work earned the praise of his immediate superiors, and even Wolseley, who arrived in Egypt in September 1884, was impressed.* Kitchener was

---

* Kitchener had clashed with Wolseley during his first spell in Cyprus when Wolseley was High Commissioner.

gazetted a brevet major in the British Army on 4 October 1884. When the desert column in the relief force began its 160-mile march from Korti to Metemmeh on 30 December Kitchener was attached to it to help with the tribes, and went on ahead with six Arab scouts.[10] The death of Gordon on 26 January 1885 affected him greatly. He was a kindred spirit – religious and, like Kitchener, an engineer whose adventurous career had been out of the mainstream of British Army life. Both had an affinity for the desert and the Arab language. Gordon, for his part, had recognised Kitchener's qualities and saw in him a future Governor-General of the Sudan.

After Gordon's death Gladstone's government had no taste for embarking on a conquest of the Sudan and when it was clear that there was to be no further military action in the Sudan Kitchener resigned his commission in the Egyptian Army. He returned to England early in July 1885, having been gazetted a brevet lieutenant-colonel on 15 June 1885. In Cairo in January 1885, while he was in Korti, he had suffered a personal loss in the death of Hermione Baker, the eighteen-year-old daughter of Gen Valentine Baker, to whom he had become attached and whom her family believed he would marry. For many years he wore under his shirt from time to time a locket containing a miniature of Hermione given to him by her father.[11] While Wolseley's reputation declined after the failure of the relief expedition, Kitchener's exploits established him as an up-and-coming man.

While on leave in England he laid the foundation of social connections which were to be important to him. With others who had taken part in the Gordon relief expedition he was presented to Queen Victoria, who was impressed by him and who took a close interest in his subsequent career. As a good-looking unmarried officer with a growing reputation he had an easy entrée into patrician country houses and in his social progress he was assisted by a renewed friendship with Pandeli Ralli, a wealthy and well-connected bachelor member of the Anglo-Greek community and recent Liberal MP, whom Kitchener had first met in Cyprus.[12] By the use of such influence as he could muster Kitchener avoided a routine posting to Ireland and instead was appointed the British member of the Zanzibar Boundary Commission, whose other members were France and Germany. On completion of its work Kitchener was made a CMG and in September 1886 was appointed Governor of Eastern Sudan and Red Sea littoral whose capital was the Red Sea port of Suakin. The area was important to Britain to protect the Red Sea route to India but inland it was under the control of the Mahdi's successor, the Khalifa Abdullahi, acting through his lieutenant Osman Digna, chief of the Hadendowas. The policy imposed on Kitchener was defensive, and to restrict the availability of arms to Osman Digna he banned trade between Suakin and the interior.

Although he had been instructed to confine his military activities to reconnaissance, and in particular not to engage his regular garrison, he attacked Osman Digna's stronghold at Handub on 17 January 1888 with a force of irregulars and regulars disguised as irregulars. The action was successful to the extent that the dervish casualties were considerably greater than the British but it was handled inadroitly and Kitchener was obliged to withdraw his force to Suakin. He was wounded in his jaw and neck and had to go to Cairo for medical treatment. Despite having exceeded his instructions his action brought congratulatory telegrams from both the Duke of Cambridge and Wolseley and a solicitous enquiry from the Queen, who made him an ADC. He was gazetted colonel on 11 April 1888.

On his return to England on leave in the summer of 1888 Kitchener stayed at Hatfield as a guest of Lord Salisbury, the Prime Minister. While there he learnt that he had been appointed Adjutant-General of the Egyptian Army under Maj Gen Sir Francis Grenfell, who had succeeded Evelyn Wood as Sirdar. Osman Digna had taken advantage of Kitchener's absence to attack Suakin and in December 1888 Grenfell, assisted by Kitchener, defeated him at nearby Gemaizeh. In August 1989 Grenfell defeated a force of several thousand dervishes[13] under another of the Khalifa's lieutenants, Wad-el-Nejeumi, at Toski near the Egyptian border. In this action Kitchener successfully commanded the Egyptian cavalry in a diversionary action for which he was awarded the CB. Kitchener agreed reluctantly to act as Inspector-General of the Egyptian police in addition to his duties as Adjutant-General. His reforms in the police force reduced the level of crime and increased the number of convictions.[14] As Adjutant-General he worked relentlessly and took little trouble to make himself agreeable to his fellow officers. His working methods were chaotic and he was unwilling to delegate but he made up for it with a formidable grasp of detail. In contrast to his assiduous cultivation of influential people in England he disdained expatriate social life in Cairo, preferring the company of wealthy Levantines who shared his artistic interests.

In April 1892 – to the dismay of his fellow officers and of the local British community – Kitchener was appointed Sirdar of the Egyptian Army with the local rank of major-general, on the recommendation of Grenfell, who was returning to the British Army, and of Sir Evelyn Baring, who since 1883 had been Britain's Agent and Consul-General. Baring, who was virtual ruler of Egypt, had early on formed a high opinion of Kitchener's ability, and not least of the qualities which commended Kitchener to him were his zeal for economy and head for business. This new appointment marked the beginning of a long period of preparation for the reconquest of the Sudan and the avenging of Gordon's death. In 1894 Kitchener was made a KCMG as a mark of the British government's confidence in him after he fell out with the twenty-year-old Khedive, Abbas Hilmi II, during an inspection of units of the Egyptian Army. Kitchener overreacted to the insecure young man's critical comments and let slip the opportunity of accepting graciously his sincere apology.[15] By 1896 his 18,000-strong army, now including six battalions of Sudanese troops,[16] was ready to invade the Sudan. In March of that year the British government authorised an expedition to capture Dongola, about 200 miles up the Nile from the Egyptian border. Kitchener himself commanded the expeditionary force which on 7 June won a decisive preliminary victory at Firket, where his Egyptian troops performed well against a force of 3,000 dervishes. With the assistance of a small fleet of armed steamers and gunboats, including four of the new Zafir class which Kitchener himself had helped to design, he captured Dongola on 23 September 1896. He was made a KCB and promoted major-general in the British Army.

So far, the invasion of the Sudan had been constrained by the decision that it should be financed wholly by the Egyptian government. This allowed an advance only as far as Dongola, where it was intended to pause for two to three years, but moves by France to extend its interests to the Upper Nile made it desirable to continue, and Cromer* sent Kitchener to London to lobby the British government for financial help, in which attempt he was successful to the extent of £500,000. During 1897 a railway was built across the desert between Wadi Halfa on the Egyptian border and Abu Hamed, 230 miles to the south-east, thus short-circuiting the 530-mile western loop of the Nile, including three of the worst cataracts. For this project, dismissed by many as impracticable, Kitchener relied on a team of young sapper officers led by Lt Percy Girouard, a French Canadian who had worked on the construction of the Canadian Pacific Railway (he later played an important part in the Boer War as the Director of Railways). On 10 September 1897 Kitchener occupied Berber, unaccountably vacated by the Khalifa's forces, but by the end of the year the progress of the expedition looked likely to be halted again by the lack of funds. The problem was resolved when Reginald Wingate, Kitchener's intelligence officer, reported that 100,000 dervishes were preparing to advance on Berber. Money was found to complete the railway as far as Atbara where the river of that name flowed into the Nile and a British brigade under Maj Gen William Gatacre was sent to join Kitchener.

In March 1898 a force of 20,000 dervishes under the young emir, Mahmoud, reached the Atbara. He planned to move down the river toward its junction with the Nile and take Berber in the rear but in

---

* Sir Evelyn Baring had been raised to the peerage as Lord Cromer in June 1892.

anticipation Kitchener had moved 35 miles to the south. Faced with the necessity of a wide sweep across waterless desert Mahmoud dug in on the right bank of the Atbara on 21 March[17] surrounding his force with a zariba.* When Kitchener realised that Mahmoud would not be lured out of his stronghold he attacked it on 8 April after an artillery bombardment. The zariba was breached and after brief but fierce fighting Mahmoud was defeated. While British casualties were under 600, some 3,000 dervishes were killed and 4,000 were wounded or taken prisoner.[18] After Mahmoud had been interrogated by Wingate he was forced to follow the cavalry in the victory procession in Berber in chains and with a halter around his neck, sometimes walking, sometimes being made to run. He bore himself with dignity and did not appear to resent the ritual humiliation which Kitchener considered necessary and which his Sudanese troops would have expected. This was not the last occasion on which liberal opinion in Britain regarded Kitchener's conduct as barbaric. He was also criticised for having pared his medical services to the bone in his drive for economies, to the detriment of the wounded. However, he received telegrams of congratulation from those who mattered to him – the Queen, the Prime Minister and Cromer – but Wolseley in congratulating him chided him gently for his apparent display of indecision in seeking Cromer's advice before deciding to attack the dervish stronghold.[19]

The final battle with the Khalifa took place in September 1898 on the Kerreri plain north of Omdurman, the town established by the Mahdi on the west bank of the Nile across the river from the ruins of Khartoum. With the addition of a second infantry brigade and two squadrons of the 21st Lancers, the strength of the British division under Gen Gatacre was now 8,200 and that of Gen Hunter's Egyptian division, including Sudanese troops, was 17,600, bringing the total strength of Kitchener's Anglo-Egyptian force to 25,800.[20] In addition, an irregular force of 2,500 Arab 'friendlies' under Maj Stuart-Wortley guarded the eastern bank of the Nile. Following the experience at the Atbara, medical support had been improved. The Khalifa's force was at least twice the size of Kitchener's, but its weaponry of swords, spears and outdated rifles was no match for Kitchener's arsenal of Lee-Metford magazine-loading rifles, eighty guns and forty-eight Maxim machine-guns. Approximately half the guns and Maxims were borne in the British fleet of ten gunboats† and five transport steamers.

* A dense barrier of thorns.
† One of these, the *Zafir*, sank on 30 August 1898.

Omdurman was first sighted on 23 August from the top of the Jebel Royan, a hill nearly forty miles away, reputedly by Maj 'Monkey' Gordon, the nephew of the man whose death Kitchener had come to avenge. On 1 September Kitchener set up camp at the village of Egeiga on the Nile which looked westwards to a plain bounded to the north by the Kerreri Hills and to the south by a solitary hill called the Jebel Surgham, about 300 ft high. From this hill, approximately five miles north-east of Omdurman and one mile from the Nile, a spur ran eastwards towards the river and a long ridge ran westwards into the desert obscuring the view of Omdurman and the plain immediately north and west of the town. On the same day the British gunboats, profiting from the failure of the Khalifa's attempts to mine the Nile, bombarded the town and the forts protecting it, damaging in particular Omdurman's chief architectural feature and spiritual symbol, the great yellow dome of the Mahdi's tomb. The bombardment was effective enough to cause the Khalifa to abandon any thoughts of keeping his army in the town and luring Kitchener into it where in the mêlée of street fighting the advantage could well have been with the dervishes.

As the dervish army came in sight just before 6 a.m. on 2 September it appeared to be heading not for Egeiga but for the Kerreri Hills to the north, which extended for some four miles westwards from the river. The British artillery, followed by the Egyptian artillery and the gunboats, opened fire at 6.25 a.m. at a range of 2,700 yd, causing a group of some 10,000 dervishes to alter course towards Egeiga. A further group of about 8,000 appeared from between the Jebel Surgham and the river. Of the rest of the Khalifa's army around 20,000 remained with him out of sight behind the Jebel Surgham and about the same number continued to advance towards the Kerreri Hills where Col R.G. Broadwood awaited them with the Egyptian cavalry, the Camel Corps and the horse artillery. By 8 a.m. the two wings threatening Egeiga had spent themselves with fanatical courage against continuous artillery fire and, when they got closer, intensive rifle and machine-gun fire. Few got within 300 yd of the zariba.

The left wing of the Khalifa's army pressed on towards the Kerreri Hills and Broadwood drew about half of them away to the north by making a fighting retreat. He ordered the less mobile Camel Corps back to Egeiga which they were able to reach under covering fire from the gunboats. Later he too returned with his cavalry to Egeiga where the first phase of the action had ended by about 8.30 a.m. Before advancing towards Omdurman Kitchener ordered the 21st Lancers to reconnoitre the area between the Jebel Surgham and the Nile and to head off dervish survivors seeking to return to Omdurman. Encountering what appeared to be a force of a few hundred dervishes Lt Col Rowland Hill Martin ordered the Lancers to charge. When it was too late for him to change his mind a further 2,000 or more dervishes, Hadendowas under Osman Digna, appeared from their place of concealment in a watercourse. The Lancers charged through

95

them, re-formed, dismounted and engaged the dervishes with their carbines, driving them away to the north-west. This action, which in public esteem rivalled the Charge of the Light Brigade at Balaclava, won three VCs, ended the regiment's long record of never having been in action, and had no effect on the eventual outcome of the battle, in which it accounted for most of the British dead. Kitchener was not impressed, since as a result of the action the Lancers were no longer in a position to provide him with intelligence about the Khalifa's forces outside Omdurman.

The advance towards Omdurman began at 9 a.m. in the direction of the Jebel Surgham and the space between it and the Nile. In the process a gap of half a mile opened up between Col Hector MacDonald's predominantly Sudanese 1st Egyptian Brigade on the right and the rest of the force, exposing him to attack by two successive waves of dervishes, which he fought off with great skill and the assistance of Brig Gen A.G. Wauchope's 1st British Brigade on his left. Kitchener ordered the ceasefire at about 11.30 a.m. As the survivors from both repelled forces retreated the 21st Lancers to the south and Broadwood's Egyptian cavalry to the north headed them off from Omdurman. The battlefield was strewn with dervish dead and wounded, so thickly in places that it was difficult to see the ground.[21] There is no doubt that some enemy wounded were killed. This was partly in self-defence since it was not unusual for a wounded dervish to try and kill one or two infidels before dying. Apart from this, Kitchener's Sudanese troops had personal scores to settle, and to a lesser extent British troops were also involved. It is unlikely, as has been alleged, that Kitchener gave specific orders that enemy wounded should be killed. On the contrary there were accounts of his trying to spare lives when he had the opportunity to do so, but it is possible that he was not as zealous as he might have been in making his disapproval clear.[22]

Total British casualties in the battle were 56 killed and 434 wounded, native troops accounting for the majority in both categories. Of the 27 British dead 21 were killed in the charge of the 21st Lancers. An estimated 11,000 dervishes were killed, 16,000 wounded and 6,000 taken prisoner. While the improved medical services were more or less adequate for the British wounded the dervish wounded were for the most part left to fend for themselves, in many cases to die. While news of the victory was received in Britain with general acclaim, liberal opinion was offended by the scale of the dervish casualties and the fate of the wounded. A few days after the battle Kitchener, fearing that it would become a focus for a further uprising, gave orders that the Mahdi's tomb should be razed to the ground and that his remains should be cast into the Nile. Whether on his instructions or on the initiative of a subordinate the Mahdi's skull was retained and given to Kitchener, who kept it in a kerosene tin while deciding what to do with it. Having toyed with the idea of using it as a desk ornament, Kitchener proposed to donate it to the museum of the College of Surgeons where he understood Napoleon's intestines to be. A press corps, antagonised by Kitchener's offhand treatment of them during the campaign, was not slow to inform the British public about this episode; to the disquiet felt in some quarters about the enemy casualties was added outrage at what was seen as the desecration of the Mahdi's tomb. Even the Queen, one of Kitchener's staunchest admirers, was shocked by his proposal for the skull, arguing that despite all his cruelties the Mahdi was a man of certain importance. The skull was later buried discreetly in a Muslim cemetery at Wadi Halfa.

After the battle Kitchener had opened sealed orders from the Foreign Office instructing him to deal personally with a French incursion on the Upper Nile by a small party under Capt Jean-Baptiste Marchand who, having travelled 3,000 miles across equatorial Africa from the west coast, arrived on 10 July 1898 at Fashoda, 400 miles upstream of Khartoum. Accompanied by Reginald Wingate, on 10 September Kitchener took upstream a flotilla of 5 gunboats with 100 Cameron Highlanders, 2 Sudanese battalions, a battery of artillery and a number of Maxims.[23] Whatever the allegations against him of crudity in his conduct as a field commander he now showed himself, as he did later in South Africa, to be a skilful and sensitive negotiator. In Marchand he met somebody with the same gift. They first exchanged courtesies on 18 September when they were 12 miles apart. When Kitchener arrived at Fashoda on 19 September he was careful not to offend French susceptibilities. He wore Egyptian and not British uniform and instructed the gunboats to fly the Egyptian flag only. The men lunched together in the gunboat *Dal* with the utmost cordiality, Kitchener making it clear that the presence of the French at Fashoda and in the Valley of the Nile was regarded as a direct violation of the rights of Egypt and Great Britain. Marchand asserted that as a soldier he had to obey his orders and that if Kitchener chose to dislodge him by force he and his men would die at their posts, which could only result in war between Britain and France. Kitchener offered, and Marchand declined, river transport to take the French party in comfort to Cairo. Marchand having admitted that he was powerless to prevent it, Kitchener ordered the Egyptian flag to be raised to the accompaniment of a 21-gun salute on a fort 500 yd from the French flag which was left undisturbed. On his return to Omdurman Kitchener left behind the artillery and a Sudanese battalion to protect Anglo-Egyptian interests and a gift of wine and other comforts for Marchand. The matter was subsequently resolved at government level, the French agreeing to vacate the area. To remove a humiliating reminder to the French of their climbdown the name of Fashoda was changed to Kodok.

On his return to England on 27 October 1898 to receive his peerage – suggested by the Queen herself[24] – Kitchener was fêted as a hero. He took the title 'Baron Kitchener of Khartoum and of Aspall in the County of Suffolk'. The only sour note was in Parliament where the vote of thanks from both houses and grant of £30,000* was vociferously if unsuccessfully opposed in the Commons by a group of MPs outraged by the slaughter of dervishes, the neglect of their wounded and the desecration of the Mahdi's tomb.[25] In December he returned as Governor-General to the Sudan, which by an agreement signed on 19 January 1899 became an Anglo-Egyptian condominium. Here he spent a year in the congenial occupation of governing the vast territory which he had added to the empire at a financial cost of less than half what it later cost Britain to maintain the First World War effort for one day.[26] Kitchener's main achievements were the rebuilding of Khartoum, for which he was made an honorary Fellow of the Royal Institute of British Architects,[27] and attracting able recruits from Britain to found the new Civil Service. While in England he had helped to raise over £100,000 for the building of the Gordon Memorial College, which survives to this day as the University of Khartoum, an enduring memorial both to him and to Charles Gordon. His success in the Sudan was marred by discontent in the Army, engendered by his harsh methods and unsympathetic handling of his Egyptian officers' grievances about pensions and allowances,[28] which erupted into mutiny after his departure and had to be dealt with by Wingate, who succeeded him.

In the summer of 1899 Kitchener spent two months' leave in England where he took steps to further his military career. He went to Ireland to meet Roberts, who was then Commander-in-Chief there, and volunteered to serve as his Chief of Staff if he was again given command in the field. Through his influential connections he also staked a claim to a senior post in India. However, following the events of Black Week in South Africa at the end of 1899 Roberts was appointed Commander-in-Chief but, because of his age, Salisbury made the appointment conditional on a younger man serving as his Chief of Staff and the choice fell on Kitchener. He joined Roberts on the *Dunottar Castle* in Gibraltar and they sailed together to Cape Town where they arrived on 10 January 1900.

---

* About £1,200,000 at 1990s prices.

Notes

1. Repington, p. 159; Esher, *The Tragedy of Lord Kitchener*, p. 28.
2. Hamilton, *The Commander*, p. 100.
3. Amery, *My Political Life* i, p. 124.
4. Warner, p. 9.
5. Magnus, p. 7.
6. Arthur i, p. 38.
7. See Chapter Two, pp. 19–20.
8. Warner, p. 56.
9. Magnus, p. 55.
10. Arthur i, p. 109.
11. Magnus, p. 66.
12. Ibid., pp. 30, 68.
13. Estimates range from 4,000 (Ballard, p. 60) to 13,000 (Magnus, p. 76) but are confused by the large numbers of camp followers.
14. Arthur i, p. 167.
15. Magnus, pp. 83–9.
16. Royle, p. 95.
17. Neillands, p. 192.
18. Arthur i, p. 228.
19. Magnus, pp. 122–3. Kitchener's most recent biographer dismisses Magnus' account of Mahmoud's humiliation as inaccurate and exaggerated. See Pollock, pp. 121–2.
20. Arthur i, p. 231.
21. Ziegler, p. 184.
22. Ibid., p. 186.
23. Magnus, p. 138.
24. Buckle, p. 275.
25. *Hansard 4th Series*, Vol. 72 327–402, 671–94; James, L., pp. 283–4.
26. Arthur i, p. 250.
27. Royle, p. 148.
28. Magnus, pp. 153–4.

CHAPTER SIX

Kitchener, Part 2

South Africa and After

By the time Roberts and Kitchener arrived in Cape Town the broad strategy of the advance to Bloemfontein had been settled and the next month was spent in preparation. Kitchener was entrusted with the scrapping of the regimental transport system and its replacement by a centralised system. Although they were different in almost every way Roberts and Kitchener forged an effective partnership, based on mutual regard. Nominally Chief of Staff, Kitchener was used by Roberts more as a troubleshooting second in command. This was never acknowledged officially and was a potential source of ambiguity and friction in his dealings with divisional commanders, to whom he was senior in his substantive British Army rank of major-general, but who outranked him in their local rank of lieutenant-general. It was a significant factor in the conduct and outcome of the battle of Paardeberg on 18 February 1900.

At the start of the Great Flank March through the Free State, Kitchener accompanied the leading 6th Division when it left Waterval Drift on the Riet River at 1 a.m. on 14 February, but it was not until daybreak that the divisional commander, Lt Gen Sir Thomas Kelly-Kenny, was aware of the fact.[1] In the opinion of *The Times History* there was no doubt that Roberts made Kitchener accompany the division in order to hustle Kelly-Kenny and make sure of his exacting the utmost exertions from his troops.[2] During a halt at Wegdraai Drift, which the division reached at 10 a.m. on the 14th, Kitchener sent staff officers to French whose Cavalry Division had led the way to the Modder River and was holding Klip and Rondavel Drifts. They came back with information that a Boer force under Commandant Froneman was watching the cavalry, and with a request from French to Kitchener to try and get to the Modder that night as he did not want to lose another day before starting for Kimberley. Kitchener persuaded Kelly-Kenny to resume the march at 5 p.m. and despite a heavy rainfall the division reached Rondavel Drift at 1 a.m. on the 15th, having covered the 24 miles from Waterval Drift in as many hours. Its timely arrival had two consequences. Firstly, it allowed French to hand over the defences on the Modder and to embark on his celebrated charge through the Boer defences at Klip Drift on his way to relieve Kimberley later in the day. Secondly, news of the 6th Division's movements reached Cronjé late on the night of the 14th, persuading him at last that he was in imminent danger of being outflanked and that it was time to move.[3]

During the evening of 15 February Kitchener and Kelly-Kenny agreed that the following morning Col Hannay's mounted infantry, supported by Maj Gen C.E. Knox's 13th Brigade, should go to Kimberley in case French needed support. Hannay, with a force of 2,000 mounted men, set off at 4.30 a.m. on the 16th. At about 6 a.m. he received a report of a great cloud of dust beyond the line of kopjes on the eastern side of the valley through which the Cavalry Division had charged the day before. The occupants of a captured stray wagon confirmed that Cronjé's 450-wagon convoy was making its way eastwards. Hannay delayed occupying the kopjes in question, wanting first to confer with Knox who was following behind. By the time Knox came up, half an hour later, the Boer rearguard had occupied the kopjes and the opportunity was lost. Kitchener, Kelly-Kenny and Knox were by now all aware that Cronjé was on his way eastwards. Without waiting for Kitchener's order 'Objective changed; go for the convoy', Knox had gone into action, directing artillery fire onto the kopjes and ordering Hannay to go through the gap between the kopjes and the river in order to outflank the Boer positions. About a mile from the gap Hannay's column came under rifle fire both from the kopjes on the left and from the river and shortly afterwards halted suddenly, probably as a result of an unauthorised order which Hannay acquiesced in, believing it to have come from Knox. Given the unexpected gift of a stationary target the Boers brought a gun and a pom-pom to bear, and a great part of the mounted infantry, made up largely of untrained horsemen, turned and bolted for the cover of the river bank. Many horses were drowned in the ensuing panic.[4]

To repair the damage after the rout of Hannay's mounted infantry Knox sent them back to cross the river at Klip Drift in order to demonstrate on the south bank 6 miles upstream at Klipkraal Drift. At the same time he sent the Oxfordshire Light Infantry across further upstream with a field battery; in conjunction with the West Ridings on the north bank they worked upstream, clearing Boers out of the scrub and the dongas. At 9 a.m. the Buffs* succeeded in driving the Boers out of the kopjes without much difficulty, into the Drieput Kopjes, the next line to the east. By now Cronjé's convoy had gone into laager protected by those kopjes and another group immediately to the north of Klipkraal Drift. The Oxfordshire Light Infantry crossed back to the north bank and with the whole of the 13th Brigade attacked the Drieput Kopjes without dislodging the Boer rearguard. While the fighting was in progress Kitchener anticipated correctly that Cronjé would attempt to cross the river near Paardeberg, 15 miles upstream, and

* The East Kent Regiment.

he ordered Hannay to take his mounted infantry there to intercept them, but Hannay declared that his force would not be able to go beyond Klipkraal Drift where it had begun to reassemble and where it was joined by the field battery left behind by the Oxfordshire Light Infantry. When that battery opened fire on the Boer laager at a range of 3,500 yd it provoked the Boers on the river to counter-attack and the mounted infantry retired once more in confusion. When the fighting died down at the end of the day the British forces remained where they were for the time being, but Cronjé was on the move eastwards again after dark, getting a head start on the 6th Division which did not set off until 3 a.m. on the morning of 17 February. Cronjé felt confident enough to stop at midnight to rest his cattle for four hours, a fatal mistake as it turned out. By the time he had covered the remaining 15 miles to Vendutie Drift on the far side of Paardeberg, French had responded to urgent requests from both Roberts and Kitchener and sent Broadwood's depleted and exhausted 2nd Cavalry Brigade on a 30-mile dash from Kimberley to cover the drift from the Kameelfontein ridges. There his artillery opened fire at about 11.15 a.m., just as Cronjé was preparing to cross the river, and destroyed enough of his wagons and oxen to trap him on the north bank.

Of the other British units converging on Cronjé's convoy, Hannay's mounted infantry arrived before dark on 17 February and, apart from elements remaining on the north bank, occupied most of the rising ground south of Paardeberg Drift. Kelly-Kenny's 6th Division and Colvile's 9th Division arrived south of the river between midnight and 4.30 a.m. on the 18th. Tucker's 7th Division was still at Jacobsdal where Roberts was also waiting for the Guards Brigade and the naval guns which were on their way from Methuen's force at Modder River Station. He remained there on the 18th, having caught a chill, leaving Kelly-Kenny technically in charge at Paardeberg as the senior officer present, but subject to an ambiguous letter which he had written to Kelly-Kenny the day before in response to Kitchener's request for clarification of his rôle. In this he had asked him to 'consider that Lord Kitchener is with you for the purpose of communicating to you my orders, so that there may be no delays such as reference to and fro would entail'.[5] On the strength of this letter Kitchener took charge at Paardeberg.

Not long after his first sight of Cronjé's laager at daybreak, and after a brief reconnaissance, Kitchener had decided to attack it. He had cut short Kelly-Kenny's exposition of his own plan, which was to surround the laager without attacking it and to await Cronjé's inevitable surrender. That plan had the attraction of avoiding heavy casualties, but it would have required a cordon 21 miles in circumference strong enough both to contain Cronjé and to keep out Boer reinforcements, and it is questionable whether there were enough troops available for the purpose. Kitchener's instinct was to seize an opportunity which might not be repeated. He planned to engage the enemy from the south and then mount simultaneous attacks from the east and the west. He was confident that it would all be over in a matter of hours, leaving the way clear for an advance on Bloemfontein. In reaching that conclusion he had, perhaps, not taken fully into account the nature of Cronjé's defences or the lessons of the battles already fought, as set out in the tactical memoranda which, as Chief of Staff, he had issued in Cape Town on Roberts's behalf.[6]

Cronjé's laager was perched above Vendutie Drift on the north bank of the Modder River, which meandered for 10 miles in a south-westerly direction from Koedoesrand Drift, 6 miles upstream of the laager, to Paardeberg Drift, 4 miles downstream. The bed of the river was approximately 60 yd wide, but it flowed through a gorge whose banks were up to 45 ft high and were covered with mimosa thorn and other bushes, which in some places extended 200–300 yd outwards from the banks. In places the banks were entered by dongas which provided natural trenches extending outwards from the river. The largest of these was on the north bank on a bend in the river 2 miles downstream of the laager where the direction of flow changed from west to south. The donga in question extended for about 500 yd from the river in a north-westerly direction. The kopjes, called Paardeberg and Koedoesrand, both on the north side of the river and from 500 to 600 ft in height, formed the south-western and north-eastern limits respectively of an oval-shaped natural amphitheatre whose long axis was the river. On either side of the river the ground sloped gently upwards for two to three miles, mostly devoid of cover. On the south side were a number of small kopjes, including Signal Hill, about one mile south-east of Paardeberg Drift, and Kitchener's Kopje, 2½ miles south-east of the laager. On the other side of the river, Gun Hill lay about 1,000 yd north of the large donga. Apart from the drifts already mentioned the river could be crossed also at Vandenberg's Drift and Bank's Drift between the laager and Koedoesrand, but the river had risen overnight and was flowing quite strongly, making crossing more difficult. Only the laager was visible to the British, but Cronjé's main defences were the trenches and dongas on the north bank and to a lesser extent on the south bank as well, allowing effective grazing fire in all directions.

The Cavalry Division, whose achievement it was to have stopped the Boer convoy at Vendutie Drift, remained in place, containing Cronjé to the north. French declined to play a more active part in the action, beyond joining in the bombardment of the laager, because of the weak state of his division and Kitchener accepted the position. To Kelly-Kenny's 6th Division Kitchener gave the task of attacking from the south of the river and it was in action by 7 a.m. with Knox's 13th Brigade on the left and Brig Gen T.E. Stephenson's 18th Brigade on the right. The brunt of the attack was borne by the 13th Brigade (Buffs, Gloucesters, West Ridings and Oxfordshire Light Infantry), supported on the right by the

Yorkshires in Stephenson's brigade. Soon after the attack started Kitchener looked at his watch, and turning to the small group of staff officers round him said, 'It is now seven o'clock. We shall be in the laager by half-past ten. I'll then load up French and send him on to Bloemfontein at once.'[7] Intensive Boer rifle fire, reminiscent of the first battle on the Modder River, had halted the attack by midday. Some units had got as far as the river bank, others to within 400 yd. Stephenson's Welsh and Essex Regiments, to the right of the Yorkshires, were to have supported an assault on the laager from the east by Hannay's mounted infantry, but they had been distracted by the arrival at about 9 a.m. of the first Boer reinforcements from Bloemfontein – several hundred burghers under Commandant H.J. Steyn who came to the aid of a handful of Ferreira's men in the kopjes between Bank's Drift and the farm Stinkfontein. Steyn effectively kept these regiments out of the main action for two hours.

After breakfasting his troops Colvile had intended to take the 9th Division across the river at Paardeberg Drift with a view to advancing towards the laager along the north bank, but before he was able to cross Kitchener called him back and ordered him to support the 6th Division on the south side. Maj Gen Hector MacDonald's Highland Brigade was ordered to close on Knox's 13th Brigade and set off at 7.15 a.m., marching parallel to the river and some distance from it. As the leading men approached the 13th Brigade the Highlanders came under heavy Boer rifle fire and MacDonald ordered them to face the river and advance towards it in a single skirmishing line. As they approached the river the intensity of fire increased and the advance of the main body was brought to a halt at a distance of 500 yd. The Highlanders' line extended for 2½ miles with its right merging with the 13th Brigade. The extreme left extended beyond the Boer defences with the result that the companies there were not directly engaged. From 9 a.m. three companies of the Black Watch and two of the Seaforths crossed the river and joined forces with the 7th Mounted Infantry, which had been there for some time. By working along the north bank they got within 300 yd of the large donga, where they were ordered to stop because they were masking the fire of troops on the other side of the river.

Maj Gen Horace Smith-Dorrien's 19th Brigade remained in reserve until about 8.30 a.m. when Kitchener ordered Colvile to send it across the river with one field battery. According to Smith-Dorrien he received the order from Maj Hubert Hamilton, one of Kitchener's staff officers, whom he asked where he could cross. Hamilton replied, 'The river is in flood, and as far as I have heard, Paardeberg Drift, the only one available, is unfordable; but Lord Kitchener, knowing your resourcefulness, feels sure you will get across somehow.'[8] With the help of a rope sent across by the Royal Engineers the brigade succeeded in crossing the river, which was flowing strongly at chest height, by 10.15 a.m. (The Highlanders who had crossed earlier had solved the problem by linking hands.) Once across, the Royal Canadian Regiment advanced parallel to the river towards the large donga, while the Shropshires secured the area around Gun Hill, which Smith-Dorrien made his headquarters, and the Gordon Highlanders swung round to the north-east of the hill. The battery came into action north-east of Paardeberg Drift. The Duke of Cornwall's Light Infantry remained south of the river to support MacDonald and to guard the baggage. The Canadians' advance was halted by heavy rifle fire 500 yd from the large donga. Rain and cloud in the afternoon prevented communication by heliograph and Smith-Dorrien had no idea of what was happening elsewhere: 'I was in a complete fog as to what was happening, and knew nothing of the situation either of our own troops or of the Boers, beyond what I could see and infer for myself . . . The only order I received was the one to establish my brigade on the north side of the river, and I could get neither instructions nor information from anyone.'[9] At 5.15 p.m. he was 'horrified' to see troops on the right of his line rise and charge forward with a ringing cheer.[10] Unknown to him, about three hours earlier Kitchener had ordered Colvile to send all available reinforcements to his support. In response half a battalion of the Duke of Cornwall's Light Infantry, commanded by Lt Col Aldworth, had been sent across at 3.30 p.m. together with a company of mounted infantry. They had gone into action as described by Smith-Dorrien and some of the Canadians and Highlanders had joined in on their own initiative. They succeeded in getting to within 300 yd of the large donga, with heavy casualties. Aldworth was among those killed. Smith-Dorrien was criticised later for not supporting the attack but according to his account it was all over within one or two minutes of his becoming aware of it.[11]

The attack from the east was to have been carried out by Hannay's mounted infantry, supported by the Welsh and Essex Regiments in Stephenson's 18th Brigade. Kitchener had ordered Hannay to proceed to Koedoesrand at 3 a.m. on the morning of the battle and he had set off with the main body of the mounted infantry at 4 a.m. Some units had been left behind at Paardeberg Drift and another was left in passing at Kitchener's Kopje. Vandenberg's and Bank's Drifts had been secured at around 9 a.m. but for the next two hours Hannay, like Stephenson, was preoccupied with the threat from the newly arrived Boer reinforcements under Commandant Steyn to the east of those drifts. When Kitchener heard about this at around 10 a.m. he ordered them, via Kelly-Kenny, to disregard the threat and to press the attack on Cronjé's laager, and to make sure he galloped across and gave them the order himself, a practice he followed in other parts of the field during the day. By 1.30 p.m. Hannay had established a firing line north of the river about 700 yd from the laager and Stephenson's Welsh and Essex Regiments had established themselves opposite him in a group of dongas on the south bank. Hannay decided that he could advance no further and sent a message to that effect to Kitchener, who received it just after he had asked Colvile and Kelly-Kenny for further efforts and had ridden across again to Stephenson to urge him to cross the river and make the utmost effort to get into the laager with the bayonet. Hannay's message was not one which he wanted to hear. He replied: 'The time has now come for a final effort. All troops have been warned that the laager must be rushed at all costs. Try and carry Stephenson's brigade with you. But if they cannot go, the MI should do it. Gallop up if necessary and fire into the laager.'

When Hannay received the message at 3 p.m. he had succeeded in moving the firing line to within 500 yd of the laager. It is uncertain whether Kitchener intended the last part of his message as an order, but Hannay took it as such. He had no news of Stephenson, who at that point was 2 miles away across the river, and he is said to have been deeply upset by the failures of his mounted infantry during the pursuit of Cronjé. It may be that he saw Kitchener's words as a slight on his personal courage and competence. Sending his staff away on various pretexts he gathered together a group of about fifty men, ordered them to mount and then suddenly galloped ahead of them towards the laager 500 yd away. At 250 yd his horse was killed under him but he extricated himself and continued on foot until he fell, riddled with bullets, 50 yd further on. His adjutant, Capt R.M.A. Hankey, was also killed as were some of the soldiers who followed him; others were able to swerve off to the left to safety. Two officers and a handful of men actually reached the laager, where they were taken prisoner. Under cover of Hannay's charge the firing line was able to move up too, within 300 yd of the laager. Some saw his charge as a protest against Kitchener's indifference to loss of life, but Kitchener was unmoved and three years later condemned Hannay's action in a letter to Ian Hamilton: 'As regards the latter I think a defeated general or an officer who makes a serious mistake which leads to things going wrong has a perfect right to shoot himself if he wishes to do so and does not thereby imperil others, but I do not think anyone has the right to take 40 or 50 men and commit suicide with them.'[12]

Stephenson crossed the river via Vandenberg's Drift with units of the Welsh and Essex Regiments at 4 p.m. and they carried out a fresh attack on the laager at 5.30 p.m., the Welsh leading with the Essex in reserve. The attack started from further back than Hannay's and as the sky had cleared they had to advance into the sun. The Boers inflicted heavy casualties and they were unable to get closer than 500 yd.

At about 4.30 p.m. Christiaan de Wet, who had come up from Koffiefontein with 600 men, occupied Kitchener's Kopje and the adjoining Stinkfontein Farm and opened fire with shrapnel and rifle fire on the baggage of the 6th Division and the British field batteries south of the river. At much the same time the arrival from Kimberley of Gordon's 3rd Cavalry Brigade at Koedoesrand forced De Beer south of the river. Steyn's men had reoccupied the kopjes from which they had troubled Hannay and Stephenson earlier in the day, with the result that the entire line of kopjes from Koedoesrand round to Kitchener's Kopje was held by Boers. While the Buffs were able to contain De Wet they were unable to dislodge him. His coup robbed Kitchener's offensive of what little momentum it retained and effectively ended the day's fighting. The distraction also prevented the issuing of instructions to all units to remain in place for the night in order to resume the fight the next day and most colonels and brigadiers withdrew their men from advance positions. The British casualties were 1,270, the worst suffered on any single day in the Boer War, although the number killed was less than at Spion Kop. The Boer casualties at 300 were proportionately the same as the British but most of Cronjé's wagons had been destroyed and his animals either killed or scattered.

Kitchener has been much criticised for his conduct of the battle and, indeed, for having fought it at all since, it was argued, it was necessary only to surround Cronjé and wait for his surrender, as Kelly-Kenny would have done without Kitchener's intervention. However, that theory ignores the imponderables. The effective appearances during the battle of Steyn and De Wet are proof that the Boers seriously intended to rescue Cronjé and more reinforcements were on the way from Colesberg and Natal. Kitchener's decision to attack was surely right, but the conduct of the battle was marred from the start by the ambiguity of the command arrangements. Kitchener was unquestionably in command, but lacked the wherewithal to command effectively. He had the assistance of only two staff officers and two ADCs, no members of the HQ staff, no signallers, gallopers or orderlies.[13] While Kelly-Kenny and Colvile responded loyally to his orders they did so without enthusiasm or conviction. Kelly-Kenny thought he was mad. At the level of individual units the battle was fought courageously and competently but there was little coordination or mutual support. A large part of the British force was committed to sterile activity south of the river when properly directed concentrations north of the river might well have overcome the Boer defences, with lower casualties. Capt S.L'H. Slocum, the US military attaché with the British forces, quoted Kitchener as having said in his presence on the day after the battle, 'If I had known yesterday, the 18th, what I know today, I would not have attacked the Boers in the river bed; it is impossible against that rifle.'[14]

Despite that admission Kitchener was contemptuous of those who believed that he should not have attacked the laager at all. Writing to Ian Hamilton three years after the battle, he commented: 'I am quite willing to accept the full responsibility for the battle of Paardeberg. As a matter of fact, putting aside local South African rank, I was the senior officer in the Army present. . . . Instead of penitently acknowledging my error, as one writer considers I should, I maintain that it was the only course to pursue, and that had I allowed Cronje to escape after all the exertions I had called for and received from the army, I should be most rightly censured, and have lost the confidence of the troops.'[15]

Roberts arrived from Jacobsdal at 10 a.m. on the day after the battle, having recovered from his chill, and reasserted his authority. He revoked a 24-hour armistice which had been granted to Cronjé to bury his dead, believing it to be a device to gain time for the Boer relieving forces, and during the morning summoned Smith-Dorrien from across the river to a meeting to discuss future tactics. Of those present Kitchener and Colvile were in favour of resuming the attack, but Roberts was persuaded by Smith-Dorrien and French, who were for bombarding Cronjé into inevitable surrender, and he decided accordingly. However, Kitchener did not give up easily. As Smith-Dorrien was about to ride away Kitchener approached him, urging him to attempt another attack and assuring him that he would be a 'made man' if he succeeded. Smith-Dorrien said that he would not attack unless ordered to do so and rode away.[16] Roberts never criticised Kitchener's conduct of operations on 18 February but on the 22nd he sent him away from Paardeberg to Naauwpoort Junction to supervise the opening of railway communications with Bloemfontein.

The business in Naauwpoort did not detain Kitchener for long and he left matters there in the capable hands of the Director of Railways, Lt Col Percy Girouard, who had built his desert railway in the Sudan campaign. He went on to De Aar junction on the Cape Town to Kimberley line where on 28 February he met Maj Gen H.H. Settle, whom Roberts had put in charge of dealing with a rebellion which had broken out in the North-Western Cape Colony. On 16 February a commando under Gen P.J. Liebenberg and Commandant Lukas Steenkamp had captured the town of Prieska, just south of the Orange River and about 100 miles north-west of De Aar. Liebenberg had proclaimed the annexation of the area to the Orange Free State and within a week 300 rebels had been armed and organised into a commando.[17] Signs that the rebellion was spreading had alarmed Milner, for whom the possibility of a general uprising in the Cape Colony was an ever-present fear. Kitchener arranged with Settle for the dispatch of three small columns, none above 600 strong, and returned to Roberts in time to accompany him on a visit to Kimberley, where they discussed with Methuen arrangements for the relief of Mafeking. Following the actions at Poplar Grove and Driefontein during the advance to Bloemfontein, Kitchener had to return to the Cape Colony after Liebenberg – in an engagement at Houwater, 50 miles north-west of De Aar – had driven back to Britstown the column

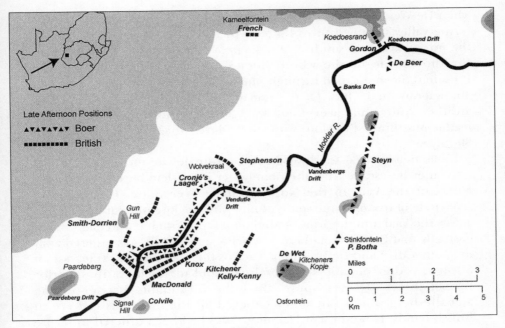

The Battle of Paardeberg – 18 February 1900

commanded by Col Adye, one of the three sent out on Kitchener's earlier visit. He accompanied the column after reinforcements had brought it up to a strength of 3,000 men and occupied Prieska on 18 March.[18] Liebenberg and Steenkamp fled across the Orange River and the rebellion subsided.

In Bloemfontein Kitchener returned to staff work. He played little part in shaping the tactics of the advance to Pretoria, but devoted himself to organisational matters. In particular he took steps to lighten the loads carried by horses, in order to prolong their lives.[19] When De Wet, following his successes at Sannah's Post and Mostert's Hoek, laid siege to Wepener Kitchener superintended the relief operation. He was armed with a letter from Roberts confirming his authority to act as his representative in terms similar to the letter to Kelly-Kenny on which Kitchener relied when he took command at the battle of Paardeberg. Some saw this as evidence that Roberts had not lost confidence in him as a result of his conduct of that battle.[20] Kitchener remained with Roberts during his advance to Pretoria, but during the battle of Diamond Hill he went back to the Free State to try and put an end to De Wet's depredations on the railway line north of Bloemfontein. While there he narrowly avoided capture. He was back in Pretoria when De Wet, with 8,000 men, was forced into the Brandwater Basin, a fertile valley hemmed in to the east by the Basutoland border and to the north, west and south by a half-circle of mountains. De Wet's plan for the escape of the whole Boer force miscarried, but he and President Steyn escaped through one of the passes with 2,600 men and 400 wagons on 15 July. Of the remainder a small number escaped by another route, but over 4,000 were left behind under the veteran leader Marthinus Prinsloo, who surrendered to Archibald Hunter on 30 July.

Kitchener hurried south again to coordinate the pursuit of De Wet who, after his escape from the Brandwater Basin, had been driven to the banks of the Vaal in the North-Western Free State. He formed a semicircle of troops to the south of him with the intention of driving him across the Vaal into the arms of Methuen. But Methuen, who had divined correctly that De Wet would cross by Schoeman's Drift, was ordered away to another drift and De Wet slipped across the river into the Transvaal on 6 August. After pursuit for several days and nights by vastly superior British forces De Wet approached the formidable barrier of the Magaliesberg where Kitchener believed all the main passes were in British hands. However, Ian Hamilton, who had been ordered to secure the pass at Olifants Nek had delayed getting there and De Wet crossed to safety on 14 August. It was some consolation for the failure of this operation, the first of three so-called 'De Wet hunts', that it brought Kitchener into a position where he was able on 16 August to relieve Lt Col Hore and 300 men besieged by De la Rey at Brakfontein on the Elands River. Thereafter, he was mostly in Pretoria until he succeeded Roberts as Commander-in-Chief on 29 November 1900.

In view of Roberts's confidence that the war was nearly over it is not surprising that the British government was looking for a reduction in military expenditure in South Africa. After the Khaki Election in October 1900 the Marquess of Lansdowne had been replaced as Secretary of State for War by W. St John Brodrick, later Lord Midleton, with whom Kitchener was to develop a close working relationship. A week before Kitchener took up his new command Brodrick wrote to him, pointing out that the British Army in South Africa had grown from 100,000 to 230,000 over the past year with only 8,000 Boers now in the field, and expressing the hope that numbers could be reduced.[21] The figures for both sides were misleading. *The Times History* put the number of Boers still in the field – even after deducting campaign losses including 15,000 prisoners of war – at 60,000, although probably not more than a quarter were active at any time, since burghers often returned to their farms in between spells of fighting. Of the nominal British strength about half were protecting the long lines of communication and manning isolated garrisons. As a result the true disparity in the fighting strength between the two sides was not as overwhelming as the bald figures suggested.[22]

If, initially, Kitchener shared Roberts's view that the war was nearly over, he was soon disillusioned. During the last few days before he took over he was in Bloemfontein taking charge of the second De Wet hunt in the South-Eastern Free State. Evading the British at Springhaans Nek the Free State leader had seized Dewetsdorp, the town named after his father, before making an unsuccessful attempt to cross the Orange River into the Cape Colony. Although he was turned back, only to escape again through Springhaans Nek, Kritzinger and Hertzog crossed into the colony on 16 December. Botha and Ben Viljoen were both active in the Eastern Transvaal, the latter fighting in the last conventional action of the war against Gen Paget at Rhenoster Kop on 29 November, the day on which Kitchener became Commander-in-Chief. In the Western Transvaal, relatively quiet since Kitchener's intervention at Elands River in August, De la Rey captured a British supply convoy at Buffelspoort, north of the Magaliesberg, on 3 December. Ten days later, in conjunction with Beyers, who had come down from the Northern Transvaal, he fell on Clements's camp at Nooitgedacht, under the southern face of the Magaliesberg. These independent actions over a wide area marked the beginning of the prolonged final phase of the war of which Capt Maurice Harold Grant wrote in the preface to volume 4 of *The Official History*:

From December 1900 to May 1902 was waged incessantly guerrilla warfare of the purest type and on the most extensive scale between an army of 195,400 men on the one side and of 30,000 to 50,000 men on the other. The contest was remarkable in many respects but in none, perhaps, more than its duration. When it is considered that at the moment at which this narration opens the Boer forces were already beaten, inasmuch as their cause was irretrievably lost, their long sustained effort to ward off the end requires some military explanation. It is to be found in the fact that in their expiring struggle they reverted to weapons which were peculiarly their own and precisely those in which their opponents were least practised. Casting off the trammels of formal warfare, and disintegrating into a thousand bands, they compelled the British Army to conform, and agitated the whole vast theatre of war with an infinite complexity of movement which never for a moment desisted, nor for more than a moment was marked by any distinguishable trend.

In adapting his army to this new mode of warfare Kitchener had above all to increase the effectiveness of his mounted infantry, by improving its quality and increasing its strength. It helped that a year had now passed since many of its new recruits had barely been able to ride, but many of the irregulars and colonials, who had signed up for a year only, now chose not to re-enlist, and it was considered impolitic to try and force them to do so by law. Their replacements were not always of the same quality, whereas the Boers, by a gradual process of shedding the faint-hearted and incompetent were now more effective than ever.[23] By mid-January 1901 the British government had accepted the need for reinforcements and by the end of May over 30,000 were in place, half of them from a new contingent of British yeomanry and the remainder largely from local and colonial sources.[24] The change in the methods of warfare was accompanied by a change in the method of control of the British Army in South Africa. Divisions and brigades were largely superseded by the column as the operational unit. There were thirty-eight of these when Kitchener took over and their number doubled in due course.[25]

Kitchener inherited from Roberts the policies of farm burning and the use of concentration camps, characterised by Sir Henry Campbell-Bannerman as 'methods of barbarism', but history has heaped most of the opprobrium on Kitchener. This is partly because of the conventional perception of Roberts as kindly and genial and of Kitchener as ruthless, but mainly because of the different uses to which they were perceived as having put the policies. Roberts introduced concentration camps largely as a means of protecting surrendered burghers and their families and also, in the Cape Colony and Natal, as accommodation for civilian deportees from the Boer republics. He started burning farms essentially as a punitive measure linked to Boer attacks on the railways. Under Kitchener concentration camps became, in the first instance, instruments of military policy intended to induce Boer combatants to surrender, by the wholesale removal of their families. As the counterpart of this policy he ordered systematic devastation of the countryside in order to starve out the combatants. By the time of Roberts's departure at the end of November 1900 there was little difference in practical terms between the policies of the two commanders. Under Roberts farm burning had become more or less indiscriminate and an increasing proportion of concentration camp inmates were the dispossessed families of Boer combatants. Kitchener made a distinction between denuding the country of supplies and livestock, which is what he required, and the destruction of farms and properties, to which he declared himself opposed except as a penal measure.[26] It was not a distinction which carried much weight with his column commanders and he exercised as little control over them in this respect as Roberts had done.

Kitchener's first memorandum on the subject of concentration camps, issued to all commanding officers on 21 December 1900, made clear his intention of using them as a countermeasure to guerrilla warfare:

The General Commanding in Chief is desirous that all possible measures shall be taken to stop the present guerrilla warfare. Of the various measures suggested for the accomplishment of this object, one which has been strongly recommended and has lately been successfully tried on a small scale, is the removal of all men, women and children and natives from the district which the enemy's bands persistently occupy. This course has been pointed out by surrendered burghers, who are anxious to finish the war, as the most effective method of limiting the endurance of the guerrillas as the men and women left on farms, if disloyal, willingly supply burghers, if loyal, dare not refuse to do so. Moreover seeing the unprotected state of women now living out in the Districts, this course is desirable to ensure their not being insulted or molested by natives.

Lord Kitchener desires that General Officers will, according to the means at their disposal, follow this system in the districts which they occupy or may traverse. . . .

The memorandum went on to specify two categories of camp inmate:

1st. Refugees, and the families of neutrals, non-combatants and surrendered burghers. 2nd. Those whose husbands, fathers or sons are on commando. The preference in accommodation, &c., should, of course, be given to the first class . . .[27]

The intended discrimination in living conditions extended to food. In the Transvaal camps this meant that the second category received no meat, but the distinction was eventually abandoned. Administration of the camps was transferred from the military to the civil authorities from 1 March 1901 in the Transvaal and Orange Free State and from 1 November 1901 in Natal.[28]

Although most of the concern, both in Britain and internationally, was focused on the camps for whites, there were also separate camps for Africans. Originally these were for the families of farm labourers made homeless by farm burning, but later Africans were moved from their own areas for fear that they would provide the Boers with food, and in order to provide male labour for the British Army. Kitchener's memorandum of 21 December 1900 stipulated that Africans removed to camps were to be available for any works undertaken, for which they would receive pay at native rates. In the Transvaal initially, no rations were provided for African inmates, the expectation being that they would support themselves and their families out of their wages.[29] Later, rations were provided for those who could not support themselves and from August 1901 onwards extensive areas of land were made available for the cultivation of crops by the inmates of African camps.[30]

By the end of the war there were over forty camps for whites[31] and over sixty for Africans.[32] In both cases the inmates were predominantly women and children, mostly the latter. In both white and African camps the death rate reached alarming proportions during the last months of 1901. More accurate figures are available for white deaths than for African. It is generally accepted that over 26,000 Boer women and children died in the camps; the figure inscribed on the Women's Monument in Bloemfontein is 26,370, of whom most were children. For African deaths, Professor Spies arrived at a total of 13,351 from available figures, but estimated that the true figure was considerably in excess of that.[33] White deaths began to rise sharply in July 1901 and in October reached a monthly peak of over 3,000. They began to fall sharply in February 1902 and by May were under 200. African deaths peaked and fell later. A common factor in the high death rates was the prevalence of epidemic diseases, the worst of which was a virulent strain of measles with pulmonary complications, including pneumonia. Also present was typhoid, which was endemic in South Africa and which in the course of the war killed more British soldiers than did enemy action. The effect of these diseases was aggravated in the concentration camps by overcrowding, poor sanitation and over-stretched medical resources.

Well before the disastrous rise in death rates the concentration camps had attracted the attention of Emily Hobhouse, the formidable 41-year-old spinster daughter of an English archdeacon. She had arrived in South Africa in December 1900 in order to distribute money on behalf of the South African Women and Children Distress Fund, which she had started.[34] In Cape Town she learnt about the concentration camps and decided to visit them and see for herself. Kitchener refused to allow her into the Transvaal, but she visited camps in the Orange Free State and the Cape Colony. She was appalled in particular by what she saw in the Bloemfontein camp, where even at that stage there were twenty-five deaths a day. On her return to England in May 1901 she took steps to bring conditions to official and public attention. She encountered a great deal of hostility but she also secured the support of powerful allies such as Lloyd George and the Leader of the Opposition, Sir Henry Campbell-Bannerman. It was shortly after his first meeting with her that Campbell-Bannerman used the phrase 'methods of barbarism'.[35] Largely because of her efforts, in July 1901 the government appointed an all-women committee of inquiry, three members from Britain and three from South Africa, under the chairmanship of Millicent Fawcett. Emily Hobhouse was pointedly excluded and she was refused permission to visit the camps again. Fears that the committee would produce a whitewash proved to be unfounded. Their report was thorough and workmanlike, and even before it reported in December 1901, a number of their recommendations had been implemented.[36] The committee did not visit African camps nor, for lack of time, had Emily Hobhouse although she later tried unsuccessfully to persuade the government to take an interest in them. In October she sailed for South Africa, but her arrival in Cape Town coincided with the extension of martial law to the ports in the Cape Colony. On Kitchener's orders she was arrested and forcibly sent back to England. She instituted and then, on legal advice, abandoned proceedings against Kitchener for the wrongful use of martial law.[37]

Contrary to some accounts Kitchener did visit camps on occasion,[38] but in the case of the visits to four camps in December 1901 recorded by his ADC, Frank Maxwell, his purpose appears to have been to speak to surrendered Boers rather than to inspect conditions.[39] He refused to accept any responsibility for poor management of the camps and blamed the high death rate on the unsanitary habits of Boer families. At one point he even went so far as to suggest that there were grounds for bringing manslaughter charges against some of the Boer mothers.[40] He referred to Emily Hobhouse as 'that bloody woman'.[41] In the case of some of the less resolute combatants the camps may have induced some surrenders, but for the hard core of 'bitter-enders' they probably had the reverse of the intended effect since these men were able to fight on in the knowledge that the British were taking care of their families. This is confirmed by the fact that towards the end of the war Kitchener reversed the policy, instructing his column commanders not to bring in families. The burden put on commandos by the need to care for such families was one of the most acute concerns expressed by representatives from the areas concerned at the Vereeniging peace conference.

In addition to concern aroused in Britain by his policies, Kitchener faced opposition locally from Milner who saw farm burning and the use of concentration camps as a threat to his vision of a prosperous British South Africa after the war. He foresaw correctly that they would leave a legacy of bitterness and he would have preferred a policy of extending British protected areas. He was responsible for one of the few redeeming features of the camps, namely the provision of schooling, in English, for those who wanted it, and by the end of the war there were nearly 30,000 children in schools in the white concentration camps.[42] An attempt to introduce schooling into African camps was vetoed largely on administrative grounds.[43] Milner was also frustrated by delays in resuming economic activity in the existing protected areas, but Kitchener did allow the resumption of gold mining on the Rand. Seven mining companies were in production by June 1901 and fifteen by October. Although their personal relationship was cordial Milner found Kitchener difficult to work with. He listened politely but took little notice of Milner's opinions. Once, Milner suggested that there should be not one Commander-in-Chief in South Africa, but three regional commanders reporting, effectively, to him. Later he tried to have Kitchener replaced by Lyttleton, but the British Cabinet was not persuaded.

Kitchener tried to hasten the end of the war by enlisting the aid of prominent surrendered Boers and non-combatants in burgher peace committees, whose purpose was to persuade those still in the field to give up the unequal struggle. Inevitably these emissaries were regarded as traitors and the initiative was a failure. Meyer de Kock was arrested, tried and shot by an open grave by Ben Viljoen's forces. J.J. Morgendaal, who was travelling in custody with De Wet's forces was shot in cold blood, allegedly on the orders of De Wet, when he appeared to be putting the commando in peril by deliberate delay.[44] Kitchener was more successful in persuading surrendered Boers to help the British forces, to the extent that at Vereeniging, Botha expressed the fear that there would soon be more Boers fighting for the British than against them.

During Kitchener's time as Commander-in-Chief the main type of large-scale military operation was the 'drive', a term embracing any concerted attempt to round up Boer combatants within a defined area. The first and much the most successful of such operations had taken place under Roberts's command in June and July 1900 when Archibald Hunter and others had driven 8,000 Free State Boers into the Brandwater Basin on the Basutoland border, subsequently capturing over 4,000 of them. Although drives became more sophisticated under Kitchener, the results in terms of Boer losses and surrenders – he had to be discouraged from referring to these in his correspondence as 'bags'[45] – were measured in hundreds rather than in thousands, and often in the low hundreds. Linked to the evolution of the drive was the extension of the blockhouse system. These miniature forts were used from January 1901 onwards to protect the railway lines. Near important bridges they were substantial stone-built structures, but for the most part their walls were of double-skinned corrugated iron filled with earth and gravel and pierced by loopholes. Their shape was soon simplified from hexagonal to circular and the distance between them was reduced from about a mile and a half to a few hundred yards. As a further refinement they were linked by barbed wire and a telephone line, and later a deep trench was dug in parallel to the barbed wire. The result of this process, which was substantially complete on the Transvaal and Free State railways by May 1901, was not only to improve the protection of those lines but also to transform them into barriers.[46] From July 1901 spurs were sent out from the railways, following the lines of roads, to subdivide the vast sphere of operations into more manageable areas.[47] By the end of the war some 8,000 blockhouses had been erected,[48] providing the links in 3,700 miles of fortifications.[49]

The first of Kitchener's major drives began in the Eastern Transvaal – without the benefit of the blockhouse system – at the end of January 1901 under the overall command of French. Seven columns, with a fighting strength of 14,000 men and 58 guns,[50] set out to sweep an area three times the size of Wales between the Delagoa Bay and Natal Railways as far as the Swaziland and Zululand borders. At the end of the ten-week operation it was estimated that 600 burghers had been killed, wounded or captured and that a further 730 had surrendered voluntarily,[51] but most of the commandos and their leaders, including Kemp and Beyers, escaped. Thereafter, the majority of the drives were in the Free State, where the Central Railway provided a fortified barrier between east and west. It was the essence of the drive that the enemy should be forced against a barrier, either an actual one or a human barrier in the form of other British columns. Before the extension of the blockhouse system the drives would usually be implemented by columns moving inwards from all sides of the chosen area. That the drives were, on the whole, unsuccessful in the primary purpose of rounding up Boer combatants was due partly to the difficulty of avoiding gaps in lines of mounted troops extending for many miles, and partly due to the skill of the Boers in slipping around the flanks of columns by day or through picket lines by night.

In the Eastern Transvaal night raids were an effective alternative to drives during the latter half of 1901, particularly as developed by Lt Col G.E. Benson of the Royal Artillery.* Relying on intelligence gathered by the South African-born Lt Col Aubrey Woolls-Sampson, Benson marched his column up to forty miles at night and attacked Boer laagers at dawn. He was killed after his column was overwhelmed at Bakenlaagte on 30 October by a superior force under Botha and he was succeeded by Maj Gen Bruce Hamilton as the principal scourge of the Boers in the Eastern Transvaal. Hamilton had a considerably larger force at his disposal and, with the help of Woolls-Sampson's intelligence skills, applied Benson's night raiding techniques to considerable effect until January 1902. With a widely extended blockhouse system in place at the beginning of 1902 Kitchener launched a series of intensive 'new model' drives in the North-Eastern Free State. These failed to trap Christiaan de Wet and President Steyn[52] who succeeded in joining De la Rey in the Western Transvaal as large-scale drives were being implemented there. Up to this point Kitchener himself had exercised direct control of seventy to eighty individual columns scattered throughout South Africa,[53] but in April 1902 Ian Hamilton, who had returned to South Africa in November 1901 to act as his Chief of Staff, was placed in overall command in the field of the Western Transvaal drives, and in the same month Bruce Hamilton took overall command of 15,000 men in the final drive in the Eastern Transvaal.

* As a major he had guided Wauchope's Highland Brigade into action at Magersfontein.

Although Kitchener's main military preoccupations were in the Transvaal and the Free State, events in the Cape Colony were a constant source of anxiety. Here Afrikaners greatly outnumbered their English-speaking fellow citizens, and in theory they could have ended the war at any time by rising en masse in support of the Boers in the two republics to whom they were linked by kinship and by a common culture. This was a hope which sustained the Boers and a fear which haunted the British. In fact they were mostly loyal or, at worst, sullenly passive, but there was always the possibility they might be provoked into rebellion by harsh administrative measures like martial law or conscription, or encouraged to rebel by signal Boer successes or, most probably, by the appearance in the Cape Colony of Boer commandos.[54] This had happened in the Eastern Cape, where five districts had gone over to the Boers following the invasion by Free Staters early in the war,[55] and also at Prieska in the North-Western Cape, where Kitchener had put down a small local rebellion in March 1900. The withdrawal from the Cape of Boer commandos following Cronjé's surrender at Paardeberg had left behind thousands of rebels. The rank and file were disenfranchised, but the question of how the ringleaders should be dealt came to be a sticking point in subsequent peace negotiations between Britain and the republics.

A decision to reinvade the Cape Colony was taken by Steyn, Botha, De la Rey and Smuts when they met at Syferfontein in the Western Transvaal in late October 1900. It was intended that this should be done in concert with a new invasion of Natal, but without waiting for that, De Wet, accompanied by Steyn, tried to invade the Cape in December. He was foiled by 6,000 British troops in nine columns, in the operation known as the second De Wet hunt, but while he kept his British pursuers occupied, both Hertzog and Kritzinger slipped across the Orange River into the Cape Colony. Hertzog went west, reaching the Atlantic Coast 120 miles north of Cape Town before turning back to meet De Wet after his renewed and initially successful attempt to invade the colony in January 1901. After their pursuit by twelve columns under Lyttleton both Hertzog and De Wet were driven back into the Orange Free State on 28 February in the culmination of the third (great) De Wet hunt. Kritzinger, meanwhile, had gone south to the Cape Midlands where he and his young commandants Scheepers, Fouché and Malan were thorns in the side of the British for many months. At the end of April 1901 he returned briefly to the Free State, taking back with him to the Cape four more commandants – Lötter, Myburgh, van Reenen and Lategan.[56] Although Kritzinger and his subordinate commanders were successful in attracting local recruits to their commandos there was no sign of a general uprising. Kitchener at first resisted the temptation to divert significant resources to the Cape Colony, but in June 1901 he sent French to take overall command there. By the end of June French had 5,800 men under his command,[57] which had risen to 9,000, excluding the 20,000 colonists raised for local defences, by the middle of September.[58]

At the meeting of the Transvaal and Free State governments at Waterval on 20 June 1900 it was decided to mount a new invasion of the Cape, by seasoned fighting men under a leader of sufficient energy and authority, to impose some coherence on isolated guerrilla activities. De la Rey offered to supply the men and Jan Smuts undertook to lead the expedition.[59] His invasion force consisted of 340 men under 4 commandants. Making their way south through the Free State in early August they became entangled in Kitchener's most extensive drive up to that time, involving 15,000 men in 17 columns.[60] As a result, by the time Smuts reached Zastron in the South-Eastern Free State on 27 August for his rendezvous with Kritzinger, his force had been reduced in size to 250.[61] There they were surrounded by British troops and had Kitchener not diverted Hart, whose column was waiting for them on the south bank of the Orange River, they would probably have been captured.

Smuts and his small band, now under two commandants, Jacobus van Deventer and Ben Bouwer, crossed the Orange River via Klaarwater Drift during the night of 3 September and were immediately attacked by mounted Basutos, losing six men and thirty led horses before escaping.[62] Smuts's men were mostly in a parlous state, with their clothes in tatters and short of ammunition. Deneys Reitz was down to his last four rounds. When he adapted a grain bag to serve as a tunic he was at first laughed at and then emulated. In their progress through the mountainous country of the North-Eastern Cape they were constantly in danger of capture by British patrols and encountered appalling weather – during one bitterly cold night fourteen men went missing and were never heard of again, and many horses died of exposure.[63] Early on they were surrounded by British troops in the Stormberg mountains, apparently with no hope of escape until they were led to safety in the dark by a hunchbacked farmer. On 17 September, entering a gorge leading to the Elands River Valley, they were warned of British troops ahead. Desperate to replace his horses and get a supply of ammunition Smuts decided to attack and, with the advantage of surprise in misty weather and superior marksmanship, overcame a squadron of the 17th Lancers, which had been forced by a swollen river to camp on the farm Modderfontein in a position overlooked by high ground. Out of 145 Lancers 26 were killed and 39 wounded.[64] Smuts's casualties were 1 killed and 6 wounded.[65] As he had intended, his men helped themselves to horses, arms, ammunition and stores. Many also took advantage of the opportunity to replace their rags with Lancers' uniforms, ignorant of Kitchener's edict that Boers captured wearing khaki would be summarily shot, with the result that several later paid for this luxury with their lives.

His successful action against the 17th Lancers gave Smuts access to the Cape Midlands. Pressing on via Tarkastad and Adelaide he reached the Southern Suurberg mountains near Port Elizabeth, getting to within sight of the city's lights. Here he decided to make for the Atlantic seaboard and the established districts of the South-Western Cape. For safety, and to lessen the provisioning burden on districts through which they were to pass, he divided the commando in two, sending one half under Van Deventer to proceed independently to the far west.[66] He himself led the other half via the Camdeboo and Swartberg mountains to Touws River Station on the Cape Town to Kimberley railway line, which he crossed on 31 October. From there he went on via Elands Vlei to Vanrhynsdorp, near the Olifants River, where he established a base. He was now in an area without railways, making it difficult for the British to concentrate troops quickly, and over the next few months he effectively established control over the 300-mile swathe of the Western Cape between the Olifants and Orange Rivers, apart from a few isolated British garrisons. In doing so he linked up with Manie Maritz – who had been operating there with 500 to 600 men since March 1901 – and with the other half of his own commando under Van Deventer. In April he attacked a cluster of British-held villages near the Orange River. He had captured Springbok and Concordia and was besieging the copper-mining settlement at Okiep when he was summoned to proceed under safe conduct to take part in the peace negotiations.

Early on in the war martial law had been declared in districts of the Cape Colony close to Boer invasions. After the fall of Pretoria, and the expectation that the war would soon end, there had been a partial withdrawal of martial law, but following the invasions of Hertzog and Kritzinger it had been extended to cover the whole of the colony except the ports. These were excluded despite the fact that recruits, ammunition, supplies and correspondence were known by the military authorities to be passing through them to the enemy.[67] The Cape government, determined to avoid military control of areas which housed the supreme court and the principal public offices of the colony, resisted Kitchener's urgent pleas that the ports should be included.[68] He finally got his way on 9 October 1901, just in time, as it happened, to prevent Emily Hobhouse from landing in Cape Town when she tried to return to South Africa. From 12 April 1901 jurisdiction over the trial of rebels in areas subject to martial law had passed from special commissions set up by the Cape government to the military authorities. In a proclamation dated 22 April 1901 Kitchener had warned all British subjects and residents of the Cape Colony who took up arms against the Crown, or incited or assisted others to do so, that on arrest they would immediately be tried by court martial, and on conviction 'be liable to the severest penalties of the law'.[69] His

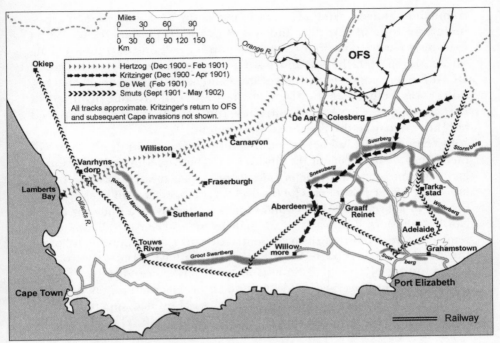

Principal Boer invasions of the Cape Colony – December 1900 to May 1902

readiness to use his powers to execute rebels captured in the field was curbed by a War Office instruction on 17 June to the effect that the fact of rebellion alone did not justify the death penalty and that this should be reserved for those who had committed 'outrages' of one sort or another. In the exercise of the discretion given to him by the War Office the death sentence was passed on rebels who had been found guilty of sniping, train wrecking, the burning of buildings and of the murder of native Africans employed by the British.[70] Of 700 rebels sentenced to death by courts martial Kitchener confirmed the sentences in the cases of 35 only. These included a few burghers of the republics captured in the colony who were convicted of similar offences on the grounds that they were breaches of the laws and customs of war.[71]

Two executions in particular attracted international opprobrium. On 5 September 1901, the day after Smuts's invasion, Hans Lötter's commando had been captured near Cradock following a night raid by Col Henry Scobell. He was found guilty by a court martial at Graaff-Reinet on nine charges including two of murder, and was shot on 11 October. On that day his fellow commandant, the 23-year-old Gideon Scheepers, was captured after he had become seriously ill and sent his commando away to safety. He was found guilty on twenty-nine charges, including four of murder, and was shot on 18 January 1902. When Kritzinger was tried on four charges of murder and one of train-wrecking on 29 March 1902 he was more fortunate, possibly because he could afford the services of an able advocate,[72] and was acquitted on all charges. Lötter was held to be a citizen of the Cape Colony, but disputed it. Kritzinger was a Free State burgher and Scheepers was a Transvaal burgher on loan to the Free State governments.[73]

In February 1902 Kitchener confirmed the sentences of death on two of three Australian officers of the Bushveldt Carbineers who had been found guilty by court martial in Pietersburg as principals or accessories in twelve murders of Boer prisoners. The Bushveldt Carbineers was an irregular unit formed in February 1901 to counter guerrilla activity in a wild part of the Northern-Eastern Transvaal. Nearly half its men were Australian and the remainder were mostly British or South Africans.[74] The murders followed the death in action on 6 August 1901 of Capt P.F. Hunt, the former commanding officer of B Squadron, who was succeeded by Lt H.H. (Breaker) Morant, a 35-year-old Englishman of uncertain origin, who had lived in the Australian outback for many years. Hunt had apparently been killed brutally during a skirmish at a Boer farmhouse. The fact that his body was reported to have been found stripped and mutilated led Morant to assume that he had been tortured and, in his case at least, the subsequent murders of Boer prisoners were motivated mainly by revenge. It was also pleaded in justification for the murders that Hunt had previously received and given verbal orders that no prisoners were to be taken. Although a number of witnesses testified to his having given such orders, no evidence was provided to support the contention that he had received them from a superior officer, and none has emerged since. Furthermore, the pattern of Boer surrenders throughout South Africa was not consistent with such orders having emanated from Kitchener or his staff.[75] In addition to Morant those sentenced to death were Veterinary Lt P.J. Handcock and Lt G.R. Witton. Apart from the murder of Boer prisoners there was a strong suspicion that Handcock, at the instigation of Morant, had murdered a missionary who was a witness to some of the murders, but both had been acquitted for lack of evidence. Kitchener confirmed the sentences of death on Handcock and Morant, but commuted the sentence on Witton to life imprisonment on the grounds that he was under the influence of the other two. At the time it was Witton's life sentence, rather than the execution of Morant and Handcock, that aroused strong feelings in Australia and also in South Africa. After representations on his behalf Witton was released in July 1904.[76] Later, stimulated by the publication in 1907 of Witton's book *Scapegoats of the Empire*, criticism focused on Kitchener's supposed motives for confirming the death sentences on Morant and Handcock. The two were cast as victims of a desire to present British justice as even-handed and to placate Germany in connection with the murder of the missionary, the Revd C.A.D. Heese.[77] Thomas Pakenham has suggested that Kitchener was motivated simply by anger at indiscipline in his own army.[78] Whatever the pressures on him, the seriousness of the offences would have left him little scope in the exercise of his discretion. Cape rebels had been shot for less.[79]

In March 1902 an offer by the Dutch government to mediate a peace settlement in Europe between the Boer delegation there and the British government was turned down by Britain with thanks in accordance with its usual policy of resisting foreign intervention in the war, and on the grounds that the necessity for the Boer delegation to travel to South Africa would have been too time-consuming. But Britain also expressed the view that the proper forum for negotiation was in South Africa between the Boer leaders there and the British Commander-in-Chief. By passing the correspondence on to Schalk Burger, acting President of the Transvaal, Kitchener made it possible for both sides to enter into negotiations, without either having overtly to seek them. A meeting in Klerksdorp on 9 and 10 April between the Transvaal and Free State governments was followed by meetings in Pretoria of the Boer leaders with Kitchener and Milner, the meeting of Boer representatives in Vereeniging, and the signing of the peace treaty in Pretoria on 31 May 1902.

More than a year earlier Kitchener and Botha had met at Middelburg to discuss a possible peace settlement. It is a measure of the rapport between them that in the course of a one-day meeting on 28 February 1901 they were able to produce a comprehensive draft settlement. Its essential basis was a complete surrender of Boer independence, to be followed by progress towards representative self-government under the British Crown; but both men were too far ahead of their colleagues. The amended terms which came back from London and which were rejected by Botha were considerably less conciliatory than those agreed provisionally by Kitchener. In particular the British government had hardened the conditions relating to financial assistance, the future rights of native Africans and, reflecting Milner's advice, the question of amnesties for rebels in the Cape Colony and Natal. While Milner was a convenient scapegoat for the failure of the negotiations, it is unlikely that Botha could have persuaded men like Steyn, De Wet and De la Rey to stop fighting for independence at that stage of the war.

In the months following the breakdown of the Middelburg talks Kitchener had applied his twin policies of drives and devastation with increasing severity, but his frustration at their failure to break the Boer will to resist had led him to advocate more extreme measures. These included confiscation of the property of combatants and the permanent banishment of prisoners of war and their families to places such as

Madagascar, Java and Fiji. Chamberlain dismissed these proposals as absurd,[80] but Kitchener was authorised, while acting as High Commissioner during Milner's absence, to issue a proclamation dated 7 August 1901 threatening all Boer officers who failed to surrender by 15 September 1901 with permanent banishment from South Africa. In addition it threatened that the cost of maintenance of the families of all burghers in the field who had not surrendered by that date would be a charge on the property of those burghers. The proclamation was received with contempt by the Boer leaders and probably provoked Botha's attempted second invasion of Natal.[81] In November Kitchener was compelled to cancel an announcement to the effect that he proposed to start transporting overseas irreconcilable Boer women from the concentration camps.[82]

By the early months of 1902 both sides were suffering from war weariness. So complete was Kitchener's devastation of the countryside that Boer combatants in some areas were finding it impossible to continue. The enthusiasm for the war of the British public had cooled and Kitchener himself was prone to exhaustion. After De la Rey's defeat and capture of Methuen at Tweebosch on 7 March 1902 he refused food for two days.[83] The time was ripe for peace talks. In the negotiations that followed there was a convergence of interest between Kitchener and conciliators like Botha and Smuts, and between Milner and the Boer hard-liners, like Steyn and De Wet. While Kitchener may have had personal reasons for wanting to bring the war to an end he also saw the wisdom of an honourable settlement. Botha and Smuts both foresaw the destruction of the Afrikaner nation if the war continued for much longer. On the other hand Milner and the Boer hardliners, for their own reasons, would both have preferred the war to continue to the point of unconditional surrender. Milner believed that to be essential to ensure British supremacy in South Africa. For their part those Boers who wanted to fight on recognised that acceptance of peace terms would bind them in honour to observe them, whereas an unconditional surrender would leave them free to fight again at some time in the future. Kitchener handled both Milner and the Boer leaders with considerable skill showing, as he had done at Fashoda, that the stern and unrelenting soldier could transform himself into an accomplished and empathetic diplomat when the situation demanded it. The terms on offer were little different from the British government's final offer after Kitchener's meeting with Botha at Middelburg fifteen months earlier. In the meetings of the sixty Boer representatives who gathered at Vereeniging, decisive contributions came from Smuts, who dashed any lingering hopes of a general uprising in the Cape Colony, and from De la Rey who, despite his own recent successes, concluded sadly that the bitter end had come. Steyn, too ill to continue, had left the conference before the end and De

Wet was persuaded privately at the end by Botha and De la Rey to vote for settlement in the interests of unity. The final vote was fifty-four in favour of accepting the peace terms and six against.[84]

Kitchener returned to England and many honours. He left for India on 17 October 1902, spending time on the way in Egypt where he inspected the Aswan Dam, and the Sudan, where he opened the Gordon Memorial College* on 8 November. He landed in Bombay on 28 November. He served as Commander-in-Chief in India for nearly seven years until September 1909, a period during which he introduced a number of important military reforms, but which is best remembered for his quarrel with Lord Curzon, the Viceroy from 1898 to 1905.

The difference between the Viceroy and his Commander-in-Chief centred on the position of the Military Member of the Viceroy's Council. This official, a senior uniformed military officer, acted as the Viceroy's second adviser on military policy and headed the Military Department in the Indian government, which handled the army's finances and administration.[85] At the time of Kitchener's arrival the Military Member was Maj Gen Sir Edmund Elles, a capable and ambitious Indian Army officer. Throughout his time in India Kitchener was a full general. While the Commander-in-Chief was the second-ranking member of the council[86] he attended only when military matters were discussed. The Military Member attended all meetings, whether or not military matters were on the agenda. Furthermore, any military proposals by the Commander-in-Chief to the Indian government had to be routed through the Military Member, who was entitled to make whatever observations he thought appropriate. To a man of Kitchener's temperament and accomplishments it was intolerable that his plans should be subject to the approval of a junior officer and that he should be required to operate at one remove from the Viceroy.

Kitchener had been Curzon's own choice as Commander-in-Chief, against the advice of friends,[87] because he saw in him the means of effecting much needed reforms in the Indian Army. Before he left for India Kitchener had been persuaded by Horace Smith-Dorrien, who had resigned as Adjutant-General in India early in 1902 on the issue, that he would find the rôle of the Military Member a problem. Kitchener had gone to India determined to absorb that rôle within his own responsibilities. Curzon was equally determined to assert the supremacy of the civil power over the military. In wishing to preserve the position of the Military Member, he had the support, initially at least, of such influential figures as Lord Roberts, a former Commander-in-Chief in

* Now the University of Khartoum.

India, and Lord Lansdowne, a former Viceroy; but he failed to get the measure of his relentless opponent. He relied on the strength of his argument and observed scrupulously the constitutional niceties. Kitchener had no such inhibitions and in his manipulation of opinion he was fortunate in his connections. Among them was Alice Salisbury, formerly Lady Cranborne, a long-term correspondent and admirer, whose husband was a first cousin of A.J. Balfour, the Prime Minister. Gen Sir Edward Stedman, the military secretary at the India Office, was a supporter, and at the War Office the Prime Minister's private secretary was Capt Raymond Marker, who had been on Kitchener's staff in India and who had been jilted by Curzon's sister-in-law.[88] Later, when Kitchener found it desirable to use the press, he enlisted the help of H.A. Gwynne, the editor of the *Standard* and Col à Court Repington, the military correspondent of *The Times*, who had been on his staff in Egypt.[89]

Valuable though Kitchener's active supporters were, perhaps the most fortunate circumstance for him was the appointment in October 1903 as Secretary of State for India of St John Brodrick, who had been War Minister when Kitchener was Commander-in-Chief in South Africa. He was also a lifelong friend of Curzon, of whose talents he was said to be jealous.[90] He declared himself to be impartial but, on the whole, his actions favoured Kitchener. By havering about procedural difficulties Curzon lost the opportunity of having the question of dual control considered by a three-man commission under Lord George Hamilton, a former Secretary of State for India. As its other members were to have been Roberts and Lansdowne it would almost certainly have found in his favour. When a committee was finally appointed in April 1904 it was chaired by Brodrick himself, it was larger, and its membership was heavily weighted in Kitchener's favour. Although it took evidence from distinguished experts, who backed unanimously the retention of the Military Member, their evidence was not reported. Its recommendation was a compromise. The Military Member was to be stripped of his most important responsibilities and to be redesignated the Military Supply Member. When Brodrick vetoed Curzon's nomination for the post of Maj Gen Sir Edmund Barrow – the one general who had not supported Kitchener's views on dual control – Curzon resigned as Viceroy on 21 August 1905 and Lord Minto was appointed in his place.

Kitchener was not tempted by feelers put out by Lord Esher, with the tacit approval of the Prime Minister, about the possibility of his accepting an appointment to the newly created post of Chief of the Imperial General Staff.[91] He knew that he was not suited to staff work – he had resisted earlier attempts by Brodrick to persuade him to go to the War Office after completion of his work in South Africa[92] – and he wished to stay on in India in the hope of succeeding Minto as Viceroy. If that prize eluded him he would have wished to be the British Agent in Egypt or the ambassador in Constantinople.[93] In December 1905 Balfour's Conservative government was succeeded by a Liberal one under Sir Henry Campbell-Bannerman. Since most of Kitchener's powerful social connections were in the Conservative camp he lost much of his influence. He got on well with the new Viceroy, a former professional soldier, but his relationship with John Morley, the Secretary of State for India in the new government, was less cordial. As a result of Morley's desire to reduce military expenditure, some of Kitchener's projects, including the building of strategic railways, were scrapped and his Army reforms were spread over ten years instead of five. In April 1907 Kitchener accepted a two-year extension of his command from November that year. These were two comparatively uneventful years, leaving him more time for leisure pursuits, official entertaining and his interest in fine art. His ardour as a collector of porcelain, art and antique furniture[94] manifested itself increasingly at this time in covetousness of the possessions of others, which he contrived to secure at knockdown prices or as gifts. According to his biographer, Sir Philip Magnus, 'Dealers learned to close their shops, fellow-collectors to be suddenly indisposed, whenever it was known that the Commander-in-Chief was engaged upon an artistic prowl, as he frequently was, especially during his last two years in India.'[95]

In July 1909 the Liberal government tried to persuade Kitchener to an accept an appointment, based in Malta, as Commander-in-Chief in the Mediterranean. He did so only when the King was induced by the government to request him personally to accept the appointment, believing that acceptance would not prejudice his being considered for appointment as Viceroy of India.[96] On relinquishing his Indian command on 10 September 1909 he was promoted field-marshal. Before taking up the Mediterranean command Kitchener proceeded with a previously sanctioned tour of Japan, Australia and New Zealand at public expense. He was accompanied by Capt Oswald Fitzgerald, who in 1906 had succeeded Frank Maxwell as his ADC, and who in that capacity and later as his personal military secretary, served him for the rest of his life. In Japan Kitchener represented Britain at the annual manoeuvres of the Imperial Japanese Army, and in Australia and New Zealand, where the cruiser HMS *Encounter* was placed at his disposal, he advised the two governments on defence policy. From there he went on to the United States, but cut his visit short to return to London at the end of April 1910, having been warned by friends that his prospects of succeeding Minto as Viceroy of India were receding. Although he was the choice of both the King and the Prime Minister, the decision was left to Morley as Secretary of State. Believing that it would be wrong to appoint a soldier at a time when the government was committed to liberalisation in India he chose Lord Hardinge, the Permanent Under-Secretary at the Foreign

Office. Before that decision was made the King had given Kitchener his permission to refuse the Mediterranean command,[97] which he did immediately after learning from Morley that he was not to be Viceroy.

Finding himself without active employment for the first time in many years Kitchener spent the summer and autumn of 1910 in England and Ireland and entered into negotiations for the purchase of Broome Park, near Canterbury.[98] In November he left for a holiday and shooting trip in the Sudan and East Africa, travelling by way of Constantinople and Egypt. He was recalled from East Africa in March 1911 to command the troops at the coronation of King George V on 22 June. He performed the task with his usual thoroughness, his instructions running to 212 pages. Early in 1991 Sir Eldon Gorst, the British Agent and Consul-General in Egypt, had become seriously ill with cancer. The Liberal government had reservations about Kitchener's suitability as a successor, but Cromer who had previously advised against his appointment now supported it, as did the King. Gorst died on 10 July and Kitchener's appointment was announced in the House of Commons six days later. He left for Egypt on 16 September.

Kitchener was welcome in Egypt, a country which he described as his spiritual home. Gorst had begun to implement the Liberal government's plans for progress towards representative government, but in doing so had allowed nationalist activity to get out of hand. Given the need to rein back, Kitchener was the ideal successor. In a country where there was a long tradition of personal government he ruled with a mixture of autocracy and benevolence. He sacked or moved staff who were not sympathetic to his plans and closed five radical newspapers;[99] but he was motivated by a genuine concern for the fellahin who accounted for 80 per cent of the population. He improved their lot by irrigation projects, agricultural reform, clinics, better housing and sanitation, and a law exempting smallholdings from repossession for debt. Contrary to custom he socialised freely with Egyptians but, having had himself installed as president, expelled or forced the resignation of all Egyptian members from the exclusive Gezira Club, when a few of them abused their membership by indulging in political activity.[100] One man who did not welcome Kitchener's appointment was the Khedive, Abbas Hilmi II, whom he had humiliated in 1894.[101] The dislike was mutual and Kitchener had little patience with the fiction that the Khedive ruled Egypt on Turkey's behalf. Ostensibly to weed out corruption, he deprived the Khedive of his sources of patronage by removing from him the control of Muslim religious charities and the award of honours. That further humiliation was compounded when, on Kitchener's advice, the King declined to see Abbas Hilmi when he visited Europe in 1914. He ended his European tour in Constantinople, where he remained after the outbreak of the First World War, in which the Turkish Empire was an ally of Germany.[102]

Shortly before returning to England on his summer leave in June 1914 Kitchener had been created an earl. On Monday 3 August 1914, on his way back to Egypt, he was recalled from Dover to London by Herbert Asquith, the Prime Minister, and two days later invited to take up the appointment of Secretary of State for War. He accepted with reluctance, the first serving officer in any Cabinet for 250 years,[103] and, although without formal party affiliation, a Conservative at heart in a Liberal Cabinet. At his first Cabinet meeting on 6 August he was alone in predicting that the war would be of long duration, his first estimate was three years. He also dismissed the conventional wisdom that the Navy would provide the main thrust of British strategy, coupled with limited military support to France as required. He believed that the war would be fought out on the European continent and he announced that, as a start, he proposed to raise a new army of a least 1,000,000 men.[104] He subsequently refined this target to a expansion of the Army over three years to a total of 70 divisions from its existing 6 regular and 14 Territorial divisions. Apart from this great task he was responsible for munitions and supplies, and for the supervision of British military strategy throughout the world, but it was in the expansion of the Army that he made his greatest contribution to Britain's war effort. In achieving this he bypassed the Territorial organisation, preferring to create a new citizen's army. His potency as a recruiter, epitomised in his 'Your Country Needs YOU' poster, was formidable. Some 750,000 men had enlisted by the end of September 1914 and 2½ million before voluntary recruitment came to an end in March 1916.[105] His creation of a great new army was one of the decisive factors in the eventual victory of Britain and her allies.

In the discharge of his other responsibilities Kitchener was less successful. Early on in the war there was a shortage of high-explosive shells on the Western Front, not because of any failure by Kitchener, but as the historian Basil Liddell Hart put it, as a result of the 'passivity as well as parsimony of Parliament and people in the face of the growing danger of war'.[106] At one point Kitchener was driven to exclaim, 'Did they remember, when they went headlong into a war like this, that they were without an army, and without any preparation to equip one?'[107] But he neglected adequately to inform the public, the Army or his political colleagues of his problems or of the efforts he was making to overcome them[108] and he resisted attempts to lighten his load. In May 1915 he was the target of a sustained attack by Lord Northcliffe's papers *The Times* and *The Daily Mail*, ostensibly on the question of shells, but driven by Northcliffe's wish for Lloyd George, Chancellor of the Exchequer, to replace Asquith as Prime Minister or failing that to replace Kitchener at the War Office.[109] French, the Commander-in-Chief of the British Expeditionary Force, fuelled this press campaign after he had sustained heavy casualties in the battle of Neuve Chapelle (10–13 March), which he blamed on the shell shortage. During the opening phase of the war Kitchener had upset French by appearing in France in field-marshal's uniform to order him to halt his retreat. French had also learnt that in November 1914 Kitchener had discussed with Gen Joffre the possibility of replacing him with Ian Hamilton.[110] Although press correspondents were banned from the Western Front, the military correspondent of the *The Times*, Col à Court Repington,* was at GHQ as a private guest of French, who had shown him correspondence on the subject of shell shortages between the War Office and the BEF. French had also, behind the backs of Kitchener and the Prime Minister, sent two officers to England with copies of the correspondence, not only for Lloyd George, Kitchener's fiercest critic in the Cabinet, but also for the two Opposition leaders, Andrew Bonar Law and Arthur Balfour. When a coalition government was formed in May 1915 Kitchener handed over responsibility for munitions to a Ministry of Munitions under Lloyd George. The success of that Ministry was built largely on foundations laid by Kitchener.

Kitchener had not taken easily to Cabinet government. Collective responsibility, consensus and the need to persuade colleagues were concepts foreign to his nature and to the methods by which he had achieved success in the Sudan and in South Africa. His self-sufficiency had been a strength in those relatively limited campaigns, but the supervision of Britain's military strategy in the First World War was an undertaking of an altogether different order of magnitude and his reluctance to delegate or consult now became a weakness. Furthermore, there was no established government machinery for waging a major war as there was in the Second World War, least of all for operations involving both land and sea forces. Winston Churchill, as First Lord of the Admiralty, was responsible independently for naval operations and Kitchener for war on land. These shortcomings, organisational and personal, became most apparent in the opening of a second front in the Near East.

Kitchener was torn between the rival claims of those who believed that all resources should be devoted to overcoming Germany on the Western Front and those who believed that she should be outflanked, or her war effort dislocated, on another front. Of the possibilities canvassed, an attack on Constantinople via the Dardanelles, as advocated by Winston Churchill, found the most support. It promised the advantages both of opening up a new supply route to Britain's ally, Russia, and of defeating Germany's ally, Turkey. Kitchener's initial judgement was that 150,000 men would be required to take the Dardanelles[111] but, like others, allowed himself to be persuaded that the narrow channel could be forced

---

* In the same capacity in 1904 Repington had helped Kitchener in his quarrel with Curzon.

by the Navy alone, after massive bombardment of the forts by battleships. This proved to be a fatal misjudgement. By the time it became apparent that the Army would be needed the advantage of surprise had been lost. Ian Hamilton, the general chosen to command the land campaign, was unable to launch his invasion until 25 April. As a result of the delay the Turks, under their German commander, Gen Liman von Sanders had ample time to defend the Gallipoli peninsula in depth, employing 84,000 men in six divisions, compared with Hamilton's 75,000 men in five divisions.[112] Within the limitations of the resources available to him Hamilton's plan was sound, but it was doomed by its late start and hampered in its execution by the rugged terrain, failure to exploit successes, a shortage of ammunition and the ability of the enemy to more than match Allied reinforcements. Despite hard fighting and heavy losses little was achieved beyond the establishment of beachheads in the south at Cape Helles and on the west coast at Anzac Cove. A later landing further north at Suvla Bay by new troops on 6 August was initially more successful but was stopped by determined Turkish opposition. The chance of a subsequent breakthrough was lost when Kitchener decided to allocate the further reinforcements which Hamilton had hoped for, to a new offensive on the Western Front, culminating in the battle of Loos (25–6 September 1915) with 50,000 British casualties.

When Asquith's Liberal government was succeeded by a coalition government under his premiership in May 1915 Kitchener retained his position as Secretary of State, albeit without responsibility for munitions. He retained the confidence of the public – there was wide approval when the King conferred on him the Order of the Garter in June – but he began to lose the support of his ministerial colleagues as a result of his secrecy, his apparent indecisiveness, the heavy casualties at Loos and the failures of the Dardanelles campaign. In October Ian Hamilton was recalled from Gallipoli and after his successor Sir Charles Monro recommended evacuation, Kitchener was sent to the Dardanelles in early November to assess the situation and make a personal report to the Cabinet. Conscious of the hostility of his colleagues, he took his seals of office with him believing, wrongly, that this would prevent his dismissal while he was away.[113] His recommendation of a partial withdrawal, telegraphed to the War Committee on 22 November was not accepted. Instead the committee unanimously recommended to the Cabinet a complete evacuation. Kitchener ignored suggestions that he should remain in the Near East and returned on 30 November to London where he immediately offered Asquith his resignation. During Kitchener's absence Asquith, acting as Secretary of State for War, had arranged for the replacement of French by Haig as Commander-in-Chief on the Western Front and had transferred some sections of the War Office to the Ministry of Munitions. He now refused Kitchener's offer of resignation, but asked him to allow the Chief of the General Staff in future to replace the Secretary of State as the government's principal adviser on military strategy. He persuaded Kitchener to remain in office as 'the symbol of the nation's will to victory'.[114] Kitchener agreed to this and later accepted Asquith's choice as the new CIGS, Gen Sir William Robertson, the blunt ex-private who had been French's Chief of Staff.[115] Robertson took up his appointment on 23 December and laid down stringent conditions, which made him the sole channel of advice on military strategy to the government and of communication with the Army regarding military operations. This left Kitchener with executive responsibility only for recruiting and the administration of the War Office.

Driven as ever by his strong sense of duty Kitchener endured the diminution of his rôle with fortitude. Despite the indifference of his ministerial colleagues he still stood high in public esteem. He got on well with Haig, whom he visited many times in France, and who, unlike French accorded him the courtesy of a guard of honour.[116] He remained on the War Committee and, as Secretary of State, took a close interest in the development of tanks and air warfare.[117] In May 1916 he responded with enthusiasm to an invitation from the Czar to visit Russia and the Russian Front and the government raised no objection to his acceptance. On 2 June, three days before his departure, he addressed a large meeting of backbenchers at the House of Commons. His impressive performance 'evoked round upon round of applause'.[118] He lunched with the King the following day and spent the morning of Sunday 4 June working in the garden at Broome, before returning to the War Office to sign official papers. That night he left London for the naval base at Scapa Flow in the Orkneys, where he was to embark for Archangel.

The ship chosen to take Kitchener to Russia was the 10,850-ton County class cruiser HMS *Hampshire*, first commissioned in 1905. She was commanded by Capt Herbert Savill RN, and on 1 June had fought unscathed in the battle of Jutland. Despite severe weather Kitchener was insistent on leaving for Russia without delay and the *Hampshire* sailed from Scapa Flow at 4.45 p.m. on 5 June. Because of the weather conditions, Adm Jellicoe had given orders to follow – out of the three possible routes past the Orkneys – the so-called North West Triangle course, which hugged the west coast. This was less frequently swept for mines than the other two routes, one to the east of the islands and the other further west, and it was not normally used by warships, but merchantmen and fleet auxiliaries had used it unharmed. As the cruiser made her way up the coast the gale increased in strength and backed from north-east to north-west. Her two destroyer escorts were unable to keep up in the heavy seas and at 6.20 p.m. Capt Savill ordered them to return to Scapa Flow. At about 8 p.m., when the *Hampshire* was just under a mile and a half off the coast between Marwick Head and the Brough of Birsay, an explosion was heard and the ship sank by the bows within fifteen minutes. It proved impossible to launch the lifeboats in the raging seas, but three rafts got away with over 150 men.[119] However, few of them reached the rocky shore and of those who managed to climb to safety some died of exposure, so that only 12 men survived out of a ship's company of over 600. There were no officers among them. The last man to see Kitchener described him as standing on the quarterdeck talking to members of his staff.[120] It is unlikely that he ever left the ship. The Admiralty's reticence gave rise over the next twenty years to various theories to account for the tragedy,* the least implausible of which was that a German or an Irish Republican bomb had been smuggled on board, but private diving expeditions in 1977 and 1983 confirmed that the damage to the ship was external.[121] This supported the official view that the *Hampshire* struck one of the mines laid by the German submarine U-75 shortly before the battle of Jutland with the intention of impeding the movements of the Grand Fleet. It may well be that better weather forecasting and the attachment of greater weight to intelligence reports about German submarine activity would have averted the tragedy[122] but if in the malign combination of circumstances that led to Kitchener's death any one factor was predominant, it was his own impatience to get to sea before the weather abated sufficiently to allow minesweepers to operate.

The public were stunned by Kitchener's death. Whatever reservations his Cabinet colleagues may have had about him he personified Britain's war effort to the man in the street and to the soldier in the trenches. Lloyd George wrote in his war memoirs:

> . . . a pall of dismay descended on the spirit of the people. Men and women spoke of the event in hushed tones of terror. The news of a defeat would not have produced such a sense of irreparable disaster. The tidings of the advance of March, 1918, did not send such a shudder of despair through Britain as did the news of the tragic end of this remarkable man. I am not capable of analysing Lord Kitchener's attributes or gifts. But he was one of the great personalities of the War who exercised an indubitable effect on its course and thus on the destiny of the whole world.[123]

When Lloyd George became Prime Minister in December 1916 he proved to be an outstanding war leader, but he could not have done the job without the great citizen's army which Kitchener had created.

---

* Collected and reviewed in *The Mysterious Death of Lord Kitchener* by Donald McCormick.

Notes

1. *OH* ii, 30.
2. *TH* iii, 418.
3. *OH* ii, 30, *TH* iii, 391.
4. *TH* iii, 404–6.
5. *TH* iii, 419.
6. See Chapter Four, p. 56.
7. *TH* iii, 424 n.
8. Smith-Dorrien, p. 150.
9. Ibid., p. 152.
10. Ibid., p. 152.
11. Ibid., p. 154.
12. Quoted in Hamilton, *The Happy Warrior*, p. 154.
13. Arthur i, p. 281.
14. Slocum and Reichmann, p. 31.
15. Quoted in Arthur i, pp. 287–91.
16. Smith-Dorrien, p. 155.
17. *TH* iii, 493.
18. *TH* iv, 4–5.
19. Ballard, *Kitchener*, p. 141.
20. Arthur i, p. 305.
21. Arthur i, p. 321–2.
22. *TH* v, 67.
23. *TH* v, 71–2.
24. *TH* v, 79–84.
25. *TH* v, 89–90.
26. Spies, *Barbarism*, p. 175.
27. Quoted in full in *TH* v, 86 and Spies, *Barbarism*, p. 183.
28. *OH* iv, Appendix 12, 661.
29. Spies, *Barbarism*, p. 228.
30. Ibid., pp. 228–30.
31. Ibid., p. 363 n. 37.
32. Ibid., p. 230.
33. Ibid., pp. 265–6.
34. Roberts, *Those Bloody Women*, p. 133.
35. Ibid., p. 171.
36. Spies, *Barbarism*, p. 255.
37. Roberts, *Those Bloody Women*, pp. 226–7.
38. Spies, *Barbarism*, pp. 222, 367 n. 99.
39. Maxwell, pp. 91–2.
40. Spies, *Barbarism*, p. 223; Magnus, p. 181.
41. Magnus, p. 180.

42. Spies, *Barbarism*, pp. 86, 200.
43. Ibid., pp. 230–1.
44. See Chapter Eight, pp. 196–7.
45. Kitchener Papers, PRO 30/57/22, Y/99, Brodrick to Kitchener, 1 November 1901, quoted in Spies, *Barbarism*, p. 246.
46. *TH* v, 256–60.
47. *TH* v, 324–5.
48. *TH* vi, 337.
49. *OH* iv, App. 2, p. 570n.
50. *TH* v, 161.
51. *TH* v, 181.
52. See Chapter Eight, pp. 202–4.
53. Hamilton, *The Commander*, pp. 100–1.
54. Le May, *British Supremacy*, p. 49.
55. Walker, p. 490.
56. *TH* v, 310.
57. *TH* v, 311–12.
58. *TH* v, 320, 539.
59. *TH* v, 296–8.
60. *TH* v, 307.
61. *TH* v, 309.
62. *TH* v, 319.
63. Reitz, *Commando*, p. 223.
64. *TH* v, 388–9.
65. Reitz, *Commando*, p. 230.
66. Ibid., p. 248.
67. *TH* vi, 560.
68. Le May, *British Supremacy*, p. 118.
69. Ibid., p. 100; *TH* vi, 558; Cd. 981, p. 75.
70. Ibid., pp. 100–1.
71. *TH* vi, 563.
72. Meintjes, *Sword in the Sand*, p. 172 n. 23 and p. 181 n. 27.
73. *TH* vi, 564; Meintjes, *Sword in the Sand*, p. 188.
74. Davey, pp. xvii–xviii.
75. Ibid., pp. xl–xli.
76. Ibid., pp. 161–5.
77. Although Heese was of German descent and employed by the Berlin Missionary Society he was born in the Cape Colony and a British subject. See Davey, p. 36.
78. Pakenham, p. 539, cited by Davey, p. lvi.
79. For details of death sentences under martial law see Cd. 981, pp. 121–30 and Cd. 1423, pp. 77–82.
80. Chamberlain to Brodrick 20 August 1901, quoted in Spies, *Barbarism*, p. 237.
81. Moore, pp. 10–12.

82. Magnus, p. 187.
83. Magnus, pp. 187–8; Hamilton, *The Happy Warrior*, p. 187.
84. For a fuller account of the peace negotiations see Chapter Eight, pp. 204–7.
85. Gilmour, p. 252.
86. Ibid., p. 252.
87. Ibid., p. 249.
88. Ibid., p. 279.
89. Ibid., p. 298.
90. Ibid., p. 267.
91. Magnus, pp. 227–8.
92. Arthur ii, pp. 118–20.
93. Magnus, p. 230.
94. Cassar, p. 485.
95. Magnus, p. 239.
96. Ibid., p. 241.
97. Ibid., p. 248.
98. Arthur ii, p. 307.
99. Royle, p. 244.
100. Magnus, p. 269.
101. See Chapter Five, pp. 92–3.
102. Magnus, pp. 272-4; Royle, pp. 245–6.
103. Ibid., p. 278.
104. Ibid., p. 284.
105. Taylor, *English History*, p. 20.
106. Liddell Hart, p. 143.
107. Arthur iii, p. 265.
108. Magnus, p. 331.
109. Esher, *Journals and Letters* iii, p. 240.
110. Hamilton, *The Happy Warrior*, p. 268.
111. Taylor, *English History*, p. 23.
112. Liddell Hart, p. 172.
113. Magnus, p. 361.
114. Ibid., p. 367; Jenkins, p. 384.
115. But see Arthur iii, pp. 297–8. According to Sir George Arthur, Kitchener had identified Robertson much earlier as the ideal choice, but had been reluctant to deprive French of his services.
116. Magnus, p. 372.
117. Royle, p. 353.
118. Magnus, p. 377.
119. McCormick, p. 46.
120. Ibid., p. 36.
121. Royle, p. 385.
122. Ibid., pp. 366–70.
123. Lloyd George, *War Memoirs* ii, pp. 759–60.

CHAPTER SEVEN

Botha

Of the senior Boer generals Louis Botha was the most able all-rounder. A politician by temperament and a farmer at heart he also had outstanding military gifts based on his power of command, his 'splendid faculty for common sense'[1] and his ability both to read the country and to anticipate the intentions of the enemy. He was a big man, nearly 6 ft in height and well built, swarthy in complexion with violet-blue eyes and a black goatee beard. In middle age his bulk increased considerably and his eyes became slightly protuberant. He had an extraordinary gift of empathy and even his political enemies acknowledged his geniality, but the counterpart of those attributes was an excessive sensitivity to criticism. Not obviously vain or ambitious he none the less expected the recognition due to his rank. He usually rode a white or grey horse and, in an army in which men wore their everyday clothes, he wore a simple uniform tunic. Prone at times to despair and irresolution he was implacable once he had made up his mind.

As a general he was at his best in the early phase of the war characterised by set-piece battles, notably in the Natal campaign when, at the age of thirty-seven, he took over command of the Boer forces on the Tugela. In the later war of attrition after the departure of Lord Roberts he had to divide his talents among three rôles – Commandant-General of all the Transvaal forces, military adviser and minder of the peripatetic Transvaal government and local commander in the Eastern Highveld. Although he had notable successes at Blood River Poort and Bakenlaagte he never quite equalled the single-minded brilliance of De Wet as a guerrilla leader. He fought as determinedly as anybody for the independence of the Boer republics but his rôle became increasingly political as the war dragged on and he recognised the need for an honourable end to it if the Afrikaner people were to avoid extinction. Also, perhaps because of his English-speaking family connections, he was driven by the vision of a postwar partnership between the two white races in a united South Africa. Hardliners like De Wet became suspicious of him and as early as his abortive peace talks with Kitchener in Middelburg in February 1901 the seeds were sown for the divisions in Afrikanerdom which were to dominate his time as South Africa's first prime minister.

Louis Botha was born a British subject in Greytown, Natal on 27 September 1862. His father, also Louis, was a prosperous farmer of Dutch and Huguenot descent whose family had been among the earliest settlers of the Cape in the mid-seventeenth century. In 1867 he moved with his family to the Harrismith area of the Orange Free State and farmed near Vrede where the young Louis grew up, the eighth child in a family of six boys and seven girls. Two of his brothers, Philip the eldest and Chris his junior, were also to serve as generals in the Boer War. Louis had little more than two years' formal schooling[2] but from an early age he began to show the qualities which marked him out as a leader of men and it is said that his older brothers deferred to his opinions.[3] During his father's long final illness he delegated to Louis the management of the family farm. When his father died he proposed to his brothers and sisters that instead of parcelling the land out among them, in accordance with time-honoured custom, they should appoint him to manage the farm for the benefit of all of them, but he failed to persuade them.[4] He left the area and sought out Lucas Meyer, an old friend of his father's and the *landdrost* (magistrate) of Utrecht, and shortly afterwards, in 1884, he joined Meyer in an 115-man expedition to Zululand to support Dinizulu in his bid to succeed his father Cetewayo as King of the Zulus against his rival Usibepu. Botha knew Zululand, having taken the family flocks there for winter grazing, and he spoke Zulu in addition to Sesuto, the language of the Basutos.

A very tall and powerfully built man, Lucas Meyer was sixteen years older than Botha, who held him in high regard and was to be closely associated with him for many years to come. Usibepu was a capable warrior who had led the attacks at Isandlwana and Ulundi in the Zulu War of 1878–9 and, other things being equal, he was more than a match for Dinizulu. However, when the two rival armies clashed at Itshana the rifle fire of Lucas Meyer's small force was decisive and Usibepu was defeated.[5] In return for their services Dinizulu ceded to Lucas Meyer and his followers a 3 million-acre tract of Zululand adjoining the Transvaal. It was proclaimed as the New Republic, independent of both the Transvaal and the Orange Free State, with Lucas Meyer as its first President. Botha undertook the tasks of surveying the site for the capital, Vryheid, and supervising the pegging out of the farms to be allocated by lot to those who had taken part in the campaign and to others who, to the resentment of Dinizulu, applied for farms without having done any fighting. Botha exchanged the farm he obtained for another one 24 miles east of Vryheid. Named Waterval it was 3,500 acres in extent with a homestead sited near a stream. The original thatched cottage was later replaced by a substantial stone dwelling.[6]

In 1886 Botha married Annie Emmett, an English-speaking South African of Irish parentage, one of whose ancestors was Robert Emmett, the Irish patriot. A well-educated and lively woman she was an ideal consort for a man destined to play a leading role in his country's fortunes. Her brother Robert Cheere (Cherry) Emmett, a close friend of Botha's, had also taken part in the Dinizulu expedition and was later to serve as a general during the Boer War. For some years Botha served as a field-cornet and collector of customs in the Vryheid district, where he prospered as a farmer. In 1895 he accepted an appointment as Resident Justice and Native Commissioner in Swaziland and lived for a short while in Mbabane before returning to Vryheid where he became Native Commissioner as well as a field-cornet. When the New Republic, unable to stand on its own feet, was absorbed into the Transvaal Louis Botha became a citizen of the Transvaal. In 1893 he had supported Piet Joubert in his unsuccessful bid for the presidency against Paul Kruger and in 1896 he and Lucas Meyer were elected to the Volksraad as the two members for Vryheid. Through astute management of his affairs he had become a man of independent means. By 1899 his assets were valued at £30,000* and included 16,000 acres of land.[7] In the Volksraad he took a moderate line and in a secret session with Lucas Meyer and De La Rey, he is said to have opposed the issuing of the ultimatum of 9 October 1899 which led to the outbreak of the Boer War, but the minutes contain no record of a vote.[8]

Apart from his reservations about the wisdom of war with Britain, its prospect confronted Botha with painful family conflicts since some of his sisters had married Englishmen, but once war was inevitable he threw himself into it wholeheartedly. With war looming Meyer had been appointed the general in command of the South-Eastern Transvaal commandos and he had made Botha his second in command, without any formal rank.[9] For over two weeks before the expiry of the Boer ultimatum, armed burghers had been massing on the Transvaal border – from 7,000 to 11,000 in the west facing Mafeking under Cronjé, assisted by De La Rey, and 14,000 under Joubert, the largest body of whom was near Volksrust on the border with Natal. Meyer and Botha were with the Piet Retief, Utrecht and Vryheid commandos, from 1,500 to 2,000 strong, near the Doornberg, 20 miles north-east of Dundee.[10] In addition some 6,500 Free Staters under Marthinus Prinsloo were getting ready to cross the Drakensberg into Natal.

The Boer mobilisation had been delayed by transport difficulties, but in any event a mounted army dependent on good grazing could not move effectively until the spring rains had brought the veld to life and it was largely this consideration which delayed the ultimatum until early October. However, it allowed time for the arrival in Natal from India of 5,600 British troops, the reinforcements necessary to secure Natal against invasion in the estimation of the resident garrison commander, Maj Gen Sir William Penn Symons, who had a low opinion of Boer fighting ability. In his early service in South Africa and later in Burma and on the North-West Frontier he had gained a reputation as a dashing and skilful

* About £1 million at 1990s prices.

commander, but it was decided that a more senior officer should take charge in Natal until the arrival in South Africa of Buller's Army Corps. The choice fell on the 65-year-old Gen Sir George White VC, a former C-in-C in India and since 1897 the Quartermaster-General at the War Office. He arrived in Durban on 7 October and his initial judgement was that it was unrealistic to attempt to hold the narrow and hilly northern wedge of Natal against a superior force and that he should concentrate his forces in Ladysmith. Symons had by now modified his view that he could hold the whole of Northern Natal, but he was convinced that he could hold it as far as the important coal mining town of Dundee, 40 miles north-east of Ladysmith. He was supported in this by the Governor of Natal, Sir Walter Hely-Hutchinson, who feared the effect on the native African population and on white loyalists of abandoning the town, and White agreed against his better judgement to defend it.

The war began at 5 p.m. on 11 October 1899 and the Boer invasion of Natal began the next day, Joubert's force operating in four columns. Erasmus with 4,000 men made straight for Newcastle which he occupied on the 15th, and Kock with 800 men of mixed nationality, together with Ben Viljoen's Johannesburg commando advanced on the town by a westerly route. Lucas Meyer, with a force increased in strength to 2,900[11] by reinforcements from the Krugersdorp, Middelburg and Wakkerstroom commandos, moved towards Dundee. On the 13th Botha led a reconnoitring expedition to De Jager's Drift on the Buffalo River, 17 miles north-east of Dundee. Here he captured an observation post manned by five men of the Natal police, who were unaware that the war had started. Botha thus shared with De La Rey – who the day before had captured an armoured train at Kraaipan on the western front – the distinction of taking the first British prisoners in the Boer War.[12] Joubert followed on behind having ascertained that not only had the British neglected to mine the Laing's Nek tunnel, but that they had left the railway into Natal virtually intact. He entered Newcastle on the 16th. The Free Staters moved independently towards Ladysmith.

The town of Dundee lies near the centre of a circular hollow some five miles across surrounded by hills, the most prominent of which is the table-topped Impati to the north, rising 1,200 ft above the town. To the east are a pair of smaller hills, Talana and Lennox, both about 600 ft high and linked by a col named Smith's Nek. The British camp lay ¾ mile to the west of the town, and about 5,000 yd from Talana. Symons had arrived in Dundee on 12 October to take over from Brig Gen J.H. Yule and a force of 3,280 infantry, 497 cavalry and 18 guns.[13] When White became aware of the Boer strength and dispositions he decided that the town should be evacuated but once again allowed Symons to persuade him that it should be defended.

The Boers planned a two-pronged attack on the town. Lucas Meyer, advancing from the east, was to occupy Talana, and Erasmus was to advance on Impati from the north-west. Symons received ample intelligence of Boer movements on 19 October, but he disdained to make any preparations, confident that he could deal with any eventualities as they arose. During the night of the 19th Meyer and Botha with 900 men and 3 guns occupied Talana, and 600 men occupied Lennox and Smith's Nek. The remainder of Meyer's force was left outside the area of fighting.[14] Erasmus, with 2,000 men, reached Impati at about 5 a.m. on the 20th to find it shrouded in mist.[15]

At about 5.30 a.m. the British saw figures on the top of Talana and shortly afterwards a shell from the hill landed in the town, followed by another which fell close to Symons's tent but failed to explode. However remiss he had been in preparation Symons responded to the situation with commendable speed and competence. The artillery was in action within 15 minutes at a range of 3,650 yd and soon silenced the Boer guns, forcing their withdrawal behind the crest of the hill. Under cover of the artillery fire the infantry were formed up in the bed of a stream at the base of Talana for a frontal attack on the terraced hill. Between the stream and the summit a blue-gum plantation and the buildings of Smith's Farm provided further cover. The infantry were held up for some time in the wood by heavy Boer rifle fire and at about 9 a.m. Symons, impatient with the lack of progress, galloped across to the wood and dismounted to hurry things on. When he went through a gap in a wall at the edge of the wood to appraise the situation for himself, he received a mortal stomach wound. He was helped back to the camp and Gen Yule resumed command. The crest was carried at about midday but had to be evacuated because of friendly artillery fire which resulted in a number of casualties. It was finally occupied at about 1.30 p.m. and most of the Boers were put to flight.

There is little contemporary evidence of the part played by Botha, but Meyer is said to have been ineffectual and afterwards it was Botha who sent a brief report of the battle to Pretoria.[16] The British victory was won at a cost of 500 men killed, wounded and taken prisoner compared with Boer casualties of less than half that number. Moreover, it was a tactical victory only since Dundee was at the mercy of Erasmus's artillery, including a Long Tom, on Impati. After two days of indecision, Yule accepted that the town was untenable and embarked under cover of darkness on an epic 60-mile march to Ladysmith in appalling weather. He left the field hospital and its wounded – including the dying Symons – to the mercy of Erasmus and abandoned three months' provisions, much ammunition and the kits of both officers and men. So precipitate was his departure that he neglected to give orders for the burial of most of the British killed in the battle for Talana.[17]

In a more successful action on 21 October Gen French and Col Ian Hamilton skilfully dislodged the 1,000-strong force, commanded by Gen Kock, from the small coal mining settlement of Elandslaagte, 17 miles north-east of Ladysmith on the railway line to Dundee. Patrols from Kock's force had captured the station and a supply train two days earlier and he had injudiciously gone ahead with his whole force to occupy the position. Casualties were heavy on both sides. The British lost 260 killed and wounded and the Boers about 200 with as many again taken prisoner. French and Ian Hamilton were in action again on 24 October near Rietfontein Farm in a demonstration against the Free Staters holding the high ground south of Elandslaagte who threatened the exposed northern flank of Gen Yule's 4-mile long column as it covered the last few miles to Ladysmith. The column entered the town in a state of exhaustion on 26 October. The Boer forces too were now concentrating on the town and the scene was set for the battle of Ladysmith in which both Louis Botha and Christiaan de Wet were to establish their credentials as fighting commanders.

White decided that he unless he dealt the enemy a decisive blow, his forces would face the prospect of isolation in Ladysmith, a town surrounded by hills where most of the advantages were with the besiegers. The Transvaal laagers lay beyond the crescent of the hills to the north and east of the town. White agreed to, and then cancelled at the last moment because he thought it too risky, Ian Hamilton's proposal for a night raid on 27 October on the large laager to the east of Farquhar's Farm, where it was estimated that 4,000 to 5,000 burghers and several guns were located. Part of the Free State force was to the west of Tchrengula, a long flat-topped kopje to the north of Ladysmith. In all some 7,500 Boers[18] confronted approximately 13,000 British troops. On Sunday the 29th the Boers cut off the town's water supply and were observed building a platform for a Long Tom on Pepworth Hill to the north-east. White's staff advised against an attack on the sabbath for fear of arousing the enemy's religious zeal and he decided to launch his attack on Monday the 30th. French's latest reconnaissance patrols and the observation balloon revealed that in addition to their presence on Pepworth the Boers were established in strength on Long Hill, the next hill round to the east, and White based his plan on this firm indication that Long Hill marked the left flank of the Boer positions.

An infantry brigade under Col Grimwood was to take Long Hill in flank and then to join a brigade under Ian Hamilton in attacking Pepworth. French's cavalry were to sweep around behind the Boer positions in pursuit of the fleeing enemy after Grimwood and Ian Hamilton had dislodged them. To prevent the Free Staters from interfering with the cavalry's pursuit a 1,000-strong column under Col Carleton was to occupy Nicholson's Nek at the northern end of

Tchrengula and he set off at 11 p.m. on Sunday night. French, Grimwood and Hamilton moved out in the small hours of Monday morning. The plan soon went awry. Pepworth had been the bait in Joubert's plan to draw the British out of Ladysmith. Apart from that he intended to dispose his forces as required by circumstances. As part of that plan, or perhaps simply because the Boers preferred to sleep in their laagers, Long Hill had been vacated on Sunday night and on Monday morning Lucas Meyer's division was in position to the east and well to the south of the hill, with the result that French's cavalry was hemmed in.[19] As it moved towards Long Hill, Grimwood's brigade became separated from its artillery and reserve battalions. At about 7 a.m. White learnt that Carleton's pack mules had bolted at the southern end of Tchrengula, taking with them most of the reserve ammunition and the mountain guns. To top the Boer's good fortune the ineffectual Lucas Meyer, whose health had been indifferent ever since Talana, collapsed early on and the command of his 2,000-strong division passed informally to the 37-year-old Louis Botha. Grimwood's brigade swung around to meet the threat from the east and was reinforced to the south by French's cavalry, the combined force extending along a front of 4 miles. At about 11.30 a.m. White decided that the effectiveness of the Boer rifle and artillery fire made the British position untenable and he decided to withdraw his forces. As they streamed back to Ladysmith they were saved from disaster only by the steadiness of the British artillery which covered them, by the remarkable intervention of naval guns which had arrived in Ladysmith from Simonstown via Durban only that morning,[20] and by the failure of Joubert – despite the entreaties of his subordinates – to pursue them. He is reputed to have said to one of his generals: 'When God holds out a finger don't take the whole hand.'[21] In the early afternoon, after fighting all morning at the southern end of Tchrengula, Col Carleton surrendered his column to Christiaan de Wet who, as an acting commandant, led the Free Staters in this action. Thus, on 'Mournful Monday', began the siege of Ladysmith.

After the battle of Ladysmith Botha's position as Assistant-General in command of Meyer's division was confirmed. With his new authority he urged Joubert to allow an expedition deeper into Natal. Joubert agreed reluctantly but insisted on accompanying the 3,000 to 3,500 burghers who set out from Colenso on 14 November. The small British garrison there had withdrawn earlier under pressure from the Free Staters' artillery and joined the 2,300-strong force in Estcourt, the only significant concentration of British forces outside Ladysmith. The expedition's first success was the capture the following day of an armoured train at Chievely, in which Winston Churchill was present as a correspondent of the *Morning Post*. While Botha commanded the operation, there is no

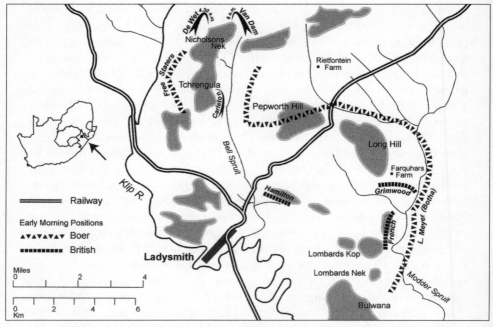

The Battle of Ladysmith (Modderspruit and Nicholson's Nek) – 30 October 1899

truth in the story that it was he himself who took Churchill prisoner, but both men found it politic to pretend to this pleasant conceit, which helped to cement their friendship after the war.[22] After this incident Joubert split the forces in two and with Botha led the larger portion to the west of Estcourt while his nephew David took 1,000 men to the east. They linked up again to the south of the town, which in the meantime had received further reinforcements, bringing the total British strength there to about 5,000.[23] On 23 November the Boers repulsed an attempt by Col Walter Kitchener, under Maj Gen Hildyard, to clear them off a hill called Brynbella near Willow Grange. During this action there was a violent thunderstorm in which one burgher and several horses were killed by lighting. Botha had his horse shot from under him. The following day his hopes of pressing on deeper into Natal were dashed when Joubert suffered internal injuries after his horse had stumbled.[24] At a *krygsraad* on the 25th a decision was taken to return to Colenso. Apart from the problem of Joubert, more British reinforcements were on the way, the Free Staters were calling for some of their commandos for the western front and heavy rains raised the prospect of being cut off to the north by a swollen Tugela River. The expedition returned to Colenso on

144

27 November with hundreds of wagons containing looted property, and many herds of cattle.[25]

On 30 November Joubert returned to his farm near Volksrust to recuperate, leaving Botha in command of the Boer forces on the Tugela. Five days earlier Gen Buller had arrived in Durban and was now making his preparations, with some 18,000 men and 44 guns at his disposal, to cross the Tugela and relieve Ladysmith. At a *krygsraad* before Joubert's departure a decision had been taken to entrench along a 7-mile front from Red Hill to the west of Colenso to Hlangwane to the east. This was on the strength of Botha's belief that Buller, with his large supply train, would want to remain close to the railway which ran through Colenso to Ladysmith. Botha persuaded his fellow officers, mostly older than him, that to gain the advantage of surprise, the Boer defences should be in the low kopjes close to the river and not in the higher range of hills behind. The defences were prepared with great care with an eye to concealment, using dummies to deceive the British, and the work was supervised assiduously by Botha himself. Against Buller's 18,000 men and 44 guns he had about 4,500 men and 5 guns, including a 120-mm Krupp howitzer and a pom-pom.[26]

Like some of Buller's junior officers, but unlike Buller himself, Botha was acutely aware of the tactical importance of Hlangwane on the Boer left, dominating the other Boer positions and isolated from them by the river. He received an early setback to his plans when, unnerved by Buller's opening bombardment on the Colenso positions on 13 February, most of the men defending Hlangwane abandoned it during the night. However, Botha replaced them with a force of 800 to 1,000 men from various commandos, drawn by lot, under Commandant Jozua Joubert of Wakkerstroom. The bombardment continued for another day, doing little harm and, as insisted on by Botha, evoking no response. Early in the morning of the 15th lights in the British camp alerted Botha to the start of Buller's attack, confirmed at daybreak by the sight of soldiers advancing on a 2-mile front towards the river. It was Botha's plan to allow the British to advance to well within rifle range and for the Boers to hold their fire until he gave the signal by firing the big howitzer, located in the Colenso kopjes. When the British were fully engaged, the Boers on Red Hill were to cross the river and counter-attack. (It had been intended originally also to launch a counter-attack from Hlangwane on the Boer left, but Botha had agreed that the replacement force on Hlangwane should exercise a defensive role only.)

By early afternoon the battle was virtually over. When Hart, on the British left, led his Irish Brigade into the salient formed by the big loop in the Tugela the Boers held their fire, as ordered, until Hart's infantry was within 500 yd and his artillery within 1,500 yd. When they opened fire the result was devastating, but the elderly Gen Christiaan Fourie, put in command at the last moment of the Boer right failed to order the planned counter-attack, despite repeated messages from Botha. Hart extricated his brigade, after incurring heavy casualties, with the assistance of Lyttleton. In the centre Hildyard's brigade, flanked in support on the left by Lyttleton and on the right by Barton, was still well back when Col Long raced his twelve field guns far ahead of the infantry to within 1,000 yd of the river opposite the Colenso kopjes. The Boers opened fire as soon as Long's guns came into action, Botha himself having abandoned the plan to hold fire until the infantry were close to the river. The guns had to be silenced, as they were after half an hour. Buller later blamed Long's impetuosity for the debacle at Colenso, but in reality, as Botha testified after the war, it was Long who saved the British from far greater casualties by springing the Boer trap.[27]

On the British right Dundonald had secured a foothold on the slopes of Hlangwane, as ordered, but had been unable to do more because of Barton's unwillingness to support him without orders from Buller. He was recalled at 11 a.m. when Buller decided to abandon ten of Long's guns, heroic rescue attempts having saved only two. At 2.30 p.m. Field-Cornet (later Gen) Cherry Emmett, Botha's brother-in-law, crossed the river with a small party to take possession of the abandoned guns, at the same time capturing twelve full ammunition wagons and taking 150 men prisoner. At about 3 p.m. Buller ordered a general withdrawal. The British casualties were 1,127, of which nearly a half were in Hart's brigade,[28] compared with 38 Boer casualties, including 7 killed.[29] Of Botha's 4,500 men he estimated that only 3,000 had been involved in the fighting.[30]

During the period of inactivity after the battle Botha expected a further attack on Colenso and took steps to strengthen his defences, particularly on Hlangwane. The burghers resumed their routine with interruptions from thunderstorms and periodic shelling by Buller's naval guns.[31] When Buller began his advance westwards to Potgieter's Drift on 10 January Botha urgently called for reinforcements in order to defend the Upper Tugela without weakening his defences at Colenso, where Barton's brigade was still in position. By the 15th when Buller's force reached Potgieter's, some 4,000 Boers were in position on the Upper Tugela in four commands. From east to west, Tobias Smuts commanded the sector from Doornkop to Vaalkrantz, Andries Cronjé's Free Staters were entrenched on Brakfontein and Schalk Burger's force was behind Spion Kop and the Twin Peaks. A 500-strong force of Free Staters and Pretoria men under Commandant Pistorius and Field-Cornet 'Red Daniel' Opperman respectively was all that was available to defend the 3-mile Tabanyama plateau to the west of Spion Kop.[32] These dispositions, extending for 15 miles, were intended to oppose a British crossing at Potgieter's Drift and it was with dismay that Botha learnt on 17 January that Warren was crossing 5 miles further upstream at Trichardt's Drift

1. *The Executive Council of the South African Republic (Transvaal).* Back row, left to right: *A.D.W. Wolmarans, F.W. Reitz, Schalk Burger, J.H.M. Kock;* front row: *Commandant-Gen Piet Joubert, President Kruger, Piet Cronjé.*

2. *Sir Alfred Milner (later Lord Milner), who was appointed Governor of the Cape Colony and British High Commissioner in South Africa in 1897.*

3. *Jan Smuts as* staatsprocureur *(State Attorney) of the Transvaal. He played a leading part in the events leading up to the war.*

4. *Gen Sir Redvers Buller. He was much blamed for his initial failures to relieve Ladysmith, but received little praise when he did achieve this or for his subsequent successes.*

5. Lt Gen Lord Methuen was a hard-working but unlucky general who served in South Africa throughout the war. In March 1902 he was defeated and captured by De la Rey.

6. Gen Louis Botha commanded the Transvaal forces in the Natal campaign and succeeded Piet Joubert as Commandant-General in March 1900. In 1910 he became the first Prime Minister of South Africa.

7. *Gen Christiaan de Wet, Chief Commandant of the Orange Free State forces. He had a legendary reputation for his opportunistic actions and ability to avoid capture.*

8. *Gen Koos de la Rey was the most revered of the Boer generals. He masterminded the Boer tactics at Modder River and Magersfontein and later led the revival in the Western Transvaal.*

9. Marthinus Theunis Steyn, President of the Orange Free State. He tried to avoid war, but once it began he became determined to fight to the bitter end. Louis Botha called him 'the soul of the war'.

10. Boers in action at Vaalkrantz during Buller's third unsuccessful attempt to relieve Ladysmith. He succeeded on his fourth attempt.

11. Gen Sir Charles Warren. He was directly responsible for the attack on Spion Kop, a disastrous venture undertaken at short notice when Buller became impatient with his lack of progress.

12. FM Lord Roberts of Kandahar. In 1880 his victory at Kandahar after a 320-mile march from Kabul with 10,000 men made him a Victorian military hero.

13. *Lord Kitchener of Khartoum. This portrait was painted by Sir Arthur Cope* PRA *and is dated 1900; it was commissioned by officers of the Royal Engineers. Kitchener was raised to the peerage after his victory at Omdurman in September 1898.*

14. Lt Gen Sir John French was one of the most successful British generals in the Boer War and the outstanding cavalry commander of his generation.

15. Col Hannay's solitary grave at Paardeberg, marking the spot where he fell on 18 February 1900. Some saw his hopeless charge as a protest at Kitchener's supposed indifference to loss of life.

16. *British troops in action at Driefontein on 10 March 1900, the last Boer attempt to defend Bloemfontein, which Roberts entered three days later.*

17. *Roberts (seated, second right), shortly before his return to England, sitting between Milner (left) and Ian Hamilton (right). Lt Col Sir Henry Rawlinson stands behind Roberts and Hamilton.*

18. *Kitchener and Botha* (seated, second and third right) *during their abortive peace negotiations at Middelburg in February 1901, flanked by their respective military secretaries, N.J. de Wet* (left) *and Lt Col Hubert Hamilton* (right).

19. *Gen Ben Viljoen* (seated) *and his secretary, J. Visser. After fighting in Natal, at Diamond Hill and Bergendal, Viljoen became Assistant Commandant-General responsible for the North-Eastern Transvaal.*

20. *Gen Christiaan Beyers was in overall command in the Northern Transvaal during the guerrilla war and joined forces with Gen De la Rey in the battle of Nooitgedacht.*

21. *Gen J.C.G. Kemp fought in the Western Transvaal under De la Rey. He was imprisoned for his part in the 1914 rebellion but later became a Cabinet minister for fifteen years.*

22. *James Barry Munnik Hertzog, c. 1901. He was Prime Minister of South Africa from 1924 to 1939, and a judge at the age of twenty-nine before becoming an Orange Free State general during the Boer War.*

23. *Pieter Hendrik Kritzinger, seen here while in captivity, led three invasions of the Cape Colony before his capture. He was acquitted of charges of murder and train wrecking.*

24. *A blockhouse at Modder River, typical of the substantial structures built near important railway bridges. Most of the 8,000 blockhouses in South Africa were circular, corrugated-iron structures.*

25. *Kitchener and his ADC, Capt Frank Maxwell VC, who was one of the few people who knew how to humour him. He became a Brigadier-General but was killed in the First World War.*

26. *Emily Hobhouse, the daughter of an English archdeacon, drew attention to the conditions in British concentration camps in South Africa. Kitchener referred to her as 'that bloody woman'.*

27. *A group of Boer women and children in a concentration camp. Poor sanitation and overcrowding aggravated the effect of epidemic diseases with disastrous consequences.*

28. *The central motif of the Women's Monument in Bloemfontein. The inscribed panel below records the death of 26,370 Boer women and children in British concentration camps.*

29. *Public sentencing, probably of the 23-year-old Gideon Scheepers, in Graaff Reinet. It is uncertain whether Scheepers was executed in public, a practice which Kitchener was ordered to discontinue.*

30. 'The Glorious Trio' – Generals De Wet, De la Rey and Botha, shortly before their departure for Europe after the war to raise funds for distressed Boer women and children.

with 15,000 men and 36 guns, opposed by a mere 500 men on Tabanyama. He feared that Warren would press on that night and push through to Ladysmith,[33] but Warren had no intention of acting so precipitately and the following day spurned angrily the opportunity of outflanking Botha's defences secured by Dundonald's successful skirmish at Acton Homes. As a result Botha had ample opportunity to reinforce Tabanyama and to dig in on the long summit with its commanding field of fire down the slope to the false crest 600–2,000 yd away, below which Warren's force was massing. The Boer guns were placed out of sight behind the summit.

Despite the wishes of both Kruger and Joubert that he should exercise overall command on the Tugela, Botha was reluctant to offend Lucas Meyer, who had returned to Colenso, and Schalk Burger. The former had for long been his mentor and political associate and the latter was both a member of the Transvaal Executive Council and a recent presidential candidate. He therefore agreed to assist on the Tugela without a formal appointment. Confusing as this loose arrangement might have been, the rank and file had no hesitation in responding to his leadership.[34]

Such was the tactical advantage of Botha's positions on Tabanyama that 1,800 Boers, 1,400 Transvaalers and 400 Free Staters, were able to keep Warren's much greater force at bay during three days of hard fighting and intense British bombardment. Through frustration, and because he and Buller could not agree on the alternatives, Warren then embarked on the ill-considered venture to take Spion Kop, whose summit was occupied by Maj Gen Woodgate's 1,700-strong force, at about 3.30 a.m. on 24 January. In doing so it had put to flight the small picket of Vryheid burghers and German volunteers on watch there. Botha, whose headquarters were on a small kopje 2,000 yd north of Spion Kop, heard the news from some of the fleeing Vryheiders and immediately resolved that the hill must be retaken. Other fugitives raised the alarm in Schalk Burger's camp below the Twin Peaks and one of his commandants, Hendrik Prinsloo of Carolina, took charge of the counter-attack from that quarter. Placing a 75-mm Krupp gun on the north-west slope of the Twin Peaks and a pom-pom on the ridge to the west of them, he sent fifty Heidelbergers to occupy Aloe Knoll, a small kopje 250 yd from the summit of Spion Kop on the same ridge. After 7 a.m. he climbed the north-east slope of Spion Kop with sixty-five men, and encountered the British soldiers who had gone out from the main trench to the forward crest line. So close was the contact that in some cases rifles were wrenched from the tommies' hands.[35]

In the meantime, Botha had taken charge of dispositions on Tabanyama, behind which four guns were brought to bear on Spion Kop – a Krupp and a pom-pom behind Green Hill and two Creusots about three-quarters of a mile further back. He also arranged for approximately

300 men, mostly from the Pretoria commando under Red Daniel Opperman, to climb the north-west slope of Spion Kop to reinforce Prinsloo at the summit. Prinsloo had taken with him a schoolteacher called Louis Bothma who was a highly skilled heliograph operator,[36] and when the mist cleared after 8 a.m. he was able to direct the Boer artillery onto the British positions on the summit with devastating precision. The vastly greater British arsenal of fifty-eight guns on the other side of the hill had the much more difficult task of trying to locate the Boer guns, with conditions at the summit making it almost impossible to signal accurate information to the British gunners. In addition to the relentless artillery bombardment the British were subjected to crossfire from rifles on Green Hill, Conical Hill and Aloe Knoll. *The Official History* described Spion Kop as 'but a cape projecting into enemy positions'.[37] Against this background the defenders fought at close quarters with the Boers on the summit. Deneys Reitz, then a seventeen-year-old with the Pretoria commando, recorded later that the English troops lay so near that it would have been possible to toss a biscuit between them: 'Our own casualties lay hideously among us, but theirs were screened from view behind the breastwork, so that the comfort of knowing that we were giving worse than we received was denied us.'[38]

The Boers seemed likely to prevail in the struggle for the summit when, despite Thorneycroft's efforts to prevent them, 167 Lancashire Fusiliers on the extreme right surrendered at about 1 p.m., but the tide turned in favour of the British soon afterwards with the arrival of reinforcements. Botha stepped up and maintained the intensity of the bombardment which took a dreadful toll among the 2,000 men, excluding casualties, who were crowded into an area with shelter for only 1,000. However, as the afternoon wore on Botha realised that he was unlikely to win possession of the summit that day. The capture of the Twin Peaks by the 60th Rifles at about 5 p.m. led to the withdrawal of the Boer guns and the men in that vicinity.

After dark many of the Boers were despondent about the prospects for the next day but Botha drew comfort from what he perceived as a lack of will on the part of the British – their heroic but passive defence of the summit, their hesitation after occupation of the Twin Peaks, and Warren's inexplicable failure to take the pressure off Spion Kop by using his large reserves to attack the depleted Boer defences on Tabanyama.[39] In a telegram to Joubert, Botha expressed his confidence that the British would abandon the hill at nightfall.[40] By 9 p.m. the shooting had died away and most of the Boers had come down from the upper slopes of Spion Kop. Only a handful, under Field-Cornet (later Gen) J.C.G. Kemp of Krugersdorp, remained, having gone there late in the day as reinforcements. At about 10 p.m. he reported the situation by messenger to Botha and received a reply at 3 a.m. instructing him to come down before daylight in order to get his burghers away safely. Botha also reported that Schalk Burger and his commando had fled from their positions below the Twin Peaks. Before leaving the summit Kemp decided to carry out a brief reconnaissance of the enemy positions, only to learn from seven stragglers whom he took prisoner, that the British had vacated the summit at 9 p.m. the night before.[41]

At dawn, on a signal from the summit, Botha and others went up and saw the full extent of the havoc wrought by the previous day's fighting. The British dead lay in swathes in their shallow trenches, in places piled three deep. Some had been horribly mutilated by artillery fire.[42] Figures from both sides put the total British casualties – killed, wounded and taken prisoner – at over 1,000, but the Boer figure for those killed, based on a body count ordered by Botha, was more than double the figure of 312 given by *The Times History*.[43] *The Official History* put the total British casualties for all the operations on Tabanyama and Spion Kop between 15 and 25 January at 1,750, compared with 350 on the Boer side.

Buller's decision to withdraw across the Tugela after the battle enabled Botha to take the leave he had deferred earlier and he slipped unobtrusively into Pretoria with his military secretary. When the Boers got wind of Buller's intention to make a new attempt to reach Ladysmith, this time via Vaalkrantz, Joubert got in touch with Botha and told him he was needed at the front. He also heard from Schalk Burger – who had fallen back on Marthinus Prinsloo's laager near Ladysmith after his hasty departure from Spion Kop – asking if Botha was returning as he himself was too ill 'to go out'.[44] Botha returned to the Tugela and took command early on 6 February. The British were in possession of Vaalkrantz, having been opposed mainly by Ben Viljoen's Johannesburg commando, who had redeemed the reputation they had lost by indifferent performances at Elandslaagte and Colenso. Ben Viljoen himself had shown considerable personal gallantry in rescuing a Boer pom–pom under heavy fire. The Boer chain of command on the Tugela had been confused further by the appointment as overall commander, at the suggestion of President Steyn, of the Free Stater Marthinus Prinsloo,[45] but this does not seem to have inhibited Botha, who continued to report to Joubert. He believed that the best way to exploit Buller's hesitancy was to stand firm and keep up continuous pressure on Vaalkrantz, but he warned Joubert that it was going to be extremely difficult to recapture it, protected as it was by the river to the rear with the approach to the front across open ground devoid of cover.[46] He planned to maintain heavy artillery fire on all sides and he was assisted in this by the arrival from Ladysmith of the Long Tom, which was dragged up Doornkop overnight.[47] The bombardment began the following morning. Despite Roberts's uncompromising message to him that the advance should continue, Buller's irresolution led him to call a council of war at 4 p.m. at which it was agreed to withdraw from Vaalkrantz and to make a fresh attempt at Hlangwane.[48] While Buller withdrew his army Botha remained behind near Vaalkrantz. On 12 February he crossed the river at Munger's Drift with a small reconnaissance force which clashed with a squadron of Royal Dragoons. This was his last military operation on the Upper Tugela.[49]

The Boer defences near Colenso, where Lucas Meyer was in command, now extended some four miles to the east of Hlangwane via Green Hill to Monte Cristo, and thence a further 2 miles south to Cingolo. Meyer had only 3,000 men at his disposal along a front of 8½ miles, of whom 1,500 defended the vital Hlangwane to Green Hill sector. From 14 February Botha, who was indisposed, began to transfer units from the Upper Tugela to Colenso, where Meyer used them to strengthen the Boer left. Botha himself undertook to go and help at Colenso as soon as he was well. Still regarding himself as Meyer's deputy he had no wish to supersede him, although he realised that Meyer was incapable of commanding on his own.[50] When he reached Colenso on Saturday 17 February the Boer positions east of Hlangwane were already in peril. Lyttleton's forces occupied Cingolo during the day and took Monte Cristo early on Sunday afternoon. There was little that Botha could do to stem the rout from the Boer laager in the plain below Monte Cristo – it was only fortunate that Buller chose not to pursue – but he tried to introduce a semblance of order at the river crossing. Late that night he succeeded in establishing a line of defence from Hlangwane, which was still in Boer occupation, north to the Tugela. On Monday, fearing that Buller would attempt a flanking movement east of Monte Cristo, he set off on a reconnaissance of river crossings in that direction. Satisfied that the British would not find a crossing without a four to five day march, he returned later in the day to find that the rearguard he had established on Hlangwane had decided to withdraw across the river.[51] By Tuesday 20 February Buller had control of the whole of the area to the east of Colenso.

Buller's disinclination to pursue allowed the Boers time to establish a new line of defence on the left bank of the Tugela running approximately 5½ miles north-eastwards from Red Hill to Pieter's Hill. Botha commanded the sector to the west of the Langverwacht Spruit and Meyer the sector to the east of it. Their chief concern was the deterioration in the Boer morale, not helped by the news from the western front, where Kimberley had been relieved and Cronjé was surrounded at Paardeberg. Many burghers, having crossed the river, had simply continued trekking northwards. Prompted by reports from his officers that they could not guarantee to keep all their burghers in their positions Botha telegraphed to Joubert that the time might have come to raise the siege of Ladysmith, and for a general retreat northwards to the Biggarsberg. Kruger was insistent that the Tugela line must be held and that to abandon it would have a disastrous effect on Boer fortunes on the western front. He reinforced his message with a long religious exhortation to the burghers. This and the efforts of Botha and Meyer stiffened the Boer resolve and when his advance guard ran into strong resistance, having crossed the river opposite Hlangwane on 21 February, Buller accepted that more than a rearguard stood between him and Ladysmith.

There was heavy fighting over the next few days, starting in the Wynne Hills in Botha's sector on the 22nd and extending into Meyer's sector late in the afternoon of the following day, when Hart's Irish Brigade began its assault on Inniskilling Hill. By the evening of the 24th the British had lost 1,300 men without gaining possession of any Boer positions and many wounded had been left out unattended. The temporary cessation of fighting the following day, to allow the British to collect their wounded, had not been formally sanctioned by Botha or Meyer but had been agreed to by the local Boer commanders on Inniskilling Hill and the Wynne Hills, mainly because of the stench of the corpses. This informal truce was largely to the advantage of the British since it allowed Buller to start moving men and guns back across the river in preparation for his next plan of attack, and the British artillery may have profited from knowledge of the Boer positions gained during the fraternisation which took place.[52]

On Monday 26 February Botha was uncertain what to make of the great concentration of British men, guns and equipment on the other side of the river and he alerted Joubert to the possibility that it might herald another retreat. That hope was shattered the following day when the British, encouraged by the news from Paardeberg of Cronjé's surrender that morning, crossed the river via a new pontoon to the north of Hlangwane to attack in succession Pieter's Hill, Railway Hill and Inniskilling Hill, supported by massive artillery fire from the right bank. By the end of the day the Boer line on the Tugela had collapsed. After a final *krygsraad* in Meyer's laager late that night Botha telegraphed Joubert asking him to sanction withdrawal from all the Tugela positions and advising the withdrawal of all Boer forces and their supplies from around Ladysmith. The next day Dundonald entered the town, two days ahead of Buller. Botha returned to his sector and gave instructions for an orderly withdrawal to the west.[53] Elsewhere the withdrawal was anything but orderly. Botha and Meyer were able to do no more than form a small rearguard, which numbered only 150 men by the time they reached Modderspruit outside Ladysmith on 1 March, the day of Buller's formal entry. They found that Joubert's former headquarters laager had been evacuated. Joubert himself was in Elandslaagte, where Botha and Meyer arrived the next day to find the place in ruins, with the commissariat plundered and stores which could not be removed burnt, together with the buildings which housed them.[54] On 3 March Botha reached Glencoe where he sent a telegram to his wife expressing his bitterness at the loss of the Colenso positions, but drawing some comfort from the fact that he himself had not lost a single position to the British.[55]

On 9 March Joubert left Glencoe and Botha set about establishing a new line of defence on the Biggarsberg, along a 102-mile front from the Drakensberg to Vryheid. By now the focus of the British war effort had shifted from Natal to the Free State and on 13 March Bloemfontein fell to Roberts with little resistance. Botha sent off 1,200 of his 6,000 men to the Free State to help oppose Roberts's advance. He was not present at the historic *krygsraad* in Kroonstad on 17 March which was presided over by Steyn and attended by fifty to sixty officers of both republics, but his brother Philip was there in his capacity as a Free State general.[56] Joubert had returned from Kroonstad with a heavy cold and died on 27 March in Pretoria. He was buried three days later on his farm Rustfontein near Volksrust. At the church service in Pretoria the day before, Kruger had revealed that it had been Joubert's wish that Botha should succeed him as Commandant-General and Kruger announced that Botha would act in that capacity until it was possible to hold an election for the position, as required by law.[57]

When Roberts began his advance from Bloemfontein on 3 May, less than 5,000 Boers opposed him, mostly Transvaalers under De La Rey. Botha, ordered to the Free State by Kruger to assume overall command there, arrived at Virginia Siding on 7 May with 3,000 Transvaalers, having had to exert the force of his personality to round up burghers who had overstayed their leave.[58] De La Rey now left the Free State to oppose the relief of Mafeking and on 10 May Botha was joined by 5,000 Free Staters in a stand on the Sand River in defence of Kroonstad. There was little that the Boers could do with 8,000 men and 20 guns against Roberts's force of 38,000 with 100 guns[59] and Kroonstad was abandoned during the night of the 11th. After eight days there to rest and re-equip, Roberts resumed his advance and on 27 May crossed the Vaal, the last of five rivers between Bloemfontein and the Transvaal. As they gave way at each river the Boers were able to extricate their wagons and heavy guns,[60] but they became increasingly demoralised. By the time they fell back across the Vaal many were no longer attached to commandos, but were simply so many individual burghers on their way home.[61]

In the battle for Johannesburg, fought largely near present-day Soweto, Botha had only 5,000 men at his disposal, including a few hundred commanded by De La Rey. In the battle of Doornkop, where Jameson had surrendered after his abortive raid in 1896, the Boers gave way after an assault by the Gordons and the CIV (City Imperial Volunteers) under Ian Hamilton. During his short stay in Johannesburg Botha successfully opposed the Boer plan to destroy the gold mines, before organising the withdrawal to Pretoria of the guns and heavy equipment. Always inclined to see the wider picture he realised that, whatever the outcome of the war, the wealth from the mines would be vital to the rehabilitation of South Africa. As the demoralised burghers fell back on Pretoria their leaders had accepted the futility of attempting to save the city and, like Steyn in the Free State, had resolved to carry on the business of government away from the capital. On 29 May Kruger and State Secretary F.W. Reitz, left Pretoria for Machadodorp 140 miles to the east on the Delagoa Bay Railway, where a number of railway carriages served as the government offices. Jan Smuts, the State Attorney, stayed behind with Schalk Burger, now relieved of his military responsibilities in his capacity as Vice-President, to oversee the removal of State funds and war supplies.

During the evening of Friday 1 June, Smuts was present at a gathering at the telegraph offices in Pretoria of some of the senior Transvaal generals, among whom were Botha, De la Rey, Tobias Smuts, Lemmer and Ben Viljoen. Shaken by the demoralisation and desertions of the Boer rank and file and persuaded, for the moment, of the hopelessness of the Boer cause, they sent a telegram to Kruger tentatively suggesting that the war should end at Pretoria. Smuts wrote of 'the bitter humiliation and despondency of that awful moment when the strongest hearts and stoutest wills in the Transvaal army were, albeit but for a moment, to sink beneath the tide of our misfortunes.'[62] Kruger consulted Steyn and on the following morning, Saturday 2 June, the same generals met at a *krygsraad* in the hall of the Second Volksraad to consider what steps should be taken for the defence of Pretoria. Only Botha, Smuts and at most one or two others had seen Steyn's reply to Kruger's telegram, in which he affirmed his unalterable opposition to peace, practically accusing the Transvaal leaders of cowardice and asserting that the Free Staters would fight on, if necessary alone, to the bitter end. His mood was matched by that of a number of younger Transvaal commanders present at the *krygsraad*, who had not been at the informal gathering the night before and were not privy to the exchange of telegrams between the two presidents. Danie Theron was cheered when he described those who spoke of peace as traitors and condemned the government for its desertion of the capital. After speeches in a similar vein the *krygsraad* decided that the Pretoria positions should be defended – as successive Boer positions had been defended during Roberts's advance – by a fighting retreat.[63]

In the new mood of defiance Boer forces rallied to Botha in the Magaliesberg to the north-east of Pretoria so that by 10 June when Roberts realised that there was going to be no surrender, Botha was able to deploy some 6,000 men and 23 guns[64] along a series of ridges to the east of the city. As a further boost to Boer morale news arrived of De Wet's success at Roodewal.[65] The ensuing battle, called Donkerhoek by the Boers and Diamond Hill by the British, ended inconclusively on the night of 12 June when Botha withdrew all his forces.[66] Many burghers lost heart, returned home and surrendered their weapons, although in some cases they buried their precious Mausers and handed in obsolete Martini Henrys and even older weapons, family heirlooms that had not seen service since the Great Trek.[67] In due course many relented and rejoined the fight.

The struggle now concentrated on the control of the Delagoa Bay Railway which joined Pretoria to Lourenço Marques in Portuguese East Africa and which provided the Boers with their only connection with the world outside. It also, for the time being, provided a relatively secure home to Kruger and the Transvaal government in its railway carriages at Machadodorp. Botha had accepted that there was no realistic prospect of defeating the British and he had no fixed plan beyond retaining control of the railway and protecting the government for as long as possible, while he prepared for the guerrilla war which he now saw as inevitable. As far as possible he deployed his commandos in their own areas and began to equip Lydenburg and Barberton, lying in mountainous country to the north and south respectively of the railway line beyond Machadodorp, as ultimate rallying points. He also rationalised the commandos into larger units, weeding out in the process six of his least successful generals, and making Ben Viljoen a general. Botha had now to reckon not only with Roberts but also with Buller, who during June had fought his way into the Transvaal via the Drakensberg, and who for the next few weeks was to secure control of the railway linking Natal to Johannesburg before striking across to join hands with Roberts's forces on the Delagoa Bay Railway.

Roberts's advance eastwards was delayed by the activities of De La Rey and others in the Western Transvaal and it was not until 27 July that French occupied Middelburg 80 miles along the line from Pretoria. Roberts paused there for nearly a month before resuming his advance eastwards. Nine of his columns were engaged in the first De Wet hunt, while Olivier in the Free State was occupying his attention after his escape from the Brandwater Basin. Roberts was also waiting for Buller, who began his advance towards the Delagoa Bay Railway on 7 August with a force of 9,000 men, mostly Lyttleton's 4th Division, and 42 guns accompanied by a supply train of 761 wagons.[68] On the 15th he made contact with the right flank of French's cavalry near Twyfelaar.

Botha chose as his last line of defence in the east the Dalmanutha plateau near Belfast, practically the last rim of the Highveld. It had formidable defensive advantages which helped to redress the numerical imbalance between the two sides. It commanded a level plain to the west and the valley behind it afforded shelter to men and horses.[69] To the north mountainous country stretched to Lydenburg and to the south bogs and streams effectively inhibited cavalry movements. The Boer positions extended for 50 miles between Lydenburg and Barberton, with half of Botha's estimated 5,000- to 7,000-strong force on the left wing and half on the centre and right. He had 20 guns, including 4 Long Toms brought together for the first time. Roberts and Buller's combined forces totalled 18,700 men with 82 guns and 25 machine-guns.[70]

By 25 August Buller was 12 miles south of Belfast and on that day he, French and Pole-Carew met in the town to receive Roberts's orders. Buller was to attack the Boer left, and French's cavalry, supported by Pole-Carew's infantry, was to attempt to turn the Boer right. Buller resolved to concentrate his attack on Bergendal Farm near the Boer centre and in particular on the boulder-covered kopje of the same name which formed the apex of a salient angle in the Boer line and which he perceived to be its weak link.[71] The kopje was held by only 74 men, members of the Johannesburg police, with 100 men of the same force on the farm behind. The adjoining positions were manned by the Johannesburg, Krugersdorp and Germiston commandos, all seasoned fighting men, but they were unable to afford much help to the exposed kopje because of the lack of communication trenches between commandos, and the Boer artillery was relatively inactive. From 11 a.m. on 27 August Buller's thirty-eight guns pounded the kopje in a bombardment whose intensity had not been seen since the Tugela battles of Vaalkrantz and Pieter's Hill. Apart from its demoralising effect the bombardment left the well-entrenched defenders of the kopje relatively unscathed. At 2.30 p.m. the 2nd Rifle Brigade and 1st Inniskilling Fusiliers began their assault over 1,500 yd of uncovered ground, and from 1,000 yd away up to the last 150 yd encountered a rate of fire so continuous that Lyttleton thought that there were 300 men on the kopje. However, the resolute defenders could not prevail against the combination of the determination of the British infantry, the effectiveness of the supporting artillery fire – honed to precision by experience – and the sheer force of numbers. When they finally succumbed, forty of the seventy-four Johannesburg police on the kopje had been killed, wounded or captured. The seizure of the Bergendal kopje and the threat posed by French to the north led to the collapse of the entire Boer line and an orderly retreat. After the war Botha told Lyttleton that the Boers had hoped to hold the Dalmanutha line for a month.[72]

Roberts, believing that the war was all but over, annexed the Transvaal to the British Crown by proclamation on 1 September. In the immediate aftermath of the battle he had lost touch with the Boer commandos and waited four days before sending Buller and French in pursuit – Buller to

Lydenburg and French to Barberton. While Ben Viljoen had remained near the railway with the Johannesburg and Krugersdorp commandos, Botha had moved towards Lydenburg with most of the commandos who had been north of the line. The commandos south of the line had stayed to defend the approaches to Barberton, to which the Boers had sent the women and children whom Roberts had expelled earlier from Pretoria.[73] Buller's operations around Lydenburg were in mountainous country in which the advantages were with the pursued rather than the pursuers. As Lyttleton described it the roads were mere pathways and place names such as 'Hell Gate' and 'Devil's Knuckles' only feebly described the nature of the terrain.[74] Ian Hamilton joined Buller from the west, bringing his total strength up to 12,000 men and 48 guns, and he occupied Lydenburg on 6 September. Botha, holding the high ground to the east of the town at Paardeplaats had 2,000 men, 2 Long Toms and several field guns. In an action on 8 September his force was dislodged but got away under cover of an evening mist, thanks to a skilful rearguard action.[75]

Leaving a small force behind, Botha returned to the railway at Nelspruit to which the Boer government had now moved. Here a reluctant Kruger was persuaded that he should go to Europe, in theory on six months' leave of absence to solicit the support of friendly powers. In truth he was too old and frail – and his capture too rich a prize for the British – to be constantly on the move, as would be required by the new circumstances of guerrilla warfare, so he left Nelspruit on 11 September and sailed from Lourenço Marques on the 19th in the Dutch cruiser *Gelderland*. The British government gave an undertaking to the Dutch government not to interfere with the arrangements.[76] Kruger never saw his native country again, but his embalmed body was returned to South Africa for burial when he died in Switzerland in July 1904. Schalk Burger, as Vice-President, became the acting head of government, but in reality the mantle of leadership of the Boer cause now fell on Louis Botha.

At this inopportune moment Botha succumbed to an acute throat infection and went down the line to recover at Hectorspruit, 17 miles from the Portuguese border, as Roberts's army closed in. On 13 September French occupied Barberton, having traversed mountainous country every bit as difficult as that encountered by Buller to the north. Opperman's* Swaziland commando had left the town, but French found there 2,500 refugees, a very large quantity of stores, 44 locomotives and 2 trains.[77] On the same day Hutton took Kaapsche Hoop, between Barberton and the railway, and Pole-Carew, who had remained near the railway after Bergendal, was already moving eastwards from Waterval Onder.

* Commandant (later Gen) J.D. Opperman, not to be confused with Field-Cornet (later Commandant) D.J.E. (Red Daniel) Opperman.

Those commandos that had not escaped to the south-east after Bergendal now concentrated at Hectorspruit. With the Portuguese border behind them, the British Army to the south and west, and the fever-ridden bushveld to the north there seemed little hope of escape. Only to the north, where Roberts's recall of Ian Hamilton to the railway had left Buller fully stretched, was there any reasonable prospect of slipping through. President Steyn had shown the way, after his two-week stay with the Transvaal government, when he headed north from Nelspruit on 11 September with a small escort, and reached the Highveld via Pilgrim's Rest. In preparation for an escape by the same route Botha sent to Komatipoort on the Portuguese border 3,000 Boers who, lacking either horses or resolve, were ill-equipped to continue the fight. After their remaining artillery pieces, except for one Long Tom and some field guns, had been destroyed and thrown into the Crocodile River[78] Botha and Viljoen set out on 17 September with 2,000 men. Heading north through the Sabi Valley they made for the foot of the mountain range which Steyn's small party had climbed to safety six days earlier. Here news reached them of the approach of Buller from the west and, judging that the whole of his force would not get through the pass in time, Botha ordered Viljoen to take the greater part of it north along the foot of the escarpment to Leydsdorp and thence west to Pietersburg, to which he brought it, more or less intact, on 19 October. With the government party and what remained of the Johannesburg police, Botha himself followed the route taken by Steyn back to the Highveld. When Pole-Carew reached Komatipoort on 24 September most of the Boers left there had crossed into Portuguese territory and surrendered their arms. He found a chaotic mass of stores and railway materials, including a 9-mile length of rolling stock and eighty locomotives.[79]

Botha and the Transvaal government party, including Schalk Burger, F.W. Reitz and Lucas Meyer, joined Steyn in Pietersburg in early October. Here they were able to discuss matters such as new command arrangements in comparative safety. Botha accompanied Steyn on his return journey to the Free State as far as the Swartruggens area of the Western Transvaal, where on 27 October they joined De La Rey and Smuts on the farm Syferfontein to discuss future strategy. De Wet was unable to join them. Acknowledging that continued resistance by Boer forces in the Transvaal and the Free State would lead to an escalation of the British policy of farm burning, they resolved to revert to the original strategy of invading Natal and the Cape Colony on the grounds that the British would not feel able to exact reprisals against the civilian population in their own territories. As a prelude to the invasions the plan to destroy the Rand gold mines, previously opposed successfully by Botha, was resurrected as being justified in the new circumstances. In

January or February 1901 a force of 12,000 to 15,000 was to attack the mines and thereafter to split into three forces, one of which under Botha was to invade Natal while forces under De Wet and De La Rey were to invade the Cape Colony.[80]

In the meantime, implementing decisions taken at Pietersburg, Botha, while retaining overall command of all the Transvaal forces, took charge as the local commander on the Eastern Highveld, assisted by his brother Chris Botha in the adjoining South-Eastern Transvaal. Viljoen commanded in the north-east on the other side of the Delagoa Bay Railway. De La Rey commanded in the west, assisted by Jan Smuts and later by J.C.G. Kemp, and Beyers was to command in the north, at the same time acting as a link between the eastern and western commands.[81] Botha had to contend with continuing local surrenders of burghers and, with the ruthlessness that underlay his geniality, wrote to commandants: 'Do everything in your power to prevent the burghers laying down their arms. If they do not listen to this, I will be compelled to confiscate everything movable and immovable and also to burn their houses.'[82]

On 29 November Roberts handed over to Kitchener and on that day, in the last set-piece action of the war, Viljoen with 650 men successfully defended a line of hills at Rhenoster Kop against Paget's force of 2 infantry battalions, 9 guns and 1,200 mounted men, before slipping away during the night.[83] An Australian officer, writing home the day after the action, described it from the British point of view as 'a very close shave of a terrible disaster'.[84] In most actions at this time the Boers were the attackers. In the Magaliesberg in early December De La Rey with Smuts captured 138 wagons and 75 men at Buffelspoort and with Beyers captured the British camp at Nooitgedacht. At the end of the month Viljoen attacked the post at Helvetia, south of Lydenburg, capturing 250 men and a 4.7-in gun. Ten days later he collaborated with Botha in simultaneous attacks on Belfast, Machadodorp and other stations on the Delagoa Bay Railway.

These minor actions served notice on Britain that the war was far from over but the great Boer offensive planned at Syferfontein was only partially implemented. In December Hertzog and Kritzinger invaded the Cape Colony under cover of De Wet's own failed first attempt. De Wet himself succeeded in entering the colony in January 1901 but soon had to abort his invasion in the face of the large British force awaiting him. As De Wet was chased back into the Free State, Botha's planned invasion of Natal was thwarted in the South-Eastern Transvaal by the first of Kitchener's drives, which began on 27 January.[85] However, in the small hours of 6 February he carried out a daring attack with 2,000 men on Smith-Dorrien's camp near Lake Chrissie, north of Ermelo, penetrating the outer defences by sending back stampeding British horses. Although the attack was soon repulsed, Botha and most of his men escaped

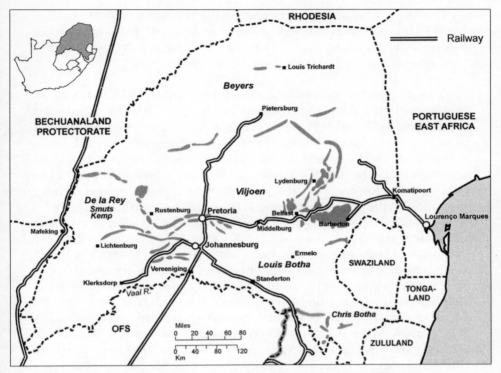

The Transvaal showing the areas of the principal Boer Commands during the Guerrilla War

through or around the British lines.[86] Other commandos, which Botha had left to cover the eastward flight of civilians, had in due course mostly fled to the north.

At this time Botha's wife Annie was living quietly with her children in Pretoria and, using her as an intermediary, Kitchener sent a verbal message to Botha to the effect that he was prepared to meet to discuss terms for peace on the clear understanding that the independence of the Boer republics was not on the agenda. Botha accepted the invitation and the conference took place in Middelburg on 28 February. Kitchener's first impression of Botha was favourable:

Botha came in at 10 a.m. and left about 3 p.m. He has a nice, unassuming manner, and seemed desirous of finishing the war, but somewhat doubtful of being able to induce his men to accept peace without independence in some form or another. He repeated that he and his people felt bitterly losing their independence. . . . He said, incidentally, that he could carry on for some time. He was very bitter about those who had surrendered. Botha is a quiet, capable man, and I have no doubt carries considerable weight with his burghers; he will be, I should think, of valuable assistance to the future Government of the country in an official capacity.[87]

Two months later, in frustration at the continuation of the war, Kitchener denounced Botha as 'an excellent actor . . . with the mind of a pettifogging attorney'.[88] However, despite this waspish comment, their meeting at Middelburg was the start of an enduring mutual regard.

The draft terms agreed to by Kitchener were appreciably more conciliatory than the British government's final terms conveyed to Botha in a letter signed by Kitchener dated 7 March 1901. In particular the government had hardened the provisions relating to financial assistance, the future rights of native Africans and, reflecting Milner's advice, the question of amnesties for rebels in the Cape Colony and Natal. On 16 March Botha declined the terms offered, without giving any explanation. Kitchener blamed the failure of the negotiations on Milner's intransigence on colonial amnesties, but in truth the Boer leaders were not yet ready to contemplate the surrender of their independence. For Botha the outcome was more satisfactory than for Kitchener because it had established the minimum terms which were likely to be available to the Boers if in due course they were defeated. As it turned out, the final terms agreed at Vereeniging over a year later were much the same but somewhat better than those offered after Middelburg. There is a charming story that Kitchener invited Botha to dinner during the evening after the Middelburg conference and taught him to play bridge, but it is difficult to reconcile it with Frank Maxwell's account of the day's proceedings, according to which the Boer delegation left at 5 p.m. and was followed by 'three solid hours of cipher to Brodrick, Milner & Co., telling them all the details of the meeting'.[89]

After the publication of the British terms Botha sent two circular letters to his burghers telling them about the negotiations and their outcome. The second of these letters stated in part:

The spirit of Lord Kitchener's letter makes it very plain to you all that the British Government desires nothing else but the destruction of our Afrikander people and the acceptance of the terms contained therein is absolutely out of the question. Virtually the letter contains nothing more, but rather less, than what the British Government will be obliged to do should our cause go wrong. . . .

Let us as Daniel in the lion's den, place our trust in God alone, for in His time and in His way He will certainly give us deliverance.[90]

Robust as this letter was, Botha was criticised by Boer hardliners for having discussed peace at all and from this time on De Wet, in particular, became suspicious about his dedication to the Boer cause. The two men had met at Vrede shortly after Middelburg[91] in the first of a number of meetings between various Boer leaders. On 10 May Botha, his brother Chris, Ben Viljoen and Jan Smuts met on the farm Immigratie near Ermelo in a mood of despondency about continuing surrenders, low reserves of ammunition, the dying hopes of foreign intervention and their declining authority. Without consulting the Free State they resolved to ask Kitchener's permission to send a delegation to Europe to confer with Kruger about the future course of the war. Steyn was told of this in a letter of 10 May, to which he reacted with predictable indignation and demanded a meeting between the Transvaal and Free State governments. In the event Kitchener refused consent for a delegation to go to Europe, but allowed the Transvaal leaders to send an enciphered telegram to Kruger. After a preliminary meeting between Steyn, De Wet and De La Rey near Reitz early in June,[92] the two governments met on the 20th on Botha's farm Waterval near Standerton. Steyn was pleasantly surprised to find a new mood of resolve in the Transvaalers, brought about partly by his own and De Wet's influence, but also by Kruger's uncompromising reply to the telegram, and a military success on 12 June at Wilmansrust on the Middelburg to Ermelo road. Here Ben Viljoen's lieutenant, Muller, had taken over 200 prisoners after storming the camp of 350 men of the Victorian Mounted Rifles.[93] The meeting resolved to fight on and in particular in was decided that Smuts should lead an expedition into the Cape Colony.[94]

After the failure of the Middelburg negotiations Kitchener had devoted all his energies to crushing Boer resistance. Hand in hand with the development of the blockhouse system and drives to round up Boer combatants he applied with increasing ferocity the measures against civilians initiated by Roberts, which were to be characterised by the leader of the Liberal Opposition in Britain as 'methods of barbarism'[95] – burning farms, destroying crops and livestock and removing women and children to concentration camps, where many died of disease. Botha has been accused of ambivalence towards these measures. Kitchener told Roberts that he did not raise the question of farm burning at Middelburg,[96] and later at Vereeniging Botha is quoted in an unofficial version of the minutes as commenting that it was reassuring to know that Boer families were under the protection of the British.[97] After the war Botha rejected emphatically any suggestion that he had condoned the concentration camp policy, stating that his correspondence with Roberts and Kitchener bore ample testimony to his protests.[98] In fact no Boer leader was more distressed than Botha about the suffering of civilians and it was his fear of the destruction of the Afrikaner nation that lay behind his willingness to consider an honourable peace settlement. His own farm in the Vryheid district, together with those of Lucas Meyer and Cherry Emmett, was destroyed at the end of July.

In May Botha's wife Annie had left for Europe and his nine-year-old son Louis had joined him on commando. At the same time Milner had returned to England on leave and, during his absence, Kitchener added the role of High Commissioner in South Africa to his role as Commander-in-Chief. At the instance originally of the Governor of Natal, on 7 August 1901 Kitchener issued an ill-judged proclamation to the effect, firstly, that all Boer officers who failed to surrender by 15 September 1901 would be banished permanently from South Africa and, secondly, that the cost of maintenance of the families of all burghers in the field who failed to surrender by that date would be recoverable from those burghers.[99]

Steyn, De Wet and Botha all replied defiantly to the proclamation. It also provoked Botha into a practical demonstration of the Boer's willingness to continue the struggle. French had frustrated his attempt earlier in the year to invade Natal. He resolved to try again. In combination with Smuts's invasion of the Cape Colony this was effectively a revival of the failed Syferfontein plan of December 1900 and as envisaged then Botha entertained the possibility now of entering the Cape through Griqualand East after penetrating Natal.[100] He set out from the farm Blaauwbank near Ermelo on 7 September with about 1,000 seasoned fighting men from the Bethal, South Middelburg, Carolina and Standerton commandos. As he moved through the South-Eastern Transvaal it was intended that he should gather reinforcements from the local commandos under the overall command of his brother Chris Botha. He issued strict instructions to all his officers, dealing not only with military matters but also with their conduct towards civilians, and making each officer responsible for seeing that his men did nothing contrary to the principles of civilised warfare.[101]

Botha's progress was hampered by heavy rain but by 17 September he had reached Blood River Poort, a long river gorge about eighteen miles south-east of Utrecht. With the addition of the Wakkerstroom, Piet Retief and Utrecht commandos his force now totalled 1,700, and a further 300 men of the Vryheid commando awaited him at Scheeper's Nek, another 7 miles to the south-east.[102] The initial concentration of commandos near Ermelo had alerted Kitchener to the possibility of a fresh attempt on Natal and Lyttleton, who had taken over the chief command in the colony early in September, prepared to oppose it. His first dispositions, based on scant intelligence, had brought near to Blood River Poort two columns of approximately 800 and 600 men respectively under lieutenant-colonels H.K. Stewart and H. de la P. Gough.[103] When in the early afternoon of 17 September Gough saw the small Boer force at Scheeper's Nek he agreed with Stewart, about one and a half miles behind him, that they would attack it together at dusk, but he abandoned the plan and decided to attack immediately when the Boers moved towards Blood River Poort with the apparent intention of setting up camp for the night. They were in fact going to join Botha who, unknown to Gough, was at that moment coming through the gorge. As Gough galloped his force across the last 1,000 yd of open ground he was fallen upon by two mounted bodies of Boers, each about 500 strong, one on his right flank and one in front. After a mêlée of about twenty minutes the fight was over and of Gough's force 20 had been killed and 24 wounded; 235 were taken prisoner, but Gough and a few others escaped that night and the remainder were released later, having been relieved of their horses, arms and ammunition.[104] Stewart succeeded in saving Gough's transport and wisely fell back on De Jager's Drift on the swollen Buffalo River, thus blocking off Botha's most direct route to Dundee. For the Boers the action at Blood River Poort was a brilliant tactical victory, the result of opportunism rather than of planning, but it effectively ended Botha's hopes of a direct invasion of Natal since it gave the British their first concrete intelligence of his presence, strength and objective. Gough was not blamed for the setback and went on to a distinguished military career.[105]

After eleven days of wet and cold weather Botha's horses were in poor condition, requiring him to rest his force for a while near Blood River Poort. With nine British columns and a swollen Buffalo River barring his access to the northern frontier of Natal, Botha decided to try and get into the colony through Zululand. After a brief incursion into the Nqutu area he went southwards, establishing his headquarters on the farm Gelykwater near Babanango Mountain on the Transvaal side of the border during the last week of September.[106] After unsuccessful attacks on two small but well-defended British posts just inside the Zululand border, at Itala and Fort Prospect, Botha abandoned his invasion attempt, blaming the failure of his expedition on bad weather and poor intelligence.[107]

With British columns closing in from the south and west he headed northwards towards the clump of mountains to the east of Vryheid, roughly resembling a funnel in shape with its exit to the north. Adjoining the complex to the east lay Botha's own farm, Waterval, on which the British had destroyed his home a month earlier.[108] Walter Kitchener, who commanded the nearest British column, secured the known wagon routes through the mountains, but Botha left his wagons behind and during the night of 5 October took a depleted force across bridle paths on to his farm.[109] The Vryheid men had been left behind, while the Utrecht and Wakkerstroom commandos had earlier filtered away in small parties to their own areas.[110] By 14 October he was back at Ermelo.[111]

Although ostensibly a failure Botha's Natal expedition had made his intended political statement in response to Kitchener's proclamation of 7 August. It had also taken pressure off Smuts in the Cape Colony and De La Rey in the Western Transvaal by diverting 20,000 British troops. Later in the month Botha narrowly escaped capture when his laager on the farm Schimmelhoek near Ermelo was nearly surrounded by the columns of colonels Rawlinson and Rimington with a combined strength of 2,000 men and 8 guns. When, after a night march, Rimington reached a hill overlooking the farm early in the morning on 25 October he saw Botha, his young son and a few companions galloping away to the north. Botha left behind a hat and personal papers.[112]

From the end of July onwards the main concern of the Boers in the Eastern Transvaal had been the night raiding techniques developed by Lt Col G.E. Benson of the Royal Artillery.* Relying on intelligence gathered by a brilliant, if eccentric, intelligence officer, the South African-born Lt Col Aubrey Woolls-Sampson, Benson had been marching his column up to forty miles at night and attacking Boer laagers at dawn. By the time of Botha's return to the Eastern Highveld Benson's success had begun to be self-defeating since the Boers had responded by keeping their laagers constantly on the move, never camping in the same place twice and saddling up in the small hours. However, his methods had engendered considerable fear and hatred, compounded by the mistaken belief of the Boers returning from the Natal expedition that Benson was responsible for the destruction they found in Ermelo.[113] Botha ordered that the Highveld should 'be rid of Benson's restless column'.[114]

Early in the morning of 30 October Benson set out from Syferfontein near Bethal en route to Brugspruit, 35 miles away on the Delagoa Bay Railway, intending to camp that night on the farm Bakenlaagte. His 1,400-strong column consisted mostly of men with virtually no recent fighting experience who had replaced his seasoned soldiers during a rest at Middelburg. The 180-strong rearguard was commanded by Maj Gore Anley. At about 1.45 p.m. the advance guard and supply column was approaching Bakenlaagte an hour ahead of the rearguard, two of whose wagons got stuck in the mud of a drift. During the march the rearguard had been harried in mist and rain, but not impeded, by mounted Boers. Woolls-Sampson had become uneasy about the way Boers kept on appearing and disappearing in the undulating country, which provided concealment for attackers but no defence against them, and he had warned Benson to look to his rearguard. Botha had joined the Boer force

* As a major he had guided Wauchope's Highland Brigade into action at Magersfontein.

with reinforcements around midday. Benson, who disagreed with Anley's decision to abandon the troubled wagons, established a gun position on a ridge, subsequently known as Gun Hill, to cover the rearguard and then took two squadrons of Scottish Horse, intending at first to help extricate the wagons. He soon gave the order to retire and as the rearguard moved towards Gun Hill it was attacked by a double wave of 1,200 Boer horsemen. By the time Benson had regained Gun Hill and turned to face the enemy Botha's force had swollen to 2,000 who, when checked by rifle fire, dismounted and spread out in a 1,200-yd firing line. Benson's defence of Gun Hill ranks among the epic last stands of British military history. Thrice wounded he calmly directed his men, and one of his last acts was to send a survivor to the camp to call gunfire onto Gun Hill. By the time the 280 defenders of Gun Hill had been overwhelmed, 231 had been killed or wounded. Benson was taken to the camp at 9 p.m. and died the following morning. The Boers' hatred of him was replaced later by admiration but there is evidence that in the heat of action the conduct of some of the Boers towards wounded British soldiers fell below its usual chivalrous standard.[115] According to one of his commandants Botha did not press the attack on the main British camp at Bakenlaagte because of the presence within it of twenty-five Boer families and forty-four prisoners.[116]

Benson's role as the principal scourge of Boer combatants in the Eastern Transvaal was taken over by Maj Gen Bruce Hamilton with a considerably larger force than Benson's at his disposal. In addition to four columns directly under his command he was able to summon the cooperation of a further eight columns as required, giving a total of 15,000 men potentially under his direction.[117] After an initial sweep to the Swazi border involving all twelve columns he applied Benson's night raiding techniques, relying as Benson did on Woolls-Sampson's intelligence skills, to considerable effect. In December 1901 and January 1902 these methods accounted for 850 Boer prisoners.[118] The development of the blockhouse system in the Eastern Transvaal continued during the remaining months of the war, further restricting Boer mobility and, by providing secure supply lines, relieving Hamilton of the encumbrance of large supply convoys such as had impeded Benson. He also had the advantage of fixed bases at Ermelo, Bethal, Carolina and Wakkerstroom. All this confronted Botha with the dilemma of dispersing his forces sufficiently to avoid capture and at the same time exercising enough control to produce concerted action. A Boer success on 4 January at Bankkop, 25 miles east of Ermelo, was marred by the death of Gen J.D. Opperman, one of Botha's most able lieutenants. In the North-Eastern Transvaal Ben Viljoen was captured on 25 January near Lydenburg. Botha retired south-eastwards to the Vryheid district in February where he eluded Bruce Hamilton's intensive operations until he was summoned to attend the meeting of the Transvaal and Free State governments in Klerksdorp on 9 and 10 April, which marked the beginning of the final peace negotiations. Compared with 87,000 Boer combatants at the start of the war there were at this time some 21,000 still in the field, of whom approximately 11,000 were in the Transvaal, 6,000 in the Free State and 4,000 in the Cape.[119] There were 37,000 prisoners of war.[120]

At Klerksdorp and the ensuing meetings of Boer delegates at Vereeniging it was Botha who argued most strongly for peace on negotiated terms. This was not out of defeatism but out of the conviction that to pursue the unequal struggle risked the extinction of the Afrikaner nation. He was supported by Schalk Burger, the acting President of the Transvaal, but for the Free State Steyn and De Wet were emphatic that there could be no question of surrender without full independence. If it proved impossible to fight on they preferred that surrender should be unconditional. Untrammelled by agreed terms this, they believed, would leave the Boers morally free to fight another day. Botha was convinced that it was essential to seek terms in order to alleviate the suffering of Boer civilians, to obtain civil rights for returning prisoners of war and to protect the rebels in the Cape Colony who had fought for the Boer cause. At the first Vereeniging meeting he was supported by Smuts, who dashed any hopes of a Boer uprising in the Cape and, crucially, by De La Rey, who despite his recent successes, concluded that the bitter end had come. The final British offer was a marginal improvement on the Middelburg terms of more than a year earlier and at the second meeting of the Boer delegates at Vereeniging the offer was accepted by a vote of fifty-four to six. After a private meeting with Botha and De La Rey before the vote was taken De Wet had reluctantly accepted the need for the leaders to present a united front and had persuaded many dissenters to support the terms.[121] The peace treaty was signed in Pretoria late in the evening on 31st May.[122]

Like other Boer leaders Botha cooperated with the British in securing the surrender of arms and he consoled his former commandos as best he could. In his farewell near Vryheid to his staff officers he said: 'It oppresses me that I can do nothing else for any of you, and that I can give you no more than thanks. One consolation remains to all of you: You can now go and rest a little. As for me, my real work only begins at this hour. The day when rest will be mine, will be the day when they lower me into the grave. The sacrifices we had to make were terrific; but we are going to see a greater South Africa.'[123]

The visit to Europe after Vereeniging of the 'glorious trio' – Botha, De Wet and De La Rey – failed in its main objective, the raising of a substantial fund to alleviate the distress of Boer women and children.

The sum of approximately £105,000* which they did raise, much of it pledged before they left South Africa,[124] was a drop in the ocean compared with the enormity of the problem. Nor were they much more successful in their meeting with Chamberlain, who refused to increase the sum of £3 million specified in the peace treaty as a 'free gift' for rehabilitation and the relief of war losses, or to give any commitment on amnesties for colonial rebels, which he regarded as a matter for the colonial governments. However, six weeks later both by letter and in the House of Commons he undertook to look sympathetically at the problems of Boer widows and orphans.[125] At the personal level the trip gave Botha the joy of reunion in Holland with his wife and children, including his youngest son who had been born in Europe. Delayed by illness Botha did not return to South Africa until December 1902, just in time to meet Chamberlain who went there to see things for himself. The delay enabled Botha to meet prominent Englishmen who had taken an interest in the war, including Sir Henry Campbell-Bannerman, the Liberal politician whose 'methods of barbarism' speech in June 1901 had earned him the gratitude of the Boers.[126]

Botha did not immediately involve himself in politics on his return. Like other war leaders he had first of all to rebuild his own life. Because Vryheid had been annexed to Natal and because of unhappy associations with the home there which had been destroyed by the British, he established a new home near Standerton on the farm Varkenspruit, renamed Rusthof (Haven of Peace). Apart from his military and political gifts he was a skilled livestock farmer and an astute businessman. He returned the £900 cheque which he received in response to a £20,000 claim for war losses, but since his land holdings were intact he was able to borrow to buy additional land in the Standerton area; by 1912 he owned 10,000 acres there. He was also able to restore his finances by acting as a commission agent and by other land deals.[127] In 1904 he bought a house in Pretoria, where he made himself available as an adviser and helper to former combatants, prisoners of war and civilians readjusting to peacetime life.[128]

Milner applied himself energetically to reconstruction, aided by his 'kindergarten' of gifted young civil servants. He did much good work in the fields of administration, agriculture, water supply and transport but his hopes of creating a predominantly British Transvaal by large-scale immigration were thwarted by economic depression. He was assailed by both English- and Dutch-speaking sections of the population demanding the replacement of Crown colony government by responsible, that is, fully representative, government. Botha, Smuts and De La Rey declined politely an invitation to serve on the nominated Legislative Council. The

---

* Approximately £3.7 million at 1990s prices.

demise of Milner's authority in South Africa was hastened by his decision to allow the Rand gold mines to import indentured Chinese labour to supplement the depleted African workforce. At a time of heightened Afrikaner national consciousness following the funeral of President Kruger in Pretoria in December 1904, Chinese labour was one of the issues providing a focus for political activity. In January 1905 Botha emerged as the leader of Het Volk (The People), a new political party dedicated to healing the rift between former Boer 'bitter-enders' and 'hands-uppers', to conciliation between Boer and Briton, and to obtaining of self-government. Portrayed in Britain as 'slavery' the Chinese labour question contributed to the defeat of Balfour's government and Campbell-Bannerman became Prime Minister of a Liberal government in December 1905. Soon afterwards he persuaded his Cabinet to grant full responsible government to the former Boer republics, and in the first election in the Transvaal in February 1907 Het Volk gained a clear majority over all other parties. Botha became Prime Minister with Smuts as his principal colleague.

The main aims of his Transvaal premiership were a continuation of the work of reconciling Afrikaans and English-speaking South Africans, the ending of Chinese labour in the mines and streamlining an overstaffed civil service while at the same time giving opportunities within it to Afrikaners. A controversial decision was the gift to King Edward VII in 1907 by the Transvaal government of the massive 3,025-carat Cullinan diamond as an addition to the Crown jewels. Overshadowing all these preoccupations were the moves towards a political union of the four self-governing colonies of South Africa, increasingly at odds as a result of diverse interests within their customs union and railway operating agreement. Botha played a leading role in the National Convention which negotiated a draft constitution, starting work in Durban in October 1908 and finishing in Cape Town in February 1909. His effectiveness in this work was enhanced by his friendship with Sir Starr Jameson,* begun when they had attended the 1907 Imperial Conference in London together.[129]

The convention rejected a federal solution for South Africa and chose a unitary constitution with the four colonies as provinces, but the degree of compromise necessary to achieve this was reflected in the choice of not one but two capitals; Pretoria and Cape Town were to be respectively the administrative and legislative capitals and, as sop to the Free State, Bloemfontein was to be the seat of the Supreme Court. The price of Union was the abandonment of any hope of extending to the rest of South Africa

---

* Prime Minister of the Cape Colony from 1904 to 1907 and as Dr Jameson, leader of the notorious Jameson Raid in 1895.

the access enjoyed by non-whites in the Cape to a qualified franchise. Botha went to London in 1909 with Lord de Villiers, the National Convention chairman, to present the draft Act of Union to Parliament. It received the royal assent as the South Africa Act in September 1909 and the Union came into being on 1 June 1910. In advance of a general election Botha was invited by the new Governor-General, Lord Gladstone,* to form a government and recruited his six-member Cabinet from the Cabinets of the four colonies. Smuts was Minister of Defence, and also took the portfolios of the Interior, and Mines. Hertzog was Minister of Justice. Botha himself, as he had done in the Transvaal government, combined the portfolio of Agriculture with the premiership. A coalition of parties under his leadership obtained a clear majority over all other parties in the first general election in September 1910, but Botha found himself without a seat, having been persuaded to abandon his safe Standerton constituency to fight the marginal Pretoria East against Sir Percy Fitzpatrick.† He was narrowly defeated but was able to find a new constituency at Losberg, to the east of Potchefstroom. In November 1911 the coalition parties merged to form the South African Party.

One of Botha's first acts as Premier was to release the Zulu chief Dinizulu, in whose cause he had gained his earliest military experience and who had been imprisoned in 1909 for his alleged complicity in a poll tax rebellion. In 1911 Botha visited Britain again for the quadrennial Imperial Conference. Highly regarded there he refused all honours, but accepted the honorary rank of general in the British Army. This third visit to Britain in four years was a touch too frequent for his critics among hardline Afrikaners, with whom reports of his attendance as a guest of King George V in court dress, including silk stockings, did not go down well.[130] This, together with the Cullinan diamond affair and his friendship with Jameson reinforced the belief among such Afrikaners that Botha was too much in thrall to Britain. Hertzog articulated their fears for the survival of their language and culture. Whereas Botha believed that both English- and Afrikaans-speaking South Africans should merge their racial identities in a common citizenship of a South Africa drawing strength from its membership of the British Empire, Hertzog advocated a 'separate stream' policy within South Africa – a sort of white cultural apartheid – and took an extreme view of the extent to which local interests should take precedence over those of the empire. His habit of speaking his mind in public put him under pressure from his

---

* The youngest son of William Ewart Gladstone.
† A prominent member of the Transvaal Opposition and formerly secretary of the Reform Committee in Johannesburg at the time of the Jameson Raid. Author of *Jock of the Bushveld.*

colleagues to resign and when it was clear that he would not, Botha himself resigned and formed a new government without him. At the 1913 annual congress of the South African Party, Christiaan de Wet led a walkout of dissidents, most of them Free Staters, as a prelude to the formation of the National Party with Hertzog as leader.

In the same year Botha faced a violent strike of white miners. The immediate cause was a petty dispute with the manager of one mine, but it arose against a background of concern about trade union recognition[131] and the high incidence of lung disease[132] in the Rand gold mines generally. Botha and Smuts intervened personally to mediate a settlement on the spot but not before lives had been lost. Early in 1914 a strike of white railway workers nearly led to a general strike. It was dealt with ruthlessly, Smuts deporting the leaders out of South African jurisdiction before the courts were aware of it.

The 'Native question' was not then, as it was to become, the predominant issue in South African politics, but the Native Land Act of 1913, which dealt with the subject of land ownership between blacks and whites, set the scene for future conflict and gave the newly formed African National Congress its first experience of political lobbying. Gandhi, then a Johannesburg advocate, negotiated with Smuts a settlement of the grievances of the large Indian community in the Transvaal and Natal, using his methods of 'passive resistance'.[133]

The 1914 rebellion, prompted by Botha's decision to accede to Britain's request for an invasion of German South West Africa (Namibia)* was essentially a bitter Afrikaner family quarrel. To avoid racial conflict Botha largely excluded English-speaking troops from the operations against the rebels, which he commanded himself, and relied on the old commando system. As a result former Boer comrades in arms were in open conflict. This caused Botha deep personal sorrow, particularly when after the rout of De Wet's rebel force at Mushroom Valley he came across the body of one of his best Boer War commandants.[134] The rebellion was over in six weeks. Apart from Beyers, who was drowned crossing the Vaal, the rebel leaders received long prison sentences but were released early, in De Wet's case after only a year, while most of the rank and file received the benefit of amnesties.

When Botha took the field for his 1915 invasion of German South West Africa his 50,000-strong force was composed more or less equally of English- and Afrikaans-speaking South Africans.[135] This brief and comparatively bloodless operation[136] in a largely desert area the size of France began on 15 April with a three-pronged attack, one from the south and two from the west. Windhoek, the capital, was captured on

---

* Radio stations there were of considerable potential value to the German Navy.

12 May and moving northwards Botha accepted the unconditional surrender of the main German force in Tsumeb on 9 July. He treated the defeated Germans leniently. Officers were allowed to live on parole in South African towns of their choice and the men were allowed to retain their arms, but not their ammunition.

The war brought no respite from party politics or personal attacks on Botha. In the 1915 general election the South African Party failed to get an absolute majority, but Botha continued in government with the support of the predominantly English Unionists. Hertzog's National Party staked its claim for the future by winning 27 of the 130 seats. Botha's workload increased considerably in 1916 when Smuts went to take command of operations in German East Africa as a lieutenant-general in the British Army. When the war ended in 1918 Botha travelled to Britain, and with Smuts – who had served as a member of the British War Cabinet – he went to the Versailles Peace Conference, as a member of the fourteen-strong British delegation. He urged the wisdom of clemency with only limited success but he was instrumental in thwarting Lloyd George's wish to treat the Kaiser as a war criminal.[137] Deneys Reitz, fresh from commanding a British infantry battalion in France, saw Botha at this time and thought that he looked 'ill and worn, for the long strain had told on him, and the knowledge that so many of his own race misunderstood his actions and looked upon him as an enemy was breaking his heart'.[138]

Having signed the Versailles Treaty, as did a reluctant Smuts, Botha returned to South Africa in August 1919. He did not long survive his return. Shortly before midnight on 26 August 1919 he died of a heart attack at the age of fifty-seven. For Smuts, who succeeded him as Prime Minister, this was a bitter personal blow and the end of a remarkable political partnership and deep personal friendship. At Botha's graveside in Pretoria he praised Botha's work for reconciliation and went on to talk about him as a friend: 'I have spoken of Louis Botha as a commander and statesman. But how can I speak of him in the greater quality of a friend? After an intimate friendship and unbroken co-operation extending over twenty one years, during which we came as close together as it is ever given to men to come, I have the right to call him the largest, most beautiful, sweetest soul of all my land and days. . . .'[139]

Notes

1. Spender, p. 181
2. Barnard, *Botha*, p. 1.
3. Spender, p. 26.
4. Engelenberg, p. 21.
5. Reitz, *No Outspan*, pp. 34–6.
6. Meintjes, *Botha*, p. 14.
7. Engelenberg, p. 35.
8. Barnard, *Botha*, p. 14; Fitzpatrick, *SA Memories*, pp. 200–1.
9. Ibid., p. 13.
10. *TH* ii, 123.
11. Breytenbach i, p. 216.
12. *TH* ii, 144; Meintjes, *Botha*, p. 32.
13. *OH* i, 123.
14. *TH* ii, 155.
15. *TH* ii, 16.
16. Barnard, *Botha*, p. 24.
17. Pakenham, p. 147.
18. Breytenbach i, p. 305.
19. *TH* ii, 220.
20. Jeans, pp. 187–96.
21. Reitz, *Commando*, p. 44.
22. Meintjes, *Botha*, p. 40 and Pakenham, p. 17.
23. *TH* ii, 316.
24. Barnard, *Botha*, p. 42.
25. *TH* ii, 317.
26. Barnard, *Botha*, p. 47.
27. Fitzpatrick, *SA Memories*, p. 153; Pemberton, p. 148.
28. *TH* ii, 456.
29. Breytenbach ii, p. 322.
30. Barnard, *Botha*, p. 47.
31. Ibid., p. 74.
32. Ibid., p. 84.
33. Ibid., p. 85.
34. Ibid., pp. 86–7.
35. Ibid., p. 96.
36. Ransford, p. 71.
37. *OH* iii, 383.
38. Reitz, *Commando*, p. 75.
39. Barnard, *Botha*, p. 101.

40. *TH* iii, 292.
41. Kemp, pp. 290–1.
42. Reitz, *Commando*, p. 79.
43. Barnard, *Botha*, p. 105.
44. Ibid., p. 110.
45. Ibid., p. 111.
46. Ibid., pp. 114–15.
47. Ibid., p. 115.
48. *TH* iii, 325–6.
49. Barnard, *Botha*, p. 118.
50. Ibid., pp. 122–3.
51. Ibid., pp. 125–7.
52. Ibid., pp. 138–9.
53. Ibid., pp. 143–4.
54. Ibid., pp. 145–6.
55. Ibid., p. 147.
56. See Chapter Eight, p. 182.
57. Barnard, *Botha*, p. 152.
58. *TH* iv, 11.
59. *TH* iv, 117.
60. Pakenham, p. 421.
61. Reitz, *Commando*, p. 103.
62. Spies and Nattrass, pp. 42–3.
63. Ibid., pp. 45–6.
64. *TH* iv, 280.
65. Barnard, *Boer Commanders*, p. 15.
66. See Chapter Four, p. 76.
67. Viljoen, p. 162.
68. *TH* iv, 437.
69. Reitz, *Commando*, p. 119.
70. *OH* iii, 392 and *TH* iv, 441.
71. *OH* iii, 396.
72. *TH* iv, 452–5; Lyttleton, pp. 238–40.
73. *TH* iv, 465.
74. Lyttleton, p. 241.
75. *TH* iv, 465–7.
76. *TH* iv, 475.
77. *TH* iv, 472.
78. Reitz, *Commando*, p. 125.
79. *OH* iii, 419.
80. Spies and Nattrass, pp. 124–33; Pakenham, pp. 470–3.
81. Barnard, *Boer Commanders*, p. 15.
82. *OH* iv, Appendix 12, p. 660.
83. *TH* v, 61–3.

84. Lt H.F. Trew, 30 November 1900, in *The Stawell News and Pleasant Creek Chronicle* of 10 January 1901.
85. See Chapter Six, pp. 116–17.
86. *TH* v, 166–9.
87. Engelenburg, pp. 64–6, quoting from a letter from Kitchener to St John Brodrick.
88. Magnus, p. 184, quoting from a letter from Kitchener to St John Brodrick dated 26 April 1901, Kitchener Papers PRO 30/57/22 Y/48.
89. Meintjes, *Botha*, p. 83; Trew, *Botha Treks*, p. 76; Maxwell, p. 79.
90. Moore, p. 5 and *OH* iv, 527.
91. *OH* iv, 125.
92. Arthur ii, p. 36.
93. *OH* iv, 203–4, *TH* v, 294–6.
94. *TH* v, 296–8.
95. Sir Henry Campbell-Bannerman on 14 June 1901 at a dinner given by the National Reform Union, see Spies, *Barbarism*, p. 9.
96. Spies, *Barbarism*, p. 361 n. 296, quoting Roberts Papers NAM 33/17, Kitchener to Roberts 28 February 1901.
97. De Wet, pp. 491–2.
98. Spies, *Barbarism*, p. 289.
99. Operative part of the proclamation quoted in full in Le May, *British Supremacy*, p. 104.
100. *TH* v, 333.
101. Moore, pp. 17–18.
102. *TH* v, 336–8.
103. *OH* iv, p. 223.
104. Moore, p. 36.
105. *TH* v, 339–40; *OH* iv, 217–18.
106. Moore, p. 44.
107. *OH* iv, 222.
108. Wilson, *Guerilla War*, p. 636.
109. Moore, pp. 86–7.
110. *TH* v, 352.
111. Moore, p. 89.
112. *TH* v, 363.
113. *TH* v, 331, 360–3.
114. *OH* v, 305.
115. *OH* v, 306–13, *TH* v, 365–76.
116. Engelenburg, p. 76, quoting Koen Brits's report of the battle.
117. *TH* v, 447.
118. *OH* iv, 379.
119. *OH* iv, 705, Appendix 20.
120. *TH* v, 57.
121. Van den Heever, p. 101, quoting the Revd John Kestell.

122. For a fuller account of the peace negotiations see Chapter Eight, pp. 204–7.
123. Engelenberg, p. 99.
124. *TH* vi, 7.
125. Spender, pp. 158–9.
126. Engelenberg, pp. 110–11.
127. Ibid., pp. 119–22.
128. Meintjes, *Botha*, p. 123.
129. Spender, p. 210.
130. Engelenburg, p. 244.
131. Walker, p. 551.
132. Spender, pp. 265–7.
133. Walker, pp. 547–9.
134. Trew, *Botha Treks*, p. 34.
135. Reitz, *Trekking On*, p. 68 n.
136. Total South African casualties were 424, of whom 113 were killed or wounded; see Spender, p. 312.
137. Engelenburg, p. 320.
138. Reitz, *Trekking On*, p. 254.
139. Engelenburg, pp. 303–4, quoting Hancock and van der Poel.

CHAPTER EIGHT

De Wet

Christiaan de Wet was the outstanding guerrilla leader of the Boer War, but he would not have been flattered by that assessment. To him the term 'guerrilla' had connotations of rebellion and outlawry and he argued that it could not properly be applied to forces fighting for the independence of their country under the orders of its legitimate government.[1] Undistinguished in appearance, he was of medium height and stockily built. He wore a short black beard streaked with grey and his dark eyes under a broad brow were those of a man seldom troubled about where his duty lay. As a military commander he was the scourge of laggards and the faint-hearted, sometimes literally when he wielded his *sjambok*.* Secretive and never popular with his men, he commanded respect because he was successful. His luck on occasions was so extraordinary that he ascribed it to the Almighty.

Christiaan Rudolph De Wet was born on the farm Leeuwkop in the Smithfield district of the Orange Free State on 7 October 1854. The De Wet family, probably of German extraction,[2] had come to the Cape in 1695 and Christiaan's branch of the family had lived in the Cape Colony until the 1840s. Sir Jacobus De Wet, the British Agent in the Transvaal in the 1890s, was a distant cousin. The family moved a number of times during Christiaan's boyhood and he had very little in the way of formal education. They relocated to the Reddersburg district in 1859 and in 1861 they moved to the farm Nieuwejaarsfontein, near what was to become the town of Dewetsdorp, named after Christiaan's father. This lay close to the Basutoland (Lesotho) border and when it became unsafe on the outbreak of the 1865 Basuto War the family went to the farm Paardekraal near Bloemfontein. De Wet married Cornelia Margaretha Kruger in 1873 when he was nineteen and she seventeen and in due course they had sixteen children. Initially, he farmed part of his father's farm, but he began to supplement his income by acting as a transport rider, moving supplies by ox-wagon mainly in connection with the Kimberley diamond diggings. On his journeys he also provided butchering services, slaughtering sheep and oxen. In the First Boer War in 1881 De Wet was among the comparatively few Free Staters to join the fight and he was one of the sixty volunteers chosen to scale Majuba in the action which led to the death of Gen Colley and humiliating defeat for the British.

* Rhinoceros-hide whip.

After the war he settled in the Rooikoppies district near Heidelberg in the Transvaal where he was elected a field-cornet. After moving on to Lydenburg in the Eastern Transvaal he was invited to stand there for election as the member of the Volksraad, and was persuaded to accept the nomination despite his declared intention of returning to the Free State. He was duly elected and fulfilled his duties by travelling to the Transvaal as necessary to attend the relatively infrequent meetings of the Volksraad.

In 1889 De Wet became a member of the Orange Free State Volksraad for the Upper Modder River ward, while retaining his membership of the Transvaal Volksraad. Despite this dual allegiance he was cool about the prospect of closer alliance between the two republics. Farming was now his main occupation, but in 1891 he lost a lot of money on unwise speculation in potato futures. In the 1895 Free State presidential election he supported the successful candidate, the young judge Marthinus Theunis Steyn, against Sir John George Fraser, a Scot who had risen to prominence in Free State politics. De Wet was determined that an 'Englishman' should not be president.[3] Unlike Fraser, Steyn saw clearly that the fate of the Free State was linked closely to that of the Transvaal and that the discovery of gold on the Witwatersrand threatened the independence of both republics. The Jameson raid, which took place shortly before the presidential election, swung the result decisively in Steyn's favour.

Shortly before the outbreak of the Second Boer War De Wet bought the horse Fleur and joined the Heilbron commando as an ordinary burgher. Fleur, a fine horse with Arab blood, was to remain with him throughout the war. On 2 October 1899 he and three of his sons were summoned to military service. The war began nine days later. Very soon he was elected Vice-Commandant of his commando. About 17 October[4] his commando descended the steep escarpment of the Drakensberg into Natal in order to join up with the Transvaal forces north of Ladysmith. He took part in the action at Rietfontein Farm against a British force, covering the retreat from Dundee of Gen Yule's column and his commando remained in the vicinity until Sunday 29 October when with other Free Staters they took up position on the right of the Boer line confronting Ladysmith. Some 7,500 Boers[5] now faced 13,000 British troops defending the town. The Free Staters were to the west of a long flat-topped kopje called Tchrengula, and the Transvaalers to the east of it in a line curving round via Pepworth Hill and Long Hill to Lombard's Nek on the east of the town. As part of Gen Sir George White's plan it was intended that a 1,000-strong column under Col Carleton should occupy Nicholson's Nek at the northern end of Tchrengula to prevent the Free Staters from checking the pursuit by Gen French's cavalry of the Boer forces expected to be dislodged by the British attack. The column set off at about 11 p.m. on Sunday night, an hour later than planned, and by 2 a.m. was to the east of the southern end of Tchrengula. Carleton accepted the advice of his guides that it was now too late to cover the remaining 2 miles to Nicholson's Nek by daybreak and he decided to take his column into a waiting position at the top of Tchrengula. As the column started its ascent his 200 pack mules panicked and stampeded, taking with them the mountain guns, heliographs, water and most of the reserve ammunition, leaving only twenty rounds per man. Despite this Carleton continued to the top and occupied the southern end of the 1½-mile long kopje. This end was liberally strewn with boulders which his troops used to construct sangars, and ruined African kraals also provided cover.

Just after sunrise De Wet's commando became aware of the British occupation of Tchrengula and with 300 men De Wet seized the undefended northern end. The British had the advantage of cover but they were short of ammunition and they gradually gave way under the impact of relentless and accurate Boer rifle fire. At 8 a.m. De Wet was reinforced by the arrival from the north-east of about 400 Johannesburg police under Commandant van Dam. By around 1 p.m. most of the British force had withdrawn to the southern extremity of the kopje out of sight of a small group of three officers and eight or ten men who stayed behind and believed themselves to be covering a general retirement from the kopje.[6] Having reached the point where they thought they could do no more they raised a white handkerchief, and when that proved ineffective, a white towel. This was seen by some of the British at the end of the kopje and a message was relayed to Carleton as the Boers came forward to accept the surrender; he ordered the ceasefire to be sounded and capitulated. De Wet counted 817 prisoners as they filed past him.[7] *The Times History* attests to the consideration with which they were treated and to the kindness shown to the wounded.[8] White's main operation to the east of Tchrengula had gone wrong from the start. At 11.30 a.m. he gave the order to retire and the British force was saved from disaster as it began to stream back to Ladysmith only by the determined covering fire of the artillery and by Joubert's refusal to sanction pursuit.[9] That decision caused De Wet to mutter angrily as he witnessed this lost opportunity – 'Los jou ruiters; los jou ruiters.' (Release your horsemen; release your horsemen).[10]

De Wet's success at Nicholson's Nek was immediately recognised by Steyn who requested him to go to the western front with the rank of *vecht-generaal** in command of the Free State commandos serving with Cronjé. He was reluctant to leave his Heilbron commando but Steyn persuaded him and he arrived at Magersfontein on 16 December, five days after the battle there in which Cronjé had repulsed Lord Methuen's force. De Wet admired Cronjé's courage but he disagreed with him on tactics. The old

---

* Literally combat-general.

general refused to allow him and De la Rey to take 1,500 men to attack Methuen's railway communications south of the Orange River,[11] but agreed later in the month to their taking 700 men and 2 guns to blow up a train immediately in Methuen's rear. The operation, which took place on the night of 4 January 1900, was a fiasco. Most of an unwilling force melted away on the road, the remainder arrived just after the train had passed, the guns lost their way and the burghers with the dynamite fled before the track could be blown up.[12] When De la Rey went south to Colesberg on 7 January De Wet succeeded him as second in command of the combined Transvaal and Free State forces at Magersfontein. He warned Cronjé repeatedly, but to no avail, that he would be outflanked if he stayed there and he became increasingly concerned about the presence of women in the laager.[13]

Early in February a demonstration by Hector MacDonald's Highland Brigade at Koedoesberg Drift on the Riet River suggested to Cronjé, as it was intended to, that Lord Roberts was planning an advance on Kimberley by a route to the west of Magersfontein. MacDonald had retired after being opposed by De Wet and Andries Cronjé* between 5 and 8 February, and on the 11th Roberts's forces began to concentrate at Ramdam, some twenty miles south of Modder River, in preparation for his great flank march on Bloemfontein. From reports reaching Cronjé he assumed that an attack was to be made on Fauresmith to the south-east. He sent De Wet with 450 men to do what he could to oppose it, followed up by Andries Cronjé with a further 325 men the next day. Commandant Lubbe with 400 men was already in the vicinity.

French's cavalry division was the first to move out eastwards from Ramdam on the 12th towards the Riet River, which at that point flowed in a north-westerly direction and was fordable both at Waterval Drift and at De Kiel's Drift, about five miles upstream. After a feint at Waterval Drift, where the Boers had concentrated early that morning, French crossed at De Kiel's Drift later in the day, reinforcing the impression that he was going to Fauresmith via Koffiefontein, in the vicinity of which De Wet's forces spent the night. The next day, when De Wet saw the cavalry division begin to advance northwards on a 5-mile front he realised that they were bound not for Koffiefontein but for the Modder River and he sent an urgent dispatch to Cronjé warning him that a British force of 40,000 to 50,000 was moving in the direction of Paardeberg† and urging him to get out of the way. When the dispatch rider returned he reported that Cronjé had rebuked him for his faint-heartedness and told him to go back and shoot the British and catch them when they ran.[14] Whatever De

---

* Piet Cronjé's younger brother.

† The number was nearer 30,000.

Wet intended to convey to Cronjé – and the figure of 40,000 to 50,000 comes from his own account – it appears from other sources that Cronjé gained the impression that the number was 5,000, which would explain his contemptuous response.[15]

By the evening of 15 February 1900 the long period of stalemate on the Modder River had come to end. Jacobsdal was in British occupation, French had relieved Kimberley and a shaken Cronjé was about to start trekking eastwards by moonlight in the hope of escaping to Bloemfontein. For his part De Wet had struck a blow which could well have impaired Roberts's chances of preventing Cronjé's escape. Faced with the sheer size of Roberts's force, on the 13th De Wet had opted for discretion as the better part of valour. He remained out of sight with his 350 burghers, awaiting an opportunity to make an assault on the British rear. The 9th Division crossed at Waterval Drift on the 14th and was followed by a supply column comprising some 200 wagons and 3,000 cattle, which remained on the north bank during the morning of the 15th to allow the cattle to rest and graze while the 9th Division continued its advance. De Wet attacked the convoy at about 8.45 a.m.[16] The 200 defenders – reinforced later by mounted infantry and a field battery – held their own, but when they tried to get the wagons away De Wet's men opened fire on the cattle which stampeded towards the Boers. Further British and Boer reinforcements arrived during the day, by the end of which it was clear to Roberts that he could spare neither the troops nor the time to recover the convoy without endangering the momentum of his advance. He decided that he must abandon the convoy, believing that for him his troops would make the strenuous efforts required of them on reduced rations. The next morning the Boers were greatly surprised to find that the British had gone. In one day's fighting De Wet had deprived Roberts of 170 wagons, 150,000 men's rations, 30,000 forage rations and 500 slaughter cattle.[17] In addition he took 40 prisoners and 1 gun.

Having seen the booty on its way to Edenburg De Wet set off in the direction of Paardeberg but he was diverted by the opportunity of capturing an isolated pocket of fifty-eight British troops. Then, having learnt of Cronjé's eastward trek, he went to Koffiefontein to rendezvous with Philip Botha, and with a combined force of 300 men[18] they set out for Paardeberg early in the morning of 18 February. From far away they heard the thunder of bombardment as the battle of Paardeberg began at about 7 a.m. Having got within 6 miles by 4.30 p.m. they saw Cronjé's laager perched above the far bank of the Modder River and surrounded by British troops. Between them and the laager lay the farm Stinkfontein on the right and a hill, afterwards known as Kitchener's Kopje, on the left, both lightly held by the British. While Philip Botha seized the farm De Wet occupied the kopje, which lay 2½ miles south-east of the laager. During the night his men dragged up a Krupp gun and a pom-pom. Under covering fire from these weapons the next day commandants Froneman and Potgieter with 100 men were able to gallop out of Cronjé's laager and through the British lines, but Cronjé would not abandon his wagons and womenfolk in order to escape with the remainder of his force. De Wet was able to resist attempts to dislodge him from his commanding position on Kitchener's Kopje until the 21st when he made his escape while the British were distracted by a skirmish with a force under Andries Cronjé. Boer reinforcements were now arriving from Natal and elsewhere bringing the total Boer strength outside Cronjé's laager to 3,500. On 23 February De Wet joined with other commanders in an unsuccessful attempt to retake Kitchener's Kopje and all the ridges between it and Koedoesrand on the north bank. After this failure they abandoned any hope of rescuing Cronjé and in a final attempt to avert his defeat De Wet sent a message to him via the intrepid scout Capt Danie Theron, who on 25 February crossed the British lines and swam the swollen Modder River. He tried to persuade Cronjé to fight his way out to a pre-arranged rendezvous, but Cronjé was unable to raise enough support for the venture among his burghers and Theron made his way back to De Wet. Cronjé surrendered on 27 February with nearly 4,000 men and the dejected Boers outside the laager withdrew to Poplar Grove, 9 miles upstream.

Following the death of Ignatius Ferreira in a gun accident on 19 February, De Wet was appointed acting Chief Commandant of the Free State forces. He had no illusions about the devastating effect on Boer prospects and morale of Cronjé's surrender but he was determined to fight on. While Roberts rested his troops De Wet consolidated his commandos at Poplar Grove, where the Boer positions straddled the river extending outwards for about ten miles on either side. The Boer strength, mostly Free Staters with some Transvaalers under De la Rey, was about 5,000.[19] The British attacked from about 7 a.m. on 7 March and under threat of being outflanked by the cavalry the Boers began to retreat along the whole of the front south of the river at 11 a.m.[20] Earlier that morning President Kruger had arrived to exhort the burghers and he had had to be bundled away quickly for his own safety. As the British advanced on the north bank the Boers on that side of the river joined the retreat, which could not be stemmed by De Wet or even Kruger whose carriage was overtaken by fleeing burghers. Casualties were little more than fifty on each side, neither of whom could take satisfaction from the results of the action. The Boers fought a more determined action on 10 March 20 miles further on at Abraham's Kraal and Driefontein, with higher casualties on both sides, but it delayed the British for no more than a day.[21] Despite extensive defences prepared by De Wet on the outskirts of Bloemfontein the city fell to Roberts, with little resistance, on 13 March.

After the fall of Bloemfontein the seat of the Free State government moved to Kroonstad where on 17 March 1900 there took place an historic *krygsraad* presided over by Steyn and attended by fifty to sixty officers of both republics including Kruger, Piet Joubert and De la Rey. In addition to De Wet the Free State generals present were Philip Botha, Froneman and A.P. Cronjé.* Two important decisions were taken, firstly, to dispense in future with the encumbrance of wagon trains and to rely solely on mounted men and, secondly, to tighten up on discipline, especially in the matters of bogus sick certificates and absence without leave. Shortly before this De Wet had sent home his demoralised commandos for two weeks on the assumption that Roberts would need to rest his troops in Bloemfontein. Challenged about this decision by Joubert he replied, 'I cannot catch a hare, General, with unwilling dogs.'[22] He was vindicated when most of the burghers returned on 25 March invigorated by their respite and with their fighting spirit restored.

Within ten days De Wet had given a further boost to their morale by taking nearly 1,000 British prisoners in two separate actions. On the evening of 28 March he set out from Brandfort with 1,600 men and 7 guns with the intention of attacking the pumping station for most of Bloemfontein's water supply which lay 21 miles east of the city on the left bank of the Modder near Sannah's Post. To throw the British off the scent he moved off in a north-easterly direction towards Winburg, misleading his own men in the process since he had resolved in Kroonstad that in future he would keep his plans to himself.[23] He soon turned south and the next day learnt from scouts, firstly, that Sannah's Post was defended by only 200 men and, secondly, that Gen Olivier who had come up from Stormberg with 5,000 men was closing in on Thaba 'Nchu, where Gen Broadwood with a 1,800-strong mounted column had been distributing copies of Roberts's proclamation of 15 March, which offered burghers the right to return to their farms if they surrendered their weapons and took an oath of neutrality. De Wet resolved both to seize the waterworks and to oppose Broadwood when he returned to Bloemfontein via Sannah's Post. At the same time he demonstrated his insistence on tougher discipline by reducing a commandant to the ranks for defying the Kroonstad embargo on wagons.

After an overnight march his force reached Sannah's Post at about 4 a.m. on 31 March in two parts. His brother Piet De Wet commanded the larger part, placed to the east of the Modder, comprising 1,200 men and the guns, while De Wet himself commanded 400 men placed on either side of the drift where the road from Thaba 'Nchu to Bloemfontein

* A.P. Cronjé of Winburg, not to be confused with Andries (A.P.J.) Cronjé, the younger brother of Piet Cronjé.

crossed Koorn Spruit, a tributary of the Modder lying 2½ miles to the west of it, and joining it 5 miles to the north. The plan was for the eastern force to drive Broadwood's column into the Koorn Spruit drift which, lying in a 15-ft deep hollow, was invisible from the waterworks.[24] Immediately to the south of the Bloemfontein road was the embankment of a partially constructed new railway with the incomplete buildings of Sannah's Post station lying about three-quarters of a mile east of Koorn Spruit.

Shortly before dawn De Wet learnt that Broadwood had left Thaba 'Nchu for Bloemfontein the previous night and daylight revealed his bivouac on the west bank of the Modder. Piet De Wet opened fire at 6.20 a.m. prompting the rapid departure towards Koorn Spruit of Broadwood's transport, followed by mounted men and two batteries of horse artillery. De Wet's men in the spruit allowed the leading transport to cross, enjoining silence under pain of death. Some wagons were allowed down to the drift but subsequent arrivals were relieved of their drivers and left on the bank. As troops arrived they were disarmed – De Wet commented later that his hasty temper was sorely tried by his burghers' constant request for instructions.[25] The first battery was captured but one of its officers was able to warn the following battery, which retired under a hail of Boer fire towards the station buildings, where it came into action at 8 a.m. Broadwood was eventually able to extract the greater part of his force by about 11.15 a.m. by crossing Koorn Spruit to the south. He had lost 159 men killed and wounded; 421 men were taken prisoner and he left behind 7 guns and 83 wagons laden with stores.[26] It was three weeks before a British force under Ian Hamilton was able to recapture the waterworks. Until then Bloemfontein had to rely on its tainted wells for drinking water, a factor which aggravated the typhoid epidemic, already taking a heavy toll of British troops in the city.[27]

The day after his success De Wet set off with a small party to reconnoitre in the direction of Dewetsdorp to the south-east. Learning of the presence in the town of a small British force without guns he sent back to Piet De Wet for reinforcements and himself gathered up 110 burghers who had returned to their farms in response to Roberts's proclamation. The British contingent in Dewetsdorp formed part of Gen Gatacre's 3rd Division and he had sent them there in response to Roberts's order to take the town if it could be done without casualties, but after Sannah's Post Roberts ordered its immediate withdrawal. The 500-strong force was commanded by Capt McWhinnie of the Royal Irish Rifles and comprised three companies of infantry and two of mounted infantry. When De Wet learnt on 2 April of its withdrawal he shadowed it by advancing on a parallel course in an adjacent valley to the north until it reached Mostert's Hoek, a horseshoe-shaped ridge about five miles south-east of Reddersburg. By the morning of the 3rd reinforcements had brought De Wet's strength up to about 2,000 men and 3 Krupp guns.[28] McWhinnie was able to hold the ridge that day and in the evening sent a message to British forces near the railway, 20 miles to the west, asking for reinforcements. The Boers carried the eastern end of the ridge the following morning and, surrounded on all sides, the British force surrendered. The Boers took 470 prisoners. De Wet found it incomprehensible that the British, with substantial forces nearby, had not come to the aid of their troops at both Sannah's Post and Mostert's Hoek, but he regarded the failure in the second case as the more culpable.[29] Roberts apparently agreed and Gatacre, his record already blemished by his Black Week defeat at Stormberg, was sent home.

De Wet, instead of seizing the opportunity to wreck Roberts's railway communication to the south or to invade the Cape Colony, now allowed his judgement to be swayed by his emotions. While he had no love for the British he respected them as opponents, but he despised those Cape and Natal colonials who were prepared to fight with the British 'for five shillings a day' against their fellow South Africans.[30] Learning that a force of colonials under Col Dalgety was in the small town of Wepener near the Basuto border, De Wet decided to take the town and by 4 April had assembled a force of around 6,000. But the 1,850-strong British force, consisting mostly of men from Brabant's Horse and the Cape Mounted Rifles, had entrenched itself skilfully in a 7-mile circle of hills outside the town on the Free State side of the Caledon River. Surrounded on all sides, its spirited defence kept the Boers at bay until 25 April when, fearing the arrival of British reinforcements, De Wet withdrew his force, having wasted three weeks on the siege of an unimportant town.

Roberts started his advance northwards from Bloemfontein on 3 May 1900. First De la Rey and then Louis Botha joined the Free Staters in opposing him, but with his 38,000 men and 100 guns there was little that 8,000 Boers with 20 guns[31] could do to stop him and, after a brief encounter on the Sand River, he entered Kroonstad on 12 May. Pausing there for 10 days, he covered the remaining 85 miles to the Transvaal without opposition, crossing the Vaal on 27 May. The Free State government chose successively Lindley, Heilbron and Frankfort as its new capital before being forced into a peripatetic existence for the rest of the war. The governments of both republics had decided that the Free State forces should remain in the Free State even if the British should advance into the Transvaal. This accorded with De Wet's wishes as he recognised the importance of harrying the enemy in the rear as well as opposing them in front.[32] It also meant that he was able to concentrate his energies in the cause he held most dear. Zealous as he was in the interests of both republics he was essentially a son of the Free State and he was passionate in his determination that it should remain independent.

Roberts occupied Johannesburg at the end of May and Pretoria on 5 June. The speed of his advance left his extended lines of communication dangerously exposed and the Free State forces, with a total strength at this time of around 8,000,[33] were not slow to exploit the advantage. On 31 May Piet de Wet took 500 prisoners when Lt Col B. Spragge, commanding the 13th Imperial Yeomanry, allowed his force to be surrounded by 2,000 Boers outside Lindley, effectively ending the career of Gen Colvile, who was told by Roberts that 'he might return to England'.[34] Four days later Christiaan de Wet took 160 prisoners and captured 56 wagons at Zwavelkrans near Heilbron. On 7 June, splitting his force into three, he attacked a 30-mile stretch of railway line north of Kroonstad. While Commandant Steenkamp overcame the small British garrison and captured stores at Vredefort Road Station to the north of him and Gen Froneman blew up the Rhenoster River bridge to the south and took 500 prisoners, De Wet took 200 prisoners and captured stores worth £100,000*[35] at Roodewal (Rooiwal) Station. The haul included a large supply of ammunition, together with winter clothing and mail for Roberts's army. What could not be taken away was burnt, but not before De Wet had given permission both to his own men and to the British prisoners to help themselves to the contents of the mailbags.[36] These depredations prompted Roberts to send Kitchener to restore control and he narrowly avoided capture when De Wet attacked a construction train in which he was travelling on 14th June. The series of attacks on the railway ended on 21 June with another three-pronged attack, this time only partially successful. While De Wet and Froneman cut the line to the north and south of him Olivier was repulsed at Honing Spruit.

De Wet's railway exploits had raised Boer morale, both in the Free State and the Transvaal, from the low point to which it had sunk as a result of Roberts's successes and Buller's breakthrough from Natal, but they also made Roberts determined to achieve the control that still eluded him in the North-Eastern Free State. Following his proclamation of 28 May annexing the Orange Free State to the British Crown, it had been renamed the Orange River Colony. The Boers regarded the annexation as a constitutional fiction, with some justification as the government of the republic continued in being until the end of the war, although from henceforth it was continually on the move. The British effectively conceded the point at the end of the war when it was agreed that the Vereeniging peace treaty should be signed by the Boer leaders on behalf of the two republics.[37] At the end of June President Steyn moved to Bethlehem which became the focus of British operations in the Free State.

* Approximately £4 million at 1990s prices.

For most of June 1900 Boer forces, growing with new arrivals to about 4,000, laid siege to Lindley, which had changed hands seven times between 17 May and 1 June.[38] It was now occupied by a force under Maj Gen Arthur Paget, who had little difficulty keeping the Boers at bay. De Wet arrived around 21 June and had to deal with a challenge to his leadership. This arose out of uncertainty about the position of Marthinus Prinsloo, a veteran commander who had resigned as Chief Commandant of the commandos guarding the Drakensberg and had been succeeded by Paul Roux, a chaplain before he became a *vecht-generaal*. To De Wet's surprise, because he had no illusions about his popularity, his position as Chief Commandant of the Free State forces was confirmed overwhelmingly in an unofficial ballot of officers in the vicinity.[39] The siege of Lindley was raised when reinforcements arrived under Maj Gen R.A.P. Clements, who set off with Paget's force towards Bethlehem on 2 July. When he realised that the town was under threat De Wet went there to organise its defence and to arrange for the evacuation of the President and of women and children to the Wittebergen, a mountain range about fifteen miles to the south-west. His force of 7,000 was well placed and was only slightly smaller than the combined forces of Clements and Paget, but they had 18 guns to his 7 or 8,[40] and other British forces were on the way. The Boers held out for two days and retired on 7 July to the Wittebergen, leaving Bethlehem to be occupied by the British.

The Wittebergen and the adjoining Roodebergen formed a 75-mile mountainous horseshoe enclosing a fertile valley to the south, in which lay the town of Fouriesburg. Known as the Brandwater Basin after one of the rivers which drained it, the valley's southern boundary, about forty miles long, lay on the Caledon River on the Basutoland border. It was in the mountainous ramparts guarding this haven that virtually the whole of the Free State forces now concentrated. In the meantime, the arrival of further columns brought the British strength in the area to around 20,000 under the overall command of Lt Gen Sir Archibald Hunter, who as Chief of Staff to Sir George White had been the mainstay of the British resistance during the siege of Ladysmith. Within days De Wet and others realised that the Brandwater Basin was a trap from which there would be no escape even if the Boers succeeded in holding the mountain passes against a much superior force. At a *krygsraad* presided over by Steyn it was decided to divide the Free State force into three parts and break out before the British were able to secure the passes. It was intended that the first division under De Wet himself – accompanied by the President, Piet de Wet, Philip Botha and 2,600 men – should leave on 15 July in a north-westerly direction towards Kroonstad and that the remainder should leave the following day, the second division under Assistant Chief Commandant Paul Roux in a south-westerly direction towards Bloemfontein, and the third under Gen Crowther to the north, leaving a small contingent under Prinsloo to hold the passes.

As planned, De Wet's column, accompanied by 400 wagons, broke out though Slabbert's Nek after sunset on 15 July and in a tight, disciplined formation passed undetected within a mile of a British camp; but to have left the others to follow independently was a fatal error. No sooner had they lost De Wet's unifying influence than leadership squabbles broke out and, in an election of questionable validity, Prinsloo took the place of Roux as Assistant Chief Commandant by a bare margin. The 61-year-old Prinsloo had made his name as a fighting man in two Basuto Wars in the 1860s and had served for many years as a member of the Free State Volksraad. Having already resigned one command on the grounds of age and ill health he was not up to the task now confronting him. Under his ineffectual leadership the escape plan was abandoned and an attempt was made to defend the passes. By 24 July the British had captured the main passes at Retief's Nek and Slabbert's Nek and Fouriesburg was captured on 26 July. Prinsloo surrendered three days later, and by 9 August 4,314 men had surrendered. In addition to capturing three guns, including two British guns lost at Sannah's Post, together with large numbers of cattle, sheep and good horses, the British destroyed 2,000,000 rounds of ammunition.[41] Apart from De Wet's column, approximately 1,500 Boers escaped, with 7 guns. Among the officers who escaped were Froneman and Olivier.

The escape of De Wet and President Steyn from the Brandwater Basin marked the start of a new phase in their relationship and in the British attitude towards them. Henceforth the seat of the Free State government was wherever Steyn was, and for most of the time for the rest of the war he was with De Wet on commando. De Wet had a profound admiration for the younger man and Steyn had complete confidence in De Wet as a military leader. As a pair they were a much sought after prize in the eyes of the British. The Free State, having entered the war as a reluctant junior partner of the Transvaal, had by now become much the more determined of the two republics to fight it out to the bitter end. Whenever the Transvaal wobbled Steyn stiffened its resolve. Louis Botha called him 'the soul of the war'.[42] De Wet set the example of what could be achieved by determined military resistance. Neither man could have thought that there was any serious prospect of defeating the might of the British Empire, but both were motivated by faith in the justice of their cause and an uncompromising view of where their duty lay. They were not alone among Boer leaders in their resolve. De la Rey in the Transvaal and Hertzog in the Free State were also implacable 'bitter-enders', but the British believed that if they could capture Steyn and De Wet Boer resistance would crumble.

Although his aggressive instincts were unimpaired and he seldom missed an opportunity of inflicting damage on the British if he thought the odds were right, De Wet's main preoccupation from now on was to survive in order to fight another day. Over the next six months his talent for survival was put to the test again and again in a series of 'De Wet hunts' in which at various times the British deployed a large number of generals and many thousands of men. The first De Wet hunt began as Steyn and De Wet moved away from Slabbert's Nek with 2,600 men and 400 of the wagons which were anathema to De Wet. With them also were two young men who were to provide De Wet with the intelligence which helped him to outwit the British during this first hunt. Each in command of a corps of scouts, they were the 29-year-old Danie Theron, who had distinguished himself by getting through the British lines both into and out of Cronjé's laager at Paardeberg, and the 22-year-old Gideon Scheepers, who was later executed by the British in the Cape Colony. Despite the encumbrance of the wagons, De Wet was able to outdistance a pursuing column led by Broadwood, bent on avenging his humiliation at Sannah's Post, and by the morning of 19 July he was about thirty miles to the north and slightly west of Lindley. Here, as he was about join Steyn for breakfast in the farmhouse of C.C. Wessels, his brother Piet approached him to ask if he still saw any chance of continuing the struggle. 'Are you mad?' shouted De Wet, turning away to enter the house as Piet de Wet rode off to surrender.[43] It is said that after his brother surrendered De Wet ordered his men, if they saw him, to shoot him down like a mad dog.[44]

Evading Broadwood and a second column, under Col M.O. Little, De Wet crossed the railway line on the night of the 21st. Moving on towards the Vaal River he reached the hills between Vredefort and Reitzburg on 24 July, having travelled the 150 miles from Slabbert's Nek in 9 days. Here he established his main laager on the farm Rhenosterpoort, commanding a Vaal crossing point at Schoeman's Drift, and protected to the east by a 20-mile line of hills running south to the Rhenoster River. For a while he rested in this relatively secure position, gathering in supplies and increasing his strength to about 3,500[45] by persuading burghers who had taken the oath of neutrality to rejoin the struggle. During this time he learnt of Prinsloo's surrender in the Brandwater Basin and of the escape from it of Froneman and others. Hertzog was dispatched to make contact with them.

From the beginning of August Kitchener began to implement Roberts's plan of forming a semicircle to the south of De Wet with the intention of driving him across the Vaal into the arms of Methuen. Broadwood's and Little's columns were joined by forces under major-generals Charles Knox and Fitzroy Hart, to bring the total British strength to about 11,000.[46] North of the river Methuen, with a force of approximately 3,000, Maj Gen C.E. Knox was ordered to watch the Vaal from Scandinavia Drift to Lindeque Drift 45 miles downstream and 30 miles upstream respectively of Schoeman's Drift, the crossing nearest to De

Wet's laager. To the north forces under Smith-Dorrien, Ian Hamilton, Baden-Powell and Carrington were ready to support him, bringing the total potential strength ranged against De Wet on that side of the river to about 18,000 men.

De Wet had to choose between attempting to break through the cordon to the south or to cross the river. The first choice would have meant persuading his Free Staters to abandon their precious wagons, and the second required him to overcome their reluctance to leave their own country and enter the Transvaal. He chose the second course and induced his men to go over the river by sending the wagons ahead of them. On 6 August he traversed the river by Schoeman's Drift unopposed, Methuen having been ordered away by Kitchener to Scandinavia Drift. When Methuen learnt of the crossing he set off in pursuit and engaged a Boer rearguard at Tygerfontein, but De Wet eluded him and progressed north-eastwards through the complex of hills on the north bank of the Vaal. Kitchener moved to head him off at Lindeque Drift in the belief that he would attempt to negotiate the river there and get back into the Free State. De Wet encouraged him in this belief by sending Theron on a feint to the south-east, but he himself turned north to the Gatsrand, a range of hills south of the railway line from Potchefstroom to Johannesburg. He met up there with Gen Liebenberg who was holding the passes for him and Methuen arrived on 10 August just in time to see De Wet disappearing through the Gatsrand. After a night march De Wet crossed the railway line early on 11 August, wrong-footing Smith-Dorrien who had been waiting for him north of the Gatsrand, and whom he now left behind him. He turned westwards for about twenty miles and then headed north to the Magaliesberg, the formidable mountain barrier west of Pretoria.

So far, De Wet had enjoyed two advantages over the vastly superior British forces pursuing him. He could generally rely on the support of the farmers he encountered and he moved faster. He himself said, 'We knew very well that an Englishman cannot keep up with a Boer on the march, and that if he tries to do so, he soon finds that his horses and oxen can go no further.'[47] An American correspondent with Broadwood's column estimated that De Wet seldom failed to cover 25 miles a day to his pursuers' 20 miles.[48] However, with the Magaliesberg looming ahead of De Wet the hunt should now have ended, with the capture of Steyn and himself. Of the three passes across the mountains Commando Nek to the east was held by Baden-Powell, Ian Hamilton had been instructed to secure Olifants Nek, south of Rustenburg, and Methuen was hurrying to prevent De Wet crossing via Magato Nek, west of Rustenburg, or alternatively going round the Magaliesberg to join De la Rey on the Elands River. But Ian Hamilton was too late and on 14 August De Wet crossed the Magaliesberg at Olifants Nek. Writing home three days later

Capt Frank Maxwell, later to be Kitchener's ADC, expressed his admiration for De Wet:

De Wet is still at large, though we presume Hamilton is after him. He is a wonderful man. How he managed to escape us is extraordinary . . . [he] must have been trekking at the rate of nearly thirty miles a day, and fast, too, and always harassed by one force or another of us, and yet this wonderful fellow managed to clear away, losing only one gun and fourteen waggons [sic] to Methuen (out of some 300 waggons), while we, with mostly mule waggons, had to leave them behind hopelessly tired out. Nor did we see a single dead ox on the road. Ask our oxen to do twenty miles a day, and they are dead beat in three days.[49]

To avoid British troops who were coming over the mountain to the west De Wet followed the Pretoria road eastwards for 30 miles to Commando Nek, where he issued a tongue-in-cheek invitation to Baden-Powell to surrender, hoping to ascertain the strength of his force. Believing that he would be unable to force the pass before the British caught up with him from the west he turned northwards and 15 miles north of the Magaliesberg camped at Zoutpans Drift on the Crocodile River.[50] Here he split his troops. Steyn set out to meet President Kruger and, after travelling through the bushveld with a small escort, found him at Machadodorp in the Eastern Transvaal on 25 August. Commandant Steenkamp, with most of the force and what was left of the convoy, went north and De Wet himself set out to return to the Free State with 200 men. With him also were Gen Philip Botha, Commandant Michal Prinsloo and Gideon Scheepers with his corps of thirty scouts.

When he returned to the Magaliesberg on 19 August De Wet found himself threatened on three sides by British forces near Wolhuter's Kop and, assuming that the main passes were guarded, he decided to climb where only a goat track led over the mountain, a path considered too steep even for cattle.[51] An African whom he questioned said it was a long time since a man had crossed there, but confirmed that baboons walked across. That was enough for De Wet and almost in sight of the British he and his men led their horses up the precipitous ascent and over the mountain.[52] The first De Wet hunt effectively ended at this point. *The Times History* described his success in evading capture during the five-week hunt as being due 'partly to the mistakes of his adversaries, but also in great measure to his own fiery rapidity of decision, his mother wit in seeing how to turn an awkward situation and his knowledge of human nature, both Boer and British'.[53] Having got across the Magaliesberg De Wet marched by night, evading a British force under Hart, and made his way to the Gatsrand where he met up with Danie Theron. On 22 August he crossed the Vaal and returned to the site of his former camp at Rhenosterpoort.

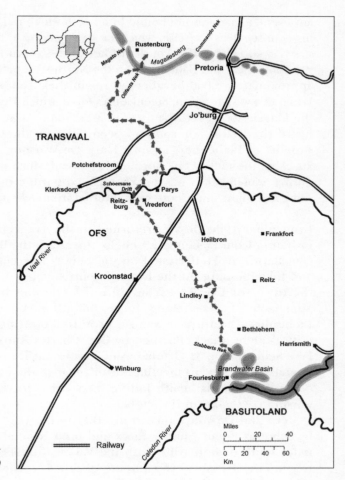

The first De Wet hunt –
July to August 1900

Having returned to the Free State in August 1900 De Wet went back briefly across the Vaal to obtain supplies of dynamite in Potchefstroom. While there he was photographed holding the 200th Mauser rifle to have been repaired after retrieval from a British bonfire. Leaving to Scheepers and his small band of scouts the task of attacking the railway line north of Kroonstad he brought back under his supervision the Vrede and Harrismith commandos, who had escaped from the Brandwater Basin under Piet Fourie, Froneman and others, and he set about the task of persuading to rejoin the struggle those burghers who, in response to Roberts's proclamation, had surrendered their arms and taken an oath of neutrality. De Wet had no moral qualms about inducing these men to break their oaths, arguing that Roberts had reneged on his promise to respect their property and to allow them to remain peacefully on their farms and that, in

191

any event, a man was not bound by an oath which ran counter to his duty to his country. This exercise, which he delegated to three of his lieutenants, was very successful. Piet Fourie in the North-Eastern Free State, Hertzog in the South-West and Badenhorst in the North-West between them persuaded approximately 3,000 burghers to rejoin their compatriots in the field.[54] While this was going on, Steenkamp's force, which De Wet had left north of the Magaliesberg, returned to the Free State. At about this time De Wet heard that Danie Theron had been killed in the Gatsrand, fighting in support of Liebenberg against Hart. De Wet now joined Scheepers in attacking the railway line north of Kroonstad which was cut in many places during September. It was quickly repaired but the British virtually stopped using it at night, and troops were diverted from field operations to protect it.

In October 1900 De Wet returned to the Transvaal in response to an invitation from Liebenberg to help him attack the British garrison under Gen Barton in Frederikstad on the railway line between Potchefstroom and Johannesburg. At the head of approximately 1,500 men he invested the town for five days from 20 to 25 October but withdrew on the approach of a relieving force, blaming the lack of success on Liebenberg's failure to send a promised contingent in support of a critical night attack. Pursued by Gen Charles Knox he returned to the Free State, but on 31 October went back to the Transvaal to meet Steyn in Ventersdorp after his meeting with Kruger in the Eastern Transvaal. The old president, his health failing, had sailed for Europe in the Dutch warship *Gelderland* on 19 October.

Steyn and De Wet returned together to the Free State, pursued again by columns under Charles Knox and on 5 November camped about six miles south of Bothaville, with the Valsch River between them and the town. The British were camped 10 miles to the north of the town. Without the scouting skills of Theron and Scheepers to warn him De Wet allowed himself to be surprised by a small British force early the following morning while his 800 men were asleep. Those who could get away fled in panic, many leaving their saddles behind. While De Wet tried to rally those who had decamped, about 150 men who had become separated from their horses took up position in a walled garden and held the attackers at bay. They were supported by a small number of men in a stone pigsty to the west and a house to the east. The British staff unwisely occupied a small house 120 yd to the north, the interior of which was visible from the walled garden and in which Col Le Gallais was killed and Col Ross seriously wounded. At about 9.30 a.m. after the arrival of British reinforcements and the start of a bayonet charge the Boers in the garden surrendered. As a result of this action De Wet lost all his guns, a fact which he accepted with equanimity as there was no more ammunition for them. He sent most of his men back to their farms to rest and re-equip.

The events which led to the second De Wet hunt had their origin in a meeting on the farm Syferfontein in the Western Transvaal where Steyn, on his way back to the Free State from seeing Kruger and accompanied by Louis Botha, met De la Rey and Smuts at the end of October. Here the Boer leaders decided to extend the guerrilla war to the Cape Colony and Natal where it could be pursued without provoking the destruction of the countryside – it would have been politically disastrous for Britain to destroy the farms of Boer sympathisers in her own colonies.[55] Steyn had been warned before the outbreak of war by Jan Hofmeyr, the leader of Cape Afrikanerdom, that the republics should not rely on the support of their colonial kinsmen[56] but the Boers still hoped, and the British feared, that the appearance of commandos in the Cape would at least provoke local uprisings.[57]

After the Bothaville setback Steyn and De Wet decided that the time was ripe to carry out the invasion project. Roberts was busy clearing his desk before returning to England and Kitchener was visiting Natal and Harrismith. Kritzinger and Scheepers were already in the Southern Free State with small forces, awaiting an opportunity to cross the Orange River, and a great gathering of the Afrikaner Bond was due to take place at Worcester near Cape Town on 6 December. It was hoped that this would be set aflame by the news that commandos were at hand. With 200 men De Wet and Steyn crossed into the North-Eastern Free State and arrived at the Korannaberg, where reinforcements brought the strength up to 1,500 men with 1 Krupp gun, for which there were a bare 16 rounds of ammunition. They were also joined here by the Revd J.D. Kestell, a Dutch Reformed Church minister of British descent who was to become a close friend to both of them. On 15 November they told the assembled burghers of the plan to invade the Cape and set off on the 120-mile journey south to the Orange River.[58]

Immediately ahead of them lay a line of British forts, backed by a series of hills, between Bloemfontein, Thaba 'Nchu and Ladybrand. Under cover of six rounds from the Krupp[59] the force crossed the line during the afternoon of the 16th through a wide defile at Springhaans Nek,* with negligible casualties, and continued south to Dewetsdorp, familiar to De Wet from his childhood and named after his father. He resolved to capture the town, which was defended by a 480-strong British garrison under Maj W.G. Massey RE. De Wet began his assault on the 19th. Massey offered a determined resistance but his force was spread too thinly, the Boers cut off his water supply and reinforcements were tardy in setting

---

* Springhaan is presumably a variant of Sprinkhaan (locust). Kestell refers to the location as Sprinkhaans Nek but De Wet, *The Times History* and *The Official History* all use Springhaan in one way or another.

out to relieve him. He surrendered on 23 November and De Wet resumed his progress to the south with 400 prisoners, who had to follow the mounted Boer force on foot. The British officers declined an offer of wagon transport, preferring to share the privations of their men, which were considerable. De Wet was unsympathetic when they complained about the length of a night march, riposting that Lord Roberts had undertaken longer marches.

De Wet's breakthrough at Springhaans Nek had alerted the British to his intention to invade the Cape and Roberts sent Gen Charles Knox, who was visiting him, back to the Free State to head off the Boer advance. He was to become one of De Wet's most persistent hunters. Assuming command of three mobile columns he set out eastwards from Edenburg on 25 November in search of the Boer force. After an inconclusive encounter at Vaalbank on the 27th he lost contact for five days until De Wet turned up 12 miles north of Bethulie on the Orange River. Here De Wet was joined by reinforcements, bringing his total strength to 2,500. Drought conditions had taken a heavy toll of his horses, accustomed as they were to graze off the veld, but he was able to replenish his stock from surrounding farms to the point where most of his men had two to three horses in reserve, and some as many as five, led by Africans.[60] He was joined here also by Hertzog who, it was agreed, would enter the Cape to the west between Norvalspont and Hopetown, while De Wet entered between Bethulie and Aliwal North. The 34-year-old Hertzog was the most remarkable of De Wet's subordinate generals. A future prime minister of South Africa, he had become a judge in the Supreme Court of the Orange Free State at the age of twenty-nine. Despite his scholarly appearance he was a stern disciplinarian and an able commander.

An engagement took place between Knox's and De Wet's forces at Goed Hoop on 2 and 3 December, with the Boers getting the better of it until they retreated eastwards on the appearance of British reinforcements and then marched for 27 hours to Kareepoort on the Caledon River, a tributary of the Orange which joined it at Bethulie. The drought was now broken by heavy rainfall and on the 5th De Wet's force and its 400 prisoners crossed a swollen Caledon River, leaving behind the Krupp gun which was by now down to its last round of ammunition. When they reached the Orange River near Odendaalstroom that evening they found not only that it was in flood but that the Guards Brigade were waiting on the south bank. De Wet accepted that his invasion of the Cape would have to be deferred. He released all his prisoners except the officers and turned north.

Knox, a day behind De Wet, had succeeded in getting part of his force across the swollen Caledon River and the remainder pressed on eastwards to Smithfield. Hemmed in by swollen rivers De Wet headed for the Commissie Bridge on the Caledon. Thwarted in his attempt to cross there by the determination of a small body of Highlanders he forced a passage 7 miles further upstream at Lubbe's Drift[61] and felt confident enough to rest his force for two days on a farm about four miles north of the drift. Moving north to Helvetia on 10 December he decided to make a further attempt to enter the Cape by marching westwards to cross the railway line near Edenburg, but Kitchener, who had succeeded Roberts as Commander-in-Chief on 29 November, forestalled him by sending a force under Col Sir Charles Parsons to head him off at Reddersburg. De Wet now marched eastwards to Dewetsdorp and on the 13th reached the ridges at Driefontein to the east of the town, where he made a pretence of establishing a position. Then, marching all night, his force reached the approaches to Springhaans Nek at dawn on 14 December. Kitchener had placed forces under Col Byng to the west of the gap and Col Thorneycroft to the east. Immediately ahead of the 2,500-strong Boer force, led by Piet Fourie while De Wet brought up the rear, lay a 2,000-yd gap between two fortified posts. Michal Prinsloo, who had got through the gap with his Bethlehem commando before dawn, was keeping Byng occupied to the west, but Thorneycroft was closing in from the east. Fourie decided to force the gap and a small body of Boers galloped ahead to seize an abandoned kraal between the fortified posts. Under their covering fire the Boer force poured thorough the gap for the next two hours. Remarkably only two men were killed.

Of the De Wet hunts the second, which ended at this point, was the least spectacular in terms of the numbers of British troops involved – approximately 6,000 in nine columns[62] – but it succeeded in keeping De Wet out of the Cape Colony at a critical time. The episode provided a further illustration of De Wet's agility. Since he had left the Magaliesberg no British column had succeeded in keeping in touch with him for more than twenty-four hours and rarely for twelve hours. Erskine Childers, writing in *The Times History*, saw him as a valuable instructor to the British: 'His practice of carrying nothing on the men but their arms and ammunition, his superb night marches, his ruses, doublings, twistings, his bold use of ground and, to a certain extent, his skill in handling a convoy, became eventually the methods of his foes.'[63]

Although De Wet had failed to invade the Cape the diversion enabled Hertzog and Kritzinger to do so on 16 December, the former with 1,000 men via Sand Drift and the latter with 700 men via Odendaal Drift. Over the next few weeks they penetrated deep into the Cape, Kritzinger, with Scheepers, southwards and Hertzog, with George Brand, westwards towards the Atlantic coast, some of his burghers reaching Lamberts Bay 120 miles north of Cape Town. Here, instead of meeting the expected merchant ship with arms and supplies from European sympathisers, they were greeted by a salvo from a British warship, HMS *Sybille*.[64]

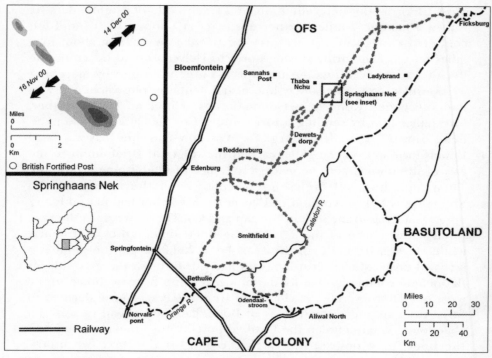

The second De Wet hunt – November to December 1900

There now occurred one of the most controversial episodes of De Wet's career, following the establishment by Kitchener of burgher peace committees, composed of prominent surrendered burghers. On 28 December 1900 J.J. Morgendaal, a JP in Kroonstad, and Andries Wessels, a wealthy farmer from the same area and a former member of the Free State Volksraad, volunteered to take out to commandos Kitchener's circular about the treatment of surrendered burghers. After discussion with Boer officers they were taken to De Wet in Heilbron, and on 6 January 1901 they appeared before a military court charged with treason. They were referred to a higher court and forced to accompany a commando under De Wet and Froneman, the latter warning them that they would be shot if they moved without permission from the cart conveying them. Before sunrise on 9 January the Boer officers received a report that a British column was approaching and immediately ordered the commando to get moving. From the evidence available it is probable that Froneman thought Morgendaal was deliberately procrastinating and lashed out at him from his horse with his *sjambok*. Morgendaal grabbed the *sjambok*, whereupon it is alleged that De Wet shouted to Froneman to

196

shoot him, which he did, wounding him in the side. Morgendaal died ten days later. The report of an approaching British column was later found to be mistaken. On 10 January Wessels appeared before a military court presided over by De Wet and was sentenced to death for high treason, but Steyn decided that the sentence should not be carried out and Wessels was subsequently freed by the British. Kitchener at first regarded the shooting of Morgendaal as murder, but later was inclined to believe that it was manslaughter. The matter was not pursued after the war when the emphasis was on reconciliation, and neither Froneman nor De Wet was denied the benefit of the amnesty for acts committed during the war.[65]

Following their invasion of the Cape Colony the success of Hertzog and Kritzinger in drawing British troops away from the Orange River encouraged De Wet to plan another invasion. Acknowledging the reluctance of his fellow Free Staters to leave their own country he agreed that of the commandos concerned half of the men should remain behind in their own districts. Those selected for the expedition assembled in the Doornberg on 25 January 1901, the force totalling 2,500 with 2 guns. Steyn was to accompany them as before and among the commandants were Froneman, Piet Fourie and Michal Prinsloo. With so many people involved Kitchener got wind of De Wet's intention and he ordered generals Charles Knox and Bruce Hamilton to the Doornberg to nip the venture in the bud. De Wet had started out before they reached him but they caught up in time for a clash in the Tabaksberg on the 28th and 29th in which the Boers captured a pom-pom.

The third, or great, De Wet hunt had begun. De Wet continued southwards avoiding Springhaans Nek and crossed the line of forts to the west of Thaba 'Nchu. Knox and Bruce Hamilton went on by rail to head him off at the Orange River. Learning that the river was heavily defended to the east of the railway De Wet turned to the west, sending part of his force under Froneman to cross the railway north of Jagersfontein Road while he took the remainder across to the south. In the process Froneman captured a well-laden supply train. Joining forces north of Philippolis they crossed the Orange at Sand Drift on 10 February 1901, capturing a party of 90 British troops attempting to mine the drift. At the last moment 800 burghers, including the Bethlehem commando led by Michal Prinsloo, had refused to leave the Free State.

Knox and Bruce Hamilton, hurrying along the north bank from the east reached Sand Drift fifteen hours behind De Wet's rearguard, but twelve British columns, under the overall command of Gen Lyttleton, awaited him to the south of the river. Among the group and column commanders were three future field marshals – Haig, Plumer and Byng. That part of the Cape Colony which De Wet's depleted force had now entered was particularly well served by railway lines, bounded as it was on

the west by the line from De Aar to Orange River Station, on the south by
the line between De Aar and Naauwpoort and on the east by the line
from Naauwpoort to Norvalspont. A 120-mile stretch of the Orange River
formed the northern boundary of this quadrilateral 'box' whose centre
was near Philipstown. Of the waiting commanders it was Plumer,
commanding a force of over 1,000 Australians and New Zealanders in two
columns, who first made contact with De Wet and engaged him over a
wide front at Wolvekuil, north-west of Philipstown, on 14 February. De
Wet was saved by two heavy thunderstorms. Reaching the Western Railway
later that day he crossed it south of Potfontein, but the rain caused him
to abandon his convoy in a quagmire immediately to the east of the
railway where he left Fourie with 100 men to fight a rearguard action.
Plumer was able to capture 40 wagons and take 30 prisoners while Fourie
escaped to the south. Having fled from the Philipstown box De Wet
intended to rendezvous with Hertzog near Prieska, nearly 100 miles to
the north-west, and then to go south with him towards Cape Town. Knox
had now joined Plumer in pursuit of De Wet, and Kitchener deployed his
remaining columns along the Western Railway with the intention that
they should advance westwards to head off any Boer advance to the south.
If they failed they were to return to the railway so that they could be
transported further south to try again. As it happened the plan was
unnecessary since De Wet was trapped in the angle of the Brak and
Orange Rivers, both in flood as a result of the heavy rain, and many of his
burghers were now on foot having abandoned their exhausted horses.
Instead of continuing to the west he doubled back eastwards along the
Orange River on the 19th. Plumer continued the pursuit but Knox
overshot to the west. When he turned back he unwittingly placed himself
between De Wet and Hertzog who crossed the Brak River on the 21st.
Hertzog was reunited on the other side with Brand, whom he had
diverted to Britstown to get supplies. They now advanced eastwards in
parallel with De Wet, who continued to hug the swollen Orange River
trying drift after drift in the hope of getting back to the Free State, always
just managing to keep clear of the British. After nine days of pursuit
Plumer withdrew for a while as De Wet crossed the Western Railway back
into the Philipstown box on the 23rd. He left a small force to continue
shadowing De Wet while other columns took up the chase.

On the morning of the 27th, in a feat of coordination never matched
during the hunt by the British, De Wet, Hertzog and Fourie all converged
near Sand Drift, where De Wet had crossed two weeks before, but which
was now impassable. Continuing for a further 20 miles upstream the
Boers came the following day to Botha's Drift, near the destroyed
Colesberg road bridge, just as the river began to fall. It was the fifteenth
drift De Wet had tried since he turned back and it was found to be
passable. His force returned with relief and rejoicing to the Free State.

The railway had proved unequal to the task of getting British troops in position in time to prevent De Wet's escape, Plumer in particular having been delayed on his 225-mile journey around from Orange River Station. In addition, the British failure to post signallers on the prominent Coles Kop had contributed to a lack of communication among the pursuers.[66] Three hours after the Boers had crossed the river it was again in flood. Reaching Philippolis De Wet dispersed his commandos and Steyn left him. Over the next few days De Wet moved northwards with a small force, keeping to the west of the railway, with Plumer again in pursuit but always a day or so behind. De Wet crossed the railway north of Brandfort on 8 March, reaching Senekal on the 11th. Plumer abandoned the hunt at the railway.

While it demonstrated once again De Wet's extraordinary talent for survival the third De Wet hunt was on balance a British success since it achieved Kitchener's main objective of thwarting De Wet's invasion of the Cape. While Kritzinger, Scheepers and others continued for some time to wreak havoc in the Cape Midlands, there was never again a serious prospect, if indeed there ever had been, of a general uprising of Boer sympathisers in the colony. But as long as De Wet and Steyn were at large the war would continue at immense cost to Britain in terms not of only of the resources needed to keep a vast army in the field, but also of the damage to her international prestige as that army was kept fully stretched by a Boer army a fraction of its size and as, increasingly, the war was seen to oppress Boer women and children.

Compared with the exertions of the three De Wet hunts the next seven months were for De Wet a period of relative inactivity. Basing himself in the North-Eastern Free State he dispersed his commandos into small groups, frustrating British attempts to bring the area under control. It was not until November 1901 that he entered the field again at the head of a force of any size. Botha's peace negotiations with Kitchener at the end of February had foundered on Milner's intransigence on the question of amnesties for colonial rebels and in May Steyn had reacted angrily to a letter from the Transvaal government suggesting further peace moves.

As Kitchener applied his organising talents to the task of ending Boer resistance in the Free State 'hunts' gave way to 'drives', the term 'drive' embracing any concerted operation aimed at the rounding up of Boer combatants within a defined area. He had increased considerably the proportion of mounted troops in his army and, learning from their opponents, they travelled lighter and became more mobile and self-reliant, but a high proportion were ill trained and no match for the seasoned Boers to whom they provided an essential source of ammunition, weapons and equipment. By this stage of the war captured

British rifles had largely supplanted the Mauser as the principal weapon of the Boer commandos. Discouraged by Boer leaders earlier in the war the practice of *uitskudding* – the stripping of prisoners – became commonplace as the Boers were deprived of any other source of clothing, despite the sanction of execution if captured wearing British uniforms. Except in blatant cases of deception Kitchener took a fairly lenient view of the offence.[67]

Hand in hand with the development of the drive went the evolution of the blockhouse system, on whose completion there were over 1,000 miles of fortified lines in the Free State alone. De Wet was contemptuous of the system, arguing that, because of the scale of diversion of manpower first in constructing them and then in manning them, the blockhouses prolonged the war by at least three months. He asserted also that when drives were successful it was because Boers were surrounded by British troops and not because they had been contained by blockhouse lines.[68] As it turned out those lines seldom proved impenetrable but De Wet underestimated their value as a deterrent against railway raids and their efficacy as lines of communication and supply.[69] The extension of the blockhouse system was accompanied by the removal of Boer women, children and other non-combatants into concentration camps and the destruction of farmhouses, crops and livestock in order to deprive the commandos of sustenance. De Wet's wife, Cornelia, was confined in the Pietermaritzburg concentration camp from July 1901.[70]

Two events stand out during the period of De Wet's relative inactivity. In June De la Rey came south to confer with Steyn and De Wet in the vicinity of Reitz. News came to them during their meeting of the capture nearby at Graspan of a women's convoy fleeing from Frankfort to Reitz. This had become a common event in the Free State and neither Steyn nor De Wet thought that it merited intervention, but De la Rey thought otherwise and they deferred to their guest. A force of seventy to eighty, drawn from the bodyguards of the three leaders, set out to dispute possession of the convoy with a force of about 200 British. They succeeded initially in capturing the convoy, but then relinquished it on the approach of British reinforcements. Each side accused the other of sheltering behind women and children.[71] In July a British intelligence coup led to the capture of nearly every member of the Free State government as they slept in Reitz. Steyn himself escaped on horseback clad in a nightshirt. After this event both De Wet and Hertzog were made members of the Executive Council.

On 7 August Kitchener issued a proclamation to the effect that all Boer officers who failed to surrender by 15 September 1901 would be banished permanently from South Africa. Steyn's long reply, sent in both Dutch and English to avoid misrepresentation, was an admirable summary of the causes and conduct of the war as seen by the Boers. Disputing

Kitchener's assertion that the whole of the country was now effectively under British control he observed 'Your Excellency's jurisdiction is limited to the range of your Excellency's guns.'[72] Louis Botha and De Wet reacted with contempt to yet another in a series of British proclamations, described by the Boers as 'paper bombs'. De Wet's reaction was summed up in the words 'bang maak is nog niet dood maak'[73] – 'threats never killed anybody'. In the event only two Boers surrendered.

In November 1900 De Wet assembled an elite 700-strong 'flying' commando with the intention of going on the offensive. The commando set out after a *krygsraad* on 28 November on the farm Blijdschap, west of Reitz. At this time construction of the two great east/west limbs of the blockhouse system in the North-Eastern Free State was well advanced. In the north a blockhouse line of over 120 miles was to join Heilbron to Botha's Pass in the Drakensberg via Frankfort and Vrede, and to the south of it a line of over 160 miles was to join Kroonstad to the Drakensberg via Lindley, Bethlehem and Harrismith. It was in the Bethlehem to Harrismith section, still under construction, that De Wet found his opportunity.

The first major engagement was an abortive ambush on 18 December of a 1,200-strong mounted column commanded by Brig Dartnell, riding out from Bethlehem to Harrismith. When the time came only 200 of De Wet's force, swollen to 900 for the occasion, responded to the signal to charge and on the approach of another British column the Boers retired. De Wet concealed his force near the Tigerkloof Spruit to await the next opportunity. This came when the British force covering the construction of the blockhouse line moved westwards from the Elands River bridge to occupy a commanding hill called Groenkop on the farm Tweefontein, about twenty miles east of Bethlehem. The force was weakened on the morning of 24 December by the withdrawal of 150 infantrymen to guard another camp, leaving behind the 11th Yeomanry, about 500 strong with 2 guns, under the command of Maj Williams.

Groenkop rose about 600 ft above the surrounding country with a summit approximately 250 yd in diameter, with steep slopes to the north and south, a gentle slope to the east and a nearly precipitous cliff on the western side. By observation from a nearby hill and as a result of a reconnaissance patrol drawing fire from the hill, De Wet knew that apart from the guns on the commanding western side of the hill the heaviest defences were to the east. He deduced that an attack would be least expected from the west and chose the precipitous face on that side for his assault. Having concentrated earlier that day at Tigerkloof, a force of 1,000 Boers, reinforced by men under Brand and Coetzee who were visiting De Wet and volunteered to join in, assembled after dark on Christmas Eve in the dead ground at the bottom of the cliff. At 2 a.m. on

Christmas morning they began their ascent via two gullies and it was not until the leading men had virtually reached the top that they were challenged by sentries. Spilling over, the Boers stormed the camp. About a third of the British defenders fled to nearby camps but the remainder fought valiantly, holding out for about an hour. At the end 116 had been killed or wounded and 240 taken prisoner. Maj Williams was among those killed. In addition the Boers captured the two guns, many rifles, much ammunition and twenty well-laden wagons;[74] thirty-two Boers were killed or wounded. After a British doctor had been killed, De Wet rigidly enforced the protection of the British hospital[75] and assisted in getting water to the wounded. Africans in the British camp received shorter shrift.

By the end of January 1902 the blockhouse system in the North-Eastern Free State was virtually complete and the stage was set for Kitchener's 'new model' drives. As now conceived, a vast mounted human dragnet was to sweep clean the areas contained by the blockhouse lines. Experienced and capable as the column commanders appointed to this task were, little was required of them by way of personal initiative since they were given pre-assigned roles and coordinated by Kitchener's HQ in Pretoria. There was no overall commander in the field. The first of the new drives was a westward sweep to the Central Railway of 9,000 men in four columns, commanded by Maj Gen Elliot and colonels Rimington, Byng and Rawlinson, stretched out in a 54-mile line at their starting point between Frankfort on the northern blockhouse line and Kaffir Kop on the southern line, 50 miles away from the railway. In addition to the four columns 17,000 men and 300 blockhouses on the perimeter completed the cordon, or 'kraal' as the Boers called it. Within the cordon were De Wet and 1,800 burghers, and a confident Kitchener travelled south to see him captured. The dragnet began its 50-mile sweep to the railway on 6 February, and as it moved west some commandos went their own way while De Wet with 700 men and a herd of cattle moved south, coming up against the southern blockhouse line in the dark that evening near Doornkloof. Despite the fact that they were only 100 yd from a blockhouse they were able to cut their way through undetected. The cattle came through the gap some time later giving rise to the erroneous belief that the Boers used stampeding herds of cattle to break through the lines. As the columns continued their westward course De Wet doubled back across the southern blockhouse line to Elandskop, between Lindley and Frankfort, and the burghers returned to their own districts. The sweep ended at the railway on the evening of the 8th with 286 Boers killed wounded or captured, half of them accounted for by Rawlinson's column.[76]

The second drive, which began only five days later, was an altogether more ambitious and complex operation, taking in most of the area between the Central Railway and the Drakensberg, bounded on the north by the Natal Railway and on the south by a line from the Doornberg to Harrismith. While Elliott with five columns swept north-eastwards from the Doornberg on a 50-mile front, leaving a further two columns to guard the southern flank, Rimington, Byng and Rawlinson advanced eastwards between the northern blockhouse line and the Natal Railway before wheeling to the south on 20 February to sweep the area between the Wilge River and the Drakensberg. In the mobile columns and in the forces guarding the perimeters some 60,000 British troops were involved,[77] with an estimated 3,000 Boer combatants within the area.[78]

Steyn and members of the government had been outside the area of the first drive and on 18 February 1902 De Wet joined them on the farm Rondebosch, 8 miles north-east of Reitz. Learning of Elliot's advance they moved south-eastwards on the 21st, crossing the Wilge River into the path of the columns sweeping down from the north, while behind them Elliott occupied the drifts on the Wilge. In addition to the government, there had gathered round De Wet some 800 to 900 fighting men, a large number of non-combatants, both old and very young with transport of every description, and a great herd of cattle, the whole convoy stretching for some six miles.[79] De Wet resolved to fight his way through the driving line and moved northwards to a small tributary of the Wilge, the Holspruit. He introduced a semblance of order into the vast throng accompanying him by organising the fighting men into two wings ahead of the civilians and the cattle. Engaging the British line at Langverwacht late at night on 23 February he forced a gap where Rimington's column joined Byng's; 600 of the best men, and Steyn's party, fought their way through but most of the civilians and the cattle were left behind.[80] Among those, and subsequently captured, was De Wet's son Kootie, who had become separated from his father when his horse was shot from under him.[81] The drive continued southwards for the next four days and it was only on the last night that it achieved a major success with the capture of 571 men of the Harrismith commando under Jan Meyer. This brought the total of prisoners taken as a result of the drive to 778. In addition to those captured, 50 Boers were killed, and 25,000 head of cattle and 200 vehicles were seized.[82]

After their escape from the second drive De Wet, Steyn and the government party returned on 2 March to the farm Rondebosch near Reitz, which they had left on 21 February. Here they found themselves in the path of the third drive, advancing westwards from the Wilge River. Steyn decided that the time had come to move to the comparatively peaceful western districts of the Free State in the belief that his departure from the north-east would diminish the intensity of British operations there. De Wet was reluctant to be thought to be fleeing from the enemy but he was persuaded, by Hertzog among others, that he should go with the party. Some even argued that his burghers in the north-east would be glad of his absence in the hope of a quieter life.[83] The party set out on 5 March and were joined the next day by the Vredefort men, who welcomed the opportunity of returning to their own district under De Wet's leadership. Taking a wide sweep to the north they travelled 180 miles and crossed three blockhouse lines – the northern line a few miles east of Heilbron, the railway north of Wolvehoek and the Vaal River to Kroonstad line on 15 March near Bothaville. Having got close to the border they decided not to stay in the Free State but to cross into the Transvaal in order to meet De la Rey, both to confer with him and to enable Steyn, whose eyesight was failing, to consult his doctor. Having crossed the Vaal by a footpath drift near Commando Drift they met De la Rey at Zendelingsfontein, north-east of Wolmaransstad on 17 March, where they were cheered by the news of his recent defeat and capture of Lord Methuen.

Towards the end of March 1902 De Wet left Steyn in order to organise the commandos in the Western Free State, but before he was able to achieve anything he learnt from Steyn of the first moves that were to lead to peace. Kitchener had forwarded to Schalk Burger, acting President of the Transvaal, copies of correspondence between Britain and the Netherlands originating in an offer by the Dutch to mediate in peace negotiations between Britain and the Boer deputation to Europe. The British government had declined the offer with thanks in accordance with its policy of excluding foreign intervention in the war and because the necessity for the deputation to travel to South Africa for consultations would be too time-consuming. It expressed the view that the proper place for negotiation was in South Africa between the Boer leaders there and the British Commander-in-Chief. Burger had taken this as an indication of Britain's willingness to negotiate and on Kitchener's advice had gone under safe conduct with members of his government to Kroonstad as the best place from which to contact Steyn.[84] He now sought a meeting between the governments of the two republics, which took place in Klerksdorp in the Transvaal on 9 and 10 April. This led to meetings in Pretoria on 12 April with Kitchener and on the 14th with both Kitchener and Milner. It was soon clear that Britain would not settle on any basis other than a surrender of Boer independence. Both Milner and Kitchener accepted Steyn's argument that the government representatives had no power to give up independence without the consent of the people and agreed that negotiation should be deferred until there had been an opportunity to consult them. It was agreed that 'the people' were effectively the commandos still active in the field and while Kitchener stopped short of granting a general armistice, he readily agreed to local suspensions of military activity as necessary to allow

Botha, De Wet, Hertzog and De la Rey to visit the commandos, to explain to them the basis of negotiation, and to arrange for the election of representatives to a peace conference at Vereeniging, on the Transvaal bank of the Vaal.

This took place from 15 to 17 May, with thirty representatives from each republic present. Smuts attended by invitation in his joint capacity as a general and as State Attorney of the Transvaal. The Transvaal representatives ranged from plain burghers to generals and included two *landdrosts* (magistrates). The Free State representatives were with only one exception generals and commandants. The meeting was chaired by Gen C.F. Beyers, and the Revd J.D. Kestell acted as secretary.* After the preliminaries the conference heard reports from every district and, although the local conditions varied widely, a picture emerged of devastation, famine, the shortage and poor condition of horses, the plight of women and children in those districts where they had not been removed to concentration camps, the burden on local commandos of protecting and sustaining them and, in the Transvaal more than in the Free State, the increasing hostility of the native African population on whom some commandos depended for food. Fourteen districts of the Transvaal were reported as being unable to continue the struggle. The reports from the Free State were on the whole more confident in tone if not in substance. Fresh from his 1,000-mile incursion into the Cape Colony Smuts disposed of any remaining illusions about the possibility of a general uprising there.

A practical difficulty arose from the fact that while some representatives had been given wide authority by their districts, others, and in particular the Free Staters under the influence of De Wet, had been mandated to agree to nothing that required the surrender of independence.[85] Hertzog, as a judge, advised that the law required representatives to exercise their independent judgement whatever their brief might be, in other words that they were not delegates but plenipotentiaries. Smuts agreed and the conference accepted their advice. Of the leaders who spoke Botha believed that the Boer cause was losing rather than gaining ground. He discounted the possibility of intervention from Europe and urged on the conference its duty to consider settlement if necessary to avoid the destruction of the nation. De la Rey, despite his recent successes and his personal aversion to laying down his arms, concluded sadly, having heard the reports from other districts, that the time had come to negotiate. De Wet, predictably, was for continuing the war rather than contemplate the

---

* In two of his own books, and in appendices to De Wet's book, *Three Years War*, Kestell has left detailed accounts of this and the subsequent meetings in the peace negotiations.

surrender of independence. He acknowledged the difficulties but declared, 'For me this is a war of religion, and thus I can only consider the great principles involved. Circumstances are to me but as obstacles to be cleared out of the road.'[86]

At the end of the third day the conference appointed a five-man commission to negotiate with Kitchener and Milner on the basis of a proposal for limited independence, involving the cession to Britain of the Rand goldfields and Swaziland and the exercise by Britain of control over foreign affairs. Botha, De Wet, De la Rey, Smuts and Hertzog met Kitchener and Milner in Pretoria on 19 May. Of the two, Kitchener, the pragmatic soldier with his own reasons for wanting an end to the war, was more inclined to be helpful than the inflexible Milner, but neither was prepared to accept the Boer proposal for limited independence. All that was on offer was a refinement of the Middelburg terms discussed by Botha and Kitchener more than a year earlier. These envisaged a complete surrender of independence followed by progress towards representative self-government under the British Crown. Much of the detailed work of drafting was delegated by the Boer commission to the young lawyer generals, Smuts and Hertzog, who negotiated with Milner and his legal adviser, Sir Richard Solomon. The final proposal which came back approved with slight amendments by the British Government on 28 May was little different in substance from the Middelburg terms, but the ex gratia sum to be made available to assist those suffering financial hardship as a result of the war was increased from £1 million to £3 million, and was supplemented by a promise of loans on favourable terms. Thanks to the efforts of Smuts and Hertzog the preamble acknowledged that the Boer leaders signed as representatives of the two republics, thus effectively negating Roberts's annexations. They also secured a widening of the amnesty for acts carried out in the execution of the war and, dealt with separately in a letter, a measure of amnesty for rebels in the Cape Colony. This did not extend to rebels in Natal, whose government insisted that the law must take its course.

The British government had made it clear that the final proposal was for acceptance or rejection without amendment and on this basis it was considered by a further full conference of the Boer representatives at Vereeniging from 29 to 31 May. They had only three choices – acceptance of the final terms, unconditional surrender, or a continuation of the war. Of the leaders only De Wet, confident that Britain would negotiate again in due course on better terms, spoke in favour of continuing the war. Hertzog was anguished but undecided. Smuts urged the conference not to sacrifice the Afrikaner nation on the altar of independence. At the end Botha and De la Rey privately persuaded De Wet in the interests of unity to join the majority in favour of the settlement and he in turn persuaded most of the Free State dissenters. The final vote was fifty-four for acceptance and six against. On the 30th Steyn, unable to continue as a result of his illness but still implacably opposed to settlement, had resigned and left the conference. De Wet was appointed acting President of the Free State in his place and in that capacity was one of those who signed the treaty in Pretoria late in the evening of 31 May 1902. The bitter end had come.

Before it broke up after the signing of the treaty the Vereeniging conference appointed a committee to alleviate the hardship of Boer women and children, of which three members, Botha, De Wet and De la Rey were chosen to visit Europe in order to raise funds for the purpose. They sailed for England in the RMS *Saxon* at the beginning of August and during the voyage De Wet worked on his book *De Stryd Tusschen Boer en Brit* (published in English under the title *Three Years War*), assisted by the Revd J.D. Kestell. They arrived in Southampton on the eve of the Coronation Review at nearby Spithead and went straight on to London, having declined an invitation to stay and witness the Review. This was ostensibly for lack of suitable attire for a ceremonial occasion[87] but was probably to avoid an overt association with a symbol of British military might.[88] For a similar reason De Wet later declined to visit the battlefield at Waterloo.[89] However, they returned to Spithead for a day to meet King Edward VII in the royal yacht *Victoria and Albert*. They were impressed with the warmth of their reception by the British public but in their meeting with Chamberlain they failed to achieve any improvement in the financial terms of the peace settlement. Their reception in Europe and especially in Holland was even warmer than in England, but in Germany the Kaiser declined to meet them for fear of offending Britain. Overall the financial result of their visit was disappointing. De Wet returned to South Africa ahead of the rest of the party.

In the immediate postwar period the Boer leaders devoted their energies to reconstruction, both of their country and of their own lives. When the new colonies were granted a measure of self-government Botha became Prime Minister of the Transvaal and De Wet became an active and popular Minister of Agriculture in the Orange River Colony. He participated enthusiastically in moves towards a Union of South Africa, which came into being in 1910. Botha was the first Prime Minister of South Africa, with Smuts as his Minister of Defence and Hertzog as his Minister of Justice. Although he continued to be keenly interested in national politics De Wet did not seek office, but in 1912 he was appointed a member of the Council of Defence, the supreme advisory body on military matters.[90]

Although De Wet spoke cordially of Botha in public, he nurtured a private dislike of him originating in a violent argument at the time of the

Vereeniging peace conference when he accused Botha and Smuts of negotiating with Kitchener and Milner behind the backs of the rest of the committee.[91] Rifts began to appear in the publicly united front of the former war leaders in 1912 when Botha dropped Hertzog from his Cabinet after dissension on the issue of grants for the Royal Navy. Botha's and Smuts's vision of an active role for South Africa in the British Empire was not shared by men like Hertzog and De Wet who believed that South Africa, and in particular the rehabilitation of the Afrikaner, must come first. The following year Hertzog, De Wet and others walked out of the annual congress of Botha's South Africa Party and Hertzog went on to form the National Party, of which De Wet was a founder member. On the outbreak of the war in Europe in 1914 Hertzog opposed in Parliament Botha's proposal to invade German South West Africa at the request of Britain. Although Parliament passed the measure by a large majority it was deplored by many Afrikaners including officers in the Union Defence Force (UDF), among whom was the most senior, Gen C.F. Beyers. On 15 September 1914 Gen De la Rey was killed when the car taking him and Beyers through Johannesburg was fired on after it had passed through police road blocks set up to capture the criminal Foster Gang, who were then terrorising the city.[92] In the atmosphere of suspicion which followed this tragic accident Beyers resigned as commandant-general of the UDF and spoke publicly in the Transvaal against the government's German South West Africa policy, while De Wet addressed meetings in the Free State. On 12 October the government declared martial law after Lt Col 'Manie' Maritz, the former Boer War general, rebelled and went over to the Germans in the Northern Cape where he had 1,500 UDF men under training, most of whom he handed over to the Germans as prisoners of war when they refused to follow him.[93] After an unsuccessful meeting between Botha and a deputation from De Wet's district in the Free State, at which he was not present, De Wet raised a force of approximately 5,000 men. At this stage he probably had no more in mind than an armed show of strength and there is no evidence that he was in collusion with Maritz. However, after an unexpected clash with a government force near the Doornberg, in which his son Danie was killed, he resolved to fight. He was nearly surrounded by a superior force in Mushroom Valley, about twenty miles south-east of Winburg, but escaped through a gap left as a result of a failure to pass a signal to one of the government commanders.[94] De Wet moved to the north-west but his force began to dwindle as many of his men lost heart and accepted Botha's offer of amnesty. He sent most of the remainder home and with a handful of men and their horses crossed the Vaal by night, intending to make for South West Africa. He retained all his old skills of evasion, but his pursuers were no longer mounted, as in the past, but motor driven, and he was run to ground in Bechuanaland (Botswana). He accepted his capture with equanimity and tipped with a plug of tobacco the Coloured policeman who drove him in a horse-drawn trap to the nearest railway station at Vryburg.[95] With the capture of De Wet and the death by drowning of Beyers as he tried to escape across the Vaal, the rebellion effectively came to an end.

De Wet was found guilty of sedition and sentenced to six years in prison with hard labour and a fine of £2,000. The fine was paid out of the proceeds of a public subscription and he was released after a year, on 20 December 1915, in return for an undertaking of good conduct.[96] He devoted his remaining years to farming, moving more than once and settling finally on the farm Klipfontein near Dewetsdorp, close to the farm Nieuwejaarsfontein, where he had lived as a child. His health deteriorated and he died on 3 February 1922 at the comparatively early age of sixty-seven. Despite his part in the rebellion he was accorded a state funeral and was buried at the foot of the Women's Monument in Bloemfontein beside President Steyn and Emily Hobhouse.

Notes

1. De Wet, p. 282.
2. Rosenthal, p. 2.
3. Meintjes, *Steyn*, p. 50.
4. Breytenbach i, pp. 176–8.
5. Ibid., i, p. 305.
6. *TH* ii, 249–50.
7. De Wet, p. 24.
8. *TH* ii, 253.
9. See Chapter Seven, pp. 142–3.
10. Reitz, *Commando*, p. 43.
11. De Wet, p. 36.
12. *TH* iii, 112.
13. De Wet, p. 38.
14. Ibid., p. 46.
15. Breytenbach iv, pp. 190–1.
16. *TH* iii, 398.
17. *TH* iii, 400.
18. De Wet, p. 51.
19. Breytenbach v, pp. 37–8.
20. See Chapter Four, pp. 64–6.
21. See Chapter Nine, pp. 223–4.
22. De Wet, p. 78.

23. Ibid., p. 85.
24. *TH* iv, 31.
25. De Wet, p. 90.
26. *TH* iv, 44.
27. See Chapter 4, pp. 69–70.
28. *TH* iv, 52.
29. De Wet, p. 99 n.
30. Ibid., p. 104.
31. *TH* iv, 117.
32. De Wet, p. 117.
33. Ibid., p. 125.
34. *TH* iv, 257.
35. *TH* iv, 265.
36. De Wet, p. 135.
37. The British were not alone in proclaiming the annexation of enemy territory. Gen Liebenberg 'annexed' the Prieska district to the Orange Free State during the rebellion in February 1900.
38. *TH* iv, 302.
39. De Wet, p. 154.
40. *TH* iv, 34.
41. *TH* iv, 342.
42. Meintjes, *Steyn*, p. 206.
43. De Wet, p. 170.
44. *TH* iv, 262.
45. Howland, p. 135 (De Wet's own figure was 2,500, see p. 177).
46. *TH* iv, 421.
47. De Wet, p. 180.
48. Howland, p. 180.
49. Maxwell, pp. 68–9.
50. *TH* v, 2.
51. *OH* iii, 363.
52. De Wet, pp. 187–9.
53. *TH* iv, 431.
54. De Wet, pp. 200–3.
55. Spies and Nattrass, pp. 124–33; Pakenham, pp. 470–3.
56. Meintjes, *Steyn*, p. 98.
57. Le May, *British Supremacy*, p. 49.
58. Kestell, p. 145.
59. De Wet, p. 220.
60. *TH* v, 34.
61. Kestell, p. 156.
62. *OH* iv, 59.
63. *TH* v, 42.
64. *TH* v, 130–1.

65. Spies, *Barbarism*, pp. 202–5, 295 and 359 n. 240; Wilson, *Guerilla War* pp. 307–9.
66. *OH* iv, 89.
67. *TH* v, 255.
68. De Wet, pp. 321–2.
69. Pakenham, pp. 546–7.
70. Rosenthal, pp. 120–1; Spies, *Barbarism*, p. 224.
71. De Wet, p. 316, quoting Steyn to Kitchener, 15 August 1901 (full letter pp. 309–18) and Wilson, *Guerilla War*, p. 770.
72. Steyn to Kitchener 15 August 1901.
73. De Wet, p. 308.
74. Ibid., p. 345.
75. *TH* v, 440.
76. *TH* v, 481.
77. De Wet, p. 356.
78. *TH* v, 487.
79. Kestell, p. 254.
80. Ibid., p. 257.
81. De Wet, p. 361.
82. *TH* v, 491.
83. Kestell, p. 263.
84. Ibid., p. 275.
85. De Wet, p. 406.
86. Ibid., p. 431.
87. Rosenthal, p. 164.
88. Roberts, B., p. 265.
89. Rosenthal, p. 166.
90. Ibid., p. 182.
91. Meintjes, *Steyn*, p. 175.
92. See Chapter Nine, pp. 244–5.
93. Reitz, *Trekking On*, p. 51.
94. Rosenthal, p. 241.
95. Ibid., p. 250.
96. Ibid., p. 269.

CHAPTER NINE

De la Rey

Of the leaders on either side in the Boer War, Koos de la Rey was one of the most admirable. He was a prominent figure in the Western Transvaal before the war and he represented Lichtenburg in the Volksraad, in which he spoke rarely. A fine-looking man with piercing dark eyes, an aquiline nose, an ample beard and a grave manner, he was an 'elder' of his church in his early thirties.[1] He was among the few members of the Volksraad to oppose war with Britain, but once the war had begun he came increasingly, with Steyn and De Wet, to represent the hard core of Boer resistance. A man without pretensions he had a directness and simplicity which took him to the heart of things and which contributed to his rare tactical insight. With the capture of an armoured train at Kraaipan on 12 October 1899 and the defeat and capture of Lord Methuen at Tweebosch on 7 March 1902 he scored the first and the last significant Boer successes in the war.[2] In that final action, at a time when 'the last of the gentlemen's wars' had degenerated into much unpleasantness on both sides, he behaved with generosity to the wounded British general, sending him back to his own lines having let his wife know that he was safe, notwithstanding the fact that Methuen had ordered the destruction of his farm. After the war, like other leading Boer generals, he played a part in national politics but he lacked the guile and ambition to thrive in that milieu. In the events leading up to the 1914 rebellion he was torn between allegiance to the legitimate government and his passion for Afrikaner independence. Before he had to make a final choice he was killed in a tragic accident at a police road block.

Jacobus (Koos) Herculaas de la Rey was born on 22 October 1847 in Winburg in what was later to become the Orange Free State. His father Adriaan was a Voortrekker whose family came from the George district in the Cape Colony. In August 1848 he fought as a commandant in the battle of Boomplaats in which the Governor of the Cape, Sir Harry Smith, reasserted British authority in the recently proclaimed Orange River Sovereignty. After the confiscation of his farm Adriaan moved with his family to a farm near Wolmaransstad in the Western Transvaal where Koos de la Rey grew up with five brothers and five sisters.[3] He gained his first experience of warfare in the Basuto War of 1865 under Louw Wepener and became a field-cornet when he was nineteen, the youngest age ever recorded for such an appointment.[4] In October 1876 he married

212

Jacoba Elizabeth (Nonnie) Greeff and soon after his marriage took part in President Burger's campaign against the Bapedi chieftain, Sekekuni. In 1880 he fought in the First Boer War. For the first eight years of their married life he and his wife farmed on land given to them by her father about five miles west of Lichtenburg, but in 1884 they moved closer to the town to the farm Elandsfontein. In 1885 De la Rey was elected a commandant and in 1893 he became a member of the Transvaal Volksraad, representing Lichtenburg. Like Louis Botha he was one of the moderates, supporting Piet Joubert against Paul Kruger. He came to public notice in 1896 as a member of the force under Piet Cronjé which surrounded and captured Dr Jameson's raiding party at Doornkop. De la Rey had been with Cronjé during the First Boer War and was to be closely associated with him during the opening stages of the Second.

In the secret session of the Volksraad which debated Kruger's proposed ultimatum to Britain in October 1899 De la Rey expressed his reservations about the wisdom of provoking war with Britain. Kruger, who was intolerant of opposition, got up to denounce all who refused to accept his proposal, effectively accusing them of cowardice. De la Rey continued calmly after the interruption, repeating his main points and prophesying that, if the decision was for war, he would be found in the field fighting for independence long after Kruger had left the country. Botha and Lucas Meyer reputedly shared De la Rey's reservations. The minutes of the meeting make no reference to a vote having been taken, but the final decision is said to have been unanimous in favour of the ultimatum.[5]

When war broke out there were only two Boer generals of any reputation or experience, both in their sixties. They were Piet Joubert, the Commandant-General, and Piet Cronjé, who had made his name in the First Boer War as the 'Lion of Potchefstroom'. Afterwards he had played a prominent part in Transvaal affairs as a close political associate of Paul Kruger, serving at various times as a member of the Volksraad and of the Executive Committee. *The Times History* listed the qualities that commended him to the more warlike of his compatriots as 'his fearlessness, his truculent and stubborn energy and his dour patriotism'.[6] While Joubert took charge of the Boers' opening thrust into Natal, Cronjé commanded the Western Transvaal commandos, a force totalling 6,000.[7] Under him were generals De la Rey and J.P. Snyman. De la Rey additionally acted as 'adviser' to Cronjé, a frustrating role since Cronjé was not amenable to advice. The force was assembled along a 25-mile front on the border with Bechuanaland near Mafeking, which lay 200 miles to the north of Kimberley on the railway line from Cape Town to Bulawayo in Rhodesia (Zimbabwe). Mafeking was a natural target for seizure. Apart from its commanding position on the railway, the Jameson Raid had shown that the town was a convenient point from which to launch an attack on the Transvaal.[8]

De la Rey did not share the general admiration for Cronjé's military ability. He disagreed with the decision to lay siege to Mafeking, advocating a swift attack before Baden-Powell was able to consolidate his defences. Cronjé's reputation from the First Boer War rested largely on the siege of Potchefstroom, but De la Rey regarded prolonged sieges as futile since they immobilised both besieged and besieger.[9]

On the outbreak of war De la Rey had crossed the Transvaal border 25 miles south of Mafeking with 800 men, with the intention of engaging a 1,000-strong police contingent believed to be defending Kraaipan station. There was no sign of them but, instead, De la Rey's men broke up the railway line on either side of the station and on 12 October, in the first engagement of the war, captured the armoured train *Mosquito* on its way from Vryburg to Mafeking with two 7-pounder guns and ammunition for Baden-Powell. In his memoirs De la Rey recalled his horror at the scalding of the driver after the boiler had been pierced by a shell.[10] They then went north to Mafeking, breaking up the line as they went. By the end of the first week of the war the Boers had gained possession of the railway line on both sides of Kimberley and had cut it at Riverton Road 16 miles to the north and at Modder River 20 miles to the south, where the bridge was eventually destroyed. At a *krygsraad* in Cronjé's laager on 17 October it was decided that De la Rey should take the Lichtenburg and Wolmaransstad commandos to the Kimberley area, collecting the Bloemhof commando on the way, in order to help the Free Staters. On his way south De la Rey occupied Vryburg, halfway between Mafeking and Kimberley, on 21 October.[11]

Lord Methuen began his advance from the Orange River with a force of 8,000 men on 21 November, intending to proceed to Kimberley along the line of the railway. He met his first opposition on 23 November 35 miles south of the Modder River in a complex of kopjes east of Belmont station defended by Jacobus Prinsloo, the Free State commander, with 2,000 men.[12] De la Rey had hurried south from Kimberley with 600 to 700 men as soon as he received news of the British advance but he was too late to assist in the battle. The Free Staters were driven from their positions and withdrew to the north-east. The next battle took place two days later and 15 miles further up the line at Rooilaagte between Graspan and Enslin sidings. Once again the Boers were holding a complex of hills providing a natural defensive position in otherwise featureless country. De la Rey, who had reached the area late on the 23rd, occupied the kopjes to the west of the railway and Prinsloo those to the east, their combined forces totalling 2,000.[13] In fierce fighting the British were able once again to take the hills and the Boers withdrew northwards. De la Rey began immediately to make preliminary dispositions for a defensive stand on the Riet River where it was joined by the Modder River near the railway station of that name.

Cronjé arrived to take overall command during the afternoon of 26 November, bringing with him artillery, ox-wagons and 300 men.[14] He did not interfere with the dispositions, which were based on De la Rey's realisation that the Boer's tactics hitherto of defending the tops of kopjes made them vulnerable to modern artillery, and that the dead ground on the slopes afforded protection to attackers. De la Rey had also recognised that the Mauser's flat trajectory and smokeless powder made it a much more effective weapon if employed from concealed positions at ground level. A bullet which missed one man had a chance of hitting others. The Riet River provided an ideal opportunity for implementing his ideas since, like the Modder, it flowed through a depression scoured out of the soft earth 100–200 yd across and 25–30 ft deep. The river bed itself was much narrower. To the south lay a featureless plain with only sparse vegetation. The general direction of both rivers was east to west, but immediately upstream of their junction the Modder made a wide loop to the north, creating an island bounded on three sides by the Modder, with the Riet providing its southern base, having turned sharply to the west after flowing northwards for about two miles from a fordable point at Bosman's Drift.[15] Two miles to the west of the junction lay the village of Rosmead on the north bank opposite a dam built across the river to provide boating facilities for Kimberley residents. The disposition of the Boer trenches on the sloping banks of both sides of the river effectively gave them three lines of fire. The guns were placed on the north bank, with reserve pits so that they could be moved around.[16] The positions extended for approximately two miles on either side of the railway line with the centre held by De la Rey's Lichtenburgers, the right by Prinsloo's Free Staters and the left by Cronjé's Klerksdorp and Potchefstroom commandos commanded by his younger brother Andries. The Boer force totalled probably not more than 2,200[17] with 6 Krupps and 3 or 4 pom-poms, compared with Methuen's force of around 7,000.

Early on 28 November Piet Cronjé, De la Rey and Prinsloo breakfasted together at the Island Hotel at the junction of the two rivers. Conscious of the weakness of their exposed flanks they were none the less confident that Methuen would march straight to the Modder River bridge.[18] They were not disappointed. The British force had camped the previous evening about six miles south of the bridge. Reports of activity near the rivers had not altered Methuen's belief that the Boers would make their next stand at Spytfontein, about ten miles north of Modder River. He himself had reconnoitred the area close to the bridge without becoming aware of the Boers dug in on both banks of the Riet.

The British infantry started their advance shortly before 5 a.m. on the 28th, the 9th Brigade under Maj Gen Pole-Carew, reinforced by the Argyll and Sutherland Highlanders, leading off on the left, followed half an hour later by the Guards Brigade under Maj Gen Sir H.E. Colvile on the right. The Boer's first sight of the advance was at around 7 a.m. when an eyewitness on the Boer left described the British troops as looking like 'a swarm of locusts all over the veld'.[19] The first exchanges were between British artillery and guns which Cronjé had moved hurriedly to his extreme left when he misinterpreted the initial direction of advance as a flanking movement on Bosman's Drift. Earlier that morning advance patrols of the British cavalry had drawn heavy fire at 1,500 yd from the Modder River bridge but Methuen, ignorant of the topography through lack of an adequate map, had not grasped the implications of what was happening and the infantry continued to advance, extended over five to six miles and unaware of what lay in store for them.

At about 1,200 yd the Boers opened fire, sending a sheet of bullets across the veld 'in solid streaks like telegraph wires'.[20] They had opened fire too soon, a mistake initiated by Cronjé's men on the Boer left,[21] but the effect was to pin down the British infantry about 800 yd from the river for much of the day. The veld was without cover, apart from a scattering of ant hills, rocks and low bushes, and the slightest movement was enough to attract Boer rifle fire. The fierce sun caused acute discomfort from thirst and, in the case of the kilted Highlanders, from blistering sunburn. Furthermore, the troops had not eaten that morning expecting that they would breakfast at the river. Despite these difficulties the British artillery continued relentlessly with its bombardment and under its cover Pole-Carew on the left was able to gain possession of a farmhouse on the south bank opposite Rosmead village during the early afternoon, and later to get 400 men across by the dam. He took and secured the village but lack of reinforcements and the danger from friendly artillery fire prevented him from exploiting the position further. However, the Free Staters, whose morale and discipline had been poor even before the battle started,[22] were unnerved by the bombardment and withdrew despite attempts to rally them. This proved to be the turning point of the battle. Expecting to resume the fighting the following day the British found that the Boers had departed.

The day had ended in personal tragedy for De la Rey when, at sunset, his eldest son Adriaan (Adaan) was fatally wounded close by him by shrapnel in his stomach. At around 8 p.m. when De la Rey, himself injured in the shoulder, was with a party bearing his wounded son to Jacobsdal, his distress was exacerbated by the arrival of Cronjé, who asked him how the battle had gone. De la Rey, believing that Cronjé had not pulled his weight and had left him in the lurch, rounded on him in fury and Cronjé rode off. Adaan died in Jacobsdal later that evening.[23]

Because of his son's death De la Rey had not been party to the decisions take by Cronjé and Prinsloo immediately after the Modder River battle.[24] The Boers had fallen back initially on Jacobsdal where they had been joined by the remainder of Cronjé's reinforcements which had arrived too late for the fighting. On 30 November the Boers crossed the Modder and established a main laager at Rondavel Drift, the bulk of the force pressing on to within 10 miles of Kimberley, where at Spytfontein and Scholz Nek they dug in on the high ground on either side of the railway. Here they were joined by further reinforcements, bringing Cronjé's total strength to about 8,000 men. De la Rey did not share Cronjé's conviction that Methuen would immediately resume his march on Kimberley believing, correctly, that the British would need a period of rest and recuperation after the punishment they had taken at the Modder River.[25] Furthermore, he feared that the Spytfontein and Scholz Nek positions would be vulnerable to British long-range artillery fire.[26] Enlisting the support of President Steyn, who visited the Boer positions between 3 and 5 December,[27] he persuaded Cronjé to move south to a complex of ridges and kopjes running diagonally across the railway line at Merton Siding, some four miles north of Methuen's camp at Modder River Station.

The area immediately to the east of the railway line was occupied by a group of four kopjes lying on or near the farm Magersfontein and dominated at its south-east corner, some two miles from the railway, by Magersfontein Hill, steeply sided to the south and east and standing about 200 ft above the plain between it and the British camp. On the other side of the railway a lower ridge ran for about three miles to the north-west to Langeberg Farm. The road from Modder River to Kimberley passed to the east of Magersfontein Hill and between it and the Modder River lay an arc of rising ground curving round to Moss Drift, 6½ miles east of Methuen's camp. By 10 December the Boer defences extended for most of the 9 miles from Langeberg Farm to Moss Drift.

De la Rey was responsible for selecting and preparing the new positions.[28] Profiting from his experience in the recent battle, he placed these not on the high ground, but on the low ground in front of the hills in discontinuous lines of relatively deep and narrow trenches. Accounts vary as to the extent of the defences at various points, but it is not in dispute that the section immediately below Magersfontein Hill, extending for approximately 1,000 yd,[29] was prepared with great thoroughness. Here the trenches were 3–5 ft deep, vertically sided, and narrow to afford maximum protection against shrapnel. They had been placed some 150–200 yd forward of the actual foot of the hill, a factor which was to prove critical in the forthcoming battle, and they were disguised with earth and scrub. There was a gap in the trenches on either side of this central section. Despite his initial reluctance Cronjé was quickly converted to the superiority of the new positions of De la Rey's scheme which *The Times History* described as 'one of the boldest and most original conceptions in the history of war'.[30] To draw British artillery fire, defences were also constructed on the high ground to be occupied by Boers with the old Martini Henry rifles using black powder. The main laager was moved forward to Brown's Drift, about nine miles to the east of the British camp.

That the Boers had gained nearly two weeks to prepare a further stand is a vindication of the tactics adopted by De la Rey at the Modder River. But the pause had also allowed Methuen to increase his strength to nearly 16,000[31] by the addition of the Highland Brigade. In addition he acquired a 4.7-in naval gun, known as 'Joe Chamberlain' and, too late, an observation balloon. The pause allowed his troops an opportunity to rest and refresh themselves and it enabled him to recover from the slight wound he had received at the Modder River. In considering his next move his first intention had been a flanking movement via Brown's Drift, but he was dissuaded from this by his Chief of Staff in favour of a night attack on Magersfontein. Cronjé, meanwhile, was under pressure from Kruger to take the initiative and attack the British camp. Understandably, he dragged his heels. Not only would he have been considerably outnumbered but he was reluctant to leave his carefully prepared Magersfontein positions. Methuen resolved his dilemma by announcing an attack, first by a few ranging shots from 'Joe Chamberlain' on 9 December, followed by a bombardment of Magersfontein Hill with most of his artillery on Sunday the 10th, starting at 3.30 p.m. It was impressive in its intensity and assumed to be devastating in its effect, but its only result was to kill one Boer and lightly wound another three.[32] There was no response. A sergeant in the Black Watch deduced the presence of trenches by the colour of the earth thrown up by shell bursts on the low ground but his hunch was ignored.[33]

To carry out the attack Methuen chose the Highland Brigade, regarded as Britain's finest fighting unit. It was commanded by Maj Gen A.G. (Andy) Wauchope, an officer much loved by his men, who had been wounded in three of the major engagements he had fought in.[34] He expressed misgivings about the night attack, but did not persist in them despite a staff officer's encouragement to do so, and declined to postpone the attack when it began to rain heavily. According to some accounts his feelings were stronger than reservations about the wisdom of the attack and included a premonition of his own death,[35] but this did not impair the vigour with which he undertook the operation. Alerted by the bombardment the Boers prepared for the attack. The positions had already been assigned and all burghers were ordered to be in them before dawn. The right wing, west of the railway, was under Cronjé's brother Andries, commanding the Klerksdorp commando and part of the Potchefstroom commando, supported on either side by Free State commandos. The centre was held primarily by the Potchefstroom commando, previously Cronjé's own, and the left by various Transvaal and Free State commandos, including the Scandinavians and De la Rey's Lichtenburgers. De la Rey, who had masterminded and prepared the Boer defences, was nominally in command of the whole of the left wing, but he was not present at the battle, having gone to Riverton near Kimberley to recover from his troublesome wound.[36] Cronjé, having made his preparations and accompanied by six members of his staff, lay down to sleep on the eastern slope of Magersfontein Hill.

At 12.30 a.m. on Monday 11 December, the Highland Brigade set out in heavy rain towards the south-eastern corner of Magersfontein Hill, where Wauchope intended that they should deploy before dawn and take the eastern side of the hill at first light. Because of the difficulty in keeping the men together in the dark in bad weather they were in mass of quarter columns (the narrowest formation possible) with a frontage of 45 yd and a depth of 330 yd – nearly 4,000 men in 90 successive files, some linked by guide ropes.[37] The Black Watch led, followed by the Argylls, the Seaforths and the Highland Light Infantry. They were guided to the intended spot by Maj G.E. Benson of the Royal Artillery, who had previously surveyed the route, but the rain, which had increased in intensity during the march, made them late and Wauchope pressed on for 200 yd beyond the point where Benson had advised deployment. The deployment was then further delayed by a line of dense thorn bushes and, unaware that the enemy trenches were up to 200 yd in front of the hill, Wauchope decided to take the whole column through or round the obstruction, which added another 300 yd to the advance. These two unplanned advances had probably brought the leading Highlanders to within 400 yd of the waiting Boers, who detected them just as they began to deploy.

The British had walked into the same trap as at the Modder River two weeks before. This time the range was much closer and the potential for disaster greater. The initial casualties would have been far worse if the Boer opening fire had not been too high, but its unexpectedness, its extent and its intensity had a devastating effect on morale. In the resulting confusion there were conflicting orders including, probably, an unauthorised instruction to 'retire' and hundreds of men fled back to the line of thorn bushes, breaking the ranks of the more steadfast as they went. After the first burst of fire from the Boers Wauchope had walked ahead of the leading companies to ascertain the extent of their trenches and, having seen the gap east of the hill, sent his ADC* back to order the Black Watch and the Argylls to reinforce on the right as quickly as possible. Having delivered his message he returned to find that Gen Wauchope had been killed and he himself fell wounded a moment later.

---

* His cousin Capt A.G. Wauchope.

At dawn, Cronjé was back on the eastern slope of Magersfontein Hill with his six adjutants after an intended tour of inspection, frustrated by the rain and dark. When the firing started he and his small party had climbed the hill and taken cover at the top. In response to Wauchope's last order Col Coode had led the Black Watch forward on the right but had almost immediately been killed. Surviving officers continued to lead the advance towards the gap in the Boer trenches and were joined by the Seaforths. Two small sorties from the combined regiments had been foiled in their attempt to get up the slope of the hill, but a third party of about 100 men succeeded in getting round to the rear of the hill and began to climb it. It was defended only by Cronjé and his staff. The intensity of the rifle fire which he and his small force let loose on the climbing Highlanders was such that they assumed that the crest was heavily defended, and so checked and began to return the fire. At this point the Boers to the east of the gap in the trenches began to move in to close it and impede the advance of the main body of the Black Watch and Seaforths. This and British artillery fire effectively trapped the small climbing party. They were surrounded by the Boers, and the thirty or forty who survived were taken prisoner. Further movements to the right, mainly by the Seaforths under Col Hughes-Hallett, had extended the Highlanders over a front of about three miles by 6 a.m. at a distance of 200–600 yd from the Boer trenches.[38] Daylight had allowed the British artillery to come to their support and the guns kept up a continuous bombardment throughout the day. Despite the earlier breakdown of discipline there were many heroic but unsuccessful attempts to reach the trenches, but for the most part the day was a repeat of the Modder River action with the Highlanders pinned down helplessly in the fierce sun, suffering agonies from thirst, hunger and sunburn to the backs of their knees.

The remainder of Methuen's force was employed mainly in containing the Boer left between the Highlanders and the river. This task was undertaken by the Guards Brigade, flanked on either side by cavalry and later, at the river, by the Yorkshire Light Infantry. At around midday Methuen sent the Gordons to reinforce the Highlanders left opposite the Boer centre. By a series of rushes they succeeded in getting to within 400 yd of the Boers, but for the rest of the day they were pinned down with the Highlanders in the sun. The 9th Brigade were ordered to protect 'Joe Chamberlain', the naval gun, on the left and to make a demonstration up the railway line. Their day was relatively uneventful.[39]

The turning point in the battle came at round 1.30 p.m. when the Ficksburg commando succeeded in getting men round the Highlanders' right. Col Hughes-Hallett, having failed twice to get a message through to the Guards to cover his flank, ordered two companies on his right to swing round to meet this threat. This was misinterpreted as a general order to the Highland Brigade to retire (Hughes-Hallett was unaware of Wauchope's death and that he was now the acting brigadier). The retirement provoked a devastating outburst of rifle fire from the Boers and heavy losses were incurred, but by 4 p.m. the troops had been rallied about 1,000 yd from the trenches where food and water carts were brought up. At this point the Boer field guns, which had been silent all day, opened fire inflicting further casualties and leading to the final retreat of the Highland Brigade. This was effectively the end of the battle.

The British casualties were nearly 1,000 killed and wounded, approximately 8 per cent of Methuen's force – much the same proportion as at the Modder River – but the Highland Brigade's casualties as a whole approached 20 per cent and the figures for the Black Watch were nearer 35 per cent. The Boer casualties were around 250 killed and wounded, including the valiant Scandinavians, who had insisted on manning an exposed position on the Boer left and lost forty-three of their total fifty men.[40]

Fresh from his success at Nicholson's Nek outside Ladysmith, Christiaan De Wet came to Magersfontein to take command of the Free State forces there on 16 December. Together he and De la Rey chafed under the frustration of Cronjé's refusal to allow any of his 8,000 men to take part in offensive operations. When he relented at the end of December and permitted them to take 700 men on a raid on Methuen's railway communications, the venture was a failure. For De la Rey, escape from Cronjé came on 7 January 1900 when he went to Colesberg as a member of a four-man commission of enquiry into complaints about the command arrangements of the Boer forces there. The other members were his close friend Gen H.R. Lemmer, A.D.W. Wolmarans, a member of the Transvaal Executive Council and Abraham Fischer, the secretary to the Orange Free State government.[41]

Following the British Black Week defeat of Gen Gatacre at Stormberg on 10 December, there were two concentrations of Boer forces in the Cape Colony south of the Orange River. Gen Olivier remained in the vicinity of Stormberg with 1,100 men[42] and to the west of him a larger force was centred on Colesberg, a town with strong natural defences on the railway line from Port Elizabeth to Bloemfontein. With successive reinforcements this had grown to around 6,000 men by the time of De la Rey's arrival,[43] made up of both Free State and Transvaal commandos and commanded by three generals. These were the sixty-year-old Transvaaler H.J. Schoeman, and the Free Staters E.R. Grobler and Piet de Wet, Christiaan de Wet's younger brother. Here they confronted Gen French who, having taken Rensburg 8 miles down the line on 30 December, had been attacking Colesberg. Piet de Wet, who had superseded Grobler as Chief Commandant of the Free State commandos south of the Orange,

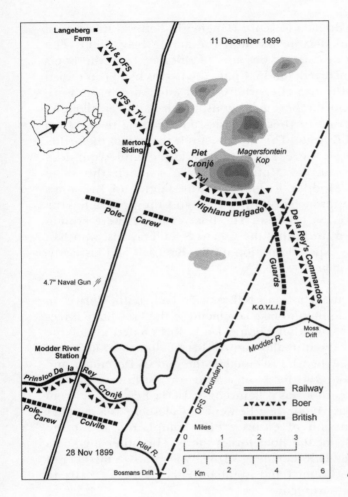

The Battles of Modder River
and Magersfontein

had complained to President Steyn about Schoeman's excessive caution
and it was this which had led to the commission's visit.[44] It found no
specific fault with Schoeman but concluded that the command
arrangements needed strengthening and it was agreed that De la Rey
should join the other generals there. He took command of the Boer left
to the east of the town with 1,000 men from the Johannesburg
commando and the Johannesburg police.[45]

When French left Colesberg to join Roberts on 6 February he left Maj
Gen R.A.P. Clements in charge with a much reduced force, but this was
not immediately apparent to the Boers who continued to send men into
the area, with the result that Clements had to defend a front of over
thirty miles against 7,000 to 8,000 Boers. By this time De la Rey's force on
the Boer left had risen to a strength of between 2,500 and 3,000.[46] Having

learnt of the depletion of the British forces he launched an attack on a group of kopjes to the south of his position on 12 February, having had to postpone the attack for two days because of Schoeman's failure to cooperate from the Boer centre as planned. The kopjes were defended by the Worcestershire Regiment (and known accordingly to the British as the Worcester Hills) who fought off De la Rey's attack, but Grobler's engagement on the Boer right was more successful and Clements was forced back to Arundel, 17 miles south of Colesberg, where he had taken up position by 14 February. He would have been in difficulty but for the fact that Roberts's great flank march was now under way, prompting President Steyn to withdraw all the Free State forces from Colesberg on 20 February in order to defend Bloemfontein. De la Rey was appointed commander of the Boer forces remaining south of the Orange River but he served in that capacity for only eight days before all Boer forces in the Colesberg area were withdrawn, following Cronjé's surrender at Paardeberg on 27 February.

De la Rey went to Bloemfontein with part of his commando to await the arrival of his unmounted men and transport. He was too late to help Christiaan de Wet in his vain attempt to stem Roberts's advance at Poplar Grove on 7 March, but he was ready at Abraham's Kraal, 35 miles from Bloemfontein, when the routed Boer forces fell back there. Many of De Wet's men could not be stopped even by President Kruger's remonstrations at the roadside, and went home to their farms. As a result the combined Free State and Transvaal forces available for a further stand against Roberts totalled probably not more than 1,500 with 12 to 16 guns.[47] Their positions extended for some ten miles south of the Modder River, concentrated on groups of kopjes at Abraham's Kraal itself, at Driefontein to the south and at Damvlei, between those two positions and slightly to the east of them. This was a strong combination of defensive positions held by a force of high calibre, the war-weary and the faint-hearted having deserted, but Roberts had 34,000 men with 112 guns.[48] In the action on 10 March, despite the disparity in numbers, the Boers held back the British for most of the day. De Wet had returned in time for the battle from Bloemfontein where he had been conferring with Steyn about the defence of the city, but the burden of command fell largely on De la Rey. When he saw that the positions at Abraham's Kraal would become untenable he reinforced Driefontein, at the same time extending the Boer line southwards to avoid outflanking. The Driefontein positions were yielded only when the ammunition there ran out. Under covering fire from small rearguards the Boers were able to extricate their forces and retire to Bloemfontein. As they withdrew they heard British soldiers shouting triumphantly 'Hurrah, Majuba!' and 'God save the Queen!'[49] Casualties on both sides were higher than at Poplar Grove, the British losses totalling 438. The Boer losses were stated officially at 25, but British troops buried 102 dead Boers and a neighbouring farmer reported seeing unburied bodies after the British had moved on.[50] The action delayed Roberts for only a day and he entered Bloemfontein on 13 March, encountering little resistance.

As the Boer commandos retreated, De Wet made a virtue of necessity and sent all his burghers home on leave. No such concession was granted to the Transvaalers, many of whom went home of their own accord with the result that at one point De la Rey's force was reduced to 400 men.[51] The day before Roberts entered Bloemfontein, the seat of government of the Orange Free State had been transferred to Kroonstad where De la Rey took part in the historic *krygsraad* on 17 March 1900. Like De Wet he endorsed enthusiastically President Steyn's proposal that the Boers should eschew defensive stands against overwhelming odds in favour of offensive action by many small commandos, in particular harrying British lines of supply, and it was he who proposed that the Boers rid themselves of the encumbrance of large wagon trains.[52]

Roberts remained in Bloemfontein for seven weeks, resting his troops and replenishing his army, during which time De la Rey established himself near Brandfort, 35 miles to the north. This long period of inactivity on his part in a defensive position was contrary to the decision taken at Kroonstad in favour of more offensive action, but his scope was restricted to some extent by a shortage of horses, aggravated by the refusal of the Free State authorities to allow Transvaalers to requisition them from local farms.[53] With De la Rey was the Heidelberg commando and later he was joined by reinforcements from Natal, bringing his strength up to 3,000. These comprised the Ermelo and Wakkerstroom commandos under Gen Tobias Smuts, and the 150-strong Irish Brigade under the American Col Y.J.F. Blake. During the long wait at Brandfort burghers had got into the habit of going off to attend to their farms and other personal business. Furthermore, the Boer intelligence was not up to its usual standard so that when Roberts finally resumed his advance on 3 May De la Rey was taken unawares. Of his nominal roll of 3,000 he was able to muster only 1,500 to 1,800 men for the defence of Brandfort.[54] Roberts, with 38,000 men and 100 guns, advanced on a 15-mile front with his mounted wings on either side of the railway line thrown forward ahead of the infantry in the centre. Given the disparity in the size of the opposing forces, De la Rey could do no more than hold him back for a day before falling back on the Vet River. Here the pattern was repeated on 5 May, but De la Rey's force was even smaller this time, whittled down by desertions to between 1,000 and 1,200.[55] Although Louis Botha was on his way from Natal with reinforcements the only additional force to join De la Rey for the Vet River action was the 100-strong Afrikander Cavalry Corps, in which Deneys Reitz was serving. The Boers offered strong resistance on both flanks but their defence was compromised by a Boer prisoner who alerted the British to the existence of a lightly defended drift on the Boer right.[56] Once again it was necessary to retreat to avoid being outflanked and De la Rey fell back now to the Sand River, the last line of defence before Kroonstad, the seat for the time being of the Free State government. Botha arrived on 7 May with 3,000 men. His reputation as the hero of the Tugela had preceded him and boosted morale even to the point of stemming desertions for the time being. De la Rey was not there to greet him, having gone to confer with Piet de Wet, who with 5,000 Free Staters had set up positions on the Sand River twelve to fifteen miles to the east.

While Roberts had been advancing along the Central Railway, forces under Lord Methuen and Gen Hunter had been advancing in the west where on 6 May they defeated Gen Sarel Du Toit at Fourteen Streams, north of Kimberley, thus threatening the Western Transvaal and promising the relief of Mafeking. De la Rey feared that this would cause Western Transvaal commandos to desert the Free State in order to protect their farms and families. On 8 May on his return from his meeting with Piet De Wet he persuaded Botha, who in turn persuaded Kruger, that he should be sent to the Western Transvaal in order to take command of all the Boer forces there and he left the Sand River on 9 May.

As De la Rey made his way to the Western Transvaal two British columns, manned largely by colonial troops, were preparing to relieve Mafeking. From the south a 1,000-strong force under Lt Col Brian Mahon had left Barkly West, near Kimberley, on 4 May. A force already in the Mafeking area under Lt Col Herbert Plumer formed the nucleus of the 800-strong Northern Relief Column comprising units of the British South Africa police, Rhodesians and Australians with Canadian artillery. Mahon's force consisted largely of South African mounted irregulars, the largest element of which was the Imperial Light Horse commanded by Lt Col A.H.M. Edwards. However, also with Mahon were 100 fusiliers chosen to represent in equal parts England, Scotland, Wales and Ireland.[57] The two relief columns met on 15 May at Jan Massibi, about twenty miles west of Mafeking on the Molopo River. Here Mahon took overall command and divided the combined force into two brigades, one under Plumer and the other under Edwards.

Three days earlier Commandant Sarel Eloff, Kruger's grandson, had with 225 volunteers carried out a bold raid on Mafeking from the west, breaking through and setting fire to the Baralong township and capturing a lightly defended fort on the perimeter. He was only half-heartedly supported by Gen Snyman, Piet Cronjé's successor as siege commander, and as a result had been surrounded and captured with about 100 of his men. De la Rey arrived in the area on 14 May and was joined by Liebenberg's commando. Men from the siege force, with little experience of fighting, brought his total strength up to about 2,000. He took up position astride the Molopo River, with his centre at Israel's Farm, about eight miles west of Mafeking. Mahon advanced on the 16th along the north bank of the Molopo with Edward's brigade on the left and Plumer's on the right. Edwards was able to outflank De la Rey to the north but it took Plumer five hours to fight his way through at Israel's Farm. At 7 p.m. that day Maj Karri Davies of the Imperial Light Horse rode into Mafeking with about ten men and was followed at 4 a.m. the next morning by the whole of the relief force, thus ending the 217-day siege. The length of the siege and Baden-Powell's spirited defence had given Mafeking a significance in British eyes out of all proportion to its strategic importance and its relief led to scenes of wild rejoicing in London.

For the Boers the relief of Mafeking was one more defeat, adding to their general demoralisation. After De la Rey's departure from the Free State Botha was no more able than he had been to hold back Roberts's overwhelming force. Kroonstad fell on 10 May and Botha, fearing that he would be outflanked, abandoned his positions on the Rhenoster River on 22 May before falling back on the Vaal. Too late he called on De la Rey to help him prevent Roberts crossing the river into the Transvaal.[58] The battle for Johannesburg was fought to the south-east of the city on 28 and 29 May. Botha occupied a ridge of hills called the Klipriviersberg and to the west of him Gen Sarel Oosthuizen occupied Doornkop, near present-day Soweto. Botha repelled French's attack on the Klipriviersberg on the first day, but on the second day French shifted his attack to Doornkop where Oosthuizen was reinforced during the action by De la Rey and his Western Transvaal commandos. The combination of the flank attack by French's mounted troops and the frontal attack by Ian Hamilton's infantry overcame the Boer defences and Johannesburg was occupied on 31 May. With its fall the demoralisation of the Boer rank and file was almost complete. When it became clear that there was no hope of saving Pretoria, which Kruger and his government had left on 29 March, it was decided to keep the British out of the city until the State gold and essential supplies could be removed. On 3 June De la Rey fought at Quaggaspoort outside Pretoria and finally in an action at Waterval in which he tried unsuccessfully to prevent the release of 3,000 British prisoners of war. When Roberts entered Pretoria on 5 June all Boer combatants had gone.

Apart from his brief involvement at the beginning and end of the siege of Mafeking, the war had kept De la Rey away from his home territory of the Western Transvaal. Like other parts of the Boer republics the area had been denuded of commandos in attempts to provide concentrated resistance to Roberts's advance. Thousands of burghers who remained behind had surrendered their arms and signed the oath of neutrality, leaving the area ostensibly under British control. At the conference of Boer leaders at Balmoral, to which Botha had withdrawn after the battle of Diamond Hill,[59] it was decided that De la Rey should return to the Western Transvaal to take supreme command there. Generals H.R. Lemmer and Sarel Oosthuizen had gone ahead of him to stir the burghers back into activity and re-form the western commandos. Lemmer had been with De la Rey at Kraaipan and Colesberg and Oosthuizen had fought in the Tugela battles and around Johannesburg. At De la Rey's request it was agreed that he should be assisted in his new role by the young Transvaal State Attorney, Jan Smuts.

In geographical terms the area known as the Western Transvaal was really the South-Western Transvaal, a wedge-shaped area nearly twice the size of Belgium, lying to the west of the railway line from Pretoria via Johannesburg to Vereeniging. The dominant physical feature was the Magaliesberg mountain range which straddled the road from Pretoria to Rustenburg before curving up to the west of that town towards the Pilanesberg. It was in the Magaliesberg that De la Rey first disturbed the apparent tranquillity of the Western Transvaal. In its 80-mile length from Pretoria to Boschoek Nek, north of Rustenburg, this range, rising to 1,000 ft above the surrounding Highveld, could be crossed by troops at only a few passes, the most used of which were Magato Nek and Olifants Nek to the west and south respectively of Rustenburg and, to the east, Commando Nek and Zilikats Nek,* 7 miles apart on either side of the Crocodile River where it flowed through a gorge at Hartebeestpoort, site of the present-day dam of that name. Of the two passes Zilikats Nek was the closer to Pretoria, only 15 miles away, but it was at Commando Nek that the road from Pretoria to Rustenburg crossed over to the northern side of the Magaliesberg.

On 10 July De la Rey arrived from the Eastern Transvaal on the northern side of Zilikats Nek where commandos were gathering. That pass, like the pass at Commando Nek, was defended on the southern side by the Scots Greys, commanded by Lt Col the Hon. W.P. Alexander, with one squadron at each pass and a third squadron 3 miles to the south near the bridge over the Crocodile River, where Alexander placed himself. It so happened that on that day the Scots Greys were in the process of being relieved by five companies of the Lincolns, all of reduced strength, under Col H.R. Roberts. The squadron of the Scots Greys at Zilikats Nek remained there overnight, as did two companies of the Lincolns destined for Commando Nek. Zilikats Nek was formed by a dip in the Magaliesberg, at the centre of which was a boulder-strewn kopje and on either side a high shoulder forming part of the range. The British

---

* Named after Mzilikatsi, the renegade Zulu chief and founder of Bulawayo, who inhabited the area for a while after fleeing from Chaka.

defenders were placed about one-third of the way up these shoulders with those troops due to move off the next day under the kopje. The guns were in the gap between the kopje and the eastern ridge with a restricted field of fire. Early on the morning of 11 July De la Rey sent off two Boer climbing parties, each about 200 strong,[60] to approach the shoulders along high ground on either side and to occupy their tops. The eastern party reached its destination at about 5.30 a.m. and at about the same time De la Rey himself led a frontal attack on the kopje, but the western climbing party was long delayed, giving Roberts the opportunity to send troops further up the western shoulder to fire at the Boer attackers. This made it impossible to capture the British guns which were, however, of little use because of their cramped positions. The arrival of the delayed climbers from the west in the afternoon enabled the Boers to drive the British off the western shoulder, to capture the guns and to surround the kopje. The British fought on but their position was hopeless and at the end of the day Roberts surrendered with 189 men, having sustained 72 casualties.[61] The Boer casualties were also relatively heavy and included two of De la Rey's adjutants, lost during the capture of the guns.[62] On the same day in an action south of the Magaliesberg, Sarel Oosthuizen was mortally wounded on his own farm, Dwarsvlei, opposing with a force of only 81 men an 800-strong column commanded by Smith-Dorrien.[63]

These two actions were typical of many which were to be fought in the Western Transvaal by De la Rey and his subordinates for almost another two years. There was no discernible pattern to them except that they were small, often involving hundreds rather than thousands of men. If they had a common purpose it was to inflict the maximum inconvenience on the British with the useful bonus on occasions of topping up Boer supplies. The Boers seldom sought to exploit or follow through their successes, preferring to disengage and await the next opportunity. The Zilikats Nek action, coming as it did after a period of apparent calm, raised Boer morale in the Western Transvaal as much as it alarmed those responsible for the British posts and garrisons there and in particular, according to Smuts, Baden-Powell, now a Major General with responsibility for the Rustenburg district. He records that De la Rey's success 'so unsettled the hero of Mafeking that his bewildered movements thereafter became inexplicable to friend and foe alike'.[64]

Among Baden-Powell's subordinates was Lt Col C.O. Hore who had been with him throughout the siege of Mafeking and who was now responsible for maintaining road communications between that town and Rustenburg. A small post had been established for that purpose at the Elands River on the farm Brakfontein, south of the road from Rustenburg to Zeerust, and was manned by a force of 505, just over 300 of whom were Australians and most of the rest Rhodesians. Its only guns were a muzzle-loading 7-pounder and two Maxims. The post was well located on a small boulder-strewn kopje surrounded by open country about half a mile west of the river on which the camp depended for its water supply. Most of the men were on the kopje but detachments held two small hills on the bank of the river. On 3 August a convoy of eighty wagons had arrived from Zeerust and was awaiting an escort to take it on to Rustenburg. That night as Hore's men held a campfire concert, De la Rey surrounded the post with a force whose initial strength was about 900 men, but which was increased subsequently to at least 2,000. Despite intense bombardment starting at dawn on 4 August – which killed over 1,000 of Hore's transport animals – and the failure of a rescue attempt from the direction of Zeerust by Gen Carrington, Hore held out.[65] On 7 August, the fourth day of the siege, De la Rey wrote to him expressing his admiration for the conduct of his men and offering to allow his officers to retain their swords if he surrendered – Hore rejected the offer. At this point De la Rey withdrew much of his force, believing that it would be better employed seeking out inactive burghers in other areas and persuading them to fight again. Hore was relieved by Kitchener on 16 August. De la Rey's efforts to reactivate Boers who had surrendered their arms bore fruit. Eventually, encouraged by the resurgence of Boer military activity, some 95 per cent of those who had surrendered their arms did rejoin the struggle, bringing the total of De la Rey's forces in the Western Transvaal to 7,000.[66] Few of them are likely to have had any qualms about breaking their oath of neutrality, believing that oath to conflict with their higher duty to their own country. An old Boer quoted by Smuts spoke for most of them when he said, 'My hand has signed this accursed thing but God knows my heart is pure and that I intend tearing it up as soon as the first commando appears.'[67]

While De la Rey was besieging Hore on the Elands River, Christiaan de Wet had been forced across the Vaal from the Free State and was heading for the Magaliesberg pursued by a large British force under Kitchener in what was later to be called the first De Wet hunt. On 14 August he crossed the range at Olifants Nek, unoccupied because of Ian Hamilton's delay. A few days later, with all the passes now occupied, he crossed again by taking his small force over the top of the mountain near Wolhuter's Kop and headed back to the Free State.[68]

By the end of August 1900 there were fragmented Boer forces in every part of the Western Transvaal, the most important of which were the Marico and Lichtenburg commandos under Lemmer, Bloemhof under Commandant Tollie De Beer, Wolmaransstad under Commandant Potgieter and Potchefstroom under Gen Liebenberg. The Rustenburg and Krugersdorp commandos were under the direct supervision of De la Rey. The others acted independently until the middle of 1901.[69]

In October De la Rey and Smuts were at the farm Syferfontein in the Swartruggens when news reached them of the approach of President

Steyn after his meeting with President Kruger in the Eastern Transvaal. He and Louis Botha joined them on 27 October and over the next few days discussions took place which led to decisions to invade Natal and the Cape Colony again and to destroy the Rand gold mines. The Free State Postmaster-General who accompanied Steyn had brought with him a device called a 'vibrator' which made it possible to intercept British telegraphic messages and to monitor the approach of the columns converging on Syferfontein.[70] After Steyn and Botha had left, De la Rey narrowly avoided capture as he followed Smuts who had taken all the available wagon transport away to the north-west.[71]

At the end of November, Roberts, convinced that the war was all but over, handed over his responsibilities as Commander-in-Chief to Kitchener. Rustenburg was once again under British control and supply convoys were travelling the road from Pretoria with relative impunity, leading one British officer to describe it as being 'as safe as Piccadilly'.[72] However, De la Rey had been keeping an eye on the convoys with a view to replenishing his own supplies. At this time the nearest British forces were those under brigadier-generals R.G. Broadwood at Olifants Nek and G.G. Cunningham in Krugersdorp. On 2 December a fully laden convoy of 260 wagons left Pretoria for Rustenburg. Having crossed the Magaliesberg at Breedt's Nek, about fifteen miles east of Olifants Nek, De la Rey, assisted by Smuts, lay in wait at Buffelspoort with 800 men. The convoy, which extended for eight miles, was divided into two equal sections, each escorted by a force of approximately 250 men. When De la Rey attacked the leading half of the convoy at about 5 a.m. its escort, commanded by Maj J.G. Wolridge-Gorton, seized two kopjes, one on either side of the road. The higher and southern kopje was the more lightly defended and fell to De la Rey at about 1 p.m. Despite continuing and vigorous resistance by Wolridge-Gorton on the northern kopje, by nightfall De la Rey had captured 126 wagons and their much needed supplies. He returned to the south of the Magaliesberg by Breedt's Nek before the British relieving forces arrived.[73]

After the Buffelspoort incident there came into De la Rey's area of operation two of the most able of the younger Boer commanders, the 31-year-old Gen Christiaan Friedrich Beyers and the 28-year-old Commandant Jan Christoffel Greyling Kemp. Beyers was a lawyer like Smuts, whose contemporary he had been at Victoria College, Stellenbosch. A fine rugby forward, he had been in the Transvaal team for several years and had played against a British touring side.[74] One of his officers described him as 'six foot of broad-shouldered, strong-limbed resolution' with 'dark deep piercing eyes'.[75] Deneys Reitz who was serving under him at this time acknowledged his bravery but disliked him, describing him as 'a dark moody man who lost no opportunity of holding prayer meetings'.[76] Kemp was a former civil servant who had seen much action in the redoubtable Krugersdorp commando throughout the war. He was present at Spion Kop as a field-cornet and was one of the first to discover that the British had abandoned the hill.[77]

As part of the command arrangements decided on by Botha and the Transvaal government at Pietersburg in early October 1900 Beyers had been given overall command in the Northern Transvaal with the intention that he should act in concert with De la Rey in the Western Transvaal. The only British force operating in the Northern Transvaal was a column under Maj Gen Arthur Paget based on the Pretoria to Pietersburg railway. When Paget moved eastwards at the end of November to deal with Ben Viljoen at Rhenoster Kop, Beyers decided to move south. He left Warmbaths on 7 December with 100 wagons and a force of 1,500 men drawn mainly from the Zoutpansberg and Waterberg commandos under commandants Ernst Marais and Van Staden respectively, together with part of the Krugersdorp commando under Kemp. Also included were the Pretoria District commando under Commandant Badenhorst and 200 Scouts under Commandant Lodi Krause, another young lawyer, who like Smuts had been both at Stellenbosch and Cambridge.

At Bethany, 15 miles north of the Magaliesberg, Beyers rested his force in the area of Chief Koos Mamaglie. Broadwood's cavalry brigade was camped between him and the Magaliesberg. His suspicion aroused by the warmth of Mamaglie's welcome, Beyers took care to give him the impression that he intended to attack Rustenburg, a ruse which drew Broadwood off in that direction when the chief duly reported the presence of Beyers's force to the British. By an oversight the information was not passed on to Gen Clements, De la Rey's former opponent at Colesberg, who was operating on the southern side of the Magaliesberg. The diversion of Broadwood enabled Beyers to cross the Magaliesberg on the night of 11 December via an old wagon track at Breedt's Nek. The following day he met De la Rey on the other side of the Nek. Five miles to the east of them Clements had camped at Nooitgedacht under the steep southern face of the Magaliesberg, which at that point rose to 1,000 ft above the valley floor. His force was 1,500 strong with 9 guns and a pom-pom. Behind him was a wooded gorge and a stream which provided him with water for his men and animals. A further advantage was that a track leading up through the gorge gave access to the crest, from which he could communicate by heliograph with Broadwood. However, the site was dominated by great crags on either side of the gorge causing Smuts to say of Clements's choice, 'I do not think it was possible in the whole range of the Magaliesberg to have selected a more fatal spot for a camp.'[78] Beyers and De la Rey quickly agreed plans for an assault on the camp. Beyers was to attack from the Magaliesberg, from the top and along the southern slope from the west, while De la Rey was to attack from the valley, from the west against the camp itself and from the south-west to cut off Clements's retreat.

In the small hours of 13 December Beyers led a force of 750 men up the mountain, leaving Badenhorst to attack along the southern slope and a further contingent at Breedt's Nek to look out for Broadwood. Beyers himself, with Van Staden's Waterbergers and Krause's scouts, moved to deal with the British pickets on the western crest above the camp while Kemp and Ernst Marais took their commandos on the longer route to the eastern crest. Before any of them were ready to launch an assault from the top Badenhorst attacked prematurely from the west at 3.40 a.m. and was repelled by Clements's mounted infantry. Beyers's men opened their attack on the western crest at about 4.25 a.m., followed later by Kemp and Marais on the eastern crest. The outnumbered British defenders were overcome easily and reinforcements were killed or wounded as they attempted to come up the track through the gorge. By 7 a.m. the mountain was in Boer possession and the stream was running red with the blood of dead soldiers. Broadwood's heliograph message to Clements asking if he required help was intercepted by a Boer heliographer who replied that none was required. Finding it impossible to communicate with Broadwood and realising the precariousness of his position Clements left his guns behind to cover the withdrawal of his force to Vaal Kop, also known as Yeomanry Hill, 2 miles to the east. Here, having recovered his guns, he held out for several hours. When he received an intelligence report informing him for the first time of the involvement of Beyers he decided to retire to Rietfontein, 23 miles away in the direction of Pretoria. His escape was facilitated by the fact that his mounted infantry had had to leave behind in the camp most of its horses, wagons, stores and ammunition, thus providing the Boer rank and file with opportunities for looting which they preferred to pursuing him. Total British losses were 628, of whom 74 were killed, 186 wounded and 368 taken prisoner or missing. The Boer losses were estimated at 100.[79]

At the end of the year De la Rey sent Smuts with 1,000 men to the Gatsrand, the 50-mile ridge lying between Potchefstroom and Johannesburg, where it was hoped that he could unite dissident elements in the Potchefstroom commando. Smuts's personal memoirs of the Boer War end at this point. On 31 January 1901 after an attack lasting 44 hours he captured the British post at Modderfontein. By early March he was operating again with De la Rey whom he assisted in an attack on Lichtenburg, De la Rey's home town. The combined Boer force, including that of Gen J.G. Celliers, totalled 1,200 men with 1 gun against a British defending force of 620 with 2 guns commanded by Lt Col C.G.C. Money.[80] De la Rey surrounded the town during the night of 2 March and on the following day succeeded in penetrating the outer defences. Despite his initial success he was unable to capture the town and withdrew after 24 hours. Gen Celliers was severely wounded in the action.

Beyers and Kemp had left the Western Transvaal at the beginning of 1901 and had operated briefly together to the east of Johannesburg. In early February Beyers had taken the Waterberg and Zoutpansberg commandos back to the Northern Transvaal while Kemp had rejoined De la Rey's command in the west, taking the Krugersdorpers back to their own district. At the age of twenty-eight he was made a general and in that capacity served in the Western Transvaal for the remainder of the war. *The Times History* described him as De la Rey's ablest and most daring lieutenant.[81] Given the task of rounding up inactive Boers south of the Magaliesberg he had, by the end of May 1901, a force of 3,000 men[82] with him at Tafelkop, a small plateau on the southern side of the Witwatersrand and about thirty-five miles south-west of Rustenburg. On 29 May he attacked a small British force under Brig Gen H.G. Dixon at Vlakfontein, approximately seventeen miles east of Tafelkop on the other side of the Witwatersrand. Under cover of smoke from a veld fire the mounted Boers charged down on part of the force commanded by Maj H. Chance and captured its guns (each side maintained that the other had started the fire). In a vigorous counter-attack Dixon recaptured both the guns and the ground which Chance had been defending.[83]

On 30 September Kemp, with others, assisted De la Rey in an attack on a force of 800 men under Col R.G. Kekewich* in their camp at Moedwil, 7 miles west of Magato Nek on the east bank of the Selons River. De la Rey's scouts had been stalking the British column for a week and he had quickly assembled a force of 1,000 when it camped at Moedwil.[84] Attacking from the river before daylight De la Rey's men fired on the camp causing the horses to stampede. Kekewich was twice wounded in the engagement, but Maj R.A. Browne to whom he delegated command dispersed the Boers on the river bank by a determined bayonet charge. Apart from De la Rey's own attack the planned supporting assaults from other sectors miscarried and he was obliged to withdraw. Kekewich's casualties amounted to 25 per cent of his force and Boer losses were put at forty-eight, probably an underestimate.[85]

The pattern of initial success followed by failure was repeated when De la Rey with Kemp and Steenkamp attacked a column commanded by Lt Col S.B. von Donop at Kleinfontein, 20 miles east of Zeerust, on 24 October. The 1,000-strong column with 7 guns and accompanied by 100 mule wagons was travelling on a road fringed by bush and dominated by thickly timbered heights when De la Rey's 500 men charged down on it.

* Commanding officer in Kimberley during the siege.

They cut through the wagon train in three places, inflicting heavy casualties on the mule teams, the gun detachments and the rearguard, but von Donop counter-attacked and was able to save his guns and most of the convoy. The Boers were left with only twelve wagons as the prize of this action.[86]

Four months later De la Rey was more successful when he attacked a 151-wagon convoy sent by von Donop on the 50-mile journey from Wolmaransstad to Klerksdorp. De la Rey was in the vicinity with Kemp, Celliers, Liebenberg and 1,200 men and could have taken the convoy, whose progress he was following, at any time during the journey. However, according to one of his officials he delayed his move until the convoy was only one day away from Klerksdorp, believing that the soldiers escorting it would fight with less determination than they would in the open veld if they knew that they could escape to a fortified refuge. The convoy left its final camping place at Yzerspruit, 13 miles from Klerksdorp, at 4.30 a.m. on 25 February 1902 and had travelled only 1½ miles when De la Rey attacked. He had planned that Liebenberg would strike from the front in order to draw the escort away from the convoy, to be followed by assault from the rear of the convoy by Celliers and then a flank attack by Kemp from the left. In the face of stiff resistance by the modest escort force commanded by Lt Col W.C. Anderson, the attacks of Liebenberg and Kemp faltered and Celliers was late in launching his from the rear. When he did attack belatedly he too encountered resistance but the Boers as a whole greatly outnumbered Anderson's force whose ammunition was eventually exhausted. De la Rey captured the convoy, the British guns, nearly 200 prisoners and large numbers of horses and mules. He had not known when he planned the assault that most of the wagons were empty, but he was able to capture ½ million rounds of much needed ammunition. Of the 490 men in Anderson's force who had been engaged 187 were killed or wounded. One wounded officer and 108 men escaped and made their way to Klerksdorp.[87]

In the course of the guerrilla war in the Western Transvaal a succession of British commanders had come and gone but Lord Methuen had remained there continuously since July 1900 when he arrived in Krugersdorp from the Free State. After taking part in the first De Wet hunt he had been put in charge of the Mafeking and Marico districts. These areas were subsequently extended to include the Northern Cape Colony as far south as Kimberley. Despite his rank of lieutenant-general and the wide extent of the area for which he was now responsible he had a relatively small force at his disposal and, in operational terms, was little more than a column commander, a task which he undertook with cheerful dedication. His area included De la Rey's farm at Elandsfontein near Lichtenburg where he called on Mrs De la Rey in December 1900 to tell her with regret that he had been ordered to burn the farm buildings.

She rejected his offer to leave one building standing for her use and also an alternative offer of a house in Cape Town, since she was not prepared to accept British hospitality and wanted to be near her husband. For the next eighteen months she lived an extraordinary life moving about by ox-wagon accompanied by six of her children, three African servants and a small collection of farm animals.[88] In the course of her adventures, about which she wrote after the war,[89] she succeeded both in keeping clear of the British and in maintaining contact with her husband. Methuen did not in fact burn the farm but used it as a billet for British officers and a local headquarters until a scout sent there by De la Rey to report on its condition shot and killed an officer who emerged in his pyjamas early in the morning and a second one who came out to investigate. Unsurprisingly the house was then burnt down. De la Rey was incensed by his scout's killing of men in cold blood.[90]

One of the effects of the Boer success at Yzerspruit was to draw Methuen in from Vryburg – to which administrative work had taken him – in order to cooperate with Kekewich in cutting off De la Rey's escape to the north-west. It was planned that he should rendezvous on 7 March 18 miles south of Lichtenburg at Rooirandjesfontein with a mounted force of 1,500 under Col H.M. Grenfell, sent out by Kekewich from Klerksdorp. Methuen's own force was 1,300 strong with 6 guns, but it was encumbered by a train of 85 ox- and mule wagons. The evening of 6 March found him 30 miles to the south-west of the intended rendezvous point. He camped at Tweebosch, below the confluence of the Little and the Great Harts Rivers, having had during the day an inconsequential brush with a small Boer force under Commandant Van Zyl of Bloemhof. He set off northwards at 3 a.m. and, believing the only immediate threat to come from Van Zyl to the south, he sent his wagons ahead. Unknown to him he was being shadowed by De la Rey, Kemp, and Celliers with 1,100 men, who were joined by Van Zyl. At 5 a.m. the Boers opened fire on Methuen's force on three sides. A high proportion of the British were an ill-assorted collection of irregulars who were unnerved and gave way under the onslaught, but the gunners under Lt T.P.W. Nesham stood firm and he himself was killed when he refused to surrender even when his guns had been captured. When the Boer attack moved on to the convoy ahead, Methuen organised the defence and held off the Boers for two hours until he was wounded and captured. Within five hours three-quarters of his force had been killed, wounded or captured. De la Rey was taken to the wounded Methuen, where he still lay near the British guns, by Beyers's secretary, J.F. Naudé, who introduced them and acted as an interpreter. De la Rey bent over Methuen and extended his hand, saying, 'I am sorry to meet you in such circumstances.' 'Oh, it's the fortune of war,' responded Methuen, 'How is Mrs De la Rey?', to which De la Rey answered 'She's still moving around safely. . . .'

Methuen replied that he had always tried to behave in a gentle and friendly way to the women whom he had conveyed to the camps and that he had only caused the removal of De la Rey's wife on the orders of his superior officers. De la Rey merely nodded.[91] Mrs De la Rey herself came to see Methuen in her husband's laager and later sent him a chicken and some biscuits.[92] To the dismay of his subordinate officers De la Rey set free his wounded adversary and allowed him to be conveyed to Klerksdorp in his own wagon, having first sent a message to Methuen's wife. The 600 other British prisoners were given rations and released.[93]

Ten days later De la Rey met Steyn and De Wet on the farm Zendelingsfontein, west of Klerksdorp, after they had escaped from one of the last of Kitchener's new model drives in the North-Eastern Free State. They were cheered by news of De la Rey's recent successes and his medical director, Dr Rennenkampf, was able to look at Steyn's deteriorating eye condition. Kitchener's reaction to De la Rey's successes was to introduce the new model drive into the Western Transvaal and during March he assembled in Klerksdorp 16,000 men in four groups under Maj Gen Walter Kitchener and colonels Kekewich, Sir Henry Rawlinson, and A.N. Rochfort. An essential complement to the Free State drives was an extensive system of blockhouse lines. While construction of these had started in the Western Transvaal in July 1901, there were none within the south-western sector, although they hemmed in the north, east and west, with the Vaal River providing a barrier to the south. It was in this sector, extending for 115 miles from north to south between Lichtenburg and the Vaal and 160 miles from east to west between Klerksdorp and Vryburg, that the bulk of De la Rey's commandos under Kemp, Celliers and Liebenberg were now located. Following intelligence reports placing large numbers of Boers within thirty miles of the Schoon Spruit blockhouse line, which marked the eastern boundary of this large area, Kitchener ordered 11,000 mounted troops under the four group commanders to position themselves 40 miles to the west of the Schoon Spruit line during the night of 23 March, and then to return to it, having deployed into driving formation, during the following day. In theory they should have trapped Kemp's and Liebenberg's commandos, and also De la Rey and Steyn returning from Zendelingsfontein with members of Steyn's Free State Council and a small escort, all of whom were in the designated area, but all of whom escaped. De la Rey and Steyn slipped through in the small hours of 24 March and Kemp at about 6 a.m. as the British were deploying. Liebenberg did not escape until the afternoon when gaps were beginning to open in the 90-mile driving line, but he had to abandon his guns and wagons. All of them joined Celliers on the Harts River, their combined forces totalling 2,500 men.[94]

After the disappointing results of the first drive which yielded 165 prisoners, 3 guns and 2 pom-poms, Kitchener conferred with the group commanders in Klerksdorp on 26 March, hampered by ignorance of De la Rey's exact whereabouts. It was decided that while Rochfort remained on the Vaal the other commanders should set out westwards in echelon over three days to set up entrenched camps at assigned points and at the same time try to make contact with the Boer forces. In Walter Kitchener's group, Col G.A. Cookson set out at 2 a.m. on 31 March with 1,800 men and 6 guns to reconnoitre the Brak Spruit, an almost dry stream which flowed westwards into the Harts River 40 miles way. At about 10 a.m. he picked up the trail of a commando and set off in pursuit until he was checked at the farm Boschbult. Here he fought a holding action while he set up an entrenched camp around two farmhouses on the northern bank of the stream. Just after 1 p.m., before he had fully completed his defences, he was attacked by Kemp and Celliers from the north and by Liebenberg from the south. After charging from the south and then again from the north-east Liebenberg joined Kemp and Celliers, but left his guns to shell Cookson's camp from the south-west. The Boers were able to drive in the British screens but could make no headway against the camp itself. De la Rey, who had made his headquarters on the farm Roodewal (Rooiwal), 7 miles to the south-west, arrived on the scene late in the afternoon and, having assessed the strength of the British defence, called off the action.[95]

On 9 April De la Rey left with Steyn and his party under a safe-conduct arranged by Kitchener to join other Transvaal and Free State leaders in Klerksdorp. This followed intimations by Kitchener, prompted by the intervention of the Netherlands government, that he would be prepared to consider peace proposals. After hearing reports by Botha, De Wet and De la Rey the government representatives drafted preliminary proposals and left on the evening of 10 April to present these to Kitchener in Pretoria. Meanwhile, Ian Hamilton had been detached from his duties as Kitchener's Chief of Staff to take overall charge in the Western Transvaal with the intention of bringing matters to a final conclusion there. He had arrived at Kekewich's headquarters at Middelbult, 20 miles south of Lichtenburg on the evening of 8 April and immediately put in hand the next operation. This was to be a drive southwards from the Brak Spruit, past the Harts River to the Vaal and then eastwards to Klerksdorp, a total distance of 140 miles, with 11,000 men in all under Kekewich on the right, Rawlinson in the centre and Walter Kitchener on the left. On the evening of 10 April the entire British force was in position on the south side of the Brak Spruit, but Kekewich placed his division ten miles too far to the east, immediately behind Rawlinson's. He partially corrected the error during the night, moving westwards towards the Harts River so that his right ended up at Roodewal, about three miles from the river.[96]

In De la Rey's absence in Klerksdorp, Kemp had taken overall command of the Boer forces comprising his own commandos, now under

Potgieter, and those of Celliers and Liebenberg. When he received reports of the British troop movements he made up his mind to attack one of the enemy flanks and, relying on reports from his scouts, decided that the British right commanded by Kekewich was more vulnerable than the left. He had expected only 300 troops at the end of the British line on the Brak Spruit but he had relied on out-of-date intelligence.[97] As his force topped the ridge about one and a half miles to the south-west of the main columns at Roodewal, it came within sight of the whole of von Donop's and Grenfell's columns, some 3,000 men in all, but according to Kemp's own account not all of these were visible to him since most were concealed in fields of maize and sorghum.[98] He continued his advance down the gentle slope towards the Brak Spruit and about a mile from von Donop's column the British saw a group of approximately 700 men detach itself and break into a gentle trot, advancing towards them in a line two, three and four files deep. As it approached it threw its wings forward like the horns of a Zulu impi and at the same time opened fire. The British closed up to meet the attack and by the time the Boers were within 600 yards, 1,100 rifles and a Maxim had been brought to bear on them. The Boers were now riding knee to knee, with their leaders in front, and firing from the saddle. Among the leaders the tall Commandant Potgieter was prominent in a blue shirt and long jackboots. Without change of pace and undaunted by the heavy fire the Boers continued to advance, throwing their wings further forward as if to envelope the British. It was not until they were 100 yd away and it was apparent that the defenders were standing firm that the Boers abandoned their charge and retreated. Potgieter was killed – shot through the head – 70 yd from the British lines. As Kemp's force retreated, the Imperial Light Horse under Col C.J. Briggs on Rawlinson's right galloped on to the scene dispersing Liebenberg's commandos who were supporting Kemp to the east.[99]

In the action at Roodewal the Boers lost 127 men, of whom 51 were killed, very low figures in the circumstances and ascribed by *The Official History* to the inadequate training in rifle drill of the many irregulars in Kekewich's force.[100] British casualties were 87 killed and wounded. Had he been present it is unlikely that De la Rey would have sanctioned Kemp's charge. It had been based on inadequate reconnaissance and lacked the advantages of cover and surprise that had made previous Boer charges so successful. However, Kemp told an interviewer many years later that his object that day was to gain a signal victory to strengthen the Boer negotiating position in the pending peace talks – cost meant nothing, all that mattered was success.[101] If he failed to gain his victory, his charge earned the admiration of the British. Ian Hamilton later lamented the fact that Winston Churchill had not been present to record the event in fitting prose.[102]

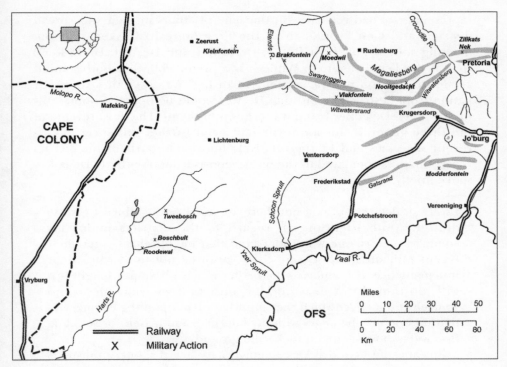

The Western Transvaal

De la Rey learnt of Kemp's defeat in Pretoria where he had gone with the other Transvaal and Free State leaders to meet Kitchener. They met him alone on 12 April and Milner joined him at a second meeting on 14 April. The result of those meetings was a failure of the Boer attempt to keep independence on the peace agenda and a re-offer by the British government of the terms rejected after Botha's meeting with Kitchener at Middelburg in February 1901. The British accepted that only the Boer people could take a decision on whether or not to surrender their independence and it was agreed that for this purpose 'the people' were the 21,000 Boer combatants still in the field.[103] The generals returned to their areas to arrange for the election of representatives from every district, thirty from each republic.

The leaders and the elected district representatives, mostly field commanders, gathered at Vereeniging where on 15 May 1902 they began their consideration of the British peace offer.[104] Beyers was elected chairman of the meeting. Among the thirty Transvaal representatives were his principal lieutenants Kemp, Celliers and Liebenberg. De la Rey did not speak until the evening of the second day when the representatives had reported on the state of affairs in their widespread districts and Gen Froneman of the Free State had asked that the meeting should now hear Botha, De la Rey and De Wet. De la Rey's speech was keenly awaited. While it was predictable that Botha would argue for an honourable settlement in order to save the Afrikaner nation from destruction and that De Wet would be opposed implacably to surrender, De la Rey had not yet shown his hand. The most revered of the three generals, his authority had been further enhanced by his recent successes and by the relatively buoyant reports of his district representatives compared to the bleak reports from elsewhere. De la Rey spoke briefly:

> I will not detain you long but there are a few points which I wish to draw to your attention. In regard to the districts under my command, every one will understand that my burghers, after their recent brilliant successes, are firmly resolved not to sacrifice their independence. If I allude to the battles which I have just fought it is with no thought of boasting, but only that you may picture to yourselves the effect which they must have had upon the enemy; and that no one may be angry with my burghers and myself for standing firm when our feet are on such solid ground.
>
> But since my arrival at Vereeniging I have heard about our districts where matters are in a far less favourable condition than in my own. So far as I myself am concerned, I cannot think of laying down my arms. Yet it appears to me that some parts of the country will be compelled by starvation to give up the struggle. It is well that those who represent these parts have spoken openly, and not left this meeting in ignorance of the state of affairs only to go and lay down their arms.

He went on to dismiss as unrealistic the hope that there would ever have been an intervention by sympathetic European powers and continued:

> There has been talk about fighting to the bitter end; but has not the bitter end already come? Each man must answer that question for himself.
>
> You must remember that everything has been sacrificed – cattle, goods, money, wife, and child. Our men are going about naked, and some of our women have nothing but clothes made of skins to wear. Is not this the bitter end?
>
> I believe that the time has now come to negotiate. England will never again give us the chance of doing so, should we allow this opportunity to slip by. . . .[105]

The meeting concluded with the appointment of a five-man delegation to attempt the negotiation of a small semblance of independence in return for the cession to Britain of the Rand goldfields and Swaziland. De la Rey, with Botha, De Wet, Smuts and Hertzog, was a member of that body which met Kitchener and Milner again on 15, 19 and 28 May. The near verbatim account of those meetings records no significant intervention by De la Rey, who left the details of negotiation to others.[106] The Boer counter-proposal was rejected and the final result embodied the Middelburg terms with minor modifications, mostly favourable to the Boers. This was to be put to a reconvened Vereeniging meeting to be accepted or rejected in its entirety. The meeting lasted from 29 to 31 May. De la Rey urged acceptance,[107] as did Botha and Smuts. De Wet was still firmly for rejection but behind the scenes he was persuaded to use his influence in favour of acceptance in the interests of Boer unity. The final result was fifty-four in favour of acceptance and six, including Kemp, against. De la Rey was one of the Transvaal signatories to the peace treaty which was signed late in the evening of 31 May 1902 in the dining-room of Kitchener's house in Pretoria. 'We are all friends now,' said Kitchener.

On the fund-raising visit to Britain with Botha and De Wet in August 1902, De la Rey was accompanied by his wife. The generals received a warm welcome but a disappointing response in the way of financial contributions. On his return to South Africa De la Rey set about rebuilding his home at Elandsfontein. Jan Smuts and his wife, both expert amateur botanists, advised and helped with the planting of trees and shrubs. On the spot where the two English officers had been shot, De la Rey planted a walnut tree.[108] In December 1903 he was asked to go to Ceylon to see the 500 Boer prisoners of war there to persuade them to return to South Africa, but also to explain that they were free to live in exile if they chose not to accept allegiance to Britain. On the way there he heard in Bombay of the death of his daughter Ada Ferreira. Another daughter Sannie Brugman had died in Pretoria shortly after the end of the war. His son Koos, who had accompanied him to Ceylon and who had gone through the war with him, died in 1907, the sixth of his twelve children to die.[109]

During the period of reconstruction under Milner from 1902 to 1905 De la Rey was active as a representative of Afrikaner opinion in the Transvaal and with Botha and Smuts he declined an invitation to serve on the nominated Legislative Council. With them, and with Beyers, he played a leading part in the formation of Het Volk, the political party of which Botha was leader and which took political control when the Transvaal was granted responsible government in 1907. De la Rey was a member of the Legislative Assembly, of which Beyers was Speaker, but did not take ministerial office. He was a Transvaal member of the National

Convention which met first in Durban and then in Cape Town in 1908 and 1909. He supported political union of the British colonies with the former Boer republics, more out of loyalty to Botha and Smuts than out of conviction. At heart he was still a Transvaal republican. When Botha became South Africa's first Prime Minister in 1910, with Smuts as his Defence Minister, De la Rey became a senator. Although he lacked the temperament and skills of a politician he was a potent force in South African politics because of the universal respect which he enjoyed. While Botha and Smuts were seen by many Afrikaners as becoming too 'English', De la Rey was seen as embodying the ideals for which the Boers had fought.[110] He had great personal affection for the two younger men, which they reciprocated, but they also needed his political support. Early in 1914 he returned briefly to his role as a military leader when the government invoked his help at the head of a commando in quelling industrial unrest in Johannesburg.[111]

The outbreak of the First World War in August 1914 had repercussions in South Africa, which aggravated the tensions within Afrikanerdom and alienated De la Rey from Botha's government. He still cherished the thought that the former Boer republics might regain their independence and he took it for granted that Botha and Smuts, for many years his close friends, shared that aspiration. He had not forgotten that at Vereeniging in 1902 Botha had assured him that an opportunity for a renewed bid for independence could arise in the future when Britain was in trouble. With that assurance in mind he had sided with Botha and used his considerable influence in the cause of peace.[112] But events had moved on – Botha now bore the responsibility of governing the whole of South Africa within the British Empire. Not only had he assured Britain that South Africa would take full responsibility for defending its own borders, but he had acceded to a request from Britain to invade German South West Africa in order to get control of the powerful radio transmitters there which threatened British ships. Although not immediately publicised, since Parliament was not in session, that possibility of an invasion became the subject of rumour and caused alarm to many Afrikaners who, while having no particular regard for Germany, found repugnant the idea of invading another country's territory on behalf of Britain. Among them were some officers in the Union Defence Force, including the Commander-in-Chief, Christiaan Beyers.

De la Rey's conduct at this time is believed to have been influenced by a strange character called Niklaas van Rensburg, a poor Wolmaransstad farmer reputed to have the gift of prophecy based on visions. He had served with De la Rey during the Boer War, in which he had been credited with some uncannily accurate predictions of British movements. While the cynics believed that his successes were based on good intelligence from native African informers,[113] De la Rey and many others, particularly in the Western Transvaal, believed in his prophetic gifts and he was known as the *Siener* (seer). Interest in his visions continued after the Boer War and the fact that he never sought to exploit his gift for personal benefit enhanced his credibility. A judicial commission later described him as 'a prophet not without honour in his own country'.[114] He left it largely to others to interpret his visions, which were symbolic and ambiguous enough to allow more than one meaning.

One such vision, disclosed to his followers long before the First World War, had been the subject of much speculation. It was about a fight among several bulls in which a grey bull had triumphed over a red bull. As war in Europe became more likely the consensus grew that the red bull symbolised the British Empire and the victorious grey bull, Germany. The *Siener* had also dropped hints that great things were in store for De la Rey, who had seen little of him since the Boer War.[115] On 11 July 1914 van Rensburg had arrived at De la Rey's farm at Elandsfontein and on the following day, in a state of some agitation, had revealed to the general a vision specifically about him. Van Rensburg subsequently related the vision to others and slightly varying accounts were in circulation, but they had in common the number 15 against the background of dark or bloody sky, De la Rey returning home without a hat, and a carriage of flowers. Hatlessness in the *Siener*'s visions was usually an omen of death and it was taken as such by both De la Rey and his daughter Polly, who was the only other person present at the first revelation.[116] The number 15 was thought to signify a date, probably the 15th day of a month. Others interpreted the vision as De la Rey returning home in triumph on such a date, having restored the republican flag.[117]

It is impossible to say how much De la Rey himself was influenced by this vision in particular and by the *Siener*'s predictions in general but he does appear to have to come to the conclusion at this time that he was called by God to play an important part in a new move for independence and also to have attached importance to the number 15. On 3 August, the day before the start of the First World War, he sent out a call for a gathering of men in the Lichtenburg district to be held on 15 August at Treurfontein, telling them to come with arms and ammunition. Since he made no attempt to keep this secret, Botha and Smuts soon heard about it and asked to meet him at Botha's home in Pretoria on 12 August. There he was told of the plan to invade South West Africa, to which he expressed his opposition, and it was made clear to him that Botha and Smuts would not support his proposed bid for independence from Britain. Botha argued that while it might be God's will to give South Africa back its liberty, it could never be his intention to bring this about along the road of dishonour and treason. After much praying together, De la Rey was persuaded to support the government.[118] This effectively defused his Treurfontein meeting. On his new instructions the 800 men who attended came unarmed and afterwards dispersed peacefully, having passed a motion of confidence in the government's ability to act in the best interests of the country.[119]

Smuts, as Minister of Defence, then met senior army officers to tell them that it would be necessary to mobilise 20,000 men for the defence of South Africa. There was no reference to German South West Africa and discussion of that subject was discouraged as it had not yet been presented to Parliament. However, Beyers, who was privy to the government's plans as Commander-in-Chief, insisted on voicing his objections and he was supported by other officers.[120] The proposed invasion was condemned at the first congress of Hertzog's new National Party in Pretoria on 26 August. De la Rey was present by invitation and spoke of the need for Afrikaner unity. On 5 September he left for Cape Town to attend a special session of Parliament called for 9 September to debate the government's intention to invade South West Africa. This was approved by the Lower House on that date by ninety-two votes to twelve, a result which overstated the extent of true support for the proposal and which reflected assiduous persuasion behind the scenes by Botha.[121] It was debated by the Senate on 12 September, when De la Rey spoke against it but declared that he would abstain. He left before the end of the debate and went by train to Johannesburg where he arrived on the 14th.[122]

Of the Union Defence Force officers opposed to the invasion of South West Africa two, both former Boer War generals, are known to have been actively plotting rebellion. These were Lt Col Manie Maritz, who was in charge of the training camps in the North-West Cape near the South West Africa border and who was already in touch with the Germans, and Maj J.C.G. Kemp, who was in charge at Potchefstroom where four mounted regiments were at a training camp due to break up on 16 September. This was the same Kemp who had fought with Beyers and De la Rey at Nooitgedacht. The extent to which Beyers was contemplating rebellion and the rôle played by De la Rey are largely matters of conjecture. Both the government and the plotters knew that De la Rey was the only man with the stature to lead a significant rebellion and his support was therefore important to both sides. Some accounts portray Beyers as persuading a troubled De la Rey to join the rebels, others conclude that De la Rey had already made his difficult choice and that it was he who stiffened the determination of an irresolute Beyers.

The two men met in Pretoria on 15 September where De la Rey apparently persuaded Beyers to accompany him to Potchefstroom and was anxious that they should leave that night and not wait until the following day as Beyers suggested.[123] They set off at about 7 p.m. in

Beyers's grey chauffeur-driven Daimler open tourer on a route that was to take them through Johannesburg. Unknown to both men the police had posted pickets on all main roads in and out of that city, in order to capture a small group of criminals, the so-called Foster Gang, who had recently murdered a policeman. When the Daimler encountered the first picket at Orange Grove on the north-eastern side of Johannesburg, Beyers could reasonably have assumed that it was intended to stop him, since his letter of resignation as Commander-in-Chief had been released to the papers for publication that day and he believed that he had been under police surveillance. After consulting De la Rey he instructed his chauffeur to ignore the instruction to stop and to go on. The police had specific instructions to open fire if a black car containing three men and a woman failed to stop and they took no action against Beyers's grey Daimler, which in the same way ignored instructions to stop at a two further pickets until it reached Langlaagte to the west of Johannesburg. Here an armed policeman lunged at a front tyre with his fixed bayonet and was flung aside as the car passed, but he recovered sufficiently to fire at a rear tyre as the car passed under a street lamp. The car drove on for another 200 yd then stopped, turned round and came back. When the chauffeur was challenged he said, 'You have killed General De la Rey.' The single bullet had richocheted off the road, pierced the rear of the car and entered De la Rey's back. A fragment of its nickel casing had lacerated his heart, killing him almost immediately.[124]

Beyers subsequently became convinced that the accident was the result of a police conspiracy directed not at De la Rey but at him. Halfway between Pretoria and Johannesburg the two men had changed places. It was a windy night and De la Rey, who had been sitting to windward, feared that the smoke from his pipe would trouble Beyers, a non-smoker.[125] Earlier that evening Dr Gerald Grace,* black-bearded like Beyers, had been killed when the police fired at his black car after he had failed to stop on the eastern side of Johannesburg.[126] A judicial commission into both deaths found no evidence to suggest that they were other than tragic accidents.[127]

Two funeral services were held for De la Rey, the first in Pretoria and the second, on 20 September, a full military funeral in Lichtenburg where nearly 10,000 people gathered.[128] The horse-drawn carriage which bore his body was covered with flowers, bringing to mind the *Siener*'s vision. Botha and De Wet both spoke emotionally, as did Beyers who denied emphatically that he and De la Rey had been planning rebellion.[129] The anger and suspicion generated by the death of De la Rey provided a focus of discontent in addition to the South West Africa

---

* A brother of the famous cricketer W.G. Grace.

issue. Maritz decamped to South West Africa on 2 October, taking with him as prisoners of war those men who refused to join the Germans. The government declared martial law on 12 October. The rebellion as it developed took the form of isolated actions involving mainly De Wet, Maritz, Kemp and Beyers. It was dealt with easily by the government, using motor vehicles against its mounted opponents. De Wet and Kemp surrendered, Maritz fled into exile and Beyers was drowned trying to escape across the Vaal.

The day after De la Rey's funeral it was resolved to erect a mounted statue of him in Lichtenburg. A donation from Methuen and Ian Hamilton towards a statue was thought by the family to be inappropriate, and was diverted to the De la Rey Memorial Hospital.[130] A mounted statue was finally erected in Lichtenburg on 27 February 1965, the 84th anniversary of the battle of Majuba.[131]

Notes

1. Meintjes, *De la Rey*, p. 48.
2. Penning, *Verdegigers en Verdrukkers*, p. 101.
3. Meintjes, *De la Rey*, p. 21.
4. Ibid., p. 19.
5. Fitzpatrick, *SA Memories*, pp. 200–1; Barnard, *Botha*, p. 14.
6. *TH* ii, 266.
7. Breytenbach i, p. 386.
8. *TH* iv, 570.
9. Meintjes, *De la Rey*, p. 49.
10. De la Rey, *Herinneringe*, A313 vol. 17, National Archives.
11. Breytenbach i, pp. 393–5.
12. Ibid., ii, p. 18.
13. Ibid., ii, p. 39.
14. Ibid., ii, p. 57.
15. Belfield, p. 39; *OH* i, 244–5.
16. Doyle, p. 141.
17. Breytenbach ii, p. 58.
18. *TH* ii, 345.
19. J.M. Lane Diary 28 November 1899.
20. *TH* ii, 350.
21. Pakenham, p. 195.
22. Van den Heever, 70–3.
23. Meintjes, *De la Rey*, p. 121–3.

24. Pakenham, p. 199.
25. Breytenbach ii, p. 98.
26. *TH* ii, 386.
27. Breytenbach ii, pp. 99–102.
28. Ibid., ii, p. 103.
29. Pemberton, p. 82.
30. *TH* ii, 386.
31. *OH* i, 466, Appendix 6.
32. Breytenbach ii, p. 120.
33. Douglas, p. 404; Pemberton, p. 86.
34. The Ashanti War (1873–4), El Teb (1894) and the Gordon Relief Expedition (1884–5).
35. Wilson, *Flag to Pretoria*, p. 180; Kruger, *Dolly Gray*, p. 128.
36. Breytenbach ii, p. 121.
37. Pemberton, p. 88.
38. *TH* ii, 405.
39. Pemberton, p. 111.
40. *TH* ii, 416.
41. Breytenbach iv, pp. 46–7.
42. Ibid., iv, p. 2.
43. *TH* iii, 138.
44. Breytenbach iv, p. 45.
45. *TH* iii, 139.
46. *TH* iii, 461.
47. Breytenbach v, pp. 67–8.
48. Ibid., v, p. 74, quoting *OH* ii, Appendices I and VI.
49. Ibid., v, p. 97.
50. *OH* iii, 229.
51. Breytenbach v, p. 119.
52. Ibid., v, pp. 156–66.
53. Ibid., v, pp. 178, 447.
54. Ibid., v, p. 417.
55. Ibid., v, p. 437.
56. Ibid., v, p. 439, *OH* iii, 48.
57. *TH* iv, 216.
58. Breytenbach v, pp. 515–6.
59. See Chapter Four, p. 76.
60. *TH* iv, 351.
61. *TH* iv, 352.
62. Spies and Nattrass, p. 92.
63. Ibid., p. 90, *TH* iv, 354–5.
64. Ibid., p. 92.
65. *TH* iv, 357–60; Spies and Nattrass, pp. 97–103; Wilson, *The Guerilla War*, pp. 60–6; Wulfsohn in *Military History Journal*, vol. 6, 3, (June 1984).

66. *TH* iv, 347.
67. Spies and Nattrass, p. 86.
68. See Chapter Eight, pp. 188–91.
69. Spies and Nattrass, p. 104.
70. Ibid., pp. 124–33; Pakenham, p. 470–3.
71. Ibid., pp. 135–6.
72. *OH* iv, 3.
73. *OH* iv, 3–7; *TH* v, 95–6.
74. Naudé, p. 20.
75. Krause, p. 106.
76. Reitz, *Commando*, pp. 134, 136.
77. Kemp, pp. 290–1.
78. Spies and Nattrass, p. 146.
79. Casualty figures *OH* iv, 20; Battle of Nooitgedacht generally Barnard, *Generalship*, pp. 157–64; Kemp, pp. 356–9; Krause, pp. 120–9; Naudé, pp. 186–93; *OH* iv, 9–22; Reitz, *Commando*, p. 132–8; Spies and Nattrass, pp. 146–51; *TH* v, 97–108; Van Warmelo, pp. 103–17.
80. *TH* v, 222.
81. *TH* v, 218.
82. *OH* iv, 184.
83. *OH* v, 281–4; Kemp, pp. 391–5.
84. *TH* v, 379.
85. *OH* iv, 297.
86. *OH* iv, 299–301; *TH* v, 383–5.
87. *OH* iv, 411–15; *TH* v, 498–9.
88. Meintjes, *De la Rey*, pp. 174–7.
89. De la Rey, Mrs General, *A Woman's Wanderings And Trials During the Anglo-Boer War*, London, T. Fisher Unwin, 1903.
90. Meintjes, *De la Rey*, pp. 230–1.
91. Naudé, p. 331.
92. De la Rey, Mrs General, p. 75.
93. *OH* iv, 417–21; *TH* v, 503–8.
94. *TH* v, 512–17.
95. *OH* iv, 494–8; *TH* v, 518–23.
96. *TH* v, 528.
97. Gibson, *ILH*, p. 345.
98. Kemp, p. 465 n.
99. *OH* iv, 499–504; *TH* v, 530–7; Kemp, pp. 462–5.
100. *OH* iv, 503–4.
101. Gibson, *ILH*, p. 345.
102. Hamilton and Sampson, *Anti-Commando*, p. 179.
103. *TH* v, 57.
104. For a fuller account of the peace negotiations see Chapter Eight pp. 204–7.
105. De Wet, pp. 428–9.

106. Ibid., pp. 436–69.

107. Ibid., pp. 479–80.

108. Meintjes, *De la Rey*, p. 287.

109. Ibid., p. 305.

110. Ibid., pp. 318–19.

111. See Chapter Ten, pp. 252–3.

112. Crafford p. 108.

113. Le May, *Afrikaners*, p. 154.

114. UG No. 10, 1916, p. 5.

115. Meintjes, *De la Rey*, pp. 139–40.

116. Ibid., p. 325.

117. Krüger, *The Making of a Nation*, p. 85.

118. Engelenburg pp. 18–19, 282–3; Krüger, *Nation*, p. 82.

119. Meintjes, *De la Rey*, p. 353.

120. Krüger, *Nation*, p. 83.

121. Ibid., p. 83.

122. Meintjes, *De la Rey*, pp. 361–3.

123. Ibid., pp. 368–9.

124. UG No. 48, 1914, p. 10; Meintjes, *De la Rey*, pp. 381–2.

125. Meintjes, *De la Rey*, p. 376.

126. Ibid., p. 377.

127. UG No. 48, 1914.

128. Meintjes, *De la Rey*, p. 383.

129. Ibid., p. 385.

130. Ibid., p. 383 n.

131. Ibid., p. 32.

CHAPTER TEN

Smuts – A postscript

Smuts's contribution ran like a thread through the Boer War – he played a significant part in the events leading up to it, in its conduct and in the final peace negotiations. From the time of his appointment, at the age of twenty-eight, as State Attorney of the Transvaal in June 1898 he was drawn into the arguments with Britain. He attended the six-day Bloemfontein conference which began on 31 May 1899 as President Kruger's chief adviser. After the failure of the conference Smuts devised the final offer to Britain, giving Milner all that he asked for on the franchise, and more, but subject to conditions which made it unacceptable. In anticipation of war Smuts prepared a strategic plan for the Boer republics and probably drafted the Transvaal ultimatum of 9 October which led to war. The initial Boer pre-emptive strikes into British territory were in accordance with his plan but the elderly generals, Joubert in Natal and Cronjé on the Western front, lost the initiative by getting bogged down in the sieges of Mafeking, Kimberley and Ladysmith. Had they pressed on to the Natal and Cape coasts, as envisaged by Smuts, the outcome of the war might have been different, particularly if a large part of the Afrikaner majority in the Cape Colony had risen in sympathy.

During the conventional phase of the war, up to the fall of Pretoria, Smuts continued to act as State Attorney. He stayed on in Pretoria after Kruger and the rest of his government had left for the Eastern Transvaal and his last official act was to remove, under threat of force, the remaining State gold from the Reserve Bank. After the battle of Diamond Hill in June 1900 he joined De la Rey in the Western Transvaal, acting as military second in command, assistant administrator and 'political commissar'[1] in an area, which because of its remoteness, the Transvaal government agreed should be administered as a separate fiefdom.[2] In many small actions, the most notable of which was the attack on Clements's camp at Nooitgedacht, he learnt the military arts from De la Rey, a man whom he revered. From January 1901 he exercised independent command in the Gatsrand area of the Western Transvaal and at the end of that month captured a small British post at Modderfontein after an attack lasting 44 hours.

In his dual rôle of State official and military commander he attended most of the important high-level councils of war. With President Steyn, Louis Botha and De la Rey he took part in the discussions about future strategy at Syferfontein in the Western Transvaal in October 1900 where it was decided to mount new invasions of the Cape Colony and Natal.[3] He was also present at the meetings at Immigratie and Waterval in the Eastern Transvaal which took place respectively in May and June 1901. At the latter meeting he was granted his wish to lead the expedition into the Cape Colony, ostensibly to prepare the way for a later invasion by De la Rey. As a Cape Afrikaner for most of his life he was a good choice for an expedition whose principal purpose was to try and encourage the long-hoped-for rising of Boer sympathisers in the British colony. He had all the qualities necessary for such a command – clarity of mind, audacity, resolution and, perhaps surprisingly to those who had known him as a reclusive student, the power of command allied to exceptional toughness and physical endurance.

Smuts's 1,000-mile incursion into the Cape Colony amid all sorts of privations and hazards was chronicled graphically by Deneys Reitz in *Commando*. Starting out with a mere 200 men Smuts succeeded in consolidating the disparate commandos already operating in the Cape and at the end had 19 commandos and over 2,000 men nominally under his command.[4] After crossing into the Western Cape he established virtual control of a 300-mile swathe of British territory between the Olifants and Orange Rivers, but his invasion had come too late in the war. There was no general rising in the colony and while he laid siege to the copper mining town of Okiep he was summoned to attend the final peace negotiations. There he played an influential rôle, not only in the meetings of Boer delegates at Vereeniging but in the negotiations with Kitchener and Milner and as the Boer representative with Hertzog on the treaty drafting subcommittee. It is said that the scale was tipped in favour of acceptance of the British terms when Kitchener drew Smuts aside during the negotiations and forecast that the probable return in England of a Liberal government would lead to the early grant of responsible government to the former Boer republics.[5] In his speech to the final meeting of the Boer delegates at Vereeniging, Smuts urged them not to sacrifice the Afrikaner nation on the altar of independence.

In the immediate aftermath of the war Smuts's main concern was for the health of his wife, Isie,* who had been detained by the British in a house in Pietermaritzburg from January 1901. He resumed his legal practice and obtained a number of lucrative briefs. This enabled him to start investing in farms, of which he had eleven by 1916 – in 1909 he established his main and lifelong home on one of these, Doornkloof at Irene near Pretoria, where he converted into a house a large wood and

---

* Sybella Margaretha Krige (1870–1954) whom Smuts married in Stellenbosch on 30 April 1897.

corrugated-iron structure, formerly an officers' mess hut, which he had bought from the British Army.[6] With Botha and De la Rey he declined Milner's invitation to serve on the nominated Legislative Council. In 1904 the sentiment aroused by President Kruger's funeral in Pretoria and the indignation provoked by Milner's decision to import Chinese labour for the mines were catalysts in the resumption of political activity on the part of the former Boer leaders. Smuts played a prominent part in the formation of the Het Volk Party which was formally inaugurated under Botha's leadership in January 1905. When Milner, discredited by the Chinese labour issue, left South Africa later that month, Smuts wrote him a generous farewell letter.[7] That same issue contributed to the demise of the Conservative government, which was succeeded in December 1905 by a Liberal government led by Sir Henry Campbell-Bannerman. Smuts arrived in London in January 1906 on a one-man mission to persuade the new government to grant responsible government to the Transvaal. He received a lukewarm reception from some ministers, including Winston Churchill, who was then Parliamentary Under-Secretary of State at the Colonial Office, but he succeeded in persuading Campbell-Bannerman who in turn persuaded his Cabinet. The Transvaal was granted responsible government at the end of 1906, as was the Orange Free State in June 1907. Het Volk won the first general election in the Transvaal with a clear majority in February 1907. The office of prime minister was probably Smuts's for the asking but he preferred to serve under Botha.[8] Botha's shrewdness and geniality allied to Smuts's intellectual gifts, his ability as a political strategist and his prodigious capacity for work made for a formidable partnership which lasted until Botha's death in office twelve years later. Both men were dedicated to healing the rifts in Afrikanerdom and to conciliation between Boer and Briton.

As one of the Transvaal representatives Smuts attended, with nineteen assistants, the 1908 National Convention called to consider the Union of the four South African colonies and he was largely responsible for drafting the constitution which emerged from it. In Botha's first Union government, formed in May 1910, Smuts took on the portfolios of Mines, the Interior and Defence. Later he gave up the first two and took on Finance. As he had done in the Transvaal government he assumed much of the burden of the legislative programme. Within two years the atmosphere of good will surrounding the Union was under strain. In 1912 the exclusion of Hertzog from the Cabinet led in due course to the founding of the National Party under his leadership. There were two major industrial strikes involving white workers – a gold mining strike on the issue of Union recognition in July 1913 and a general strike in January 1914, both attended by violence. In the first, as a result of irresolute intervention by imperial troops, Botha and Smuts were compelled to negotiate personally with the strikers and to settle the dispute. In the second the newly created Union Defence Force, under the local command of De la Rey, was more effective and Smuts summarily deported nine foreign-born labour leaders before the courts had time to consider the matter. He was much criticised at home and abroad for this unconstitutional action and incurred the lasting enmity of organised white labour. Gandhi, then a Johannesburg advocate, took up again with Smuts the grievances of the large Indian community in the Transvaal and Natal, and after a repeat of his earlier 'passive resistance' tactics* negotiated a settlement in June 1914.[9]

As Minister of Defence Smuts was intimately involved in the 1914 rebellion. One exception to the generally lenient treatment of the rebels was the passing of the death sentence on Capt Joseph (Jopie) Fourie. An officer in the Active Citizen Force, he had neglected to take the precaution of resigning his commission before joining the rebels and it was considered that he had caused unnecessary deaths by continuing to fight after the rebellion had collapsed. Smuts's dismissal of petitions for the reprieve of Fourie made a martyr of him and exacerbated the legacy of bitterness left by the rebellion. Although at the time Smuts maintained that the circumstances left him no option, he is said to have admitted later that the execution of Jopie Fourie was the greatest political mistake he ever made.[10]

The rebellion had been provoked by the intention of the Union government to comply with Britain's request to invade German South West Africa. When that went ahead in February 1915 Louis Botha himself took command in the field as the only man who enjoyed the confidence of both Afrikaans- and English-speaking troops. Smuts was responsible for mobilising and equipping the 50,000 men involved, a considerable achievement for a country which only three years earlier had no army. He left his desk in Pretoria in April to take command of the forces in the south of the territory, supporting Botha's main thrust in the north. After the successful conclusion of the campaign in July 1915 it was decided to send volunteer South African troops to support the faltering British war effort in German East Africa (later Tanganyika and now Tanzania). When Sir Horace Smith-Dorrien became seriously ill in Cape Town on his way to assume command there Smuts agreed to take his place and was made a lieutenant-general in the British Army. He took up his command in February 1916 with a force at his disposal of 45,000 men of whom 19,000 were South Africans, 14,000 Indians and the remainder British and Africans. Opposing him was the able German Gen von Lettow Vorbeck

---

* Smuts had negotiated with Gandhi on Indian grievances when a minister in the Transvaal government.

with a force of 14,000 of whom 3,000 were Europeans and 11,000 Askaris, among the best of African troops.[11]

In a vast territory, twice the size of Germany, Smuts saw no prospect of forcing his adversary into a decisive engagement and therefore resolved to manoeuvre him out of his positions. He began by dislodging von Lettow Vorbeck from his foothold in Kenya in the vicinity of Mount Kilimanjaro and then advanced southwards into German East Africa in order to secure the railway line which ran alongside the Paré and Usambara mountains to the port of Tanga. Van Deventer, his principal lieutenant during his invasion of the Cape Colony in 1901–2, advanced southwards independently, supporting his western flank. Progress was hampered by heavy rain and by malaria, to which Smuts himself succumbed. Smuts took Tanga in early July 1916 and by early September he and van Deventer, in cooperation with British and Belgian forces to the west, had taken the whole of the Central Railway line from Lake Tanganyika to Dar-es-Salaam. By the end of September the whole of the coast from that port to the border of Portuguese East Africa was in control of imperial troops. Von Lettow Vorbeck was never actually defeated but remained with a much depleted force in the south of the territory until the end of the war.[12] Some of the British regular officers in East Africa resented serving under a man they regarded as an amateur but Col R. Meinertzhagen, who was in charge of military intelligence, recorded this appraisal of Smuts in his diary for 28 July 1916: '. . . His knowledge of human nature, his eye for country, his exceptional power of imposing his will on others, his remarkable personality, reckless disregard of difficulties and very remarkable brain, compel one to respect and admire him. Perhaps it is wrong to say he is no soldier. He is a bad tactician and strategist, an indifferent general but in many ways a remarkable soldier.'[13] After the war Smuts remained on cordial terms with von Lettow Vorbeck and in the period of austerity in Germany after the Second World War sent him food parcels.[14]

Smuts arrived in London in March 1917 having been asked by Botha to go in his place to represent South Africa at the Imperial War Conference. In parallel with the conference, which was chaired by the Secretary of State for the Colonies, the representatives met as an Imperial War Cabinet under the chairmanship of Lloyd George, dealing with day to day administrative matters, the conduct of the war and the question of peace terms. Smuts carried a resolution at the conference opposing a move towards imperial federation and he proposed instead the idea of a British Commonwealth of autonomous nations.[15] He expanded on this idea when he addressed a joint meeting of both Houses of Parliament on 15 May 1917.[16] In April of that year Smuts had been offered the Palestine command but had declined it after the Chief of the General Staff, Sir William Robertson, had made it clear that operations there would be a sideshow. In June, at the invitation of Lloyd George, he became an unpaid member of the British War Cabinet, but declined a suggestion that he should seek a seat in the House of Commons. He proved to be an outstanding administrator who quickly found himself at home in Whitehall. He served on the War Policy Committee and took charge of the committee considering home defence against air raids and the future of Britain's air services, which at the time were parts respectively of the Army and the Navy. The main outcome of the committee's work was the formation of the Royal Air Force with it own Air Staff and Air Ministry.[17] He became chairman of the War Priorities Committee with power to determine the competing claims of the services on industrial production. He was even asked to deal with a potentially disastrous coal strike in South Wales.* Introducing himself as someone from far away, he told an angry crowd of miners that he had heard that the Welsh were among the greatest singers in the world and asked them to sing him some of the songs of their country. They readily responded with 'Land of My Fathers'. He appealed to their patriotism and after he had repeated the performance at other meetings the strike was over.[18]

Between November 1917 and February 1918 Smuts was charged with missions to the Italian, Western and Middle Eastern fronts and to sound out in Switzerland the possibility of a separate peace with Austria. In June 1918 his frustration with America's slowness in starting active operations on the Western Front led him, in a private letter to Lloyd George, to propose himself as field commander of the American forces. Lloyd George did not pass on this suggestion, which would have caused great offence.[19] Immediately before and after the armistice, Smuts chaired the Demobilisation Committee and prepared the British brief for the peace conference. He was instrumental in securing for the dominions separate representation within the British Empire delegation. He resigned from the British War Cabinet in December 1918 and applied his mind to the promotion of the League of Nations, of which President Wilson and he were the main sponsors, and to the forthcoming peace conference in Versailles where he was to join Botha, representing South Africa. He was a passionate opponent of imposing over-harsh terms on Germany, believing that in due course they would lead to another war. He urged 'appeasement' in the sense of conciliation from a position of strength, and not, as it came to mean in the 1930s, of yielding from a position of weakness;[20] but he was no longer at the centre of power in Britain and as the junior representative of a small country his influence was much diminished. Although his personal prestige was still high his views were

---

* The government had been told by the Navy that they had coal reserves for only one week.

against the mood of the conference. He resolved at first not to sign the peace treaty but later relented. He returned to South Africa in August 1919 as a privy councillor and Companion of Honour.

Throughout his three-year absence Smuts had continued to be a South African Cabinet Minister and MP. He had been back barely a month when Louis Botha died at the age of fifty-seven. Smuts succeeded him as Prime Minister and was to be actively involved in South African politics for the whole of the twenty-year interval between the two world wars, a period characterised by shifting coalitions and party mergers and one in which the principal issues continued to be South Africa's relationship with Britain and the relationship between the white races. Native affairs were certainly part of the legislative programmes but between the parties there was a broad consensus that there should be some degree of segregation between black and white and that there should be no extension of full political rights to the non-white population as a whole. The differences were at the margin. Of that twenty-year period Smuts was Prime Minister for only five years, from 1919 to 1924. He was confirmed in office in a general election in 1921 following the absorption by his South African Party of the predominantly English-speaking Unionist Party.

His term of office was marred by three incidents which had in common the use of force by government agencies. In May 1921 police opened fire when they were charged by members of a Native religious sect known as the Israelites, who had refused to vacate common land at Bulhoek near Queenstown despite months of patient negotiation; 163 Israelites were killed and 129 wounded.[21] In May and June of the same year the administration in South West Africa, then a League of Nations mandated territory, used force in a dispute with the Bondelswart tribe, an Afrikaans-speaking Christian community of mixed Hottentot and white blood; 115 members of the tribe were killed.[22] In early 1922 there was a renewal of industrial unrest on the Rand involving white miners, engineers and power workers, culminating in a general strike. The predominantly Afrikaner strikers were organised in commandos and serious violence, including attacks on Africans and Indians, erupted after a small Communist-inspired group of militants gained control. The government declared martial law on 10 March and Smuts himself took command of the Active Citizen Force, restoring order within three days. In all there were nearly 700 casualties of whom 153 were killed – 72 members of the police and military, 157 strikers* and 42 innocent civilians.[23] Eighteen strikers were sentenced to death for murder, of whom four were executed.

* Classified by the Martial Law Commission as 'Revolutionaries' and 'Suspected Revolutionaries'.

Away from domestic troubles Smuts played a leading part in the 1921 Imperial Conference in London, renewing his advocacy of autonomy for the dominions within a British Commonwealth. His presence in Britain and his known sympathy for the cause of Irish nationalism led to his playing an informal mediating rôle in the Anglo-Irish dispute.

Following Smuts's general election defeat in 1924 by an alliance of Hertzog's National Party and the Labour Party, Hertzog succeeded him as Prime Minster, an office he held for the next fifteen years. Four years older than Smuts, Hertzog had a similar background. He was a lawyer who had come into prominence as a young man (he had been appointed a judge in the Supreme Court of Orange Free State at the age of twenty-nine), he had been a Boer War general, and he was a cultivated man. However, he lacked Smuts's flair and his self-discipline, giving vent sometimes to intemperate and incoherent outbursts. It fell to Hertzog to bring to fruition the work begun by Smuts on dominion status, culminating in passing of the Statute of Westminster in 1931. As Leader of the Opposition, Smuts succeeded in frustrating Hertzog's attempts to curtail further the political and civic rights of non-whites, taking particular objection to statutory job reservation for whites in industry and the proposed ending of the Native franchise in the Cape. In 1933, when Hertzog's parliamentary majority was under threat, Smuts agreed to serve under him as Deputy Prime Minister and Minister of Justice and in 1934 the National and South African Parties merged to form the United Party. The rôle of main opposition party was taken over by the 'Purified' National Party led by Dr Daniel François Malan, Smuts's boyhood family friend and neighbour at Riebeek West, a former minister of religion and founder-editor of *Die Burger*, the Cape Afrikaner Nationalist newspaper. To maintain their unity Smuts and Hertzog had to some extent to bury their differences and Smuts did not oppose Hertzog's renewed attempt to end the Native franchise in the Cape, settling for improved communal representation in its place. Their unity did not survive the outbreak of the Second World War. Smuts's motion opposing South African neutrality was carried by eighty votes to sixty-seven. Hertzog resigned, the Governor-General refused to dissolve Parliament and Smuts became Prime Minister again at the age of sixty-nine.

Smuts first task as war leader was to build up the Union's neglected defence forces by the recruiting of volunteers from both the white and non-white communities, the latter unarmed and providing support services. A large proportion of both served abroad. When Kenya, Somaliland and Ethiopia had been secured, the South Africa forces there joined the British forces in North Africa. They were supported by aircraft of the South African Air Force, and small ships of the Seaward Defence Force (later the South African Naval Forces) operated with the Royal Navy in the Mediterranean. In the early stages of the war Smuts had to reckon with Hertzog's defeatism and advocacy of a separate peace between South Africa and Germany. He obtained a decisive parliamentary majority in support of continuing the war, confirmed by a general election in 1943, but throughout the war he had to deal with anti-war elements such as the Ossewa Brandwag.* In general his policy was to disarm them and to leave their leaders free but under surveillance. After the South African 2nd Division was captured at Tobruk in June 1942 Smuts recruited a replacement division. After Germany had been defeated in Africa the South African 6th Armoured Division served in Italy and on 4 August 1944 was the first Allied formation to reach Florence.[24] During the war Smuts visited North Africa five times and went to Britain four times. He formed a close working relationship with Winston Churchill and in May 1941 was made a field-marshal in the British Army. When the Suez canal was reopened, South Africa and the Cape sea route were no longer of vital strategic importance to the Allies and Smuts himself lost much of his influence in the highest councils of the war, but he was one of the first Western leaders to recognise the implications for postwar politics of Russia's military strength.[25] After the war he played a leading part in the formation of the United Nations and was the principal author of its charter.

After the war Smuts was dismayed by the strength of world opposition to South Africa's racial policies and the use by India of the United Nations in expressing that opposition. This and his own acceptance that a growing black urban population and the dependence of industry on black labour were inescapable realities, led him to place the emphasis on ways in which South Africa's different races could coexist, as opposed to the National Party's advocacy of rigid apartheid, although he was a long way from contemplating the grant of full political rights to non-whites. Before he was able to implement any liberalising measures he was removed from power by the Nationalist election victory of May 1948. His defeat marked the end of an era and it was to be almost half a century before South Africa was again to have a respected voice in world affairs. The death of his able lieutenant J.F.H. Hofmeyr prompted him to continue in politics as Leader of the Opposition, but his health began to fail from about the time of the celebrations for his eightieth birthday in May 1950 and he died at Doornkloof on 11 September of that year. His family declined the offer of a State funeral and settled for an impressive military funeral procession in Pretoria.[26]

In parallel with his career as a politician and soldier Smuts achieved recognition as a philosopher and scientist. Although the outward formalities

---

* Literally 'Ox-wagon Picket' – a Fascist-type organisation which began its life innocuously in 1938 as a cultural society to celebrate the Great Trek.

of religion became less important to him in the years after the Boer War he was a deeply spiritual man whose intellectual life was a long quest for the ultimate reality. From childhood he had a deep affinity for South Africa's landscape and natural life, in particular its mountains and plants. He had a special feeling for Table Mountain which he climbed most weekends when the House was in session during the first thirty-five of his forty years in Parliament.[27] As a botanist he could hold his own with professionals in naming at sight South Africa's many species of grasses.[28] After his 1924 election defeat he found time to write his book *Holism and Evolution*, developing the concept of 'wholes' which had first attracted him at Cambridge – it was he who coined the term 'holism' and its more widely used adjective 'holistic'. He argued that the elements which constituted matter, life and mind were associated within groups or wholes, from which were derived the organising and creative energy of evolution. He saw the process of evolution, not as a random proliferation of species, but as progress towards the development of wholes and wholeness, whose highest manifestation was the human personality. He never found time to finish his planned further book on the subject. Apart from his special interests he played a part in the promotion of science generally. In 1925 he was president of the South African Association for the Advancement of Science. In 1930 he was elected a Fellow of the Royal Society and the British Association for the Advancement of Science chose him as its president for its centenary year in 1931. At the centenary meeting he delivered a wide-ranging address on 'The Scientific World Picture Today'.[29] The University of London conferred on him the honorary degree of DSc, previously conferred only on Lords Lister and Kelvin.[30] In the course of his career he received many academic honours, but the ultimate recognition of his many-sided ability was his installation as Chancellor of the University of Cambridge in June 1948.

At a time when twentieth-century South African politicians tend to be judged by the part they played in progress towards universal equality, Smuts's reputation has lost some of its lustre. It would be easy to categorise him as a white supremacist who tolerated and even reinforced what Nelson Mandela has called the de facto apartheid which prevailed before successive Nationalist Governments replaced it from 1948 onwards by de jure apartheid.[31] But Smuts was a man of great complexity. At heart he was a humanitarian who respected all races, but he was not alone in believing passionately in the virtues of Western civilisation and he thought that its precarious foothold in Africa could best be secured by the European races. When he first became involved in national politics he saw with Botha that to establish South Africa as a modern industrial state it was necessary first of all to heal the bitter enmities among and between the white races, but he was under no illusion that ultimately the real issue in South Africa was the resolution of relations between black and white. Yet, as a pragmatist he knew better than anybody that politics is the art of the possible and he saw no prospect in his lifetime of a white electorate accepting full political rights for all South Africans. As early as 1906 he had commented that he was 'inclined to shift the intolerable question of that sphinx problem to the ampler shoulders and stronger brains of the future',[32] a sentiment which largely characterised his approach to the question for the rest of his career. When he did attempt to improve the lot of non-whites he pleased nobody – conservatives regarded him as a dangerous liberal and liberals as a reactionary. However history finally judges his contribution to South African and world affairs, it is given to few men to be born with so wide an array of gifts and to use them so fully for so long.

Notes

1. Hancock, *Sanguine Years*, p. 122.
2. Spies and Nattrass, p. 77.
3. Ibid., pp. 124–33; Pakenham, pp. 470–3.
4. DSAB i, 740.
5. J.C. Smuts, p. 83.
6. Ibid., pp. 120–1, 269–70.
7. Hancock, *Sanguine Years*, p. 198.
8. Ibid., p. 228.
9. D.W. Krüger, *The Age of the Generals*, pp. 77–9.
10. Ibid., p. 93.
11. Hancock, *Sanguine Years*, p. 411.
12. Williams, *Botha, Smuts and South Africa*, pp. 102–7.
13. Part of a longer quotation in Hancock, *Sanguine Years*, p. 419.
14. J.C. Smuts, pp. 178–9.
15. Hancock, *Sanguine Years*, pp. 428–9.
16. J.C. Smuts, pp. 187–91. The idea of a British Commonwealth was canvassed as early as 1904 by John X. Merriman, the veteran Cape politician, in his correspondence with Smuts. See Hancock, *Sanguine Years*, pp. 203–4.
17. Lloyd George, *War Memoirs* iv, pp. 1863–70.
18. Ibid., iii, pp. 1372–5.
19. Hancock, *Sanguine Years* pp. 482–4.
20. Ibid., pp. 512–3.
21. Hancock, *The Fields of Force*, pp. 89–99.
22. Ibid., pp. 100–1.
23. Martial Law Commission, quoted by Millin ii, p. 377 and Hancock, *The Fields of Force*, p. 84.
24. Keene, p. 190.
25. Hancock, *The Fields of Force*, pp. 412–13.
26. J.C. Smuts, p. 527.
27. Ibid., p. 401.
28. Hancock, *The Fields of Force*, p. 173.
29. Quoted extensively in J.C. Smuts, pp. 315–22.
30. J.C. Smuts, p. 315.
31. Mandela, p. 104.
32. From letter to John X. Merrriman 13 March 1906, document 288 in Hancock and van der Poel ii, pp. 242–3, quoted in Hancock , *Sanguine Years*, p. 221.

Bibliography

UNPUBLISHED PAPERS

Public Record Office	Kitchener Papers PRO 30/57
National Army Museum	Roberts Papers NAM 7101/23
National Archives, Pretoria	De la Rey. Versameling A.313, vol. 17, *Herinneringe*
Mr William Lane	Diary of John Moody Lane, 16 November 1899–27 February 1900

OFFICIAL PUBLICATIONS

Cd. 426 – *Proclamations issued by Field-Marshal Lord Roberts in South Africa*, 1900

Cd. 457 – *South Africa Dispatches vol. 1 (Roberts)*, 1901

Cd. 458 – *South Africa Dispatches vol. 2 (Natal Field Army)*, 1901

Cd. 968 – *The Spion Kop Dispatches*, 1902

Cd. 981 – *Papers relating to the Administration of Martial Law in South Africa*, 1902

Cd. 1423 – *Papers relating to the Administration of Martial Law in South Africa (Continuation of Cd. 981)*, 1903

Cd. 1789 – *Royal Commission on the War in South Africa – Report of the Commissioners*, 1903

Cd. 1790 – *Royal Commission on the War in South Africa – Minutes of Evidence vol. I*, 1903

Cd. 1791 – *Royal Commission on the War in South Africa – Minutes of Evidence vol. II*, 1903

Cd. 1792 – *Royal Commission on the War in South Africa –Minutes of Evidence: Appendices*, 1903

Hansard 3rd and 4th Series – Parliamentary debates

Report of Major General Roberts on the Operations in the Khost Valley in January 1879 HC 1878–9 (100) LVI pp. 757–766

Papers relating to the Proceedings of Major General Roberts in the Khost Valley on 7th and 8th January 1879 HC 1878–9 (234) LVI pp. 767–772

Union government, Blue Book UG No. 48 1914 – *Judicial Commission of Inquiry into the deaths of Senator General the Honourable De la Rey and Dr G. Grace – Report of the Commissioner*

Union government, Blue Book UG No. 10 1916 – *Judicial Commission of Inquiry into the Recent Rebellion – Report of the Commissioners*

Union government, Blue Book UG No. 42 1916 – *Judicial Commission of Inquiry into the Recent Rebellion – Minutes of Evidence*

BOOKS AND MAGAZINE ARTICLES

(First edition and place of publication London unless otherwise stated)

Amery, L.S. (ed.). *The Times History of the War in South Africa*, 7 vols, 1900–9

———. *My Political Life Vol. I*, 1953

Anglesey, Marquess of. *A History of the British Cavalry: 1816–1919 – Volume IV: 1899–1913*, 1986

Bibliography

Anon. *In Memoriam – In Memory of Field-Marshal Earl Kitchener of Khartoum K.G.*, Leamington Spa, 1960

Arthur, Sir George. *Life of Lord Kitchener*, 3 vols, 1920

Asprey, R. *War in the Shadows*, 1994

Atkins, J.B. *The Relief of Ladysmith*, 1900

Balfour, B. *The History of Lord Lytton's Indian Administration, 1876 to 1880*, 1899

——. *Personal and Literary Letters of Robert, 1st Earl of Lytton – Vol. II*, 1906

Ballard, Brig Gen C.R. *Kitchener*, 1930

——. *Smith-Dorrien*, 1931

Barnard, C.J. *Generaal Louis Botha op die Natalse Front – 1899–1900*, Cape Town, 1970

——. 'Studies in the Generalship of the Boer Commanders', *Military History Journal*, vol. 2, 5 (June 1973)

——. 'General Botha at the Battle of Colenso', *Military History Journal*, vol. 1, 7 (December 1970), pp. 1–6

Barthorp, M. *War on the Nile*, Poole, Dorset, 1984

——. *The Anglo-Boer Wars*, paperback 1991 (Or. 1987)

Bateman, P. *Generals of the Anglo-Boer War*, Cape Town, 1977

Belfield, E. *The Boer War*, 1975

Beukes, P. *The Holistic Smuts*, Cape Town, 1989

Beyers, C. (ed. in chief). *Dictionary of South African Biography* (English edition) 4 vols: I, II and III Cape Town, vol. IV Durban, 1968–81

Birdwood, FM Lord. *Khaki and Gown – An Autobiography*, 1941

Bond, B. (ed.). *Victorian Military Campaigns*, 1967

Breytenbach, J.H. *Die Geskiedenis van die Tweede Vryheidsoorlog in Suid Afrika, 1899–1902*, 5 vols, Pretoria, 1969–1983

Buckle, G. (ed.). *The Letters of Queen Victoria*, 3rd Series, vol. III, 1896–1901, 1932

Buller, Gen Sir Redvers. *Evidence to the Royal Commission on the War in South Africa*, 1904

Burleigh, B. *The Natal Campaign*, 1900

Butler, L. *Sir Redvers Buller*, 1909

Buxton, Earl. *General Botha*, 1924

Calwell, Maj Gen Sir Charles. *Field-Marshal Sir Henry Wilson Bart*, vol. I, 1927

Cassar, G. *Kitchener: Architect of Victory*, 1977

Chisholm, R. *Ladysmith*, 1979

Churchill, Winston S. *Ian Hamilton's March*, 1900

——. *London to Ladysmith via Pretoria*, 1900

——. *My Early Life*, 1937

Clarke, P. 'The Battle of Omdurman', *Army Quarterly and Defence Journal*, vol. 107, 3 (July 1977)

Colvile, Maj Gen Sir H.E. *The Work of the Ninth Division*, 1901

Crafford, F. *Jan Smuts*, Cape Town, 1946

Creswicke, L. *South Africa and the Transvaal War*, 8 vols, 1900–2

Crowe, G. *The Commission of H.M.S 'Terrible' 1898–1902*, 1903

Davey. A. *Breaker Morant and the Bushveldt Carbineers*, Cape Town, 1987

Davitt, M. *The Boer Fight for Freedom*, New York, 1902

De la Rey, Mrs General. *A Woman's Wanderings During the Anglo-Boer War* (tr. Lucy Hotz), 1903

De La Warr, the Earl. *Some Reminiscences of the War in South Africa*, 1900

De Watteville, H. *Lord Roberts*, 1938

——. *Lord Kitchener*, 1939

De Wet, Gen C.R. *Three Years War (October 1899–June 1902)*, 1902

(Defender). *Sir Charles Warren and Spion Kop – A Vindication*, 1902

Dodwell, H. (ed.). *The Cambridge History of India – Volume VI: The Indian Empire 1858–1918*, Cambridge, 1932

Douglas, Sir George, Bt. *The Life of Major-General Wauchope*, Hodder & Stoughton, 1904

Doyle, A.C. *The Great Boer War*, 17th edn (complete), 1902

Dudley, C. 'The Boer View of Buller – New Evidence', *Army Quarterly and Defence Journal*, vol. 114, 3 (July 1984), pp. 320–7

Dundonald, Lt Gen the Earl of. *My Army Life*, 2nd edn, 1934

Edwards, Dennis & Co. (publisher). *The Anglo Boer War, 1899–1900 – An Album of Upwards of Three Hundred Photographic Engravings*, Cape Town, *c.* 1901

Elsmie, C.R. *Field-Marshal Sir Donald Stewart*, 1903

Engelenburg, F.V. *General Louis Botha*, 1929

Ensor, R. *The Oxford History of England – England 1870–1914*, Oxford, 1992 (Or. 1936)

Esher, O. (ed.). *Journals and Letters of Reginald, Viscount Esher – Vol. 3 1910–1915*, 1938

Esher, R. *The Tragedy of Lord Kitchener*, 1921

Farrar-Hockley, Sir Anthony. *Goughie, the Life of General Sir Hubert Gough*, 1975

Farrar-Hockley, Maj A. (ed.). *The Commander* (by Gen. Sir Ian Hamilton), 1957

Farwell, B. *Queen Victoria's Little Wars*, 1973

——. *Eminent Victorian Soldiers*, 1986

——. *The Great Anglo-Boer War*, paperback, New York, 1990 (Or. 1976)

Fergusson, J. *The Curragh Incident*, 1964

Fitzpatrick, J.P. *South African Memories*, 1932

Fuller, Maj Gen J.F.C. *The Last of the Gentlemen's Wars*, 1937

Germains, V. *The Truth About Kitchener*, 1925

Gibbs, P. *Death of the Last Republic*, 1957

Gibson, G.F. *The Story of the Imperial Light Horse in the South African War 1899–1902*, 1937

Gilbert, M. *Churchill – A Life*, pocket edn, 1993

——. *First World War*, 1994

Gilmour, D. *Curzon*, 1994

Goldmann, C.S. *With General French and the Cavalry in South Africa*, 1902

Hackett, R.G. *South African War Books – An Illustrated Bibliography of English Publications relating to the Boer War of 1899–1902*, 1994

Hamilton, Gen Sir Ian. *The Commander* (ed. by Maj A. Farrar-Hockley), 1957

——. *The Happy Warrior: A Life of General Sir Ian Hamilton*, 1966

Hancock, W.K. *Smuts – the Sanguine Years 1870–1919*, Cambridge, 1962

——. *Smuts – the Fields of Force 1919–1950*, Cambridge, 1968

—— and Van der Poel, J. (eds). *Selections from the Smuts Papers* vol. II, Cambridge, 1966

Hanna, H. *The Second Afghan War 1878–1880*, 1899–1910

Hensman, H. *The Afghan War of 1879–1880*, 1881

Hillegas, H.C. *With the Boer Forces*, 1900

Hobhouse, E. *The Brunt of the War and Where it Fell*, Methuen & Co., 1902

Hobson, J.A. *The War in South Africa – its Causes and Effects*, 1900

Holmes, R. *The Little Field-Marshal – Sir John French*, 1981

Howland, F.H. *The Chase of De Wet*, Providence, USA, 1901

James, D. *Lord Roberts*, 1954

James, L. *The Rise and Fall of the British Empire*, 1994

Jeans, T. (ed.). *Naval Brigades in the South African War 1899–1900*, 1901

Jenkins, R. *Asquith*, paperback 1994 (Or. 1964)

Jerrold, W. *Lord Roberts of Kandahar*, 1900

——. *Sir Redvers H. Buller, VC*, 1900

Judd, D. *The Boer War*, 1977

Keene, J. (ed.). *South Africa in World War II – A Pictorial History*, Cape Town, 1995

Kemp, Gen J.C.G. *Vir Vryheid en vir Reg*, Cape Town, 1941

Kestell, J.D. *Through Shot and Flame*, 1903

Knox, E.B. *Buller's Campaign with the Natal Field Force of 1900*, 1902

Krüger, D.W. *The Age of the Generals*, South Africa, 1958

——. *The Making of a Nation*, 1969

Kruger, R. *Good-Bye Dolly Gray – The Story of the Boer War*, paperback, 1983 (Or. 1959)

Laband, J. *Lord Chelmsford's Zululand Campaign 1878–1879*, 1994

Le May, G.H.L. *British Supremacy in South Africa 1899–1907*, Oxford, 1965

——. *The Afrikaners*, Oxford, 1995

Lees, F. (tr.). *Colonel de Villebois-Mareuil War Notes*, 1901

Lehmann, J. *The First Boer War*, 1972

Liddell Hart, Capt B. *History of the First World War*, paperback, 1972

(Linesman). *Words by an Eyewitness – the Struggle in Natal*, 1901

Lloyd George, D. *War Memoirs*, 5 vols, 1933–6

Lutyens, M. *The Lyttons in India*, 1979

Lyttleton, Gen Sir Neville. *Eighty Years – Soldiering, Politics, Games*, 1927

MacGregor, Lady (ed.). *The Life and Opinions of Major-General Sir Charles Metcalfe MacGregor*, 2 vols, 1888

MacGregor-Hastie, R. *Never To Be Taken Alive – A Biography of General Gordon*, 1985

Macnab, R. *The French Colonel*, Oxford, 1975

Magnus, P. *Kitchener – Portrait of an Imperialist*, 1958

Mahan, Capt A.T. *The Story of the War in South Africa*, 1900

Malan, J. *Die Boere-Offisiere van die Tweede Vryheidsoorlog 1899–1902*, Pretoria, 1990

Mandela, N. *Long Walk to Freedom*, BCA edn, 1995 (Or. 1994)

Marais, J. *The Fall of Kruger's Republic*, Oxford, 1961

Martin, Col A.C. *The Concentration Camps, 1900–1902*, Cape Town, Howard Timmins, 1957

Maurice, Maj Gen Sir Frederick and Grant, M.H. *History of the War in South Africa*, 4 vols and maps, 1906–10

Maxwell, Mrs F. (ed.). *Frank Maxwell: a Memoir and Some Letters*, 1921

May, H. and Hamilton, I. *The Foster Gang*, 1966

Maydon, J. *French's Cavalry Campaign*, 2nd edn, 1902

McCormick, D. *The Mystery of Lord Kitchener's Death*, 1959

Meintjes, J. *De La Rey – Lion of the West*, Johannesburg, 1966

——. *President Steyn*, Cape Town, 1969

——. *Sword in the Sand – The Life and Death of Gideon Scheepers*, South Africa, 1969

——. *General Louis Botha*, 1970

Melville, Col C.H. *Life of General Sir Redvers Buller*, 2 vols, 1923

Menpes, M. *War Impressions*, 1901

——. *Lord Kitchener*, 1915

Midleton, Earl. *Records And Reactions 1856–1939*, 1939

Miller, C. *Painting the Map Red – Canada and the South African War 1899–1902*, Montreal, 1993

Millin, S.G. *General Smuts*, 2 vols, 1936

Mockler-Ferryman, Lt Col A.F. (ed.). *The Oxfordshire Light Infantry in South Africa*, 1901
Moore, D.M. *General Louis Botha's Second Expedition to Natal during the Anglo-Boer War, September–October 1901*, Cape Town, 1979
Morris, J. *Pax Britannica*, paperback, 1979 (Or. 1968)
——. *Heaven's Command*, paperback, 1979 (Or. 1973)
——. *Farewell the Trumpets*, paperback, 1979 (Or. 1978)
Naudé, J.F. *Vechten en Vluchten van Beyers en Kemp bokant De Wet*, Rotterdam, 1903
Neillands, R. *The Dervish Wars: Gordon and Kitchener in the Sudan 1880–1898*, 1996
Newman, O. and Foster, A. *The Value of the Pound 1900–1993*, Appendix 1 – 'Purchasing Power of the Pound, 1900–1903', p. 305, Manchester,
Newton, Lord. *Lord Lansdowne*, 1929
Paget's Horse. *The Cossack Post Journal of B Squadron, Paget's Horse*, 1901
Pakenham, T. *The Boer War*, 1979
Pearse, H.H.S. *Four Months Besieged*, 1900
Pemberton, W.B. *Battles of the Boer War*, 1964
Penning, L. *Verdedigers en Verdrukkers*, Den Haag, 1902
Phillipps, L. *March With Rimington*, 1902
Pienaar, P. *With Steyn and De Wet*, 1902
Pirow, O. *James Barry Munnik Hertzog*, 1958
Plaatje, S.T. *Mafeking Diary*, paperback, Cambridge, 1990 (Or. 1973)
Pohl, Victor. *Adventures of a Boer Family*, 1944
Pollock, J. *Kitchener – The Road to Omdurman*, Constable, 1998
Powell, G. *Buller: A Scapegoat?*, 1994
Rait, R. *The Life of Field-Marshal Sir Frederick Paul Haines*, 1911
Ralph, J. *Towards Pretoria*, 1900
Ransford, O. *The Battle of Spion Kop*, 1969
Reitz, D. *Commando*, 1929
——. *Trekking On*, 1933
——. *No Outspan*, 1943
Reitz, F.W. (issued by). *A Century of Wrong*, 1900
Repington, Col Charles à Court. *Vestigia*, 1919
Roberts, B. *Those Bloody Women – Three Heroines of the Boer War*, 1991
Roberts, FM Lord. *Forty-One Years in India*, 30th edn, (1 vol.) 1898
Robertson, FM Sir William. *From Private to Field-Marshal*, 1921
Robson, B. *Roberts in India – the Military Papers of Field Marshal Lord Roberts, 1876–93*, 1993
Rosenthal, E. *General De Wet*, 2nd edn, Cape Town, 1968
Rosslyn, Earl of. *Twice Captured*, 1900
Royle, T. *The Kitchener Enigma*, 1985
Ryan, A. *Mutiny at the Curragh*, 1956
Sampson, P.J. *The Capture of De Wet*, 1915
Sampson, V. and Hamilton, Gen Sir Ian. *Anti-Commando*, 1931
Selby, J. *The Boer War*, 1969
Slocum, S. and Reichmann, C. *Extracts from the Reports of Captain S.L'H. Slocum and Captain Carl Reichmann*, Scripta Africana, Johannesburg, 1987
Smit, Kmdt J.P. 'Die Dood van generaal De la Rey', *Militaria*, issue 6/3 (1976)
Smith, I. *The Origins of the South African War 1899–1902*, 1996
Smith-Dorrien, Gen Sir Horace. *Memories Of Forty-Eight Years Service*, 1925
Smuts, Gen J.C. *Holism and Evolution*, 1926

Smuts, J.C. *Jan Christian Smuts*, 1952

Spender, H. *General Botha*, 1916

Spies, S.B. *Methods of Barbarism? – Roberts and Kitchener and Civilians in the Boer Republics, January 1900 – May 1902*, Cape Town, 1977

Spies, S.B. (ed.). *A Soldier in South Africa, 1899 to 1902 – the Experiences of Eustace Abadie*, Johannesburg, 1989

Spies, S.B. and Nattrass, G. (eds). *Jan Smuts – Memoirs of the Boer War*, Johannesburg, 1994

Steevens G.W. 'The Downfall of Mahdism 1896–8', a lecture to the Aldershot Military Society, 1898

Sternberg, Count. *My Experiences of the Boer War*, 1901

Swinson, A. *North-West Frontier – People and Events 1839–1947*, 1967

Symons. J. *Buller's Campaign*, 1974 (Or. 1963)

Taitz, J. (ed.). *The War Memoirs of Ludwig Krause*, Cape Town, 1996

Taylor, A.J.P. *English History 1914–1945*, Oxford, 1990 (Or. 1965)

——. *The First World War – An Illustrated History*, paperback, 1996 (Or. 1963)

Thomas, I.G. 'Buller, the Man – Not the Barracks', *RCT Review*, vol. 1, 18 (November 1974) pp. 80–6

Trew, Lt Col H.F. *Botha Treks*, 1936

——. Letter dated 30 November 1900, in the *Stawell News and Pleasant Creek Chronicle*, 10 January 1901, Victoria, Australia.

Uys, I. *South African Military Who's Who 1452–1992*, Germiston 1992

Van den Heever, C. *General J.B.M. Hertzog*, Johannesburg, 1946

Van Warmelo, D. *On Commando*, 1902

Viljoen, Gen B. *My Reminiscences of the Anglo-Boer War*, 1902

Walker, E.A. *A History of South Africa*, 3rd edn, 1947

Warner, P. *Kitchener – the Man Behind The Legend*, 1985

Warwick, P. (ed.). *The South African War*, 1980

Warwick, P. *Black People and the South African War 1899–1902*, Cambridge, 1983

Waters, Col W.H.H. and Du Cane, Col H. (trs). *The German Official Account of the War in South Africa*, 2 vols, 1904–6

Wheatcroft, G. *The Randlords*, paperback, 1993 (Or. 1985)

Williams, B. *Botha, Smuts and South Africa*, 1946

Williams, C. *Hushed Up: A Case for Enquiry into some Suppressed Facts Concerning the Conduct of the War in South Africa*, 1902

Williams W.A. *The Life of General Sir Charles Warren*, 1941

Wilson, H.W. *With the Flag to Pretoria*, 2 vols, 1900–1

——. *After Pretoria: the Guerilla War*, 2 vols, 1902

Wilson, M. and Thompson, L. (eds.). *The Oxford History of South Africa Vol. II 1870–1966*, Oxford, 1971

Wolseley, FM Lord. *The Story of a Soldier's Life*, 1903

Wood, F. (ed.). *Young Winston's Wars*, 1972

Worsfold, W.B. *Lord Milner's Work in South Africa 1897–1902*, New York, 1906

Wulfsohn, L. 'Elands River: a siege which possibly changed the course of history in South Africa', *Military History Journal*, vol 6, 3 (June 1984)

Ziegler, P. *Omdurman*, New York, 1974

Index

Subheadings are arranged in chronological order, apart from British Army battalions which are in order of seniority in the Army List. Italic page numbers refer to maps.

Index

Index